Formative Spirituality

Volume Three

FORMATION
OF THE
HUMAN HEART

Formative Spirituality

Volume Three

FORMATION OF THE HUMAN HEART

·ADRIAN VAN KAAM·

CROSSROAD · NEW YORK

1986

The Crossroad Publishing Company
370 Lexington Avenue, New York, NY 10017

Library of Congress Cataloging in Publication Data

Van Kaam, Adrian L., 1920–
Formation of the human heart.
(Formative spirituality; v. 3)
Bibliography; p. 385
Includes index.
1. Spirituality—Catholic Church.   2. Sociology,
Christian (Catholic)   3. Catholic Church—Doctrines.
I. Title.   II. Series: Van Kaam, Adrian L.,
1920–   . Formative spirituality; v. 3.
BX2350.65.V35 1985   248   85–25506
ISBN 0–8245–0719–3

Contents

Preface

T his book is the third volume of the series on the science of formation and its articulation in the Christian formation tradition.

The first volume, titled *Fundamental Formation*, dealt with the foundations of distinctively human or spiritual formation in general. The second volume, titled *Human Formation*, was concerned with a practical theory of human formation that takes into account the relevant contributions of arts, sciences, and formation traditions. Their partial findings and insights are complemented, integrated, and reformulated in a metalanguage that is not unduly contaminated by the metalanguage of one or another perspective of a particular science, school, or tradition consulted by the formation scientist.

In the final chapters of Volume Two we introduced the concept of the human heart or core form of life, its position and function in the totality of the human life-form and human formation. We closed these considerations with a discussion of the basic disposition of the human heart as transcendent. This disposition was identified and described as awe in face of the mystery.

In this third volume, other basic dispositions of the human heart are discussed theoretically and practically. Implications for life's formation are elaborated where possible.

The author would like to warn again that the recent emergence of a science of formation should not lead one to disregard the prescientific myths, intuitions, experiential descriptions, and spontaneous convictions often handed over from generation to generation. Many of these improvisations that predate the rise of the human sciences may contain wisdom that should not be neglected. We could compare this with prescientific medicine. Some of the herbs, powders, lotions, and purgations used for centuries contained powers of healing that we did not suspect until recently.

Medical researchers study with new interest the once maligned methods and recipes of tribal medicine men, witchcraft doctors, and shamans.

Similarly the student of formation should keep an open eye for the prescientific ways of giving form to human life. Much wisdom may be hidden in popular intuitions of the past. Such probing of prescientific customs seems even more relevant for formation science than for medicine. The wisdom of formation is interwoven with human experience. This intimate source of practical knowledge was in principle available to successive generations before the era of human science. Formation science does not want to supplant this wisdom but to complement it and, if necessary, to purify it from dissonant accretions that may be a source of much suffering and failure in countless human lives.

In the next volume in this series we shall consider the way in which such completion and correction can be validly accomplished by means of a scientific methodology developed for this task that has been imposed on us at this crucial juncture in the history of human formation.

Acknowledgments

I wish to offer my sincere appreciation to all those who assisted in the preparation of this book. I am grateful to Dr. Susan Annette Muto, Director of the Institute of Formative Spirituality at Duquesne University, for her tireless editing of this work, and to Father Richard Byrne, OCSO, Ph.D., Executive Director of the Institute, for his many valuable comments. A special word of thanks is due to Eve Bauer, the excellent typist of the manuscript, and to the graduate assistants of the Institute. I especially commend Sister Mary Josephine Torborg, along with Susan Stangl, Annetta Wallace, Judy Joehrendt, and the secretary and staff of the Institute, especially Mrs. Helen Douglas, who worked diligently preparing the index. They all made the timely publication of this book possible through their generous assistance and fine cooperation.

CHAPTER 1

Dispositions of the Heart: Consonance in Congeniality, Compatibility, and Compassion

The second volume of this series on formative spirituality contained a basic consideration of the core form or heart of human life. We indicated there that our heart is formative through its dispositions. Hence, we find it desirable to consider in this volume the main dispositions of the human heart as nourished by awe, wonder, and marvel—dispositions treated thoroughly in the preceding volume.

The disposition that serves as the bridge between awe and the other formative dispositions of the heart is that of consonance. We know that distinctively human formation is based ultimately on awe and reverence. Awe is nourished by our contemplation of the splendor of forms emerging in our formation field, including our own unique form. They all reflect the splendor of the formation mystery itself. This splendor radiates from the consonance of forms. One could say that education to awe is education to contemplation of consonance. Similarly, the formation of life and world should be consonant. Only then can the lifelong task of form reception and donation appeal to our predisposition for awe. Only the awed heart can sustain fidelity to our call by the mystery. In service of this call, the heart engenders such sustaining subdispositions as those of congeniality, compatibility, and compassion. They express and protect consonant formation.

Formation aims at bringing the whole of our human form and its field to consonant unfolding. Such consonance is not an abstraction, a mere idea or a pleasing fantasy: it is the living harmony of all aspects of our formation field and the harmony between this field itself and the formation mystery.

1

Terms Related to Consonance

The science of formation uses the term *consonance* to express the inner and outer harmony of both form and formation. During their history of formation, people have used different words in interrelated ways to point to this consonance of form as well as of formation. At the dawn of history, as recorded in systematic writing, the Greek *synphonia* and the Latin *consonantia* were coined to convey this desirable harmony of each of them. *Consonantia* is related to the verb *consonare*. This verb derives from *con* ("with") and *sonare* ("to sound"), meaning to sound harmoniously together; it refers to the agreeable correspondence of sounds and hence, more generally, to any state or form of being consonant. Augustine calls consonance of form and of formation a concert of beauty. He speaks with delight about *"harmonica partium consonantia,"* the harmonious sounding together of the parts.

Another Latin word, *formosus*, related this consonance to the mystery of either form or figure or of formation. *Formosus* points to the pleasing radiance, the appealing beauty, of form or formation. The term is constituted by *forma* and *-osus*. *Forma* means shape; *-osus* is the suffix that means "full of." Hence, the beautiful is that which is filled with form or shape. Shape in this sense is not necessarily restricted in meaning to the outer shape of appearance. It can refer primarily to inner shape and meaning that shine forth in the appearance.

Another word for either beautiful form or formation is *speciosus*. In Old English *specious* means good looking, pleasantly appearing, radiant. In Latin it does not have the same negative connotation of deceptiveness as the word specious frequently assumes in modern English usage. The word *speciosus*, interestingly enough, is related to contemplation. It is derived from the verb *specere*, meaning "to behold," "to contemplate." As mentioned earlier, it is such contemplation of the form in its inherent integrity and wholeness rather than logical or scientific analysis that discloses for us the radiance of its consonance. *Speciosus*, as coformed by the word *species* and *-osus* ("full of"), thus points to the splendor of consonance that radiates from within the interior space of any form inasmuch as it manifests the pristine integrity granted to it by the formation mystery.

Consonant Formation

Formation is called consonant insofar as it stays attuned to this core of intrinsic splendor. This radiant center, this hidden seed of nobility, is the mystery's original gift of primary consonance or likeness with itself. Our fidelity to this gift means that we allow it to unfold within all the subforms we foster in our intrasphere and in the other spheres of our formation field. Formation is not only concerned with our own life; it also fosters the true formation of other persons, things, and events encountered in this field. In regard to the inter- and outer spheres of form donation, our efforts are called consonant insofar as they foster in awe and reverence that which shines forth from each form as its unique reflection of the mystery. Among other things, the creation of a consonant environment is rooted in this disposition of the human heart.

The basic disposition of the heart is to find and foster consonance that is both nourished by awe and in turn fosters this same awe disposition. Consonance is obedience to the mystery as it reveals itself in the innermost recesses of our being and its field of presence. It calls us by name; it invites us to form our life and its field in harmony with that name. This is not merely the categorical name that identifies us functionally in government records or on our driver's license or credit card. It is a secret name, one that points to our transcendent destiny, a name known fully only to the mystery of formation.

In spontaneous natural contemplation, we may be graced with the awareness that we cannot live consonant lives if we remain aloof from the still point of our soul. There the transcendent keeps naming us uniquely. To miss that name would mean the miscarriage of our life. We would remain nameless strangers to ourselves, numbed refugees with an unknown destiny, dissonant players in the mighty concert of consonance that orchestrates the universe.

Consonance is the splendor of form and formation. Our heart, therefore, should be disposed to consonance. To initiate and maintain this disposition demands courage and decisiveness. It implies the asceticism of detachment from all that distorts the purity of our own original form in the ongoing formation of our subforms and their expansion. It demands a purification of all that obscures our contemplation of any form in its pristine epiphanic beauty.

Consequences of Loss of Presence to Consonance

If we lose the art of awed presence to the consonance of form and formation, it will be impossible for us to pray or to love. Our frenzy to amass pieces of information should be balanced by contemplation of their mutual consonance within wider forms and within unifying consonant formation. Otherwise the meaningfulness of our life and its field could be dissolved into minute, isolated islands of facts and figures. No reconstruction of reality, by itself alone, can bring back the living consonance of the original form, now dissected and dissolved.

The light of awed contemplation penetrates the primordial consonance of forms. Such at-homeness with reality should be complemented but not replaced by an approach that is analytical. The longing for lost objective consonance cannot be remedied by a subjectivistic romanticism. Romanticism begins as an excited attempt to restore shattered reality to radiant meaningfulness by emotional enhancement alone. Sadly, one only ends up with a romanticized world, a beautiful dream without substance, an idle melody invented by the orphaned heart. When the dream fades, nothing remains but a sterile count of particles. Collections of isolated parts, while useful for functional purposes, cannot by themselves stir the tired heart or inspire awe, wonder, marvel, and passionate love. Idle dreams can even spoil one's taste for consonant formation. Then one's shattered human life may sink down in quiet desperation.

A fragmented field, without the promise of the joy or consonance of forms and formation, has neither luster nor inspiration. In such a field, the distinctively human task of form reception and donation loses its appeal. It is no longer self-evident why the primal call of life is the call to consonant formation. We begin to ask ourselves why we should be committed to consonance. Why not commit ourselves to its alternative, dissonance and deformation? The latter offer less challenge to our inclination to inertia.

If consonance loses its awesomeness, our concern for truth and goodness may die. Both lose their cogency when they fall out of tune with the symphony of consonance. The mechanisms of exact or exciting information, the syllogisms of logical argumentation, may keep proliferating data and abstract concepts, but by themselves alone they cannot shepherd the orphaned heart. When the language of consonance is forgotten, the mystery of formation can no longer express itself in our life. Its voice falls silent. It cannot sustain us in the forms of real community. We gather together as isolated lumps of life, chattering away wildly to maintain the illusion of meaningful togetherness.

Consonant Integration of Fragmented Aspects

People are tempted to neglect contemplative presence. They may scatter their apprehension and appreciation of forms by constant analysis and indifferent manipulation. Consonant formation implies, therefore, that we gather together and reintegrate the fragmented aspects of our life in the light of the consonance inherent in the depth of each scattered form. Such a gathering cannot be a merely logical or technical reconstruction. We should not assemble partial insights and observations as if they were separate building blocks. Rather, we should let these fractions and splinters of the form light up in the radiance of its hidden seed of consonance. This integrative core and its lucidity are disclosed to us in patient contemplation of the "speciousness" of the form. Such seeing of the form as a whole often happens implicitly and prefocally.

The splendor of the core is at the same time an implicit judgment on the consonance or dissonance of fragments and subforms and on their whole or partial availability to consonant integration. Consonance offers itself to our contemplative presence. We may resist what we see. We may insist that we cannot observe the consonance of form or formation. If we are victims of functionalism, we may almost automatically seek to reduce forms and formations to constituents that we mistakenly assume to be prior to the original form. The spirit of final analysis compels us to sneak "behind," as it were, the form's immediate givenness, to detect the ultimate elements to which it can be reduced. Doing so, we fall into a void, for only nothingness is behind forms in their pristine givenness and their inherent initial consonance.

Form as form is intrinsically consonant. No authentic form is thrown together through a chance play of cosmic forces whose analysis can fully explain by reduction its unique "form-ness" as a whole. Our seeing of form must remain loyal to the given form as such. The formation mystery and our formation field appear to us primarily in such given forms.

Human Form and Responsible Formation

Among the forms in our world, we find the vegetative, the sentient, and the intelligent. These forms of life can express themselves in subforms with a certain spontaneity. In our human form this formation potency attains a relative freedom. Hence, we are responsible for the consonant expression of the unique form granted to each of us. Consonant form reception and donation becomes a call to our freedom to respond to it in fidelity. Through our body we give form to our formation field. We are challenged constantly to act and intervene responsibly in that field in all its intra-, inter-, and outer spheres, in all its dimensions and articulations, including its historical dimension. In regard to the latter, the human form inscribes its apprehensions, appreciations, and affirmations indelibly upon the unfolding scroll of the history of formation. This scroll bears lastingly the sociohistorical imprints of human formation received over the millennia, whether they are consonant or dissonant.

The human form is not free, ethically speaking, to engage in formation in total independence of the mystery and its directives. The mystery, not the human form in isolation, is the ultimate measure of history. Any attempt at prideful isolation breeds dissonance. The human form is not the protoform of the mystery of formation, but rather its image, called to receive and give form in consonance with its inner intentionality. We are not the first word but only a response to be ruled by the laws of consonance. We are not the inventors of the original rules of consonance. They are imposed on us. We did not first impose them on ourselves.

The human form as embodied spirit is called to mirror consonantly the mystery of formation. We must seek to establish in our life the primacy of the transcendent dimension of our human form. Its light should illumine all other dimensions of our life. Through these dimensions our form is a microcosm of the world. When enlightened by the lucidity of our obedient spirit, we are able to disclose the world consonantly as the reflection and likeness of a transcendent mystery that forms it lovingly.

Our spirit immanent in the human form manifests itself radiantly through it. The splendor of our forming spirit discloses itself in the consonance of formation. But, sadly, it hides itself in moments of dissonance. Our spiritual light proceeds from the depths of the mystery. This inner light penetrates our mind and heart. Through them, it lights up our formation field. Only when our human form dwells in the sphere of the spirit can it be "true to form." The measure of this fidelity is the measure of the consonance of our life.

Practice of Consonance

Consonance is thus the central disposition of our transcendent life. The other core dispositions of congeniality, compatibility, and compassion are meant to strengthen and deepen consonance. Its practice does not involve a rigorous effort to control the lives of ourselves and others in our formation field. Such regimentation may create regularity but not the harmony that is the hallmark of the consonant life.

Gentleness is another basic disposition, yet it is not sufficient in itself if one is to persist in the practice of consonance. Gentleness has to be balanced by firmness. To become consonant, we need the firmness of discipline mellowed by gentleness. Consonance, as disclosed in gentle discipline is ultimately a gift of the formation mystery. It is not mastered by us but bestowed upon us; it is the effect not of our labor but of transcendent love.

The practice of consonance lifts into the light of day what has been shrouded in our heart as inmost longing. It is like bringing a lovely flower out of a greenhouse into the sunlit space on our windowsill. Our persistence in consonance lets the mystery shine forth in our lives.

The disposition of consonance demands an exertion that is a labor more of disclosure than of mastery. The mystery calls us to consonance. To hear this call, to let it resonate in our dispositions, demands an effort to remain open to its sound in our busy lives. There are so many voices, so many distractions, that vigilance is necessary if we are to stay attuned to the mystery of consonance. We make ourselves ready to receive this gift when we foster the dispositions of faith and hope in the mystery that bestows consonance where it meets no resistance to its generosity.

Firm and gentle vigilance is indispensable. Without vigilance, the powers that prevail in our functional existence would pull us into popular pulsations and facile achievements. They are too attractive to withstand. Hence, the seeds of consonance will be suffocated if we do not nourish them faithfully.

Path of Consonance

The path of consonance is marked by gentleness and firmness. To be more specific, the consonant life is to be lived gently and firmly in congeniality with one's foundational life-form as rooted in the formation mystery and in compatibility and compassion with others. If we cannot be gentle, we cannot be obediently congenial, compatible, or compassionate. Without these dispositions the life of consonance is unthinkable. Gentleness enables us to face joy and sadness in equanimity and to share serenely the same experiences with others. If we are not firm, we lack the strength to bear the trials life holds in store for us and to welcome them with composure. We cannot sustain others in their sufferings. Gentleness without firmness becomes flabby; firmness without gentleness grows harsh. Only in unison do they prepare us for a life of consonance in the light of the formation mystery.

Consonance has to be firm—not powerless, passive, or dependent. Like all ideals, the ideal of consonance can be abused by those in power to keep the powerless under their dominance. For them consonance may only mean keeping things as they are and counseling against reformation. But consonance means just the opposite. It is a disposition to flow with the always reforming and transforming mystery.

True consonance is not a suspension of thought and action until some dominating person sets out to reform a dissonant situation. This would be a perversion of the consonant disposition. Consonance means to enter effectively into our formation field and to cope courageously with the dissonance that emerges.

Consonance implies the disposition to be open to all nuances of the formative events of life, no matter how disconcerting they may seem. True consonance is neither effortless nor compliant. It defies our impulse to escape what is unpleasant or to battle what we cannot bear. When we see someone assaulted, we feel inclined to look aside. When someone accuses us, we are prone to bypass that awkward moment. When a guilt feeling emerges, we feel compelled to negate it. When our own demanding behavior is challenged, we try to reduce the conversation to some other, less threatening issue. If we cannot escape the awareness of such causes of dissonance, we try to battle any evidence that would force us to reformation.

Consonance invites us to transcend the alternatives of contention or evasion. It calls for a gentle yet firm acceptance of the present. It implies abiding with what is going on, seeing it through, and heeding what emerges without evasion of or premature closure to the problems at hand.

Consonance means laying aside our plans when someone needs us, suspending our fear of failure when life demands action, facing guilt when we fail to live in fidelity, remembering humbly how we lost our way. Consonance means keeping the door open for new disclosures while being ready to appraise our familiar formation field for possible surprises. Consonance is formed by these disclosures of the mystery of formation, even if they imply giving up one's present mode of mastery and risking a journey in unchartered regions.

Consonance is thus a rich disposition. It implies a partnership between such dispositions as firmness, courage, gentleness, patience, effectiveness, openness, obedience, steadfastness, and fidelity. It is both the mother and the child of such dispositions. Hence, it holds a central position in the secondary dispositional form of our life. In and through consonance, the presence of the forming mystery becomes evident. It is central in the life of formation because it enables us to share fully yet uniquely in the unfolding of human history. Consonance is a dynamic and effective disposition, marked by gentle power. It makes us living symbols of the harmonizing mystery of formation in this world.

Consonance and Formation Time

Consonance involves a dynamic participation in the struggles and sufferings of humanity in its quest for the harmonious life. As such, it makes us experience time in a less dissonant fashion. Openness to the mystery of formation not only reforms our experience of our life-form and our formation field; it also effects formation time.

To appraise what we call "consonant formation time," we must look at moments of dissonance. When we feel dissonant, say, toward people who visit us, we want them to leave. When we experience dissonance between our taste and our surroundings, we feel compelled at once to move elsewhere. When we sense our own lives becoming dissonant, we feel the urge to change ourselves overnight. Whatever form dissonance takes, we desire to overcome it at once by moving into a more soothing situation.

Expressions of dissonance manifest our desire for some kind of change. We say, "Nothing is going on around here. . . . The meals are always the same. . . . I cannot stand sitting in this waiting room. . . . How much longer will it be before the speaker finishes his paper? . . . It drives me out of my mind to stand so long at the checkout counter with all those shopping carts in front of me. . . ." Such words evidence the emergence of a secondary dissonance on top of the one we felt initially. It goes deeper and is more serious than the first because it creates a disruption between what the mystery allows to be and our lack of transcendent presence to this reality. It creates a dissonance between our vital impulses, our functional ambitions, and our transcendent aspirations. Functionally and vitally we feel driven to break loose from our unpleasant predicament instead of facing it creatively.

Our dissonant feelings may be so overwhelming that we feel unable to give meaningful form to what we experience as disruptive. We lose the power to appreciate the hidden opportunities in every situation. Imagine, for example, being in the waiting room of an office building. There are many ways to give form to this "lost" time. Through various acts, we could make it consonant with our life. We could engage in active relaxation exercises to restore our energy, begin a friendly conversation, read a book, pray, make notes, correct papers, quietly reflect. Unfortunately, we are so overcome by the dictates of our functionality that we are often blind to these opportunities. The only thing that matters is overcoming our functional-vital dissonance instead of making it a stepping stone to higher consonance.

Functional Time

The cause of this kind of dissonance is our tenacious attempt to give form to life only in terms of functional time. We plan the form-giving aspect of our life in abstract time units. Functional time can be rationed out on the basis of information provided by clocks, watches, calendars, schedules, and computers. Our formation attempts are controlled by these dissociated allotments of time: so much time to meet, date, meditate, eat, play, write, think.

Functional time is not "soul time." Its mathematical logic is foreign to the feelings of our heart. By separating the various formative moments of our life into airtight compartments, it becomes difficult to experience an inner wholeness that surpasses yet unifies our functional-vital involvements. Instead of being present serenely to the mystery as it manifests itself here and now, we are always afraid of running out of time. We become people in a hurry, living dissonant lives while missing out on relaxed togetherness with one another.

Consonant Time

Perhaps we have known moments in which we felt liberated from the tyranny of dissonant, functional time. Such moments of consonance may be the exception rather than the rule, but they remain with us as precious memories of what could be. These moments of consonance are replete with meaning; they are full-toned and fertile epiphanies of the eternal. We want to abide with such moments, for in them all things seem to coalesce. They may happen to us when visiting a friend, listening to a symphony, walking in the woods, enjoying a meal prepared with loving care, experiencing sorrow or pain, losing a loved one, or doing simple chores with a meditative awareness of their coherence with the deeper meanings of life and world.

It seems as if functional time comes to a standstill at the moment of full consonance. The mystery of our ongoing formation touches us in the present moment. It is no longer experienced as dissociated but as an integral and integrating expression of the total meaning of our life. While all moments are meant to be experienced in this fashion, they rarely are.

To exemplify such an experience of consonant time, picture a family gathered in a funeral parlor around the body of a beloved husband and father. It is their first viewing of the body before friends and visitors stream in. They feel sequestered from their everyday functional lives. This is a sad and solemn moment. The pressure of functional time is left behind. Their usual conversations about plans, projects, and practical problems are silenced. Not much is said. They feel united in their loss. They experience wordlessly the awesome truths of life and death. All share in the formation history that made them this family with this father. They experience consonance with the mystery that gave unique form to their family over countless generations. In some way they feel at one with all bereft families. They feel cradled in the great web of formative events that silently direct all happenings in space and time.

When we stand still in the face of death, functional time is dispelled and the transcendent time of consonance is disclosed instead. Consonant time is lived from within; it is experienced as replete with meanings that overflow concrete events while being miraculously mirrored and contained within them.

For many people, the experience of consonant time happens only on the occasion of striking events. Outside these islands of transcendence, life seems immersed in the gray waves of functional time. However, persons blessed with an increasingly consonant life are disposed to cultivate the transcendent time experience daily. This does not mean that they do not share in or appreciate the schedules of functional time. Without these schedules it would be impossible to give form to one's life. What makes these people different is that they try to complement these experiences with a consonant dimension: they endow functional-vital moments with a transcendent depth. Moreover, they are inclined to create many instances of consonant time in their lives.

The time of consonance resonates with a presence to what is lastingly meaningful, even if it swiftly passes in the functional-vital sense. It is symbolized in the difference between a fleeting moment of sexual gratification and an experience of lasting love. As long as we are immersed in functional time, our experience remains shallow. There is no formation in depth. Encapsulated in functionality or vitality, the moment of consonant formation escapes us. Yet we do not benefit our unfolding if we run away from displeasing events. Moments of discomfort will always be with us. Vexation and confusion are interwoven with the short and turbulent journey that is human life. Finding consonance in all of these events makes us slowly aware that they have a mysterious and lasting meaning. Transcendent time is a treasure in which we discover the benign presence of the formation mystery inviting us to share its epiphanies.

Transcendent Time

Because it embraces and sustains time that is functional and vital, transcendent time is like the sun that rises above fields and forests, persons and places, gathering them out of their isolation into a wider luminous coherence. Through such consonance, we abide in the eternal. Transcendent time fosters awareness of what is congenial for us. Our life becomes a timeless appeal to others to befriend their own call to consonance. Consonance grants us time to empathize with the congeniality of others, to feel and act compatibly with their situation and compassionately with their vulnerability. Abiding in transcendent time enables us to make time for others.

As long as we remain immersed in functional-vital time only, we have no time for compatibility and compassion, no time to attend to the call of obedient congeniality with the disclosures of the mystery. We are always getting ready for the next project. We cannot hear the cry of our own soul or sense the abandonment of our neighbor. Such intimations are perceived as interfering with our schedules. Reluctantly we grant them the minimum attention needed to escape guilt and shame, but we are too encapsulated in our own time slots to be wholeheartedly present. We lose the spontaneous enjoyment of people we meet because we are too busy to notice how they, too, are touched by the eternal. Their worth transcends the grip of functional temporality. They are more than pieces to fit neatly into our well-timed days and plans. If functional time loses its clutch on us and we begin to abide in the time of the eternal, obedient congeniality, compatibility, and compassion will become abundant.

Consonance flows into compatibility with all kinds of people and in many different situations, be they young or old, executive or employee, career woman or housewife, single or married. Consonance translates into compassion for those who are suffering, for the sick and dying, for the unemployed and hungry. We empathize more readily with those embittered by injustice.

People who are blessed with the disposition of consonance radiate a peace that lifts us out of our pressured life. Their congenial oneness with the gift of their own being, their relaxed compatibility and compassion, make us feel how much we, too, are welcomed by the mystery. At such graced moments, the events that worry us seem to lose their hold on our hearts. Our formation field is no longer imprisoned in mere functional and vital temporality. Events become pointers to the experience of transcendent time that is woven into the fabric of our daily doings. The dispositions of obedient congeniality, compatibility, and compassion sustain and express our consonant life.

Deeper Meaning of Obedient Congeniality, Compatibility, Compassion

The consonant life to which we are called includes the functional and vital dimensions while it lifts us beyond them. Vital expressions of love in a good marriage, for instance, are not restricted to bodily pleasure. They are taken up in deeper care for one another. Mutual bodily enjoyment is suffused by a distinctively human love.

All the many ways in which the consonant life expresses itself can best be brought together under the three headings of obedient congeniality, compatibility, and compassion. These dispositions are interwoven with one another, so much so that if one of them is missing, the others become deformatively dominant. For instance, if we are congenial with the mystery speaking within us but not compatible with the people around us or compassionate with their suffering, our life cannot be consonant. If we are compatible only with what is going on in the everyday scene but neglect to listen to the calling of our own life, we cannot be fully consonant. If we do not bear in compassion our own vulnerability and share the vulnerability of others, our way to consonance is again closed off. Without compassion, compatibility deteriorates into selective sharing only with those whose lives are not maimed by failure, sickness, and other aberrations. When misfortune cuts people down, we withdraw inwardly. We might speak comforting words, but we do not really share their trials. This, too, affects our congeniality and compassion, for to withhold ourselves from others is to miss the opportunity to be in touch with our own vulnerability.

A wise blending of these three dispositions, as modulated by our obedience to the mystery, is crucial for the balanced formation of human life. Let us address each of them separately while emphasizing their interconnectedness.

The word *congenial* is derived from the Latin words *genus* and *cum*, which together means "to be in tune with one's genus, kind, or nature." Our nature is human. This means it is called to subject itself obediently to the mystery speaking to it objectively. When we are disposed in a distinctively human way, we are in tune with our true obedient nature. Typical of this nature is our capacity for freedom and insight. It enables us to be unique insofar as we gain insight into the limits of our own call and situation. We can freely make the best of things for ourselves and others in our limited fashion, in obedience to this mystery, which often entails sacrificing our own plans and projects.

The word *compatible* comes from the Latin *pati* and *cum*, and the suffix *-ble*, which means ability or capacity. Taken together they mean "the ability or disposition to feel or empathize with." Compatibility invites us to empathize with people and their experiences, to share in their laughter and tears, to identify with their hopes, their customs, their concerns. It means to be immersed in the daily flow of life in its simplicity and complexity. This disposition enables us to be at home in our surroundings. It tempers the expressions of our congeniality. To be faithful to our own calling does not mean that we can allow ourselves to be obstreperous or inflexible.

Everyday compatibility prevents us from relating only to persons to whom we can show compassion because of their failings and sufferings. Some of us may only be comfortable with people when they are down. This may indicate a need in us to feel superior to them and a certain unease with those who are doing as well or better than we ourselves are.

The word *compassion* is derived from the Latin *passio* and *cum*. Taken together they mean that we are disposed to suffer with those who are hurt in countless ways. We meet suffering everywhere. Hence, we must also be in tune with the vulnerability of a life that misses the mark, that suffers illness, injustice, conflict, defeat. Compatibility is not enough. It can make us share in a complacent society, walled off from those who do not manifest the symbols of success we value too highly.

Compassion summons us to go beyond congeniality and compatibility to feel the oppression of those who are unjustly treated, to sense the burden of those bent under the weight of worry and work. Compassion makes us feel as wounded as they are. We empathize with those who are denied the power and dignity they deserve as human beings, whether they live in slums or academies, occupy unemployment lines or executive suites. We feel compassion with the suffering of the foreigner grossly or subtly discriminated against in every walk of life.

To maintain consonance, compassion must be balanced by obedient congeniality or the humble acceptance of our limits. No one can relieve the needs of all people in all walks of life. We have to find out what we can do best in view of our limitations. Nor should compassion become an excuse for disregarding compatibility with those who are not visibly suffering. They still need our sympathy. Concern for the alienated should not make us neglect courtesy for neighbors.

Neither congeniality nor compatibility nor compassion alone constitute the core of our consonant dispositions. All three are equally formative of the consonant life. All three emerge from and deepen the triad of faith, hope, and love. They grant each other a necessary modulation. In isolation they would become deformative. Our primary stance in life should not be based on any one of these but on a consonance that implies and presupposes them equally.

Dissonant Life

Contrary to a transcendent consonant life is a life centered only in functional achievement, vital gratification, or social adjustment. This life is dissonant because it is rooted in the pride-form, which opposes the consonance with the mystery we are called to image. Our functional ego does not want to live in congenial obedience to the voice of the mystery within, neither in gentle compatibility with others in everyday situations nor in compassion with the vulnerability of those around us. Functionality wants to forge an isolated ego-identity, marked by complacent, self-important efficiency and subtle, condescending arrogance. To form a merely functional identity demands competition, not compatibility and compassion, and surely not obedient congeniality with the demands of the mystery at the center of our life.

The triad of obedient congeniality, compatibility, and compassion is rooted in faith, hope, and love. It is based on the conviction that the mystery of life and world formation is itself congenial, compatible, and compassionate. The mystery is endlessly congenial with itself; limitlessly compatible with its epiphanies in people, events, and things; immensely compassionate with all kinds of suffering. The call to consonance is a call to share in this threefold analogous disposition of the mystery.

Because we are all imprisoned by the pride-form, with its bent toward functionalism and vitalism, this call requires a total conversion of heart and mind. It is a summons that goes to the roots of our functionalistic and vitalistic lives. The congeniality, compatibility, and compassion of the formation mystery itself is the basis and source of these three dispositions.

Presence and Consonance with Others

When do we feel really consonant? Is it when someone tells us what to do? When an acquaintance lends a helping hand? When people speak words of sympathy and encouragement? To some degree all of these expressions may be helpful and consoling. But what matters ultimately is that someone is present to us wholeheartedly and we sense together the mystery of formation that vibrates between us, sharing our life in regions already explored and in those still uncharted. We also know that the mystery does not take over, that we, too, are responsible for giving form to our life and world. The creation of our history is entrusted to our freedom.

The mystery will not leave us stranded in our misery. It will travel with us, sustaining us in our efforts to solve life's questions and problems. Immediate relief may not be forthcoming, but we enjoy the deeper relief of faith in an enduring presence that understands, forgives, consoles, and encourages us on our journey.

Our presence to others must be a reflection of this presence of the mystery to us. Compatibility and compassion are necessary conditions for such a presence, and so is congeniality. If we do not know who we are, if we are not faithful to this knowledge, we cannot be present to others as images of the mystery. We might say the right words, but our listeners will know that we are not truly there. They sense a void where our soul should be. Consoling words only carry weight when they are born out of consonance with the deepest meaning of our lives. Compatibility and compassion must be anchored in congeniality with our own centeredness in the mystery. This does not mean that we have to experience exactly the same conditions others have gone through. That would be impossible. A male counselor, friend, or spouse cannot feel exactly what a woman goes through when facing an unexpected and unwanted pregnancy. Yet consonance is possible and we can share the basic human feelings engendered by her predicament. As human persons we may have gone through similar feelings evoked by other situations; at least they are potentially available to us.

Empathic imagination enables us to enter into another's emotions, to feel affinity and to express it meaningfully. Such basic human feelings are not superficial or fleeting. They touch our hearts. Compatibility and compassion well up spontaneously in us. As central, powerful emotions, they generate in us tenderness and empathy. All such feelings coalesce in our consonant presence to others. They move us in our intimate sensibilities to feel the joy and sadness of people. The gift of consonance enables us to embrace everything human with compatibility and compassion.

When we teach, counsel, or heal others without this presence, we leave their souls and hearts in darkness. They may be better educated, less confused, more healthy, but they still experience an inner void. Their hearts are not relieved because, in our concern for the periphery of their life, their center has been left untouched.

Consonance and Competition

Functional acts and dispositions should be permeated by consonance. The functional life-form by itself alone tends to be ambitious and competitive. It makes it difficult for us to be congenial with our deepest selves as well as compatible and compassionate with others. Western society is functional. It fosters an ambitious bent. Being formed by this society means being trained in all sorts of competitive enterprises. We are encouraged to follow the instigations of the pride-form rather than being obedient to the inspirations of the spirit.

Early in life we learn to live in comparison. We sense that our parents compare our progress with that of the children next door. We learn that our report card places us in a certain rank of functional performance. People may make us believe that a grade indicates what we are worth in this competitive world. We are formed not in consonance but in competition. The same happens to us in sports, in dressing, in spending. We strive to equal or outdo each other.

We need the conviction that we can give form to our life and world. But a problem arises when our form potency is reduced only to our ability to give form to life functionally and vitally speaking. In this case, our deepest potency for consonance is seldom mentioned.

Consonance cannot be measured. It is a transcendent quality. Functional and vital achievement can be given a real or an imagined grade. We appraise our whole form potency by this measurement. Our pride-form moves us to define ourselves in terms of practical achievements. The disposition to appraise ourselves by comparison pervades the formation field, coloring our perceptions, affecting our relationships, cutting us off from our true nobility, and preventing us from being spontaneously compatible with others. In short, we favor competition over consonance.

Consonance invites us to go beyond our functional alienation from others. It implies the loss of the functionalistic identity in which we may have invested most of our formation energy. This may be the only identity we know because we have not yet discovered our transcendent identity. Hence, the call to consonance may cause us anxiety. The call may seem at odds with all we have learned about promotion and survival in competitive collectivities of anxious contestants.

We fear consonance more than we long for it. This fear influences many of our dispositions. We live in the illusion that we *are* our accomplishments; that our worth can be measured by the standards of society; that the approval of successful people demonstrates our real potency.

Such illusions dispose us to become more and more ambitious and possessive. We may go to any length to protect the symbols and signs of our functional achievements.

Invitation to Consonance

The mystery of formation invites us to escape the prison of functionalism. If we listen in obedience to its appeal, we will feel drawn by the flow of consonance that pervades the universe. We begin to share in the life of the mystery itself. We long to be as close to people, events, and things as the mystery is. Competition gives way to compatibility and compassion. Anxious forging of our functional identity is replaced by gentle congeniality with the unknown form of life the mystery is fashioning for us.

The mystery of consonance wants us to let go of the current form of life engendered by the pride-form so that we can receive a new current form, congenial with its inspirations. Functional achievement should no longer be the main source of appraisal of our form potency. Our deepest potency is rooted in the formation mystery itself. The consonant life depends *not* on form donation but on form reception.

This new life of consonance makes it possible for us to be compatible and compassionate. Through union with the mystery, we are lifted out of competitiveness. By sharing in the wholeness of the mystery, we enter into new interformative relationships with others. By affirming our dependence on the shared mystery, we can be with each other without aloofness or apprehension.

Consonant uniqueness, freed from possessiveness and the need for status and power, opens us to a new way of life. Compatibility and compassion are no longer pretenses in service of the fulfillment of our ambitions. They are the spontaneous manifestations of our transcendent inspirations and aspirations.

Consonance is thus much more than a sentiment of sympathy and affection. It is the embodiment of our congeniality with the mystery. It enables us to be together in the compatibility and compassion of the mystery itself. In and through this gift, we can begin to live in consonance with one another as fully and intimately as the mystery lives with us.

Concreteness of Consonance

Consonance in congeniality, compatibility, and compassion is not something abstract or indefinite. It is embodied in concrete and specific dispositions and gestures in which we reach out to others. It is a visible epiphany of the fullness of the mystery *as* consonant. People cry out from the depths of their misery for a word that will heal them, for a heart that will commiserate with their pains and their failings, for eyes that will look at them with respect and compassion. We must divest ourselves of self-importance and share in the weakness of the weak, entering into their loneliness and lack of consolation.

People feel overcome by events they cannot control, by unpredictable pressures that sway society, by arbitrary powers that impinge on their lives. The threat of war, of economic collapse, of theft, of environmental health hazards, of highway accidents, of fire, of wanton killing, and of loss of work imbue them with a pervasive feeling of vulnerability. Consonance in compassion forbids us to look away from this condition. We must make our home in its midst. Our dispositions must disclose the presence of the mystery in the trials that beset our planet.

The movement of consonance is not only one of ascent. It also means a willingness to descend into suffering, poverty, powerlessness, and oppression. Some may be called to abide there permanently, to spend their lives with those who may never make it by this world's standards. Others may be called to serve the ascent of society, to strive compatibly with others to disclose and realize opportunities for the betterment of the human race. Each has to respect the other's calling.

No matter where we are, consonance must remain the hallmark of our life. It is not a disposition that should stay dormant most of the time, only to be activated when other dispositions fail to be effective. It is our distinctively human presence in the formation field. It is the root of our secondary foundational life-form, of our formative dispositions. The same must be said of the obedient congeniality, compatibility, and compassion that flow from consonance and enable us to express it concretely in everyday life. We are ambassadors of the mystery that becomes concrete in our consonant lives.

Consonance expressed as compatibility and compassion is a way of meeting the mystery in those who prosper as well as in those who fail. When we begin to see the mystery of formation itself in all events, people, and things, we rise above the dissimilarities that separate abundance and indigence, victory and defeat, prosperity and deprivation, effectiveness and ineptitude, graciousness and awkwardness. Within the limits of our congeniality, consonance makes us feel at home with all people in compatibility and compassion. To be consonant with the mystery in them should be the main motivation of our service. Less transcendent motivations are too small to sustain us in labors of love.

If we measure only the functional effects of our assistance, we will soon give up our efforts. When no improvement is apparent, when gratitude is not forthcoming and no appreciation is shown, when no one lauds our valiant efforts, we may ask ourselves why we should go through all of this trouble. We cannot find any functional or vital reason to continue. We can only see failing, suffering, despondent people who stay that way despite our best efforts. Our loving presence may soon be eroded and finally depleted. Then the heart goes out of our work, lest we be crushed by hopelessness.

Joy and Consonance

Only when we can celebrate in the midst of misery the presence of the mystery as revealing itself through us and as hidden in those who suffer can we continue our compassionate consonance with the broken lives of countless people. One sign of the consonant life is joy. We feel joy when we are attentive to the needs of others. Our life seems widened and challenged by their presence. We experience joy in the faith that our concern does make a difference in their lives—if not a visible difference then an invisible one, in ways we cannot predict.

The conviction that we come nearer to the mystery in genuine service can be a source of unspeakable joy at privileged moments of life. Knowing that we share in the consonant presence of the mystery, no matter what happens, fills us with joy and grateful goodwill.

Social Justice, Peace, and Mercy

In relation to society the dispositions of congeniality, compatibility, and compassion generate dispositions of social justice, peace, and mercy. Congeniality, compatibility, and compassion refer primarily to the interformative sphere between individual human life-forms. The wider object pole of these dispositions embraces, beyond individual relationships, society as a whole and each one of its formation segments.

Concern to establish and maintain optimal social conditions for the congenial unfolding of people gives rise to the disposition of social justice. Its focus is the safeguarding of the right to congeniality for all members of a population.

Commitment to compatibility between societies and between their formation segments is rooted in the disposition to promote social peace.

Effective promotion of a social climate that fosters considerateness, generosity, leniency, and loving care in regard to those who are vulnerable, fail, and suffer is the fruit of the disposition of social mercy.

Confirmation, Cooperation, and Concelebration

Formation science complements the dispositions of congeniality, compatibility, and compassion, social justice, peace, and mercy with those of confirmation, cooperation, and concelebration.

The science distinguishes between affirmation and confirmation. Affirmation is an intraformative act of our free will assenting to and asserting a personal form directive proposed to the will by the apprehending and appraising mind. Confirmation is an interformative expression of wholehearted assertion of potential or actual consonant form directives of others as manifested implicitly or explicitly in their formation field.

The disposition of confirmation is complemented by the disposition of effective cooperation with others, if such cooperation is congenial, compatible, and compassionate and does not interfere with the demands of social justice, peace, and mercy.

Concelebration is the disposition to joyously celebrate with others any consonant achievement, repute, prosperity, gift, growth, generosity, or felicity that comes one's way.

Competence

A final disposition necessary for the effective incarnation of the other ones is the disposition of competence.

Competence is the disposition to acquire and continually enhance the knowledge, skills, capabilities, expertness, facility, and sensitivity that can assure the highest possible effectiveness of the process of realistic embodiment of congeniality, compatibility, and compassion, social justice, peace, mercy, confirmation, cooperation, and concelebration in one's concrete formation field.

CHAPTER 2

Dispositions of the Heart:
Appreciation, Openness, and Detachment

To live the consonant life in obedient congeniality, compatibility, and compassion, other dispositions are needed: these are, first of all, appreciation, openness, and detachment. They enable us in turn to develop the dispositions of obedience, simplicity, and reverence, which will be discussed in chapter 3.

Without appreciation, openness, and detachment, it would be impossible to know what in fact is congenial, compatible, and compassionate for us in our unique formation field. These dispositions comprise conditions for our formation in an ever more *concrete* life of consonance as lived in the image of the mystery.

Appreciation, openness, and detachment are mutually complementary. To exemplify this point, let us see how they operate in a major decision, such as whether to marry a certain person. To know if this marriage has a reasonable chance of being congenial, compatible, and compassionate, I have to appraise rightly my own limits, gifts, and affinities as well as considering my spouse, his or her background, and our future prospects. I cannot clearly appraise these factors if I am not open in humility to my limitations as well as to my assets. I must also be open to my romantic exaltation of the person I hope to marry. Such openness presupposes detachment from my own prejudices and from customary ways of living that now have to be adapted to those of my partner.

Disposition of Appreciation

The formation of human life distinguishes itself from that of the mineral, vegetative, and prehuman sentient animal forms around us. What distinguishes it, among other things, is the ability of antecedent appraisal. This means that people, unlike animals, can appraise a situation before

22

they act or dispose themselves to a certain way of acting in response to that situation. Human formation, unlike any other known to us in the universe, is relatively free and insightful.

The ongoing formation of animal life is directed by instinctive appraisal. Animal life survives, forms itself, and evolves by relatively fixed structures of appraisal. Animals do not respond; they instinctively react to the relevant stimuli of their organism and their environment. Instinctive, adaptative obedience to the biologically formative events in nature is the source of their ongoing formation.

People are called to form their lives and world by free, insightful appraisal. The more open their appraising mind is in all its historical, vital, functional, and transcendent dimensions, the richer their formation will be. Once we have appraised that our life should develop in a certain direction to be consonant, this appraisal may become a lasting disposition of appreciation.

A bride may appraise that she should care diligently for her spouse and family. She may see what a selfish, uncaring person she has been up to the present. This appraisal may lead to a lasting disposition of appreciation, making her attentive to the opportunities for care that will emerge in her home life. This disposition could be formed only because she was open to her former lack of care. What helped her to be open was humility or the disposition to be detached from self-exaltation. The disposition of appreciation will grow and deepen if she keeps on fostering openness and detachment. These dispositions will enable her to become aware of her failures in care. Appreciation is accompanied by the opposite movement of depreciation. In our example, the appreciation of care presupposes the depreciation of its opposite, of carelessness.

The consonant life is dynamic since it is lived primarily in the light of appreciation. This disposition facilitates opportunity-apprehension and opportunity-thinking. Its corresponding depreciation can never be the main focus of the consonant life.

Because we are embodied spirits, our appraisal and subsequent appreciation of people, events, and things can attain a depth and flexibility incomparably richer than the instinctive appreciations of animal life. Animal appreciations are set in advance; they are fixed and focused in few directions. The human potential for appreciative dispositions is, by contrast, flexible, dynamic, ongoing, and expansive, giving rise to ever new current forms of life.

Appraisal and appreciation involve the whole person, all that we are at this moment of our life and all that we anticipate becoming in the future. Both anticipation and memory influence our formation of appreciative dispositions. Past formative experiences do affect our present appreciations. Such experiences refine our sensitivities and expand the scope of our powers of apprehension, appraisal, and appreciation. All of the past comes into play potentially at the moment of appraisal in the present.

Disposition of Openness

The scope of appraisal is limited by a lack of openness. Openness means humility. If we are not open to the unexalted truth of who we are and what our situation is, we cannot appraise what should be done to foster a more consonant life.

Openness is a disposition that enables us to be as open as we can be to the formative and deformative meanings of our formation field. We can refuse to open our minds and hearts to these meanings and the feelings they engender. We can close ourselves off from their message and resist their warnings, inspirations, and subtle evocations. We can do so either unwittingly or by willful closure. Such a proud, deformative stance isolates us from the mystery and makes it impossible for us to grow in consonance.

One cause of such closure is the pride-form. This quasi-foundational form of life, operative in everyone since the Fall, tends to isolate us from others, from the cosmos, from the mystery itself. We acknowledge such realities only insofar as they can serve our autarchic self-actualization. The pride-form tempts us to closure. We cease to develop obediently congenial, compatible, and compassionate lives. Seldom, if ever, do we experience peace and joy in the midst of turbulence and disappointment.

To live in openness means not to exclude any disclosure of reality from our powers of appraisal. It means overcoming our blind spots when we have the opportunity to face and transcend them. Closed-off, proud people decide in advance what shall and what shall not evoke their response. They resist disclosures that may surprise them.

To form a disposition of closure, we must develop and maintain excessive safety directives. These protect us against denied realities that try to penetrate the boundaries of our effective closure. Tension, psychosomatic symptoms, deformative disorders—all may be evoked when we become aware of directives that threaten to break through our well-regulated, walled-off resistance to manifestations of the mystery.

The energies needed to form such excessive safety directives, to keep them alert and alive, tend to block the normal flow of formation energy. We are inclined, moreover, to organize our lives around measurable, utilitarian projects. Such rigidity may close us to any message not directly relevant to our functional specialization.

When our attention to smooth functioning excludes other facets of formation, it becomes a source of closure. Such denial gives rise to disobedience, isolation, and fragmentation. These dispositions harm the consonant formation of society as a whole in social justice, peace, and mercy.

Openness, Humility, and Humor

In many religious form traditions, the term *humility* means "openness." One acknowledged master of formation, Teresa of Avila, defines humility as walking in the truth of who we are. Reading the masters of other classical traditions, it becomes evident that they, like Teresa, point to humility as a necessary condition for the consonant life.

Humility is associated with the Latin word *humus*, meaning "earth" or "ground." The word indicates that we should be open to our earthiness, to our concrete, fallible reality. This openness should enable us to overcome our tendency to blow things out of proportion under the pressure of the pride-form of life. Humility also tempers pride by humor.

Humor and Timely Deflation and Demystification

Wise directors and teachers use timely humor to deflate any exaltation that may creep into the process of formation. Amusing stories and anecdotes break into a seriousness that could become puffed up. Spontaneous laughter reminds us of the amusing precariousness of all things. We free ourselves from the threat of exaltation by a comic remark or an unexpectedly playful response to a question. To be engaged lightheartedly in life's formation, as if we were not engaged there at all, is our best protection against exaltation. Humorous and playful relationships between participants in formation sessions are a means to maintain relaxed openness and detachment.

The humor that serves openness and appreciation is never denigrating. It is nonjudgmental. It describes what a human situation looks like in its exaltation when seen against the background of reality. An example would be when the anonymous author of *The Cloud of Unknowing* compares the person too eager for spiritual consolation to a greedy greyhound, or when Teresa of Avila detects an exalted concern for ecstasy in her sisters and asks them how well they are peeling the potatoes for dinner.

The exalting pride-form loves to mystify things, to consider one's efforts as terribly special. Humor helps to demystify them and to show that what seems special is only one vulnerable human way. The twinkle of an eye, the flash of a smile, these communicate the truths of formation. Humor counteracts the tendency of the pride-form to foster attachment and illusion, to become arrogant about our learning, to parade our knowledge with intellectual smugness. The author of *The Cloud* unmasks those spiritual strivers who let the world know by dramatic movements of the eyes, by sighs and a tilt of the head, that they have reached great heights of prayerful presence. Buddhist masters, too, excel in the art of demystifying humor.

Closed persons cannot laugh if their exalted concerns are not taken seriously. The boundaries of their life are too controlled to allow for spontaneous relativization. Above all, they cannot laugh at themselves. They take themselves too seriously.

To be free for laughter, one must pass many boundaries of self-importance. Humor enables us to divert our minds from preoccupation with "important things" so that we can look at our situation from a new perspective. Humor thus plays a crucial role when we have to move to a new current form of life not yet known to us in its implications.

Humor helps us to realign our apprehensions and appraisals. A good laugh relaxes our fixation on disciplines of life that were meant to liberate us. Cool logic and willful determination may dominate our days if we stifle spontaneity and relaxed openness. Humor may be the breakthrough we need to remind us that we should forget our struggles and try to be playful.

In the midst of rigorous discipline, humor can restore the sense of motion and flow. We let go of excessive attachment to events, people, and things. We relate spontaneously to the mystery of life in its playfulness, approaching each day with a sense of wonder and appreciative openness. Criticism does not despoil the basic humor and humility in which we live. In all these ways, openness facilitates congenial unfolding as well as compatibility and compassion. It fosters relaxed interformation.

Transcendent and Functional Humor

There is a difference between transcendent and functional humor. The latter is often unfree; it is neither spontaneous nor inspiring, for it is guided by an open or hidden functional project. Such humor may be used to display one's cleverness. It is at the opposite end of the spectrum from transcendent compassion and compatibility. Instead it is used as a means of combat and competition with others. Functional humor fails to evoke spontaneous joy and shared simplicity. It may produce applause for one's cleverness, even envy. It may wound those who are the butt of our jokes and fan the fires of silent anger in their hearts. Functional humor creates not relaxed intimacy but a certain remoteness. People are tense in spite of their apparent mirth and laughter.

Humor that is transcendent creates space for its participants to share in the freeing experience of the laughable relativity of life. Why take things too seriously? It helps us to release our anxious hold on worldly values and to experience joyous abandonment to the benign mystery. Such humor may not be clever, original, or complex. Most of the time it entails simply pointing to the comical side of a common situation. Humor lights up at once the same sad-funny moments. It makes us feel accepted in our shared, vulnerable humanity. We feel less victimized by feelings of insufficiency and inferiority.

The humorous disposition helps us to maintain the balance between a functional structuring of life and a vital-transcendent spontaneity. The slightly foolish and farcical, plain fun and frolicsomeness, are means to mellow the rigidity of our functional disciplines. Consonant living involves a continual interchange between structure and spontaneity. Life without smiles, laughter, fun, and lightheartedness is not far advanced on the path of consonance.

People who live the consonant life manifest something of the bohemian and the disciplinarian. This combination keeps people young in spirit, unpredictable, and surprising. Humor lifts them out of mere functional structure into the joyous openness of creative nonstructure. Both are necessary facets of consonance.

Detachment

The dispositions of appreciation and of openness or humility, with its supporting disposition of humor, need another disposition, detachment, as their support. Life grows dissonant due to inordinate attachments that obscure our appraisal by severing it from the whole of our formation field and its mysterious source. Only when we distance ourselves can we appreciate life as a whole in gentle humor and humility. We should be involved in the world while still being detached. Greed, ambition, and self-exaltation cloud our apprehension, appreciation, and appraisal. Consonant presence is, therefore, unattainable without detachment.

Certain expressions of detachment that were used in the past are admittedly ill-adapted to life today. For example, modes of mortification that made sense for desert fathers may look senseless in our age. The mistake is to identify stern conventions that have lost their meaning with detachment itself. Detachment in the deepest sense is neither world-denying nor strenuous. It is a relaxed movement towards appreciation, openness, and consonance.

Words like detachment and discipline may evoke memories of the exploitation of the powerless by the powerful, of impatience with our limitations, of the imposition of unreasonable burdens, of overwork and underpayment. The ideals of detachment and discipline were often used as weapons of degradation and unjust domination. No wonder these words left a bitter taste in many.

Only if detachment emerges from our inner center can it contribute to consonant living. Beyond infancy and early childhood, we are able to grow in insightful detachment out of inner conviction. If too much detachment and discipline are imposed on us before we are ready to appreciate them, we rebel inwardly. In that case a crisis of discipline is almost unavoidable.

Detachment does not mean that we refuse to participate in the saga of humanity, that we drop out of the struggle for social justice and the building of a better world. On the contrary, to be really involved in these quests implies detachment and self-forgetfulness.

Nor does detachment imply austerity. If detachment is not tempered by gentleness, humility, and good humor, it is liable to become austere. Austerity is the mark of deformative detachment. It becomes an end in itself instead of being a means to consonant living.

Detachment may imply temporary hardships, but we should not focus on that fact only. The essence of detachment implies growing beyond a diffuse form of living to a life that is more centered, whole, and simple. It helps us to stem the tide of images, thoughts, feelings, memories, and anticipations that crowd our hearts and minds. In gentle discipline we create zones of silence in the rush of all-too-fleeting days. We distance ourselves from the flood of information thrown at us by countless billboards, magazines, and television and radio programs. They assail us from morning until night and will impair our judgment unless we exercise detachment toward them.

If detachment becomes showy, a trick to enhance our self-image, if it is not rooted in humility and consonance, it cannot kindle the light of reality. It is thus unwise to imitate the style of detachment practiced by people famed for their generosity. Detachment has to be congenial with our own call, with the formation phase in which we find ourselves, and, above all, with the inspiration of the mystery within our ever changing formation field.

Fixation on preplanned forms of detachment may blind us to forms that are more compatible with the ongoing history of our formation. All efforts to congeal life in a stifling mold of routines and resolutions are in vain. Willful detachment defeats its goal; it limits our vision and inhibits our unfolding; it leads finally to stagnation and spiritual starvation.

The disposition of detachment is opposed to the practice of inflexible routines. It goes hand in hand with humble openness to any inspiration of the mystery in our lives. If detachment is a labor of consonance, it will be experienced far more as "giving" than as "giving up." Detachment becomes a gracious acceptance of the demands of daily life in compatibility and compassion; it is a joyful response to the mystery that forms us.

Rhythm of Detachment and Attachment

Life is a rhythm of detachment and attachment. No new attachment is possible without detachment; no detachment is meaningful without a deepening of involvement. These dispositions alternate and permeate each other on all planes of life. Engagement without detachment easily degenerates into obsession. That is why we must respect our own pace. If we refuse to accept the limits of life as set by the mystery we cannot grow toward a life of consonance. Thus we must die repeatedly to any fixated pattern of life, which curbs further growth. Life is a rhythm of death and resurrection.

This rhythm begins early in life. The newborn infant develops a disposition of receptive attachment to its mother. At this time of life, the reception of form from one's formation traditions via the mother should prevail. In some cases this disposition does not develop properly. Some infants manifest passive detachment as opposed to active receptivity. As a result they cannot receive formation via form traditions as lived by their parents. They are unable to attach themselves to their formative wisdom, be it only in a primitive or prefocal fashion. As a result they develop no formative conscience. Such infants may grow into sociopaths.

Others manifest neither active receptivity nor passive detachment. Instead they show active resistance against motherly formation. They experience only a negative bond between themselves and their mother. This generates in turn negative dispositions of withdrawal, distance, and opposition that may color their entire future formation.

If formation unfolds normally in the life of the infant, at about five months of age a kind of consonant fusion with the mother is reached. At that moment the infant begins to show signs of initial active participation in the play of interformation with the mother. The child begins to exercise vital sensing and initial functioning. On the abnormal side, this phase leads in some infants to a total denial of attachment. An emotional detachment disposition of this sort may affect their life adversely. It may make it difficult for them to relate emotionally to people later in life.

In normal development we observe in the eighteen-month-old child initial awakening of individuality. The child assumes its own role in the interformative relationship. This implies more detachment from the mother without relinquishing all attachment. At that moment the infant may go through a crisis of reattachment, characterized by an anxious return to the experience of consonant fusion that was attained around the fifth month. If this crisis is not resolved, the infant may become disposed to overattachment and fusion. Its future growth may be hindered by a disposition to be in search of a person with whom one can fuse indiscriminately. This condition, like the others, does not totally take away one's freedom of formation; it only limits it.

Another deviation that may take place during the initial individual exercise of the infant's sensing and functioning is a kind of exaltation of this experience of form potency. This could lead to a lasting disposition of self-exaltation.

If all goes well, the child attains, around three years of age, a certain constancy in its formation of dispositions of appropriate attachment and detachment. However, the story of this rhythm goes on for a lifetime. Detachment for the sake of a deeper attachment remains a necessary condition for ongoing formation in the life of the spirit.

CHAPTER 3

Dispositions of the Heart: Obedience, Simplicity, and Reverence

To live the consonant life in congeniality, compatibility, and compassion requires obedience, simplicity, and reverence. Related to them in certain religious form traditions are obedience, poverty, and chastity.

The consonant life is necessarily guided by obedience, simplicity, and reverence. This threefold path has to be lived in congeniality with the communal and personal life-form to which one is called and in compatibility and compassion with the situations in which we are inserted. These dispositions create the possibility for our wholehearted formation in consonance in the image of the mystery.

Obedience, simplicity, and reverence lead us to the mystery hidden in our heart and in our formation field. They are mutually complementary dispositions, enabling us to be present to life and world in three different and necessary ways. They help us to give form to our lives in such a way that it is possible to be consonant.

When we look at our formation field, we see that the mystery manifests its presence in three main appearances: events, things, and people (ourselves included). We do not meet these appearances of the mystery in isolation from one another. They interact in each life situation. When I go to the pharmacist for a prescription, the event is that of obtaining the right medicine. This event receives its form from the way in which I ask for the medicine. Am I shy or arrogant, impatient or patient, anxious or relaxed? The event is also influenced by the dispositions and actions of the pharmacist. Is he brusque or kind, efficient or awkward, slow or fast? Things play a role also: for instance, the pharmacist's clothing. Is he garbed in a white coat or in blue jeans and a T-shirt? Is the arrangement of the pharmacy neat or sloppy?

All of these factors can contribute to or detract from the consonance of the situation. Hence, to enhance the easy flow of consonance in our daily life, we must develop the right dispositions in regard to events, things, and people. We must be open to each of them in positive appraisal and appreciation. This positive regard is rooted in abandonment to the beneficial meaningfulness of what the mystery allows to be. The option for appreciative abandonment is nourished in turn by our faith, hope, and consonance in regard to the mystery itself. On this basis, we develop dispositions of obedience to the events that happen in our lives, of simplicity in regard to the things we possess or use in our formation field, and of reverence in regard to the people with whom we interact interformatively.

Disposition of Obedience

Our thoughts and feelings about obedience may be distorted. The word itself may be contaminated by feelings of resentment. It reminds us of grown-ups who ordered us around without kindness, of bosses who made unreasonable requests, of physicians who did not take the time to explain to us why we should follow doctors' orders, of aloof bureaucrats who told us in a cold distant way to follow their directions, or else!

The basic disposition of obedience has little to do with such negative experiences. The word itself is derived from the Latin *ob* and *audire*, meaning "to listen attentively." Obedience thus implies a relaxed, appreciative heeding of all the happenings in our life as communications of the mystery of formation. We pay attention to their meanings and directives. This gentle attentiveness is inspired by our willingness to give form to our life and surroundings in light of what we hear with the inner ear of obedience.

The more faith, hope, and consonance deepen our appreciative abandonment to the mystery, the less we associate obedience with fear. Obedience becomes the expression of our intimate, consonant relationship with the mystery. It is not associated with the anxious execution of stern orders, but with a gentle flowing with whatever is disclosed in the successive events of our life. The consonance of life, its congeniality, compatibility, and compassion, is traceable to our listening presence to the mystery in daily events. In our silent center we recollect ourselves in gentle attentiveness to the communications of the mystery. From this still point of our soul, we reach out to give form to life and world.

Obedience and the Simple Life of Consonance

The consonant life is not necessarily filled with religious heroes, giants of social accomplishment, spiritual superstars. It is the life of simple people, attentive to the invitation veiled in everyday events. They try faithfully to flow with these disclosures of the mystery by peaceful, steady attention to its appeals.

Obedience is basic to a simple life of consonance. The obedient person does not search for amazing accomplishments, stunning feats, or impressive renunciations. These would be sources of dissonance if they did not flow from listening to the small events of daily life. Achievement, heroism, and mortification are not the issue. Obedience is not a commitment to accomplish as much as possible under adverse conditions. It is a commitment to listen to the mystery speaking in the simple events of everyday life. The consonant person obeys without hesitation, without conditions or restrictions.

Whenever we separate congeniality, compatibility, and compassion from obedience we lose our consonance with the mystery. We are thrown back on our isolated potentials. We become victims of the pride-form. Exaltation replaces simplicity. Consonance, radically speaking, is congeniality with the voice of the mystery, compatibility with its manifestations, and compassion with human vulnerability through our sharing in the compassion of the mystery itself. When formation science, therefore, uses the terms congeniality, compatibility, and compassion, it always means *obedient* congeniality, compatibility, and compassion.

Challenge of the Mystery

The deepest intuitions of form traditions can be betrayed by popular applications. Misunderstanding can be engendered by the way people apply the idea of "the will of the mystery" or "the will of God." What can be deformative is the way in which this idea affects the formation of one's appraisal of events.

Painful, unjust, or oppressive events may be appraised as the enduring will of the mystery to be borne in blind submission. On the contrary, they are challenges allowed by the mystery that call forth our ingenuity, zeal, and dedication. The will of the mystery is our consonant collaboration with its healing response to suffering. Obedience is our creative yes to the challenge at hand, not our compliance with its denigration of human dignity. Resignation means literally to "re-assign" new meaning to an oppressive or painful event.

When our responses prove to be in vain—when an illness, for instance, cannot be cured, a conflict solved, a criminal converted, or oppression overcome—the challenge changes again. It becomes an invitation to disclose the deeper meaning of a suffering that cannot be alleviated by any means at our disposal. Obedience implies even then our readiness to re-enlist ourselves in attempts to improve the situation the moment new possibilities open up. In the event that nothing can be done, we can only share in the loving compassion of the mystery for people whose plight cannot be improved. Such compassion may confirm them in courage and surrender.

Obedience and Exaltation

Obedience protects us against the pride-form and its exaltation. We are constantly tempted to exalt whatever we are thinking and doing. We make these things signs of our importance. Such exaltation may manifest itself in excitement as well as in a display of outspoken wisdom, accompanied by solemn gestures and expressions. Anything we say or do is presented as a matter of major consequence. A certain pompousness colors our statements, suggesting significance or gravity. If others fall for this pretense and begin to defer to us, as though we were really wise, exalted importance may become second nature to us.

Deep down we know that our thoughts, words, and projects do not carry such earthshaking significance. To dampen the voice of truth, we seek confirmation by others. We feel offended if they do not notice us. While they go about quietly listening to their own responsibilities, we may engage in odious attempts to enlist them and entire communities in our own projects, slogans, and interests. Especially when we have some administrative power, we can suggest that others are not sufficiently community-minded or that they lack care for humanity because they do not attend the endless meetings we unnecessarily proliferate. We resent that they do not promote our plan for saving the world.

People who follow their inmost genuine call, who do not flatter us to gain our approval, are really our benefactors. They help to deflate our ballooning ego; they prepare us for the gift of failure that will diminish self-exaltation and restore the balance of obedience. Exaltation always implies a lack of obedience. We make ourselves, not the mystery, the source of our importance. We want to inspire events instead of being inspired by them. We rally people around our ideas instead of letting ideas serve people if they happen to be in consonance with the unique preformation of their life.

Polarized Attention of Obedience

Obedience is the bridge between contemplation of the whole and concrete formation, which implies that we give form to specific events within that totality. Functional formation of this sort demands specified attention. We have to narrow our apprehension, appraisal, and affirmation to the task at hand. At the moment of incarnation, this contraction is unavoidable. If we do not engage in such practical concentration, we cannot translate into concrete projects what contemplation inspires.

When a coalminer drills in the dark layers of the earth, when a teacher is at pains to explain arithmetic to unruly children, when a nurse must give an injection, when a housewife has to prepare the evening meal, all must obey the inspiration of the mystery to express its loving care in these occupations. Yet they can only realize obedience in practice if they pay attention to what they are doing. Otherwise they fail to incarnate these directives effectively.

Strategic contraction in service of concrete events ought not to cancel obedient presence to the whole. It will linger in the background of life, provided we do not absolutize any particular involvement. We should remain at least implicitly present to the mystery. Consider a few examples: A mother doing dishes is fully involved in the process of washing, rinsing, drying, yet she is aware in the background of her family; a father labors as a fireman, yet he senses in the background the wife and children who will profit from his labor; two people in love are not totally absent from one another during their working hours. No matter how meticulously these people execute their various duties, they stay vaguely aware of their close relationships.

The disposition of obedience thus sustains the polarity between the whole of the mystery and its incarnation in daily projects. One basic difference between these two poles is that the mystery is less tangible than one's family or one's beloved. We are all liable to lose ourselves in mundane involvements and forget the mystery. To do so is to make the contraction of our apprehension, appraisal, and decision more or less absolute: making money, building a career, getting a degree become our whole world. We exalt these projects beyond their passing importance.

Contracted attention closes us to the transcendent meaning of events. We are incapable of relating single events to the mystery of the whole. We begin to measure our importance in the light of the exalted status we give to these events. The polar tension of obedience is lost, namely, the tension between gentle openness to the mystery as a whole and the firm contraction of this openness in effective attention to a particular event. When the bridge of obedience is maintained, both kinds of openness remain in consonance with one another.

Obedience as Expanding Openness in Surrender

Obedient openness to events as disclosures of the mystery implies a disposition of surrender. We must be ready to yield to whatever manifests itself as a sound directive. We listen with all we have and are for the possible speaking of a formative word in our experience. We listen with our mind and heart, our memory, our anticipation and imagination, our feelings and intuitions, our experience, our expertise and learning. We listen with our spiritual, practical, and poetic dispositions, with our eyes and ears, our sense of touch, our body. We become committed listeners to the forming presence of the mystery.

This disposition to listen is dynamic. At times we resist it because we fear that listening in surrender may expose us to a directive that is at odds with a complacency we have cultivated in our life. What if we are invited to give up a grudge we have nursed for a lifetime? Obedience may challenge us to accept a responsibility we have ignored, for instance, that of becoming involved in a case of discrimination that tarnishes our community.

Interformative Dimension of Obedience

Obedience thus has an interformative dimension. To be human is to be with others in the realization that the mystery of formation speaks not only to each of us personally but also to our companions on the journey. Usually we cannot rely on what we alone hear or see. Different aspects of a life situation may be disclosed to different people due to their character, temperament, education, experience, and expertise. The formation mystery adapts itself in its disclosures to the limited abilities and perspectives of each person. All may receive different, equally important insights in a situation if they allow the mystery to enlighten and deepen their human perspectivity. These insights can complement one another.

Obedience implies that we listen respectfully in the hope that the mystery may manifest itself to us through one another. Husband and wife share what they see as relevant to the problems they must face as a family. Children ask their parents what should be done in a precarious situation. Management and employees discuss the most effective and just way of production. Scholars compare notes. Scientists keep tabs on each others' experiments. Fishermen discuss the weather and its prospects for navigation. A team of surgeons lays out a precarious procedure in a difficult operation. All of these people form their judgment mutually in shared obedience to reality. Their listening is not merely a hearing of information but a mode of engagement. One is committed in advance to give form to life in ways that are compatible with what has been heard as a disclosure of reality and the mystery that sustains it.

Obedience and Authority

In this shared obedience, not all listeners are equally equipped. Some occupy a privileged position. The seasoned scholar of worldwide fame can hear more than the young teacher just out of graduate school. The master electrician with years of expertise knows better than his new apprentice what should be done. The experienced rafter can guide us more safely over wild waters than our jittery companions who venture out for the first time. All these people can be called authorities in reference to the activities concerned.

Shared obedience implies that we listen to those who are master listeners in the specific field of action we share. This aspect of obedience has often been extolled at the expense of the other aspects discussed thus far. The powerful use it to justify their oppression of the powerless. However, authority (interpreted as one's being the author or source of special insight into the disclosures of the mystery) has a privileged position in the shared obedience of people. Good master-listeners gather together respectfully what we have heard. They synthesize it into a final decision, made in the best interests of the community as a whole.

The same applies to the form tradition to which we have committed ourselves in freedom. Each form tradition is like a master-listener. It gathers what its adherents have heard over the centuries in obedience to the mystery of formation. A form tradition represents an implicit dialogue between generations of listeners. It binds many partial views together in a unifying wisdom pertaining to the fundamental formation of human life. The more each adherent is willing to listen to the elemental wisdom of the shared tradition, the greater the opportunity for expression of personal insights, feelings, and inclinations. The conviction that every adherent will abide by the basic wisdom of the tradition guarantees that its essence will be preserved in the midst of expansion and ongoing modulation.

This unity in obedience should in no way detract from the possibility of candid disclosure of divergent feelings and opinions. An atmosphere of mutual formative respect should prevail. Each adherent can feel at home and in communion with the mystery of formation as it speaks in one's form tradition and in those who expand it in dialogue with other form traditions and with the findings of the arts and sciences.

All of this implies that obedience is not ahistorical. Obedience draws upon history. It takes into account what has been heard over the centuries by other committed listeners. Obedience participates in the unfolding of history as flowing from the formation mystery. It listens to what happens in the present and tries to anticipate what may happen in the future.

Relation of Formative Obedience to Congeniality, Compatibility, and Compassion

As we have seen already, consonance presupposes congeniality, compatibility, and compassion. Before and above all, it presupposes that these three are permeated and molded by obedience. Obedience refers ultimately to the source of our deepest consonance with the mystery itself. This mystery silently embraces the unique protoform of our life. Over a lifetime of formation it discloses this protoform to us. We may resist this disclosure or be receptive to it. Even if we are receptive, we will never know our protoform in all its secret richness and profundity during this lifetime.

Formative obedience refers to our willingness not only to listen to this disclosure but to implement its message obediently in the concrete form reception and donation of our life and its field of formation. Obedience is the opposite of autarchic self-actualization. This is the actualization of a counterfeit self, a self that pretends to find its autonomous being in its own isolated, rationalistic or romantic subjectivity.

Congeniality, compatibility, and compassion cannot be trusted unless they are pervaded by obedience. Hence, the science of formation always presupposes implicitly the adjective *obedient* as a necessary qualifier of these dispositions: namely, *obedient* congeniality, *obedient* compatibility, *obedient* compassion. This means that these dispositions are authentic only if they are fully subordinated to the mystery as it discloses itself objectively in world, in history, and in community.

We have mentioned that consonance implies congeniality on the transcendent level, congruence on the functional level, congenitality on the vital level, and compatibility and compassion on the sociohistorical levels of our life-form. Here we must add that what may appear congenial, congruent, congenital, compatible, and compassionate—when looked upon only from these levels—may still be dissonant from the viewpoint of ultimate formative obedience to the disclosures of the mystery. It is dissonant as long as it does not obediently conform to the disclosures of the transcendent through its objective symbolic disclosures in world and society.

More often than not, such obedience will imply the sacrifice of what appears or feels more congenial, congruent, congenital, compatible, or compassionate. Formative obedience, while open to the mystery in its disclosure, must take all of these aspects into account, yet never be ruled by any one of them exclusively. It should welcome them wisely as *possible* sources of what the transcendent may want for one, yet it should never absolutize any aspect as such.

Briefly, truly formative congeniality implies formative obedience first of all; it takes into account congruence and congenitality; it respects the demands of compatibility and compassion. It should also be noted here that formation science usually speaks about congeniality without explicitly mentioning obedience, though, from what we have said, it is always implied on all levels of the life-form. Therefore, congeniality that is disobedient would not only be self-destructive and deformative; it would also be a contradiction in terms.

Simplicity

The gift of consonance is a gift of harmony with the mystery as it discloses itself in our formation field. Its presence fills us with awe. We behold the manifestations of the mystery in events, things, and people. We are called to be open in faith, hope, and consonance to their deepest meaning. Detaching our minds and hearts from surface appearances, we enter into the eternal stillness, the silent abyss out of which they emerge. All forms share this silent source. It is the ground of the consonance to which they are called. All are restless until they find their rest in this holy origin.

The world to which we give form is not homogeneous. It is full of differentiated appearances. The holy assumes countless forms. Its main epiphanies can be found in events, things, and people. The historical epiphany of the holy is in events; its cosmic epiphany is in things; its human epiphany is in people. (Many traditions add to these three manifestations a fourth one, a trans-human epiphany; we will discuss this manifestation in a later volume.)

In our discussion of obedience, we focused on the appearance of the sacred in the events that coform our life's history. In this section on simplicity, we shall be concerned with the cosmic epiphany of the mystery in things, in the macro- and microcosmic appearances that coform our field of formation. In regard to this epiphany, our deepest disposition is one of simplicity, or the celebration of things in their simple givenness.

Awe and Simplicity

At times we may be aware that things arise out of a seeming nothingness that is nonetheless immensely generative, teeming, as it were, with mysterious power. A sense of awe about things and their hidden ground invades our being. We begin to muse about their formation, reformation, and transformation. We find ourselves on a journey into their depths. We sense their changeable fluidity in the presence of something "other," something "more than." Our present-day insights into the atomic and subatomic whirl of things deepens this sense of awe.

Why is there something rather than nothing? What is behind the enchanting dance of falling and rising forms in the universe? What secret do they hide? Whence come and whither goes the awesome atomic power hidden in all things? Is there something that orchestrates this music of the spheres? Something that does not diminish, break, or fade? Is there an eternal source, an unspeakable One, an unceasing nameless center of all becoming?

It is easy to lose this appreciation for things in their simple givenness. We are seldom present to them as shrines of the sacred. Our obsession with control accounts for this loss. Reasonable concern for the subjection of things and their prudent manipulation is commendable. We are the stewards of this corner of the universe. It is part of humanity's responsibility to give form to the world, to make cosmos out of chaos. Obsession with such subjection becomes deformative if it excludes other modes of presence, if, for example, compulsive control leaves no room for simple presence to things in reverence and wonder. If we become too possessive and manipulative, things lose their fascination as epiphanies of the mystery.

Analytical Approach versus Undivided Presence

In service of the formation of the world, we must approach things analytically in our textbooks, clinics, factories, and laboratories. While this approach is necessary, it should be balanced by moments of undivided presence, as when we dwell in nature, enjoy beauty, feel playful, or simply wonder about the marvel of our minds, bodies, and surroundings.

To survive and give form to our lives, we need to collect, maintain, and manipulate many things. The more complex society is, the more complicated such activities become. Without this practical interaction with things, life would come to a standstill. However, this way of involvement should not absorb all our possibilities for presence. We should create transcendent pauses in which things are allowed to emerge in their pristine simplicity as sacraments of the sacred.

In the midst of the rush of modern life, we must learn to detach ourselves and to concentrate in tranquility on the things we are doing, seeing, or using. We must be so detached that we can be present in poverty of spirit to precisely this moment and the simple things it embraces. Such presence sets us free in unexpected ways. The liturgies of various form traditions, for instance, are exercises in simplicity. Participants leave their projects behind them as they try to be present wholeheartedly to words, acts, and symbols that have been developed over the centuries in coherent structures. Together these structures point to the epiphany of the holy.

Simplicity versus Exaltation

Presence to things simply as given can set us free from exaltation and its illusions. We are less caught up in the entanglements of exalted images, memories, and anticipations. The pride-form weaves a screen between our deepest self and our formation field. The blade of simplicity cuts through the web of these exalted feelings and enables us to develop a silent reverence for things as they are. The fruits of simplicity are serenity, integrity of life, and a certain directness in all that we do. Simplicity brings us into contact with the all-embracing mystery of formation. This mystery remains elusive, in spite of the fact that everything we encounter emerges from its pervasive power. This hidden mystery is the principle of consonance.

Simplicity allows us to experience the interformative harmony of all things in nature. The rhythmical song of the seasons is revealed to us in changing leaves, in the ebb and flow of the tides, in the restoration of our health. Animals and plants, deep valleys, and distant stars point to a common source when we immerse ourselves in them simply and directly in carefree contemplation.

Simplicity lets us do things in a gentle way, without exalted willfulness. We do them as if we were not doing them. Our actions are not motivated by a desire for monetary reward or an anxious striving for compliments. Doing things in simplicity of mind and tranquility of spirit clears the way for aesthetic creation, inspired conversation, lucid thought, and right action. We feel more like celebrating the love that binds us together as people.

Being Present in Simple Appreciation

Any particular thing—be it an act, a thought, an image, a tool, an art object—can be a transcendent pointer to the mystery of formation. A single drop of dew, a leaf on a tree, the petal of a rose—each reflects infinite mystery. Presence in simplicity or poverty of spirit prepares us to heed the mystery in a single snowflake, ceramic, symphony, or flower. Food and drink are savored, not merely consumed. Our mind becomes like a motionless mountain lake, pure and clear. We are ready to reflect all things as they are without exalting them positively or negatively, without distorting them by manipulation.

Simplicity directs our attention with tranquility of mind to whatever appears in our formation field. At the moment of simple appreciation, we do not ask ourselves whether something is better than something else in our field. We simply enjoy *that it is*. We sense an inner completeness, infused by the formation mystery, in each thing we encounter. We grasp the special indwelling of the mystery in the particular and we stand in awe of its myriad ways. Our emptied mind comes to rest in the specifics of the formation mystery in each of its appearances. When the moment of simple presence is upon us, we leave behind categories and projects and want to savor transcendent meanings.

Simplicity is like a song: let everything simply be; let it announce wordlessly the mystery of its own form, its wondrous particularity. In simple appreciation, time is experienced moment by moment as the treasure it is. Things do not become an occasion for contest but an opportunity for disclosure. We begin to experience the unity at the basis of the formation field, a fusion of time and space. One thing mirrors the other, yet remains distinct. We experience each form in its particularity as well as in its connection with every other form, with the cosmic, human, and transhuman epiphanies of the mystery.

Simplicity, Ecology, and Task Fulfillment

Simplicity serves ecology. Respect for the specialness of things forbids us to impose our projects and desires heedlessly and destructively on subhuman forms of existence. We must blend our plans with the particular goodness of things that surround us in nature. We are their stewards, not their arbitrary masters. We should handle them with care and responsibility, acknowledging and cherishing the mystery that makes them be and in the end binds all of us together.

Simplicity helps us to fulfill our daily tasks wholeheartedly. We are serenely committed to whatever engages us. Even the simplest task assumes a new dimension, a deeper significance. Regardless of its simplicity, each thing we do becomes an encounter with reality as it is. When we are simply *with* the things at hand, we are wholly there. When we lose this simplicity, it becomes difficult to remain *with* and *in* what we are doing. Our presence becomes divided and dissonant. This is true not only of important undertakings; it applies even more to the seemingly insignificant actions that make up most of our days. The secret of formation, the source of serenity, is to be dedicated in poverty of spirit to the humble things and actions that bind our days together.

Everydayness and Simplicity

When we are poor of spirit, we are able to pay relaxed attention to the sounds of daily life: to wind and rain, the chirping of birds, the clamor of crickets, the footsteps of passersby, the steady rumble of traffic, the song of the steaming kettle, the hum of the freezer. We become attentive to the shape of a face, the fragrance of a flower, the form of a tree, the quaintness of a building, the flowing lines of a dress. In short, we live fully where we are and do not have to rush ahead to the next thing to be done.

Once we learn this art we may increasingly enjoy moments of wholeness and serenity. Within the limits of our abilities, we may also become more effective and practical. Lack of efficiency is at least partially the result of not being with the things we are doing. We may then overlook many details. We forget and confuse things. This would be less the case if we were truly with our task and attentive to our surroundings. Lack of involvement not only harms wholeness and serenity; it also diminishes effectiveness.

Wise Use of Things

Things in our formation field are gifts and means of the all-embracing mystery of formation. They may be natural or cultural. We may have interiorized them in concepts and symbols or in other images, memories, anticipations, and their corresponding feelings. We must form and use all of these things in a way that brings out their deepest meaning, a meaning rooted in the innermost form potential each thing received from the formation mystery.

The use of things in poverty of spirit means that we respect not only their innermost form, but also our own unique form and that of others. We may have to utilize things for ourselves, or we may have to use them with and for others. Self-centered tendencies tempt us to use things in possessive, manipulative ways that are incompatible with the demands of social justice, peace, and mercy. Simplicity implies detachment from the mere utilitarian meanings of things so that we can use them wisely in compatibility with their deepest form and with the demands of human interformation.

Living the simple life slowly pries us loose from the things that we cling to inordinately. We begin to use the gifts of nature and culture respectfully in inner detachment and poverty of spirit. We are no longer enslaved to things. Rather we strive to disclose and celebrate their deeper meanings and possibilities in the light of our life situation and in obedience to the mystery.

Relatively Unique Expression of Simplicity

The external expression of simplicity should be different for each person because each person is unique. Each differs in life call, style, and form; in physical health and strength; in sensitivity, insight, and interest; in the need for a certain amount and kind of recreation; in background, knowledge, and professional responsibility. True simplicity of spirit takes all of these factors into account. What is a wise and respectful use of things for one person may prove to be an unwise and disrespectful use for another.

There is infinite variety in the individual expressions of poverty of spirit. They vary from one person to another, and even from one period of life to another in the same person. Since each human life-form changes and grows, the expression of simplicity has to change accordingly. Most important are not the details of this expression but the spirit in which it is lived. The expression of simplicity should never become rigid and inflexible, isolated from the formation of our life as a whole. True wisdom in regard to the celebration of things is guided by openness to changes in our formation field.

Freed from mere possessiveness, we may find evidence of the mystery in a sunset, in the smile of a child, in a painting, in a sip of mellow wine, in an evening of good company. Everywhere in culture and nature, the mystery is waiting to reveal itself to the poor of spirit, no longer burdened by the need to possess or manipulate things disrespectfully. Unfortunately, we are tempted to forget this deepest human desire. We see only the glass of wine, the charming face, the lovely dress, the cozy home in which we live. Our inclination is not to go beyond the shell of things to the mystery they contain. We easily fall away from our innermost calling, from the message of a universe filled with mystery, and from our mission to disclose and celebrate its presence in the things that surround us. By our anxious, possessive preoccupation with things in isolation from their deepest ground, we may lose our joyful presence to them in simplicity of heart.

Reverence

Our lives are not formed in isolation. From beginning to end, they depend on interaction with others. The condition for consonance with people is our appreciation of their uniqueness. Each is called to be an unparalleled image of the mystery. We must revere this singular dignity because it is a gift of the holy, no matter how deeply it may be concealed under immaturity, imperfection, meanness, and hostility. We should have faith in the form potency with which people are endowed. Loving faith may awaken their shaky confidence in their own possibilities. We should nourish the hope that they can bring to light their hidden nobility. Perhaps our faith and hope is the inspiration for which they have been waiting.

Reverence for the distinctive dignity of people is a necessary disposition if we are to attain consonance. We must detach our minds and hearts from the distortions and disfigurations we see. Our loving faith must penetrate beyond the surface to the center of their wounded lives. There the mystery calls each one forth uniquely. We must share its compassion with their sufferings and failings. The sacred resides in their deepest interiority in a way that transcends its dwelling in things and events. This is the distinctively human epiphany of the holy in the midst of human misery. It endows human life with freedom and insight, with spiritual aspiration and feeling.

Because of the transcendent giftedness of humanity, our basic disposition of reverence in regard to people is different from the same disposition in regard to events and things. Events and things evoke in us the dispositions of obedience and simplicity. In regard to people, our disposition of reverence for the indwelling mystery gives rise to the disposition of distinctively human respect or loving appreciation of people in their gifted humanity. Without this disposition, congeniality, compatibility, compassion, justice, peace, and mercy cannot attain fruition.

Reverence and Appreciation

At certain moments we are touched by the mystery of others, the secret of their freedom, the holy enigma of their life. Other lives may seem so much alike, and yet, when we look at them with respectful appreciation, we discover an unparalleled distinctiveness in what each one says and does. We are moved by their vulnerability, the fragility of their hopes and dreams, their powerlessness in the face of bureaucratic power. At other moments we sense the profounder human feelings they hide so gingerly, emotions that cry out for understanding, compassion, and empathy. Embracing all of these is their human dignity, often offended and threatened. Yet it is still there as a nobility that shines forth as a silent appeal for respect from the depths of a broken life.

The reverence we should show for people is immensely different from what we may experience in regard to the presence of the mystery in events and things. We sense that people are called to be a personal manifestation of the eternal and its freely unfolding image in the flesh.

What if we have lost appreciation for people in their transcendent dignity? We may then handle them as if they were things. We forget about their relative uniqueness and try to categorize their distinctively human feelings in a numbered report. Our fascination with efficient organization and classification may betray humanity. Organization is necessary, but not fixation on organization. This is deformative, for it makes us bypass the distinctive humanity of people. We have no space and time left for their personal feelings and concerns, for their aspirations and ambitions. We begin to manipulate their feelings as if they were events and things to be controlled in the light of our projects. A certain bureaucracy can be a blessing, but to reduce all of life to red tape is devastating.

To supply the demands of modern society, we need to organize labor, production, and consumption. At times, we must look at people from the perspective of practical usefulness in a certain occupation or enterprise. It would be pernicious, however, if this became our only perspective. There must be other times in which we meet people respectfully, in the wholeness of their hoping, suffering, aspiring, feeling humanity. There must be moments of deeply felt human consonance. Without these we not only hurt others; we lose our own humanity.

Such moments of human consonance may be ours when we experience friendship; when somebody tells us about their pain and despair; when we visit a sick person, relieve poverty, or share the struggle of the dispossessed. We should create opportunities for people to be wholly themselves without fear or repression. We must be detached enough from our own plans and concerns that we can sit down with them and share in their hopes and dreams. We must offer them the gift of real understanding. If they feel really understood, they will experience our empathic participation in their formation field. This experience of compassion entails for many an unspeakable relief from isolation. It enables them to believe again in the beneficial meaningfulness of the mystery of formation as kindly imaged in unselfish human compassion.

Distinctively Human Presence and Exaltation

Presence to people in their uniqueness implies detachment from self-exaltation. The pride-form inclines us to exalt our own problems and projects to the point where we cannot see what others have to go through. The more we exalt our own concerns, the more we minimize those of others. This dense cloud of self-importance makes us oblivious to the outcries of those who do not figure in our plans. Reverence can blow the cloud away so that others may appear as they are in their woundedness and nobility.

Distinctively human presence in reverence brings out the best in people. Its fruits are compatibility, generosity, compassion, gentleness, and joyousness. It enables us to experience human consonance. We flow with the lives of others as loving companions, yet we maintain the subtle distance human privacy demands.

Distinctively human respect asks us to be gentle with people, not to force their lives into patterns we personally prefer. Our interaction is not inspired by a secret yearning for subtle control of their lives. We are moved neither by indelicate curiosity nor by profits that may accrue for us. Respect clears the way for human encounter. The respectful love we extend to people should also be extended to our own deepest self. We must love and revere our own veiled nobility as the unique gift it is.

Respect and the Chastening of Love

Some formation traditions use the word *chaste* to express this disposition of respect. The meaning of the word chaste is related to that of the verb *to chasten*, meaning "to refine," "to purify." A chaste, or respectful, love is one purified of historical pulsations, vital pulsions, and functional ambitions that are self-directed and disrespectful of the concerns of others. Such deformation breeds dissonance. It tempts us to coerce or manipulate ourselves and others at the expense of inner nobility and its silent appeal. Unchaste or disrespectful love violates the integrity of self and others spiritually and functionally, if not physically. It can violate, among other things, one's own or another's sexual integrity.

As we have seen, obedience restores our consonance with events and simplicity restores our consonance with natural and cultural things. Respect engenders consonance with the fundamental dignity and uniqueness of self and others. Disobedience, possessiveness, and disrespect are forces of isolation, fragmentation, and closure. In the realm of human relations, respect restores the consonance with others we may have lost through various kinds of alienation.

Respect for self is inseparable from respect for others. When we lose respect for our own giftedness, it becomes difficult to appreciate the gifts that others are. Chaste or respectful love of self means that we accept and affirm our life wholeheartedly. We revere it as a gift of the mystery. The height of loving self-respect implies the depth of humility. The most profound act of humility is that of full acceptance *as gift* of the limited gift that we and others are.

Respectful Service of Humanity

Loving respect for people is a healing and consoling force in society, but we should not understand this in a narrow way. Small-mindedness would restrict liberating respect to its ostentatious expressions. We may think only about the immediate relief of certain concrete needs of people for food, clothing, shelter. These are praiseworthy manifestations of loving respect, for we must incarnate our generosity in obvious expressions of compassion and concern, provided they are congenial with who we are and compatible with the situations in which we find ourselves.

We may be called as well to different, less noticeable incarnations of respectful love. In some cases these may be even more beneficial to humanity. Some are called to embody their loving respect for humanity and its formation in scholarship, artistic creation, or scientific research. It is possible that they and their colleagues serve humanity more effectively than if they would have spent their time and energy in feeding a limited number of people or teaching a small group of children. Their contribution to such scholarly, aesthetic, or scientific fields may hasten the moment in which a new insight is born. This birth of knowledge may benefit not only one small class of school children or one deprived section of the population. Untold millions may profit from their dedication. For instance, certain scientific breakthroughs may remove the causes of poverty for an entire population. The emergence of a new expression in art may bring many to the threshold of a deeper humanization.

We may have the talent and the ability to embody our loving respect for humanity in a professional engagement that would indirectly sustain common social efforts to alleviate the needs of people. In that case it would be unwise to spend our life solely in the relief of the immediate needs of a small group. We may enjoy such immediate service in loving respect of those for whom we care. Yet we may have to leave this service as a full-time task to the many admirable people called to this form of assistance.

Some may dread the thought of embodying their loving respect for people in the hidden services rendered by study, research, and artistic creation. There are no immediate rewards, grateful voices, and warm sympathy awaiting such scholars, scientists, or artists. They may strike people as somewhat cool and distant. The nature of their service demands a certain reservation to protect the solitude necessary for effective creation and reflection. They may enjoy little or no experience of concrete success. Many of them may die long before the service in which they participate yields a victory over human needs. Yet this breakthrough was only possible because numerous professional men and women spent years of research as inconspicuous servants of humanity. They may die unknown, but they will have served humanity well in the anonymity of tedious labors in their laboratory, writing den, operating room, or consulting office.

Celibate Component of Reverence

Reverence implies a celibate component that in no way inhibits or diminishes human love. Nor is it a denial of the sexual component of the vital life. The celibate moment is necessary for any human love that intends to remain truly respectful of the personal feelings, needs, and desires of the beloved. In marriage this celibate component may be experienced especially when the spouses discover in each other a uniqueness and inner solitude only the forming presence of the mystery can penetrate. The celibate disposition implies gentle respect for that ultimate mystery of each one's life. It enables spouses to respect one another's privacy when the need for silence and solitude is delicately communicated.

We may conclude that the disposition of celibate reverence is so basic to the structure of respectful human love that no true love is possible without it.

Needy Love versus Respectful Love

Human love begins in early childhood with a kind of needy love that shows little respect for others. It tends to be demanding, possessive, and imposing. We can tell that this childish love is still with us when we manifest love not out of respect for the other as emerging from the mystery but only to gain something for ourselves. Growth toward human respect must go beyond this. We must move toward a mode of love rooted in true respect for the other *as* other. Respectful love not only receives gratefully; it is ready to give graciously and to love others as they are. We reach the height of growth in loving respect when we appreciate others in their deepest calling, not merely as the imperfect persons they are, but as endowed with a personal form potency. This is the precious moment of distancing ourselves temporarily from the peripheral immediacy of others so that we can encounter them respectfully in their personal dignity and creative potential.

The movement from less to more respectful love demands constant effort and attention. At its most sublime heights, it draws one toward recollected presence to the mystery as the holy ground of the other. Daily concerns invade our awareness to such an extent that we forget that our main call, our reason for being, is respectful love. In our forgetfulness of this call, our love may regress to its earlier form of needy love.

For example, tired from daily preoccupations, we may turn to others merely for relief. If relief becomes the chief reason for loving others, it may be difficult for us to refrain from imposing on them. It then becomes almost impossible to respect the other as the gift of the mystery that he or she is. We cannot appreciate others as valuable in themselves apart from their usefulness to us.

Truly respectful persons are not demanding but facilitating. They appreciate others and try to help them be who they uniquely are. The sacred dimension of celibate respect can only emerge to the degree that the mystery of formation becomes meaningful for us. This happens when we renew our celibate presence to the mystery in solitude. Moments of celibate respect for our own and others' need for privacy flow forth from this foundation. These moments cannot be maintained for long without recurrent recollection and centeredness in the mystery as present to each of us.

Respect in Formation Counseling

An interesting illustration of the celibate component of respectful love can be found in good formation counselors. They form intimate trusting relationships with others without always and necessarily receiving loving respect in return. They are ready to revere their counselees even when there is no response or only a negative reaction from them. The celibate moment for counselors consists in their full knowledge and acceptance of the fact that they may not always receive loving reciprocation. They transcend the frustration naturally felt when their respectful presence meets a wall of indifference or hostility.

The counselor's respectful love is maintained even when a person becomes abusive, aggressive, seductive, or envious of other counselees. A counselee may demand exclusive attention and only slowly gain sufficient confidence and stability to stop imposing on the formation counselor. The counselor's unconditional respect for such a person can only be called celibate respect in the fullest sense if it is rooted in respect for the sacred ground of the counselee.

The dimension of celibate reverence for the privacy and the mystery of people is basic to all modes of distinctively human formation. It is the core of every expression of true respect that alone makes dedication to human formation possible. This is especially true when formation demands the tolerance of human inertia and resistance. In such instances one must be able to maintain respect and love without the reward of much or any reciprocity.

Distinction between Person and Personality

The foregoing considerations have highlighted for us the fundamental distinction between person and personality in the transcendent and in the functional sense. The fullness of the human personality can be reduced neither to the functional integration of an ego and superego nor to any empirically observable dimensions of the human life-form. While these constructs point to an important subordinate aspect of the human personality, they are insufficient to cover the whole of human life formation. For this reason the science of formation envisions the human person as a call to unique consonance with the mystery substantially united with each one's own preempirical center. Personality becomes the empirical expression in one's dispositional life of the relative consonance with this mystery that one has attained at any given moment of one's formation journey. Our substantial union with the mystery, which is always there, becomes increasingly a union of likeness, modulated in its personal expressions by one's significant interactions with the formation field.

A consideration of the etymological roots of the words *person, consonance,* and *respect* may facilitate our understanding of their specific mutual relationship within the formation theory of personality. *Person* and *personality* are derived from the Latin verb *personare*, meaning "to sound through." We become persons in the fullest sense to the extent that we allow the formation mystery to sound through our dispositional life-form as it develops in dialogue with our successive life situations.

Consonance is derived from the Latin verb *consonare*, meaning "to sound with" or "to sound in tune with." The mystery in its uniquely forming presence in our foundational life-form can only sound through our empirical personality to the extent that we become consonant or in tune with its basic inspirations in our dispositions and actions. The "sounding through" of the mystery in our life presupposes a "sounding with" the formative movements of the mystery that dwells in our inmost being and in all other aspects of our formation field.

This "sounding with" is only possible on the basis of our increasing respect for the presence and movements of the mystery within and without. *Respect* is derived from the Latin verb *respicere*, meaning "to look again." Only when we look again and again in faith and reverence do we become aware of the image of the mystery within us. This respectful awareness of the sacred image at the source of our personal unfolding enables us to give form to a dispositional life that is more and more in tune or in consonance with our transcendent, yet biogenetically embodied, roots. The more we grow in this union of likeness, the more the mystery itself will begin to sound through us personally. In this sense we coform our personality with the mystery of formation in dialogue with the historical unfolding of our formation field.

CHAPTER 4

Disposition of Firmness

Consonant life formation is impossible without the disposition of firmness. This is due to the fact that life must form itself in an upward movement. This attempt meets with countless inner and outer resistances, some so minute that they may go unnoticed, others so formidable as to be almost overwhelming. Be that as it may, resistances will always hinder the upward flow of our life, disturbing its peace and consonance. Not so surprisingly, the meeting between such resistances and our firmness is what gives form to life.

One could compare the forming flow of life to a river winding its way through sturdy rocks, splashing incessantly against boulders that would halt its flow, carving its course through mountain slopes and riverbanks. Without these resistances the river would not be able to give form to the rushing water. It is exactly the interchange between river and resistances that grants this body of water its unique form, beauty, and disciplined power. Without resistances the water would flow shapelessly away, to be absorbed by surrounding fields or to become an ugly swamp without sparkle.

Human life, like a river, must flow in consonance with the dance of formation in space, time, and history. This forming mystery manifests itself in the resistances of everyday life that invite us to rise up in nobility and strength. Life without resistances and the firmness of managing them wisely would soon become like a stagnant swamp, decayed and putrified, a life entrapped in pettiness, sparse in aspiration.

An effortless life without friction is an illusion, a wishful fiction, a flight from the challenges that mark our existence from morning to night. The disposition of firmness readies us to meet propitious moments of resistance. We see these not as sources of distress and despondency but as invitations to turn whatever is difficult into a formation opportunity.

Lacking such firmness, we may feel like running from resistances in mute distress. Before long our lives may wither and waste away.

Firmness and Joyfulness

One reason for refusing to meet resistances is the fear that life would be without joy were we to engage in steady struggles. Is joyfulness, which is another basic disposition of the consonant life, compatible with firmness? Does firmness necessarily lead to austerity, harshness, even ruthlessness? The latter traits could be true of a perverted firmness, but in reality this disposition is meant to be as pliable, relaxed, and gracious as gentleness and joy.

Perverted firmness does not come from openness to the mystery of formation, which allows resistances in life, but from pulsations, pulsions, and ambitions that have not yet been made consonant. This fake firmness is alive in tyrants, dictators, and oppressors of every sort, in any masochistic purveyor of a false asceticism that has become an end in itself. Their joyless fortitude is enslaved to the pride-form, which breeds a discipline that is austere rather than gentle like the transcendent mystery at the center of human life.

By the same token, we cannot assume that genuine firmness will always generate pleasant and attractive experiences. What generates deep joy can be painful and unpleasant, as witnessed in the lives of heroic people called to battle the resistances created by unjust oppressors of the poor and underprivileged. Thus we ought not to confuse pleasure and satisfaction with the deeper joy that surpasses both of them. Pleasure is a vital delight, but life often demands that we forgo its gratifications. Satisfaction is a feeling of accomplishment associated with a job well done, but it should not be our main motivation for living. To receive the gift of joy, we must be firm enough to free ourselves from entrapment in either pleasure or achievement.

At moments of detachment, we may lose the agreeable feeling of being in control of life. However, we gain a new level of courage and insight, enabling us to reform our lives accordingly. A surge of joy accompanies any rise above stagnation. Take away the timely transcendance of mere pleasure and satisfaction, and joy will elude us like a beautiful cloud we try to grasp with greedy hands. Joy cannot be captured, no matter how hard we strive to attain it. It is a gift beyond human control.

The kind of firmness that fosters joyful and dynamic life formation rests in our resolve to reform our lives in response to the resistances we meet daily. Our joy arises in the trying. If we do not receive the gift of joy, it may be because we fail in firmness. It is equally true that to be steadfast is not our achievement alone; it is an effect of our cooperation with the formation mystery. We are most firm when we apprehend that the mystery of formation itself is our strength. In the midst of failure and weakness, the mystery is present, confirming us constantly. Our firmness always implies a loving acceptance of this deeper confirmation by the mystery.

Firmness is thus the concerted yet gentle effort of ourselves and the formation mystery to discipline our lives. This cooperation generates the kind of joy that persists in spite of disappointment, pain, and misfortune. Joy does not take such trials away. Many people, however, may be so oppressed, so exploited, and so mishandled by parents, teachers, unjust rulers, and employers that they miss the most primitive conditions necessary to foster joy through discipline. Those of us who are blessed with these basic conditions should try to grow in the disposition of joyful firmness. This will enable us to fight the good fight for and with others against oppressors on all levels of society and in all social institutions. If we do not learn how to cope firmly with the small resistances in daily life, how can we hope to persevere in our fight against the unjust oppression of the poor and downtrodden?

The ongoing formation of our own life is difficult enough, but it is even harder to help the underprivileged give form to their life and world. Along the way we have to cope with many restraints that hinder both their unfolding and ours, restraints that try to halt the upward flow of life's forming energies. Without firmness it is practically impossible to cultivate a consonant way of life, either for ourselves or for the oppressed. Worst of all, without firmness we can hardly open up to transcendent joy.

Firmness and Decisiveness

We cannot go far in the formation of ourselves or others if we refuse to be decisive. Many moan about their problems and burdens as if they were comparable to the immense injustices oppressed people have to suffer for a lifetime. The fact is, giving form to life and world cannot be effortless and without friction, even for the privileged. If we want to form our lives and work to reform an unjust society, we have to cope continually with resistances. There is no use bewailing our labors for peace and justice when they do not succeed. Rather, we must rise above these setbacks with faith, hope, and love.

Firmness is essential if we are to contend with the obstacles that hinder our unfolding and delay the reformation of a merciless, mercenary world. If we allow only a little strength to flow into us from the mystery of formation, we can expect to grow only a little in the struggle for a humane, harmonious society. By contrast, if we embrace wholeheartedly the fortitude infused in our soul, we will grow strong in the battle for justice that apeals so deeply to humankind on Planet Earth.

Whether we are appraising impediments to peace and justice, prevailing over them valiantly, or bearing with them patiently, we are immersed in a harrowing venture. Opposition from without and inhibition from within call for the courage to face and handle diverse challenges. If this is not yet possible for us, we should persevere in gentle patience or passive strength until we reach the propitious moment for action. Initially we may be overwhelmed by negative feelings, such as disappointment, defeat, and self-depreciation. We may feel discouraged, guilty, shamed, indignant, angry. These sentiments can be as distressful as physical suffering. In fact, at times they are more agonizing than the worst bodily pain we may have experienced.

Distress of this magnitude may tempt us to avoid resistances. We dislike having to face both the trials in our inner life and those within our world. We ignore them in the hope that they will go away. Maybe they will go away, but usually they do not. Our best efforts to give form to life and world are bound to meet with a seemingly endless succession of resistances.

Formation as human is often wearisome and arduous. It is like swimming against a mighty stream. True formation implies suffering as well as joy. Once we acknowledge and accept this as the human condition, we will be less bothered by it. Once we are freed from the illusion that life will be smooth, we can begin to grow resourceful, resilient, even ingenious in the struggle of formation. We welcome resistances as formation events, as stimulating opportunities to grow in firmness, as signposts of the mystery, as stepping-stones to a dynamic and daring life.

In this stance of appreciation, resonances are experienced as veiled echoes of the epiphany of the mystery in our life. This is not to say that the mystery imposes resistances as such. Mostly they are traceable to other people or to the operation of our own inertia and pride. Still the mystery inspires us to respond to them in a way that resonates with its forming design. We must not expect the mystery to take suffering away. Rather, it helps us to respond to limits in meaningful, effective ways. It teaches us that joy is often born in the midst of pain.

We form life firmly by this attempt to prevail over resistances. Resistances are the crossroads that lead either to stagnation or ongoing formation. The choice is ours. Resistances invite us to grow in courage, openness, appreciation, and firm decision. Our capacity to respond creatively becomes ever more expansive and flexible. The way we handle adverse situations becomes more competent and effective. This is because resistances have forced us to become firm and flexible in the maintenance and direction of the upward flow of life.

Our spirit welcomes challenging problems. Wrestling with them forms us; ignoring them weakens and deforms us. What hurts us most can, paradoxically, be deeply formative. We learn slowly but surely that it is far better to face problems than to shy away from them, overwhelmed by dread, for nothing enduring can be built without rising above the obstacles that block generous projects for humanity.

Evasion of Resistances

Despite arguments to the contrary, most of us fail to be firm. Frightened by failure and suffering, by loss of popularity and of facile success, we try in some measure to evade or bypass the obstacles on our path. We delay confrontation, put our life in a holding pattern, drag our feet. We keep procrastinating in the hope that things will not only look better but be better tomorrow. Rather than struggling through painful issues, we choose to ignore them.

This anxious flight from what is difficult and unsettling engenders a great deal of worry and misery. It is one basic source of deformation. Since most of us suffer from this failure of courage, most of us live more or less deformed lives, at least during certain phases of our journey. At such times our joy is minimal. We may develop elaborate strategies to avoid as much as possible the awareness of trials, to escape the distress they inflict.

To elude the problems inherent in life, we may develop intricate illusions and security directives. We could become so alienated from life as it is, from the gentle discipline it demands, that only some form of direction or counseling could restore us to effective interaction. All we have accomplished is to replace the firm and reasonable facing of our problems with a suffering of our own choosing. We have chosen implicitly the deformation of our capacity to apprehend and appraise life as it is. Ironically, this substitution becomes more burdensome than the burden it was meant to relieve.

Excessively protective dispositions turn out to be the greatest resistance to free and joyous unfolding. They imprison our life by poisoning its source and inspiration, by paralyzing its dynamics, by halting its upward flow. This numbness breeds anxiety, guilt, and shame, accompanied by a sense of formation impotence. To escape these feelings, new deformative dispositions tend to proliferate, generating in turn their own afflictions. To diminish this pain, other protective dispositions are necessary, and so on. Soon we are imprisoned in a vicious circle of security directives that suffocate life itself.

Some may find both the opportunity and the courage to face this stifling deformation. With the help of formative counseling or direction, received privately or in common, we learn how to appraise anew the obstacles that life formation presents to everyone. If the deformation is too severe, formative counseling or direction may be insufficient and prolonged professional treatment becomes a necessity.

Evasion of the normal formation pains that accompany our daily dealings with resistance may lead to evasion of the opportunities these same resistances offer. In the case of chronic deformation by evasion, we lose not only the firmness disposition but also our momentum. We are encased, as it were, in the concrete of excessive safety directives. Without in-depth reformation, our imprisoned élan may not survive.

To prevent this calamity, we should form in ourselves, as well as in those entrusted to our care, the disposition of firmness. Resistances are indispensable and necessary for formation. Dealing with them requires firmness of apprehension, appraisal, and decisive affirmation. We must also be willing to bear graciously the sufferings they entail. Parents in this regard ought to provide the gift of small resistances to their children to prepare them for what life in general will surely provide.

In summation, firmness is the basic disposition we need to deal formatively with the obstacles we meet when we live in an unjust, greedy, fallen world. So central is the disposition of firmness in the face of resistances that many other dispositions are affiliated with it. We will consider some of them in the following pages. This reflection will serve to deepen our insight into the disposition of firmness itself, for in some way these related dispositions are subordinate expressions of the central disposition of firmness as such.

Disposition of Formative Suspension of
Instant Pleasure and Satisfaction

The formation theory of personality that is part of the overall science of formation draws distinctions among the *pleasures* afforded by the pulsing, vital dimension of life; the *satisfactions* gained in fulfilling ambitions of the functional life; and the *joy* that accompanies openness to the directives of the transcendent dimension. Distinctively human formation does not exclude pleasure and satisfaction; it requires only that they be consonant with the inner and outer aspects of one's formation field. To gain or to maintain such consonance, we must often suspend both pleasure and satisfaction.

In many instances formative suspension may mean only a temporary delay of the felicity or comfort of what is immediately gratifying and agreeable. For instance, we may delay the pleasure of snacking in the afternoon in order not to spoil a dinner to which we have been invited in the evening. In other situations formative suspension may imply our lasting renunciation of certain indulgences that remain available to others. Alcoholism, for instance, demands an enduring suspension of the pleasure of drinking alcoholic beverages. Diabetes or a severe heart condition may demand the suspension once and for all of certain foods one used to enjoy. A marriage commitment requires the enduring suspension of liaisons one may have indulged in before marriage, even if their attraction does not totally cease. The same goes for satisfaction. When a person chooses to excel as a concert pianist, he or she may have to forgo lastingly the satisfaction of being a successful teacher.

Ongoing renunciation of either pleasure or satisfaction is still designated a "suspension" because the impulsive desire may well remain alive. In that case only the *fulfillment* of the desire can be lastingly suspended. From the viewpoint of one's formative life direction, the desire is no longer indulged. From the perspective of vital pulsions, however, the possibility remains that the latent pulsion may overwhelm one's resolve. This happening proves that in many cases only *suspension* is involved, not *extinction* of the pulsion. Firm and effective life formation requires, therefore, that we suspend temporarily or lastingly pleasant experiences that interfere with the consonant formation of our life.

Differences in Formative Suspension

Considerable differences can be found in each person's disposition for formative suspension. Such differences in capacity for suspension mark for better or worse one's power of formation. As we know, to give unique, consonant form to life requires that we overcome many resistances. Most of them emerge ultimately from undisciplined pulsations, pulsions, ambitions, and aspirations that clamor for instant fulfillment. Distinctively human formation is, by its nature, a long-term project. We must patiently appraise all aspects of our formation field, past, present and future, to discover whether they resist or resonate with the unfolding of our life. We ask frequently how we can turn resistances into resonances, obstacles into opportunities, temptations into liberations. What characterizes human formation as human is the consistency and consonance with which it transcends momentary pulsations, pulsions, ambitions, or aspirations in their demand for instant fulfillment.

Take the example of a student who complains that she is unable to write her term papers. What is the cause of her paralysis? The formation counselor may detect that she has not been sufficiently formed during childhood in the firm direction of the pulsions of her vital dimension. Her resistance to unpleasant self-exertion finds its source in an inner dissonance. Neither the transcendent nor the functional dimension of her life form has gained sufficient firmness to direct her vital pulsions effectively.

It is normal for everyone to experience resistance to a task that requires strenuous self-exertion. Naturally such a task interferes with one's tendency to prefer agreeable, easy movement and action, a preference that signals a certain inertia and attachment to familiar routines. An ordinary experience of resistance becomes problematic when one lacks the firmness of direction and determination to suspend the more pleasant things one wants to do instead of tackling the task at hand. One must be able to postpone or forgo pleasure firmly and gently when its indulgence interferes with the consonant formation of life and world.

Early Formation of the Suspension Disposition

The disposition of formative suspension should be formed early in life. Parents form their children to suspend instant gratification by numerous exercises gently imposed, such as sharing toys and candy with others, going to bed and rising at regular times, interrupting their pleasant games to greet a visitor, taking their meals in a certain style, participating in household chores. Each of these practices obliges children to suspend the inner or outer process they would much prefer to continue without any displeasing interruptions. Their disposition for formative suspension grows and deepens through each of these exercises. Teachers can also be formative in this regard. When they impose certain tasks, their execution should neither be too demanding nor too easy in view of the age, the capacities, and the makeup of their students.

By the age of fifteen or sixteen, many young people do acquire the firm disposition to suspend instant indulgence in anything that feels good, pleasant, and agreeable when consonant life formation demands such a renunciation. They can, therefore, be effective in their daily chores, in schoolwork, and in social interaction. They are quite capable of handling the usual resistances anyone may feel in relation to everyday duties, especially when the demands of duty interfere with one's desires of the moment.

Some people may be unable to form this disposition of suspension. They cannot cope effectively with the ordinary resistances in their formation field. We could say that their resistance-tolerance is too low. They cannot bear patiently with a prolonged suspension of the fulfillment of their immediate pulsions, ambitions, and aspirations. They seek instant gratification, attainment, achievement, or enlightenment. The pulsation of their life dominates their ambitions and aspirations. Some of them may speak beautifully about their ideals and genuinely mean what they say at the moment of enthusiastic verbalization, yet their concrete life remains basically ruled by insufficiently appraised and integrated vital pulsions. Their idealism has no staying power.

We may conclude that meaningful, coherent formation in a distinctively human sense is impossible without the formative disposition of consonant suspension. People who lack this disposition are heading for failure in the harmonization of inner life with interformation, of labor with leisure.

Deformative Disposition of Evading Resistances

The impulsiveness of the vital dimension may compel the powers of functional and transcendent mind to develop ingenious strategies to avoid problems. One may become an expert in evading situations that threaten to interfere with one's easy routines and self-indulgences. Excuses for failures, omissions, and poor performances may be masterfully contrived. One may even sound quite virtuous. Initially others may be deceived, especially when the one who evades the resistance is intelligent, soft-spoken, and charming. One's apparent failure in daily performance and production, in careful attention to detail, is often compensated for by a vivid imagination about the great things one is going to do in the future, or one's hidden, unrecognized talents, one's "spirituality" or one's "contemplative bent," or the fantasy about what amazing achievements would take place instantly "if only. . . ."

People whose life-form is dominated by vital pulsions may have the gift of easy verbalization and a certain seductive charm. They may be able to veil their lack of productivity and painstaking fidelity to detail by an attractive apparent form. Playing, usually prefocally, on certain needs and dreams of countless insecure people, they may be able to live an inert, self-indulgent, yet utterly charming life. Appearances are often so deceptive that good-looking persons without inner solidity may be elected or appointed to responsible positions of administration and leadership. Their inertia guarantees that nothing of importance will happen when they are in charge. Feigning an importance that is not theirs, they are more than happy to let others do their work. Impulsively, and mostly prefocally, they may use the power and prestige of their office to avoid any problems or issues that challenge their routine responses and thereby threaten their feeling of form potency.

Other victims of the vitalistic form of life are not so fortunate. They are not endowed with innate charm and verbal facility, with good looks and melodious voices. Their life can be and often is disastrous, not only inwardly but also in the public eye. They cannot as well hide their inertia behind attractive appearances. Lazy persons who by genetic predisposition are dignified, charming, and well-spoken can often indulge their aversion from work and other resistances without incurring too much public rejection and indignation. Many people are too kind or simple-minded to see the underlying infirmity of such a life.

Persons who are not so enchanting, pleasantly verbose, cleverly social, or pompously impressive, must prove their worth by regular performance and production. Real and enduring achievement in daily fidelity to one's task is impossible without the repeated suspension of what is momentarily more pleasant and agreeable or of what flows with the ease of routinization.

Genesis of the Self-Indulgent Disposition

Formation scientists seek the origin of dispositions first of all in the period of initial formation. The concept of "formative prototypes" is helpful in this phase of the research. We prefer the term *type* to *model*, for the former term suggests more latitude for eventual personal versions of the type concerned. When one speaks about a typical teacher, one does not mean that she has modeled her teaching in every detail after that of another teacher who functions as her model. She may be typical only insofar as she assumed in her life in a personal way the characteristics common to teachers in our society. She acquires this typical set of dispositions through interformative contact with other effective teachers. They become the general prototypes, not necessarily the compelling precise models, for her own professional comportment and disposition.

In a similar way parents should function not as models but as prototypes for their children, leaving them latitude for personal appropriation of the parents' type of life as well as room to grow beyond it. Children need to develop their own life-form with its distinctive texture of dispositions, though they may adopt a personal version of the general type of life and the dispositions they appreciate in their parents. Highly influential in this interformative process is not what parents say but who they are. For instance, if their disposition to suspend instant fulfillment is finely developed, this will be communicated to their children.

Formation is always in some way interformation. Children are formed by the prototypical lifestyle of their parents. The needs of children become in turn a stimulus for the parents to form themselves in the art of consonant suspension, wherein one grows in firm yet gentle self-control through expressions of dignity and restraint.

A less excellent example of interformation between parents and children occurs when the parents are inconsistent, unsteady, and vacillating in self-discipline and decisiveness. They themselves are fickle in the execution of daily chores at home and at work. Children pick up their self-indulgent whining and complaining about what life demands of them. Instead of being honestly ambitious and resilient under pressure and resistance, they are unstable and disordered in the everyday organization of their time and space. In this case, the parents function in the life of their children as negative prototypes who promote a self-indulgent or merely routinized life.

Parental Prototypes and One's Unique Inner Protoform of Formation

The prototypical impact of parental life on the formation of children is substantial. One source of this power is situated in the presentiment in children of a formation mystery that guides all things. This presentiment is vague, implicit, and prefocal. Precisely because it is implicit, children are inclined to experience their seemingly all-powerful parents as manifestations of that unknown guiding power.

There is still another mysterious and unique epiphany hidden in the center of each child's life. This is neither awakened as yet nor disclosed to them in personal experience. We refer to their own uniquely gifted protoform of life, to their foundational life-form. Prefocally children feel inclined to identify the prototypical life of their parents with their unique inner protoform, for it is still concealed from their apprehension and appraisal. Hence, the prototypical powers of parental presence are immense.

Their dispositions may become either temporarily or lastingly the dispositions of the child. For this reason parental firmness may become their firmness, parental laxity their laxity.

Mitigation of Parental Prototypical Power

Can the formative power of the prototypical lifestyle of parents be mitigated? Can it be made less of a threat to the inner protoform of the child? Fortunately, the impact of parental formation can be tempered by the faith, hope, and love the parents themselves cultivate and manifest toward their children.

Faith, hope, and love comprise the basic unified triad that underlies distinctively human formation. This triad expresses itself in the disposition of consonant, consistent care: *consonant* because this care attunes itself respectfully to the life call of the child insofar as it discloses itself in the light of parental faith, hope, and love; *consistent* because this care is not capricious and whimsical, not at the mercy of passing pulsations, pulsions, and ambitions. The basic formation triad is rooted in the transcendent aspect of human life, which is less vulnerable to the flux and flow of passing feelings.

This basic triad effects a disposition of "abandonment to" the formation mystery as symbolized by the parents. As such, it counteracts the emergence of a disposition of feeling "abandoned by" the parents and the formation mystery they symbolically represent. Such favorable effects depend on the incarnation of this triad in a disposition of consonant and consistent care. Though this care is never perfectly realized in the human condition, our concern should be to approximate it as well as we can in all of our interformative relationships.

Consistent, consonant caring is especially significant when we try to foster in children the disposition of firmness and consequently of formative self-discipline. The triad of faith, hope, and love, expressed in care, awakens in children a prefocal sense of their own form potency. They sense that they are obviously held dear by their parents. Otherwise, why should they care so much? The parents' faith in them kindles the faith that they can make something worthwhile out of their lives. Loving care communicates that their parents never abandon hope for their well-being and success. This confirms their own emergent hope that they can give form to their life in their own way, over and beyond the prototypes they have been exposed to in childhood and infancy. The love of the parents that permeates their hope and faith enables children to live in consonance or in love with what they are called to be and become. If their parents love their uniqueness so unconditionally, it must be truly valuable and attractive.

We all know punctual, successful, firm parents who provide their children with every material advantage available. They care for them materially, not humanly. A warm radiation of the formative triad is missing. In spite of their own example of self-discipline, their own mastery of life and its surroundings, their children may lead impotent, superficial, chaotic lives.

We may also know vacillating parents who do not manifest much self-control or reasonable asceticism. Yet they possess and manifest genuine faith, hope, and love in regard to the potentialities of their children. Despite their lack of disciplined integration, their faith, hope, and love may grant the children a firm, secure life formation. Notice well that love is the greatest of the three, but it is not sufficient. It must be accompanied by formative faith that children are gifted and guided by the formation mystery, that they can do well in their own good time if others do not interfere in any violent or disrespectful fashion. Nor can love be effective in formation if its formative action is not sustained by hope for the future unfolding of the child's life under the veiled aegis of the mystery that operates at its center.

Children sense without question the presence or absence of this unified triad. They feel its chilling departure despite an abundance of material gifts. This experience cannot be expressed by them since it is usually prefocal and implicit. Even if they could talk of it, they dare not, for the prospect of negative abandonment by the parents who sensed this dissatisfaction is too frightful to face. Admitted or not admitted, the terrifying emptiness is there. It undermines a child's basis for a firm, secure life formation, often for a lifetime.

Insufficiency of Parental Love

Love that is accompanied by despondency instead of hope, by uncertainty instead of faith, cannot overcome the negative power of the prototypical life of the parents. The message is, "I love you, but I cannot really believe and hope that you are able to do as well or better than I did, be it in your own congenial fashion." Often children of successful or famous parents turn out badly. Their own potency for firmness seems to be paralyzed. Their successful, well-controlled parents may have loved them, but they were unable to convince their children through their own profound faith and hope in them that they would fare well on their own formation journey.

Parental success, mastery, and dominance can be a source of discouragement and laxity in children. Therefore, the more prosperous and thriving the parents are, the more they must radiate the faith and hope that their children can do as well or better in their own way, usually a different or less noticeable way. They must convince their children of their faith that accomplishment through firmness should not be confused with public recognition or with the type of acclaim or impressive appearance that happens to be their own. Parents should make light of these fleeting externals in comparison to the inward nobility and firmness of their children. That is what makes each human life worthwhile, in spite of the absence of applause. Applause can be encouraging, but it can also spoil the consonance of life by fostering the pride-form and its blinding exaltations.

In the realm of interformation, love without faith and hope has little effect. We must not only love people; we must also really believe and hope that they can make their life valuable, no matter how limited they are. Faith and hope, like consonant love, rest ultimately on our implicit faith and hope in the formation mystery at work in all receptive people. Parents are called to become the believing, hoping, loving collaborators of that mystery in their children's lives. The promise that children are makes it worthwhile for parents to spend time and energy on their behalf.

To help children grow in the disposition of firmness, security, and certitude demands the gift of the parents' time. Not all people can make such time available to children due to the nature of their calling and their consuming tasks. Some people may opt to live the single life, knowing that what they do for the formation of humanity and world is in its own way as crucial as what parents do for their children.

CHAPTER 5

Formation in Firmness

We naturally spend time on the things for which we care most. When we love our garden, we can pass many an hour in the tasks of maintenance and beautification. People who enjoy musical performance have to spend time in daily practice perfecting their skill. Sports fans always find time to watch their favorite teams in action. Similarly, when we care for those entrusted to us, we take the time to communicate to them our faith, hope, and love in regard to their dispositional unfolding.

It takes time to form children in firmness and patience, to watch them gently and unobtrusively. Our caring presence alerts us to the tenuous signals they send out: signals of distress in weakness; silent pleas for assistance when their faith, hope, and love seem to be sagging; cries for direction and correction when they cannot yet find or impose these on themselves. To be firm with them, we must be firm with ourselves. It is so much easier to let things slide by, to allow them their little weaknesses, to avoid their unpleasant irritation due to our interventions. We would much rather enjoy instant popularity among those for whose firmness we are responsible. It becomes especially wearisome when we share our formation responsibility with a marriage partner or with others who, because of their own lack of firmness, compete for an easy popularity among children, students, or trainees. Our attempt to form them in firmness may be acknowledged only later in life, when they succeed where others fail.

Firm direction grows from a believing and loving presence, not from anger and irritation. One takes time for observation and wise deliberation. We do not wait until the failure of firmness is so obvious and disconcerting that punishment takes place impulsively and irrationally, accompanied by sudden outbursts of anger without wisdom and compassion. Usually if we neglect the first subtle signs of laxity and allow blatant

67

misconduct to build up, we are compelled to react angrily. Our harsh measures are unable to form children in the deeper firmness they need in order to respond to their own inner resistance to self-discipline.

The art of formation is in large part the art of appropriate and timely praise and blame in ways that are congenial, compatible, compassionate, competent, and effective. Firm parents and other people responsible for formation are masters in appropriate reward and punishment. They lovingly provide their charges with the right resistances that build firmness, strength, and self-discipline. Their love is not spineless, sentimental, and blindly accommodating; it can be tough and demanding when necessary.

Firmness and Conviction of Form Potency

The science of formation presumes that faith in one's form potency as a gift and a challenge of the mystery is a necessary condition for free and joyous unfolding. Parents, clergy, teachers, and other formative persons must convey their faith in others' form potency by exposing them to new, ever more demanding resistances. In their focal awareness they may resent such obstacles and complain bitterly. Prefocally, they realize that we believe in their capacity to give form to their situation in the face of difficulties. This test, once passed, generates faith in their own form-giving capacity under adverse conditions.

Faith in one's form potency, in its firmness and resiliency in the face of resistances, is essential for the formation of a consonant life. This is the firsthand effect of the confirming faith, hope, and love of caring parents, teachers, and formation directors who do not hesitate to expose their directees to resistances. Nor do they spare them correction, appropriate punishment, and discipline.

The reality of one's form potency must be experienced early in life. Lacking this initial formation in the disposition of firmness, the stamina for consonant, consistent formation may be missing later on. To try to acquire this disposition during one's later ongoing formation is a painful, problematic enterprise. Once we are convinced of our form potency as a gift of the mystery, it is unlikely that we will ever be shattered totally by the blows of life. Undoubtedly, this is the greatest gift formative people can give to those in whom they believe.

It is not adequate that children, students, or trainees be made to feel valuable, worthwhile, or lovable. They must feel far more than that if consonant formation is to proceed. They must feel potent or capable of coping personally with obstacles. Form potency should not be experienced as an isolated power. In that case one would risk collapse when resistances to the creative formation of life and world seem unendurable. Our power must rest in faith in a higher form potency that pervades the universe benignly. Our formation history is bound to a mysterious power in which we ourselves participate.

This is why we say that simple trust of parents in their children is not enough. Children will sooner or later discover that they themselves are as untrustworthy as other people when it comes to staying firm. Their parents must manifest faith and hope in them, for faith, unlike mere human trust, refers implicitly to a higher potency, to the mystery of formation we believe in some way creates, sustains, restores, and rekindles its special epiphany in the formation potency of each person.

One's faith, hope, and consonance in regard to one's parents is transposed transfocally to the formation mystery as epiphanous and operative in one's own form potency. The faith, hope, and consonance they show in regard to us is now experienced as radiating toward us from the formation mystery itself. The deeper this faith conviction is, the less vulnerable will be our powers of endurance, resiliency, and creative coping with resistances. Such firmness of potency conviction, rooted in faith, is the birthplace of heroes and saints, those who become well-known and those whose inconspicuous heroism in the midst of poverty and adversity remains unapplauded.

Life Call and Firm Management of Time

Faith in form potency sustains fidelity to our call to foster the formation of life and world in accordance with the firmness disposition. We feel called to make our limited life span serve as best as possible the interests of emerging and suffering humanity. We experience simultaneously this appeal to potent service and the pressure of the finite time allotted to us for competent completion of this task. An awareness of these limits inspires us to foster a firm management of the time dimension of our formation field. We begin to take our time in hand, as it were, organizing it in such a fashion that we do not paralyze our potency for effective service by wasting time or by letting it disperse uselessly due to our inertia.

In the light of our calling, time appears as a precious commodity to be jealously guarded. In one sense, time and timing are everything. Outside the bounds of time, nothing happens in regard to formation, for formation is time-bound. The firm management of time determines how much we can do well during our brief sojourn on earth. Our service to humanity, therefore, depends for its effectiveness on the right use of time.

Resistances against an expedient ordering of time are legion. We meet them daily, and we often fail to master them. It seems necessary that we initiate ourselves and others in the firm, judicious management of time. Time has to be managed well if we want to pursue the most effective investment of our form potency and the energy it entails. Our best possible service of humanity, in collaboration with the mystery of formation, requires a firm, functional ordering of the time and space of our formation field. A realistic apprehension and appraisal of our form potency, together with the form energy and life call linked with it, make us appreciate even more the preciousness of time. We want to preserve this treasure and maximize our potential to discipline its use.

The threat of abandonment or of the withdrawal of faith, hope, and love by parents or other significant formation figures can be used overtly or subtly as a means of control and dominance. This makes it much more difficult for children to take their time, to wait, to trust in the good time of the mystery. The more insecure they feel due to negative abandonment, the more problematic it becomes for them to suspend instant pleasure or ambition. These children know what they have now; they feel as uncertain about tomorrow as they do about the faith, hope, and love of fickle parents. Such is the prefocal logic of these unfortunate little ones. They experience their formation field as totally unpredictable; hence, they prefer the predictable fulfillment of the moment to the unpredictable challenge of the future.

To enable them to cope with resistances that demand suspension of immediate satisfaction, these children must be exposed to firm, formative prototypes who, at the same time, communicate faith, hope, and love. Children may then dare to abandon themselves to their own form potency as a gift of the mystery. As we have seen, only when this faith, hope, and love are expressed in consistent, consonant care, at least most of the time, will children gain the security that enables them to form life firmly with the help of the resistances offered by the formation field.

Resistances and Patient Firmness

Firmness, fortitude, and strength are words that tend to evoke in us active images. Our functional society uses them mostly in a more or less aggressive way. Rarely do we dwell on passive strength, the power of endurance and forbearance, of tolerance and waiting, of quiet tenacity and relaxed perseverance. The firmness required for these approaches can be far greater and more taxing than the power needed for active fortitude. Various modes of passive firmness can be found in the disposition of patience.

Many resistances in our formation field cannot be immediately overcome. Some will be with us forever. To turn them into formation opportunities requires the art of patience. The ability to take our time is a form of patience. Taking time means that we are willing to wait for success, for the knowledge or skill we need to develop, for the cooperation we hope to enlist. Because we lack the firmness of patience, we may fail to use our minds calmly and persistently to solve a problem, to court the people we need for the execution of our projects, to prepare a tasty meal, to create aesthetically uplifting surroundings, to repair or improve in time the appliances, furniture, cars, or houses needed for our formation of life and world.

If we have developed firmness in patience, we are inclined to take the time we need to overcome many of the resistances that block the consonant unfolding of our lives. Patient firmness is formative. Patient people have given a certain form to their lives as a whole that distinguishes them obviously from impatient persons. Who they are comes through in their way of acting, speaking, and waiting, and in their movements, pace, and gestures. Interformatively, their patient presence may calm others who are overanxious or too much in a hurry, provided they are receptive to this gift. If they are not inclined to be receptive, such patience may irritate them beyond measure. They may misinterpret it as laziness or inertia. However, true patience is never inertia. It is a dynamic, poised readiness for the propitious moment, an alert waiting in composed attentiveness for any opportunity that may emerge to cope effectively with the resistances at hand.

Patience is resignation in the sense not of capitulation but of reassignment; that is to say, patience firmly assigns new meaning to an enduring resistance, and it gives it the meaning of a formation opportunity. For this reason patience is the mother of reflection. Impatience acts upon the first impulse, image, or thought that stirs one inwardly; it wants instant solutions; it cannot bear with the discomfort of unsolved problems; it is enslaved to the pleasure and satisfaction of their immediate solution.

Patient people, by contrast, have acquired the firmness to tolerate the dissatisfaction of dissonance long enough to find an appropriate response. Theirs is the patience of the good repairman, the wise parent, the dependable typist or secretary, the successful businessperson, the scholar or con-scientious scientist, the accomplished painter or musician, the well-prepared teacher, writer, formation counselor, or physician.

Disregarding Resistances instead of Appraising and Reforming Them

The worst enemy of patience is the disposition to disregard resistances in one's formation field. People who grow in the consonant life are inclined patiently to probe their formation field. They try to disclose past, present, or future resistances in themselves or in their situations. They become sen-sitive to anything that may interfere with the service they are called to render to humanity. They never try to escape resistances by disregarding their presence, for they realize that resistances do not automatically turn into opportunities. They must be thoroughly apprehended and appraised. If not, they remain a hindrance to consonant formation.

Disregarding resistances instead of reforming them into consonant op-portunities is a major obstacle to effective formation. We see it in the stu-dent who postpones preparation for an exam; in the author who loses weeks waiting for the moment of inspiration to appear; in spouses who refuse to apprehend and appraise together the mutual resistances that begin to undermine their marriage; in parents or teachers who do not see the growth of resistances in their children or who hope that the children will outgrow them; in the housewife who disregards the dirt that is accu-mulating in hidden corners or the clutter of disorder in wardrobes and drawers. Those who disregard their inner resistance to solving problems will not be inclined to start any demanding task.

The disposition to disregard resistances is related to the breakdown of the disposition of formative suspension. People typically ease into a rou-tine form of life. Routine dispositions can be excellent, but enslavement to them is pernicious. In that case we have neither the passive nor the ac-tive firmness to leave the ease of the routine life behind when coping with resistances that demand such renunciation.

Firmness and Heartfelt Responsibility

Our earlier considerations pertaining to the heart or the core form of human life gave us the insight that its main dispositions were responsibil-ity and sensibility. It is not enough for us to apprehend and appraise the resistances in life. We must be able to respond to them "wholeheartedly" from the core of our being. We must take responsibility for the consonant upward flow of our life. This implies that we assume responsibility for the resistances that try to halt or slow down this flow. Without this conviction of personal responsibility, we will be unable to reform resistances into consonant formation opportunities. Only when we accept a resistance as ours can we make it a formation opportunity. No one else can do that for us.

We should avoid the tendency to make others responsible for our resistances or to expect that they will solve them. Because most form giving happens in dialogue with resistances, we ourselves are responsible for dealing with them in a formative, consonant fashion. Life's consonant unfolding is dependent, therefore, on the way in which we dispose ourselves in regard to our formation responsibility.

Absence of All Responsibility

Some people refuse all responsibility. This may be due to genetic influences, to the experience of negative abandonment in infancy and childhood, or to other deformative factors. The life-form of total irresponsibility is psychopathic. Consonant, consistent upward formation is impossible for such persons. They are undependable and a constant threat to the formation of a just and compassionate society or global community.

Those who accept responsibility for the formation of life and world may do so in a dissonant or in a consonant way. Dissonant responsibility is not in tune with what transpires in our formation field. As a result, we may assume more than we ought to, and hence find ourselves faced with another problem: that of too much responsibility.

Excessive Responsibility

The responsibility one feels may be uncongenial with one's real form potency. We suffer from this deformation if we feel guilty when we hear of the heroic deeds other people are able to do for the poor in distant countries under dangerous conditions; or guilty for the sufferings our children bring upon themselves through their own free choice of incompatible friends or marriage partners; or harsh with ourselves due to others' rejection of us because of their own focal or prefocal envy of our talents and success. We may be tortured by feelings of responsibility for all the suffering in the world or in our society or family that we cannot relieve. If we are not firm enough to rise above such unfounded feelings of responsibility, they will inhibit the joyous upward flow of life.

We may suffer from the deformative feeling of responsibility that is incompatible with our life situation. For instance, we may feel responsible for not being as refined in dress and manner as people of a certain segment of the population are, even though we know that their upbringing and lifestyle were different from our own. We do not realize that our style is what it is because of its necessary compatibility with the inter- and outer spheres of our formation field that by necessity are different from theirs. Likewise, we may take responsibility for changes we cannot bring about in children or students because the changes are incompatible with the milieu from which they come, to which they must return daily, and in which they have to make their future.

We must find the fortitude to transcend such irrational feelings of responsibility. We must not feel tortured by a feeling of individual responsibility for the lack of compassion and mercy shown to people the world over. It is consonant, of course, to feel compassion with others and to do what we can within our possibilities to relieve their suffering. What constitutes a deviation is our feeling of personal responsibility for what is done to them beyond our power of relief and defense. The same applies to irrational feelings of personal responsibility for the illness and suffering of parents, friends, and neighbors when we can do nothing about it—even though some of them may irrationally blame us for their misfortune. Only a firm transcendence of such excessive feelings of responsibility can save us from crippling deformation.

Deficient Responsibility

Inadequate or deficient responsibility is another form of dissonance. We may not feel as responsible as we should for the congenial unfolding of our form potencies; for our lack of discipline; for the resistances we allow to fester within our own interiority; for the missing compatibility skills we do not try to acquire; for the self-centered harshness of heart that makes us insensitive and uncompassionate toward those who suffer injustice. We must develop the courage to face these deficiencies of responsibility and try to remedy them, for to refuse to do so is to grow more and more lax, to risk losing our firmness completely.

Consonant Responsibility

Consonant responsibility is the exact opposite of dissonant excessive or deficient responsibility. Few, if any, of us are ever perfectly consonant in responsibility. We all suffer from some excessive or deficient feelings in this regard. The best we may hope for is that we are on the way to consonant responsibility. Growth in this direction demands the firm discipline of continual appraisal of our formation field. Often formation counselors are called upon to assist counselees in the appraisal of the excesses and deficiencies of such responsibility dispositions as well as of the deformative, crippling consequences. Counselors should help them to gain the firmness necessary for the discipline of continual self-appraisal in the realm of responsibility. Patience is also necessary, for it is only over a long period of time that one can disclose what is really congenial, compatible, and compassionate in one's formation field. Only this deepening disclosure can relieve us from the debilitating consequences of excessive and deficient feelings of responsibility.

In summary, excessive responsibility weighs us down; deficient responsibility weakens and disperses our potency. Excessively responsible people paralyze their joy and resiliency; deficiently responsible or irresponsible persons dull and deaden the joy and resiliency of others. Here, again, initial formation plays an important role.

Parenting and the Formation of Consonant Responsibility

Parents who want to form their children in consonant responsibility are sensitive to the signs that children are trying to take responsibility for things for which they cannot be responsible, as, for example, the marital problems of their parents, the illness or irritability of their grandparents, the recalcitrant behavior of their brothers and sisters. Parents should be equally alert to the opposite symptoms, namely, those of refusal on the children's part to take responsibility for their own failures, to blame their siblings for conflicts, their teachers for grading problems, the school coach for troubles with the team.

No resistance can be turned into a formation opportunity unless we assume responsibility for this creative reformation. If we lack this kind of firmness, resistances will simply persist as resistances; they will retard or abort the upward flow of formation. Excessive or deficient responsibility, if not caught and reformed in childhood, can impair our entire lives. Instead of participating gently and effectively in the formation task of self, others, and world, we will merely drag on from day to day, never even glimpsing the fullness of peace and joy.

Resistances of Our Own Making

At times, all of us try to dodge the discomfort of taking upon ourselves, firmly and decisively, the responsibility for changing obstacles into opportunities for distinctively human unfolding. This is due to dissonant appraisal of our responsibility for the resistances we encounter. We do not honestly ask ourselves the question: How far are my resistances the consequence of my own choices? Any interformative situation is coformed by us; so are its resistances.

Do we honestly appraise whether the resistance we experience in a teacher, spouse, friend, colleague, or teammate is of our own making? How many of the resistances that we find in doing a certain task are due to our own lack of balanced living? Don't we often tend to go overboard in one or another direction? Do we really foster good nourishment, exercise, rest, and relaxation? Do we steadily try to purify depreciative thoughts and feelings? Do we nurture faith, hope, and consonance in regard to our form potency? The list could go on and on. The longer we live, the more we disclose those errors that create or contribute to resistances, that prevent us from changing these into openings for formation.

Firmness and Change of Disposition

At moments of crisis in life, we may have to do more than reform our dispositions. We may have to completely let go of ones that have been dear to us. We must drop certain dispositions because their formative object is gone. Our formation energy, though crystallized for a long time in these dispositions, must be directed elsewhere. Such trying moments demand all the firmness we can muster. What if a friend or family member suddenly dies? Because we loved that person deeply, we invested our formation energy in a disposition of special faith, hope, and love for him or her. A substantial part of our energy went into caring for their congenial unfolding. We delighted in being formed by them in turn. This disposition deepened and expanded over the years. It became more and more a part of our life-form itself, of our formation history. When this person dies, something has to die in us, too. That something is the disposition we developed toward this person.

The death of a formation disposition is a slow, painful process. The energy invested in the disposition spontaneously seeks its usual outlet. Not finding this, it searches desperately for a similar opportunity to discharge itself. Thus a reordering of our effusion of formation energy has to take place.

Sooner or later each of us will have to cope with this dispositional resistance due to the death of a loved one. The same dynamics may be active in a divorce; a separation; a conflict between friends; the loss of a home, a job, a hobby one really liked, or one's native country. In all of these situations our firmness is tested. Can we or can we not reinvest our formation energy, in spite of resistance, in other actions and dispositions, giving up a former, familiar pathway and inaugurating another?

Dispositions as Crystallized Formation Energies

The question of reinvesting formation energy makes us aware of another basic aspect of dispositions, namely, their being forms of crystallized energy. The formation of crystals causes a kind of physical energy to assume a crystalline form, which is relatively enduring. Figuratively, the term can be applied to any energy that assumes a definite or concrete form. Applied to dispositions it means that our more or less free-floating, undisciplined formation energies assume a definite direction in certain dispositions we have chosen. In and through such dispositions, we focus our energy on some facet of life or world. Any interference with that directed potency and its emission is experienced as a resistance. Once we are disposed, for example, to become an engineer, a writer, a banker, a gardener, or the like, anything that seems to block this way of life is felt as a resistance to be overcome.

In some prefocal way we are aware of the firmness that may be required of us if we bind our energy to certain dispositions. We fear preconsciously the resistances we may have to manage in the future in faithfulness to them. We are relatively free to invest our form potency in any disposition. Our fear of the demands such investment implies may make us want to escape the responsibility for such a commitment. To evade this responsibility, we may hand our freedom over to others. We forget that it is far better to fail in the formation of our own dispositions and their effectiveness than to succeed in blind compliance with the dispositions of others. In the latter case we do not succeed at all as distinctively human persons. We make ourselves formless particles in the stream of events that flow from the dispositions of others more courageous than we are.

Gradual Formation of Dispositions

We usually do not form a disposition at once. First comes the movement of gradual intensification and crystallization of formation energies. They take the form of directives that may remain passing and incidental. Then we may develop a certain direction that is more than incidental but not yet as enduring as dispositions are. Finally, we may establish lasting form dispositions. These, as well as the form directives that give rise to them or that flow forth from them, are more than merely informational.

They are called *formative* directives to distinguish them precisely from mere functional-intellectual directives, as, for example, those found on the instruction sheet that accompanies an appliance we have to assemble ourselves.

Form directives and dispositions represent the more or less affective-formative involvement of our formation energies in a person, event, or thing with whom we feel some affinity. When our familiar involvements are questioned or interrupted by resistances, our life-form itself may feel threatened. We experience this intervention as a menace because we tend to identify ourselves with the directives and dispositions currently involved in our formation field. In other words, we feel threatened in our form potency as expressed and contained in this precise dispositional involvement and direction.

We may try to escape such a discomforting experience by denying the threat or by evading the firmness we need if we want to change an affective-formation direction or disposition. In that case, form energies embedded in the disposition initially tend in the old familiar direction. Yet we have to detach ourselves from its now lost formation object. We have to refuse to indulge that customary mode of energy effusion, even if it has become part of our life-form itself. This process of detachment from a familiar mode of form-energy emission can be extremely painful. It takes a long time to achieve it totally.

The issue of radical disposition change is deeply intertwined with our form potency. This is a central concept in the science of formation. Many miss the firmness to deal effectively with disposition change. They shrink from the demanding transposition of formation energies it implies. The basic reason may be that a person is not convinced of his or her form potency. One may harbor and nurse a pervasive sense of form impotence that inclines one to shake off the burden of relatively free self-formation. This is the grandeur but also the affliction of the human life-form. We cannot grow up unless we acknowledge and accept firmly and gently our formation responsibility, which no one else can carry for us.

Distinctively human formation is a succession of personal apprehensions, appraisals, and affirmations. Subsequently, these are embodied in corresponding acts and dispositions. However, affirmation of our formation responsibility is the beginning of liberation from pulsations, pulsions, and ambitions that we have been unable up to now to discipline firmly.

Firmness of Dispositional Formation
in an Increasingly Nuanced Formation Field

Firmness is so basic a disposition for effective life formation that we can immediately recognize its necessity for such fundamental formative dispositions as gentleness, humility, apprehension, appraisal, simplicity, congeniality, compatibility, compassion, detachment, effectiveness, privacy, communality, and social presence. How could any of these be possible in an ever changing formation field without firmness? The constant refinement of our field requires the firmness of ongoing renewal or the refinement of dispositions. It invites us to call into question our routine apprehensions and appraisals as well as to purify remembered dispositions once they are challenged by new apprehensions. We must be firm enough to bracket our familiar dispositions of apprehension and appraisal so that we may appraise each formative event in its own right. We must dare a momentary "de-routinization" of dispositions to remain in consonance with an ever more nuanced formation field.

Our actual life-form implies the focusing of our energies in certain directions in accordance with our dispositions. Firmness gives us the courage to distance ourselves from our actual life-form at certain moments. We, so to speak, put it out of focus. This "de-focusing" allows our current life-form to enlarge itself through fresh apprehensions and appraisals into a new or expanded current form. This may be the direct effect of a temporary relinquishment of our actual focus of life. An indirect effect may be the enlargement of the core form or heart of life.

Our heart may expand, deepen, and be refined under the impact of new apprehensions and appraisals. The openness thus created may help us to disclose something else in regard to the basic or original form of our life. This is our inmost treasure and secret, the hidden nobility of our embodied soul and its direction. This process of periodic deroutinization and defocusing of our actual life-form is typical also of formation counseling, whether conducted in private or in common.

Firmness and Infraformation

The science of formation, as we have seen, views human life as an unfolding formation field, constituted by pre-, intra-, inter-, and outer poles. Underlying this field and all of its aspects, the theory posits a movement of infraformation. It qualifies this formation as *infra-* (which means "under," "beneath," or "sub") because it is not immediately obvious to us that this ongoing movement undergirds and deeply influences the formation of our life. For example, the infraformation of our physical-vital processes has an impact on our pre- and intraformative apprehensions, appraisals, feelings, and actions. Our interformative interaction with others is modulated by an infraformative network of prefocal mutual impressions, apprehensions, and spontaneous appraisals that are partly linked with forgotten or repudiated childhood memories. The immediate outer aspect of our formation field, namely, that of situational formation, also has its infraformative underground.

Each situation has underlying symbolic meanings of which we may be unaware. Nevertheless, they determine, at least in some measure, the impact of the situation on us. Experts in television advertising take advantage of this infraformative power. The same is true of the formation of our lives by society and world in and through the situations in which we move and act, receive and give information.

It is evident that special firmness, courage, and perseverance are needed to penetrate the infraformation of life and world. Much exertion is required to grasp this hidden movement. Our inclination to inertia shuns such effort. Once we disclose the hold of infraformation over our lives, we may feel obliged to counteract its negative impact on our appraisal powers and on our other dispositions. This may require a painful attempt to reform dispositions we have cherished for a lifetime. Infraformation thus presents another challenge to our disposition of firmness.

Various chapters of this book, at least indirectly, give some insight into the infraformative movement that influences our pre-, intra-, inter-, and outer situational life formation. What may be less obvious is the infraformative movements that influence our society and the sociohistorical world at large in which it participates. Hence, we would like to close this chapter on the formation of firmness with a consideration of its indispensable role in relation to the infraformation of society and world.

Firmness and Infraformation of Society and World

Our world view is determined in large part by apprehensions and appraisals rooted in our formation traditions. We view society and its institutions in their light. What we may not be aware of is that a whole web of hidden sociohistorical pulsations, constituted by an ongoing movement of infraformation, can penetrate and pervert even the most venerable social institutions.

One or the other formation event may make us suddenly aware of the immense power wielded by the infraformation of our social and economic institutions. It can jar our traditional apprehensions and appraisals and therewith the appreciations, dispositions, and actions directed by them. Gradually, we reappraise the ideological and religious form traditions that, up to the present, have directed our dispositions in relation both to social institutions and to our social apprehension of the formation mystery itself.

We begin to see the connection between accretions of our form traditions and contemporary pulsations that were never sufficiently appraised. Some of these accretions may incline us to condone social injustice, oppression, and violence on basis of superficial traditional justifications. Beautiful-sounding phrases cover up sociohistorical pulsations of greed and exploitation. They conceal a depraved movement of infraformation that undermines the distinctive humanness of our society and world. Many beneficial movements of infraformation have been repudiated by more powerful movements of avarice, cupidity, and inhuman enslavement of the poor. Malevolent tendencies in our infraformation may have distorted our traditional apprehension of the mystery itself. We apprehend it in such a way that it seems to legitimate institutional forms of oppression, exploitation, and discrimination.

If we have the firmness and courage to persist in the reformation of our apprehensions and appraisals, we may be able to reform our dispositions toward institutionalized violence, its victims and its perpetrators. We will gradually return to the distinctively human foundations of the great formation traditions and their underlying faith directives. We will be able to distinguish more clearly accretions from foundations, detecting also which accretions are enslaving and which are liberating. Our appreciation of the formation mystery is freed from the self-justifying attributes imposed on it by the infraformative movements of oppression and greed. The foundational layer of form traditions, disclosed in its original purity, invites us to reform our current and core forms of life in relation to the institutionalized injustice lingering in society and affecting countless victims.

Formation implies a lifelong growth in insight into the infraformation of our dispositions. We must firmly and courageously disclose and appraise in them any residues of negative infraformative pulsations in self and society. Are there any traces in us of nationalism, economic imperialism, sexism, racism, consumerism, elitism, clericalism, or vocational or form-segmental superiority? Do these dispositions contribute to the enslavement of people? Do they prevent them from sharing in the resources of humanity and the conditions necessary for a distinctively human life?

We must try to develop dispositions that foster the reformation of social institutions in such a way that they maximize the opportunities for a congenial, compatible, and compassionate life for the greatest number of people. This is no easy task, especially since we must operate within the limits of our congeniality. Anyone who has been involved in the struggle for justice in an occupied country against a ruthless oppressor knows that in extraordinary circumstances a firmness until death may be required of us if we want to live in fidelity to formative rather than deformative dispositions.

CHAPTER 6

Disposition of Gentleness

The gentle disposition has to complement firmness if our life is to remain consonant. This means that our pulsations, pulsions, and ambitions need to become the flexible disciples (hence the word *discipline*) of the transcendent dimension. Firmness would lose its humane intention if it became instead the disciple of discordant pulsions. It would deteriorate into a dehumanizing, willful harshness characterized by whipping ourselves and others into shape. Firmness as a consonant disposition disappears whenever we become uncaring or insensitive to the point of ruthlessness. Willfulness of this sort is destructive not only of others but of ourselves as well. It overrides the transcendent wisdom that could save us from impetuous overexertion or a destructive style of asceticism.

A person who has attained true firmness is guided by the wisdom of the spirit. Yet even then, firmness can be threatened by an invasion of dissonant dispositions. This distortion betrays itself by an inclination to rigidity or inflexibility. Firmness must thus be balanced by gentleness. The consonant life is a blend of firm gentleness and gentle firmness. One disposition should modulate the other. Firmness without gentleness deteriorates into severity; gentleness without firmness becomes debilitating weakness.

The gentle disposition is a facilitating condition as well as a fruit of the consonant life. Gentleness is the royal road of presence to a mystery that cannot be compelled or controlled. The ideal of gentleness has played many roles in religious and cultural form traditions. From it derives, for instance, the ideal of the gentleman. We should realize, however, that a person could develop the apparent form of a gentleman without being gentle at heart. In that case gentleness is merely bound to public appearances; it is not really a core disposition.

Oppressors of the underprivileged may only play at being gentle when they keep company with high society. In the meantime, they may be ruthless with those whom they exploit. Their gentleness may be only an imitation of genteel appearances customary in certain circles. Such surface gentility is useless for growth in the core disposition of gentleness. In no way does it bring us nearer to the gentle mystery of formation that dwells in our souls.

Self-centeredness may hide behind apparent gentility. Gentleness is charming and powerful. Clever people may eagerly imitate its appearances to further their own ambitions. A disposition can only be known by its manifestations. Hence, we should pay attention to everyday expressions of the gentle disposition. These might include an encouraging smile, a comforting embrace, a cordial handshake, a considerate gesture, a sensitive choice of tactful words, a serene movement of the body, or a peaceful facial expression. Such simple expressions of gentleness, confirmed by true and effective acts of generosity, can be an occasion for reflection on the disposition underlying them.

It is difficult to grasp the experiential meaning of these expressions if we ourselves do not try to walk the way of gentleness. We can learn from our failures in this regard. They are like the mistakes in an almost perfect painting. By pointing out what the painting should *not* be like, they tell us in a roundabout way what the real painting should reveal. This example applies to all the dispositions of the heart. We should try to make them our own, no matter how awkward we feel at first. Once we are able to ponder our limited experiences of success and failure as part of our attempt to acquire them, we can complement and compare our findings with the experiences of other people.

Nature of the Gentle Disposition

Gentleness is usually evoked by what is valuable and vulnerable. What seems precious to us, yet also somehow frail and easily wounded, arouses a feeling of gentle concern if our life is on the way to consonance. It may be an abused family in an oppressive nation, a helpless foreigner lost in one of our bus stations or airports, an abandoned child, a person covered with blood after participation in a demonstration for justice.

What is valuable and vulnerable can be deeply hidden. This is true of the nobility of our soul, the beautiful, basic form of our life. It is the fragile treasure we are called to bring to light. It is the most valuable gift we have and are, and hence it is vulnerable. But the sense of our unique form potency is easily lost. Oppressors of the soul can be found on all levels of society, in all social institutions. They threaten to take away the opportunities to be our best. They want to enlist us merely in their causes, thus paralyzing our hearts. We know many underprivileged persons whose primary human right to unique unfolding is taken away by bureaucracy, by social injustice, by merciless exploitation. The more we grow in consonance, the more gentle we feel toward all such victims of injustice.

Our best potentials may be paralyzed as well by a lack of gentleness toward ourselves. Often we are our own worst enemies. We easily forget our own fragility and woundedness. Our anxious need to please oppressors, our fear of malicious gossip, our susceptibility to contamination by popular pulsations—these and other related factors may estrange us from our mission. We do not walk wisely and gently along the path of fidelity to our calling. Rather, we run excitedly or anxiously, oblivious of the pitfalls on the road, of the sly seducers waiting to deflect us from our journey.

The more we are at home with the forming mystery, the more we sense that it silently suffuses people, events, and things. They begin to light up for us as symbols of its presence. Their veiled radiance illumines our formation field. A sense of gentle love begins to pervade our life. The disposition of gentleness may manifest itself in a refined mode of presence to all persons we meet, to all things we handle. They become for us fragile mirrors of the mystery. We sense how liable these mirrors are to be dimmed or fractured. While gently tending the people and things entrusted to us, we grow in reverence and respect.

We should be especially gentle with ourselves. Fidelity to our life call, to our incomparable dignity, is easily lost. When we feel disappointed in ourselves, we may be tempted to abuse our fortitude by exaggeration. We begin to discipline ourselves rigorously without wisdom and compassion, blunting our finer sensibilities. We silence the whisper of the mystery in our heart. The gift of gentleness should enable us, in moments of disappointment, shame, and guilt, to nurse our wounded lives compassionately and kindly.

Most frail and vulnerable is our presence to the mystery itself. It is threatened by countless distractions and popular pressures. The awareness of its consoling presence is delicate. It may close itself like a flower at nightfall, when we try to force its appearance or its abiding. Gentleness is the mild, propitious climate in which the flower of presence blooms.

Gentleness in Labor and Leisure

Without gentleness we become tense and strained in labor and leisure. Losing ease of heart and mind, we no longer feel able to muse in a leisurely

way about the meaning of life, its sufferings and joys. We become strained, willful, upset if things don't go our way. We feel the need for instant
accomplishment. Like loving gardeners, we should flow gently with
events and things that emerge in the garden of life. Ideas, symbols, and
emotions should not overwhelm us at a feverish pace.

The disposition of gentleness is linked with that of abandonment. When
we live in appreciative abandonment we can let go. We can give ourselves
over to the calming climate of a gentle lifestyle. We lose the anxious urge
to do more and more things in less and less time. The spirit of gentleness
begins to modulate serenely our pace of achievement and production.

For a wise unfolding of the consonant life to occur, time is of the essence. Gentleness allows time to play its forming role in the mystery of our
formation of life and world. Gentleness disposes us to let things be, to
abide with life as it comes, to be busily engaged, if necessary, yet to remain
gentle inwardly. The disposition of gentleness stills the greediness and aggressiveness of a merely functional life. This silencing allows us to center
ourselves in the mystery, gently to nurse distinctively human dispositions.
We become like smooth channels for the outflow of the forming mystery
in this world. Our frail formation of life will be harmonized with the veiled
presence of the mystery that fills universe and history. Any trace of vehemence may melt away.

Gentleness and Effectiveness

To be effective in our form giving to the world, we have to be strong
and shrewd in the face of social injustice in society and its institutions.
The ability to be strong and shrewd does not in itself make us unfit for
gentleness. What matters is *how* we live the disposition of form effectiveness. Our concern for effectiveness can become so exclusive that gentleness wholly disappears. The gentle disposition should always linger in the
background, ready to be activated when the time is ripe. To be sure, the
disposition of effectiveness ought to help us live up to the demands and
resistances of daily reality. But we should equally cultivate gentleness.
Otherwise we may succumb to mere functionalism without compatibility
and compassion.

Gentleness keeps our life open to the mystery. It does not demand that
we become defenseless in the face of oppression. The disposition of effectiveness implies at times strong stands and daring decisions. But our acceptance of this necessity should be rooted in a deeper receptivity. It should
be based on our disposition to listen gently to the beyond in daily life.

Effectiveness does not mean that we cannot think without strain or labor without pressure. The effective person is not necessarily impassioned or vehement, firm or tough. Nor should effectiveness make us feel that we must cram every moment with something useful to do or say. Consonant effectiveness implies that we can distance ourselves at the propitious moment from the pressures of life.

Gentleness should precede effectiveness. It enables us to appraise dispassionately the nuances that emerge constantly in our formation field. Such appraisal can help us to enhance our effectiveness in consonance with these nuances. It enables us to offer our best possible service in the changing situation.

We may neglect presence to reality and thus approach all situations only from the viewpoint of efficiency. Then we may resent the unexpected changes in our formation field. We tend to feel that they interfere with the programmatic approach of our functional mind and will, with the flawless execution of our performance or the fulfillment of our ambitions.

Effectiveness should be the flexible servant of the spirit. Unenlightened effectiveness is a rebellious servant. Arrogantly it takes over our life, running it with a calculating eye, a willful ear. The formation field becomes merely a place of duty, of profit making and strife, of survival of the fittest. To be sure, the formation field can be all of these things, but not only them, and certainly not ultimately them. Gentleness does not destroy or deny functional-vital pursuits. It puts them in their rightful place. It helps us to go beyond mere manipulation of events. We listen respectfully to what they have to tell us in the light of the mystery that allows them to transpire.

Gentleness and Presence to the Mystery

Presence to the mystery is a most precious gift. It transcends our analytical modes of thought. In functional thinking we tend to isolate what we are pondering from the larger scene in which people, events, and things appear. This horizon is the whole of our formation field. This field itself points to a wider, as yet not fully known, horizon out of which it constantly emerges. This is the mystery of formation and its epiphanies.

Effective living demands analytical thought in service of the practical organization of life and world. It should be balanced by transcendent presence to the mystery as a whole. Exclusive analytical thought would be deformative. It demands a certain mental and emotional aggressiveness, necessary to foster focal concentration on the problems and resistances at

hand. This disposition to isolate and dissect objects could harm the consonance of our life if it were to dominate all of our thoughts, feelings, and
actions. For instance, how could a married couple experience the beauty
and wholeness of intimate love if they could not let go of the analytical
and dissecting approach?

The same is true of our presence to the mystery. This presence leaves
division and isolation behind. It makes us one with an all-embracing,
forming source in peaceful simplicity. This presence is unitive, not divisive. It makes us whole. We experience a moment of consonance with a
mysterious totality that is already there. Such presence is gentle, not aggressive. It grants us a pause from practical performance; from building
theologies, philosophies, and other sciences; from techniques and efficient organizations.

Gentle presence is a healing power. It creates a climate of equanimity,
an atmosphere of stillness and repose. It heals the wounds inflicted by the
exalting pride-form. It tempers the multitude of illusions that distort our
apprehensions and appraisals, our feelings and motivations, the mirages
that make us suffer and fail. Gentle presence is a return to our original
form of loving consonance with the mystery from which we emerge. The
image of that lost paradise is buried in the silent abyss of our being. Prefocally we are in search of this treasure like people who dream and seek for the
legendary land of Atlantis. This inner form seems to draw us irresistibly.

At certain moments the mystery itself may take over and grant us a presence that goes beyond images, forms, and thoughts. It keeps us in silent
wonder, embraced by the mystery and its epiphanies. The precious power
of gentle presence is a way to oneness with the ineffable. It rescues the mysterious apophatic depth of the people, events, and things we deal with functionally in our everyday life. They radiate again for us the splendor of each
epiphany of the mystery. Our hearts are no longer tightened by pained concern about our progress. Excessive forcefulness is softened; motives are
clarified. We are liberated for one glorious moment from the curse of enslavement to popular opinion and the paralyzing need to please all people.

Anger and Gentleness

Anger can be a wholesome, human, consonant, and congenial expression of our life in unjust situations. How could we not feel indignation in
the face of the oppression of poor people or in the unjust opposition of
envious gossips who inhibit our attempts to serve those in spiritual, functional, or vital need? Gentleness does not mean that we should paralyze

this powerful emotion. A misunderstanding of gentleness would lead us to repudiate or refuse the awareness of anger. Feelings of anger should be taken into account. We should work them through, not turn them off. Only a deformed disposition of gentleness would deny our ability to be angry and indignant. It would compel us to remove from our awareness feelings of aggressiveness as soon as they appeared.

Repudiation does not do away with anger. It only hides it in our infrafocal awareness. Anger is a basic formation ability, rooted in our form potency. We can hide this ability, but we can never destroy its potential upsurge in our life. We may mask anger with apparent gentleness, but forced gentleness may only strike others as disguised irritation. This veiling of anger by a pretense of gentleness may not be a deceit emerging from our focal consciousness. Our intent to be gentle as such may be genuine. We can simulate an absence of irritation to cover up what is really bothering us. Perhaps we forced ourselves into adopting the apparent life-form of a gentle person before we were ready. We omitted the formation task of patiently apprehending and appraising our angry feelings and of gradually mitigating them in the light of transcendent inspirations and aspirations.

Gentleness does not disclaim the emergence of anger and related aggressive emotions. It helps us to accept the fact that even irrational feelings of hostility can stay with us for a long time during our formation journey. This openness or humility deepens our gentle disposition and allows it to govern other moments of life. Gentleness with our own affliction enables us to express more effectively and appropriately anger over injustice, lack of compassion, and disrespect for the uniqueness of people.

Apparent gentleness may refuse to admit anger and deal with it. It becomes an infrafocal explosive power that poisons our formation. When this repressed disposition finally bursts out in an unguarded moment, its expression tends to be volcanic and destructive. Our attempt to be gentle should not prevent irritation from coming into the open at its inception. Anger should be allowed to spend itself in a wise, moderate fashion, for instance, in a forthright conversation with a good friend or a formation counselor. Such interaction that vents anger and irritation mitigates its explosive force. It frees us to activate again the disposition of gentleness.

The gentle disposition should prevail in a life that is on the way to consonance. Anger about injustice, expressed in a congenial, compatible fashion, has a rightful place in our lives. In the end, it should be a lasting disposition that effectively forms our life and world in unjust situations while not disturbing our calm, inmost center.

The wages of repudiated anger include, in the long run, useless exhaustion of emotional energy, diminishment of functional and vital health, damage to our interformative relationships with others, and decrease in effectiveness. We should own, instead of disowning, our angry upsurges and aggressive feelings. Rather than reject them, we should accept and appraise them. If possible, we should reform those that are irrational in content or expression. Our lives should no longer be poisoned by anger we refuse to resolve.

Gentleness and the Reformation of Anger

All people get angry, saints and sinners alike. Feeling irritated, annoyed, angry, or aggressive is as human as feeling sad, delighted, tired, or lonely. Gentle people get angry like everyone else. The difference is that anger and aggressiveness do not dominate their lives. They may be momentarily angry, usually at the right time and in an acceptable manner. But they have formed their lives in such a way that they can handle their angry feelings.

Growth in gentleness does not alleviate our ability to feel anger. The unfolding of the transcendent dimension of our life, however, widens our views. It changes the vision of our formation field. Aspects of that field that aroused our anger appear in a new light. This wider perspective of the deeper meaning of things may both lessen our anger and enable us to find a more compatible, compassionate response.

A mistaken notion of what the gentle disposition should be like may have made us feel ashamed, guilty, or anxious about our angry or aggressive emotions. We do not dare to admit to ourselves how angry we sometimes are. Paradoxically, it is the gentle disposition itself that enables us to accept the resistance of irrational anger in our attempts to reform it. Gentleness helps us to respect the pace of progress in formation that is uniquely ours. Our temperamental preformation, our personal history, and the interformative situations to which we are exposed all set definite limits to this pace of improvement. Our formation in gentleness may be painfully slow. In most of us it is marked by ups and downs, by peaks and valleys. When we try to reform ourselves too fast and furiously, disregarding these limits, things may get worse instead of better.

A premature attempt to turn angry moods into gentle feelings may only lead to a denial of our anger. Then it will keep forming itself wildly. It proliferates unchecked in the infrafocal caverns of our consciousness. In that case, our pretense of perfect gentleness may be permeated by sly, mean, sweet-sounding intrusions of smoldering anger.

Initial Formation of Expressivity of Gentleness and Anger

The human form potency includes the abilities to feel angry and gentle, as well as the ability to give form to these feelings in corresponding actions and expressions. This preformation is modulated by interformation within the family. In the period of initial formation in infancy, the child, without fully understanding why, can sense the angry and gentle feelings of the parents. The parents function as prototypes in the way of giving form to such feelings and dispositions.

We may have been born into a family that allowed us to form our feelings rather freely. They were not upset by our expressions of tenderness or anger. They did not necessarily agree with its content, perhaps they found it necessary to correct the style of our expression, but at least they did not punish, condemn, or ridicule us simply for the fact that we felt angry or tender and tried in some way to communicate that feeling.

One way to prevent the free unfolding of the disposition of gentleness is to make fun of it or to make one feel sentimental, childish, weak, or lacking in fortitude. If a climate of relaxed expression of feelings prevails in a family, if it is confirmed by wise foundational form traditions, an overall atmosphere of gentleness may prevail, interrupted periodically by normal expressions of anger and aggression. When such feelings are given external form while still in their embryonic state, they cannot grow intraformatively to such a magnitude that sudden outbursts or explosions become inevitable. The other members of the family can take the communication of our nascent feelings into account. They can be worked through interformatively. In this way gentleness and peace may be restored sooner than otherwise might be the case.

In such a family, children are initiated early in life into appropriate ways of giving form to feelings of gentleness and anger. They are made to feel that loss of the foundational triad of parental faith, hope, and love is not risked by the acknowledgment of such emotions. They feel confirmed in their own form of life, even if they do not stifle their feelings or refuse to display a tenderness they do not really feel at a given moment, simply to please their parents.

Reformation of the Disposition of Feigned Gentleness

Our initial formation may have formed us in feigned gentleness. We should not blame what happened on our family, teachers, school, or community. Our impotence in the area of a reasonable expression of justified anger is not ultimately their fault. They, too, may have been forced to feign gentle acceptance, no matter how they really felt. They may have been the victims of deformative accretions of form traditions that left no room for genuine self-communication. They may suffer more than we do from the same accretions imposed on us.

To reform feigned gentleness, we must begin to express how we really feel, if this is possible in the situation without violating the rules of compassion or wise diplomacy. When we feel angry, we must not simulate a spontaneous feeling of kindness. If the situation allows, we should disclose how we feel, though we should try to do so wisely and not destructively. If we communicate our feelings when they are in an incipient state, it should not be too difficult to maintain a certain moderation in our expression. In this way we will gradually learn to express our anger appropriately in a manner that is beneficial for us and others. In thus overcoming our need for feigned gentleness, we do not paralyze our potential for the authentic disposition.

Once anger is released from our infrafocal system, we can apprehend and appraise its meaning. By lifting it into the light of transcendent aspirations and inspirations, as nourished by foundational form traditions, our anger may diminish or even disappear. Enlightened appraisal may disclose that our anger was merely a response of the functional, competitive ego, threatened in its security. It may also prove to be proper indignation, sparked by social injustice toward ourselves and others.

Denial of Indignation in Service of Irenicism

What if we were formed in a false kind of irenicism, that is to say, in a disposition to force or feign a unity of conviction between people that is not really there? We act as if we are perfectly alike at the price of remaining honestly aware of and admitting differences in our convictions. These cannot be erased without our being unfaithful to our congeniality or to the foundations of our form traditions. In service of irenicism, we may also erect a facade of gentleness toward convictions that we oppose.

Irenicism in our personal relationships may be motivated by a variety of concerns, all coming down to the desire for peace at any price. We may be afraid to displease people in any way. We dread their disapproval. To be approved means that we need not doubt our potency to give form to our relationships with others. We believe that irenicism is the best way to foster our career; to gain promotions; to be free from any feelings, opinions, or beliefs that may give rise to irritation, indignation, or uneasiness.

Irenicism may also be a way to escape the patient work of apprehending and appraising our hostility and aggravation. We shirk the task of mellowing them a little day by day. We do not want to be bothered by appraising the difference between our justified wrath and our irrational anger.

Irenicism of this sort would eradicate at once all possible indignation, justified or not, and its expression. It inclines us to an idealized image of what we should be: "From now on I have to appear as the perfectly pleasant person, at peace with everyone." Also present may be the motivation of self-protection: "If I am never irritated, others will not be so easily irritated with me." Guiding these motives is the pride-form, which would have us base our life-form on an exalted image of being a nice, regular guy or gal, a peacemaker, liked and applauded by all. We fear that any sign of irritation, any difference of opinion, may taint this pleasing picture. Approval is a security blanket: were we to provoke displeasure in others, it would be a menace to our self-preservation. Hence, we must do nothing to jeopardize our standing with others. We must play the role of the unruffled one. As long as we can keep up appearances, we feel we have the situation in hand; we do not doubt our form potency or our ability to keep the peace always and everywhere.

To practice irenicism is never to be ourselves. The constant pressure to appear gentle, while feeling coarse, demands a great deal of formation energy. Our limited strength could be invested more profitably in sincere dispositions. Sadly, our pretense does not always grant a reward. Persons who might have been able to appreciate us as we are soon feel ill at ease in our presence. Our pretense makes it difficult for them to know who we really are. What do we stand for? Our make-believe gentleness may backfire in the long run, even if we developed it with the best of goodwill.

Real peace grows only between people who genuinely apprehend and appraise their fundamental differences while they deepen their unity of conviction and their appreciation and concern for what they can honestly share. Gradually one comes to understand why others feel and think differently without denying one's own deep, though opposite thoughts and beliefs.

Enlightened Restraint without Repudiation

Allowing room for anger does not mean that we vent it indiscriminately. A certain restraint should modulate its manifestation. The ideal of restraint without repudiation may be approached when we live in openness to wider horizons. They are disclosed to us in the light of the formation mystery. Such vistas relativize every event. They grant us the wisdom of balanced proportions. We seldom restrict our appraisal of life and its vicissitudes to any immediate situation, lest one or another affront engulf us in anger, thereby veiling other equally important facets of reality.

Gentleness does not demand that we bottle up frantic emotions. Nor is firmness a license for lashing out spasmodically at people or things to relieve irritation. Eruptions may release our rage, but they also induce violence. Violence is a caricature of firmness. It builds up until we explode fiercely when faced with resistance.

Dispositions have a quality of need. For instance, once we form the disposition to find relief in the indiscriminate airing of anger, we may increasingly feel the need to indulge in this venting. The more intensely angry we are, the more pleasurable the experience of release. This pleasure tempts us to intensify feelings of aggravation so that we can indulge in an intense experience of relief. Small irritations may be enlarged by means of enraging images, memories, and anticipations.

Intensification of anger has consequences for formation. Through this process, corresponding dispositions of apprehension and appraisal are formed. We grow more and more disposed to magnify out of proportion any irritating event in order to intensify our anger and the subsequent experience of its furious release. Our reaction is usually dissonant with the real significance of what is happening. However low the incitement may be, we burst out angrily. Our fantasies, perceptions, memories, and anticipations tend to be easily inflamed. We are oversensitive to the slightest sign of opposition, injustice, or depreciation. Irate feelings flare up instantly. Such anxious watchfulness makes gentle presence to the mystery nearly impossible to maintain.

Consonant people neither bottle up their exasperation nor release it without restraint. They guard against magnifying their annoyances out of proportion. To be sure, in the beginning of our journey to consonance, we may not be able to dissipate in time the anger that accumulates in us. It may be dammed up, yet, like all emotions, it strives to form itself in dialogue with our personal actions or prepersonal behavioral patterns. Anger affects our neuromuscular and glandular systems. It strains for action, disposing us physically for aggressive expression. If we do not allow ourselves any release, we keep building tension in our body, the tension of physically straining for action while inhibiting its release.

This strain badly affects our health. It taxes our energies in needless ways. If we are not as yet able to handle our anger wisely, it may at least be helpful to relieve neuromuscular strain in physical ways that do not threaten or upset people. We may hit or kick a ball, jog or otherwise exercise, or vent out fury in conversation with a trusted friend. Our aim is not to depend on these measures, but to form ourselves in a restrained expression of anger. We should release it in the beginning, while it is still weak, and we can handle it with ease; more violent outlets of fury should function as emergency release systems only, a kind of safety valve. We should not become addicted to them, lest we risk developing a violent disposition. To vent fury convulsively may remove its burden, but it does not deplete the deeper, dammed-up sources of our rage. Only prolonged apprehension, appraisal, and corresponding reformation can drain these hidden layers of pent-up aggravation and aggression.

Interdeformative Source of Immoderate Rage

Angry people find each other. They intensify their fury by verbal, facial, and behavioral communication, unleashing together their enraged memories, images, and anticipations. They feel confirmed in their form potency when they cheer one another's excessive display of irate emotions.

Angry people may also find vicarious relief in these mutual exhibitions of aggravation. They work each other up to increasingly violent forms of expression, augmenting their inventory of aggressive words, gestures, and actions. Such interdeformation strengthens the violent disposition in rageful people and their victims.

We may feel angry for many reasons. Perhaps we experience others as threatening our position. Perhaps they evoke guilt feelings in us about our own form of life or remind us painfully of the oppression and injustice we inflict on the less fortunate. We may simply feel the need to affirm our potency by stepping on those who are beneath us on the social ladder. Defenseless and vulnerable people may evoke in us a violent urge to hurt and humiliate them. The moment this urge is satisfied, we experience a pleasurable release of tension.

If we do not purify the infra- and prefocal sources of such violence, the same urge will flare up again and again. We will impulsively pursue the alleviation of this tension by hurting those who seem to evoke it. This disposition to violate others and its pleasurable consequences may partly explain the cruel behavior of soldiers or police guards toward defenseless prisoners.

To rise beyond violence and grow in the disposition of expressing righteous anger compatibly, we must pay attention to the power of interdeformative influences. Do we prefer to consort with hostile, cynical, resentful people? Do we take pleasure in violent movies and television programs or in harsh oratory? How do we feel when we hear cruel words spoken or deeds committed? Can we distance ourselves from fiery defenses of righteous causes?

Misdirected religious zeal can be the mother of war and persecution. Its lofty principles may seem to justify the violence perpetrated in its name. Unfortunately, the adherents of many sublime faith traditions have not been as well initiated into their corresponding consonant form traditions. They learned the absolutes of their faith but not the wisdom of a formation tradition that could teach them how to live these absolutes in congenial, compatible, compassionate ways. They simply superimposed the noble truths of their faith on a dormant volcano of irrational anger, aggressiveness, and violence. They played the role of people not only informed but already transformed by the age-old wisdom of their faith tradition. Their slumbering, unpurified violence may find an outlet in some holy cause close to the hearts of the faithful. This insight may clarify in part the violence indulged in by the crusaders of religions and ideologies against those perceived as a threat to their convictions. No world peace is possible unless adherents of diverse faith traditions learn to implement the foundations of their consonant form traditions. This attempt will help to transform violent tendencies into more peaceful approaches.

It is counterproductive to attack people verbally or by unrestrained action. This tactic only serves to incite farther our angry feelings and expressions. It creates a climate that breeds violence. A more effective way would be to replace outburst by description: we can communicate, almost factually, how we are feeling. We can tell the people who provoke us, for instance, that we are really upset. Such information helps them to realize that they have hurt us more than they thought. Such communication is formative because it teaches others about us and our reactions as well as about themselves and the impact of their expressions. Many marriages and friendships have been saved by frank disclosures of this sort.

We are not naively suggesting that this interformative expression of feeling will work well in all situations. Others may intend to hurt us, or they may be so obtuse that they cannot imagine how bad we feel. The only way to alleviate such hurt may be through conversation with a trusted friend, a formation counselor, or an understanding spouse. The final answer, however, can be found in wise apprehension and appraisal of the relativity of all violent anger in the light of our presence to the mystery that forms life and world. When violent aggravation flares up, we should try not to dwell on its accompanying aggressive memories, fantasies, and anticipations directed at those who hurt our feelings. We should calm these violent emotions in reference to a more transcendent vision.

Pseudogentility

The disposition of violent anger ought to be replaced by the disposition of firmness with its concomitant capacity for righteous indignation and its complementary disposition of gentleness. We should not confuse our slow progress with its final result: the life of consonance that awaits us in the end. This consonance will most likely not be ours during our lifetime. Expecting to reach the end of the journey before we go along the road of reformation can only lead to disappointment.

We may try to shorten the road by cultivating pseudogentility or the lie of a gentleness not really felt. To keep this lie alive, we may deform our apparent form by pasting on the mask of kindness. When this tactic fails, we may resort to that of affective isolation. Avoidance of involvement with people seems to enable us to maintain our gentle status. We can stay nice on the surface by escaping any chance of conflict. This inner distance helps us to preserve our unruffled demeanor. Yet ultimately we are the losers in this game. Wise and moderate interaction with others would enable us to see ourselves as we are in the mirror of their honest responses.

CHAPTER 7

Formation in Gentleness

Our potency is a gift of the formation mystery. Our prefocal awareness of this potency manifests itself in our need to sense that we can give and receive form in life. This need plays a basic role in the dynamics of human formation and hence in our attempts to grow in gentleness.

The disposition of gentleness is one of the main conditions for congenial, compatible, compassionate unfolding. If we try to be gentle and often fail, we may feel that our potency itself is in jeopardy. We should realize that we cannot totally avoid feelings of irritation and anger. At times we have to take the offensive against those who disturb the peace, pursue war, make light of social justice, and inflict suffering on those who are defenseless and poor. There are moments when we must speak out against oppressors and the measures they use to threaten the rights of our own or others' congenial formation.

An appropriate expression of anger, aggression, and indignation can be wholesome and human. It complements the potency to form ourselves as well in gentleness, which is one of the distinctively human dispositions. Justice is another. The struggle to gain justice must often be sustained by anger and consonant aggression.

Life becomes dissonant if it forms itself exclusively around one disposition. Once again, gentleness must be complemented by firmness. At times firmness must be nourished by feelings of indignation that are consonant and suitably manifested at the proper time and place.

The conviction of form potency may be overly dependent upon popular pulsations. We may be too attached to limited expressions of our form tradition. This attachment may lead us to believe that only gentleness should be cultivated. In that case it may be difficult for us to come to terms with our aggressive feelings. We try to turn them off, while claiming that indignation as such is unworthy of people who live in true abandonment to the mystery. Such abuses of a form tradition may paralyze us.

Gentleness should not arise from fear of impotence. Nor should it emerge from the deceptive dream that it will relieve us from aggravation. Gentleness should not be an anxious expression of our need to please people. It must start from the acknowledgment of where we are in our formation history: ideally, we are simply people of goodwill who at times experience anger, resentment, and hostility.

Secret Compensation for Potency Oppression

Without a sense of form potency, the human life-form loses its dynamism, resiliency, joy, and creativity. It can no longer function as a channel of the formation mystery in which we humbly share. We each carry the burden of nourishing, maintaining, or restoring the sense of form potency in ourselves and others. The worst oppression of all is that which blocks the exercise of form potency, yet this oppression is universal due to the pride-form, which is operative in all races, cultures, formation segments, communities, and families. It often affects the infraformation of social institutions.

Most oppressive institutions are couched in symbols of justice, order, virtue, and sacredness. Yet they may limit unjustly the primary human right and responsibility to maintain a sense of form potency. Rarely are we aware of the extent of the injustice they inflict, for the oppressive disposition is usually covered by a web of justifications. The survival of the sense of form potency is best served by firm and open resistance. But oppressive people, laws, or institutions may be so powerful that effective resistance by the powerless becomes impossible. Yet one is not absolved thereby from the responsibility to preserve one's sense of potency.

The only way to save that sense may be to seek for hidden compensation. This may entail the secret appropriation of some form of restitution. One must feel that one can do something, that one is not wholly impotent. It is not so much the amount or the content of the self-initiated restitution that matters, but the experience of some "form-ability," of the feeling that "I am still able to do something." Secret compensation can make up for the paralyzing experience of the oppression of form potency. In certain formation segments, social institutions, or historical periods, this may be the only safeguard left to oppressed people.

For secret compensation to be effective, it is crucial to see it as a challenge posed by the formation mystery itself to every human being when no other way is left to overcome injustice. If the normal exercise of one's form potency is not possible, the alternative is either open fight or hidden compensation. What ought never to be stifled is one's appraisal power. Oppressors may attempt to falsify one's conscience by suggesting that it is more humane, virtuous, or holy not to resist social injustice, while they themselves may remain blissfully unaware of its gross nature.

Such sanctimonious appeals to the conscience of the oppressed can be impressive and powerful. Oppressors (or oppressive infraforms of society) increase their effectiveness when they themselves believe in the reasonableness of their case. Because of their conviction, their appeal to the conscience of the oppressed may sound humane and full of concern. To overcome the anesthesia of such pious appeals, the oppressed must mature in their conviction of their duty either to resist openly or to compensate secretly for the draining of their sense of potency by unjust oppression.

Many oppressed women, original thinkers, foreigners, and ethnic minorities have used the tactic of secret compensation successfully in oppressive societies and communities. A number of them have been able to actualize their best potential by securing positions worthy of their unusual energy, originality, and creativity. Gifted foreigners, for instance, may go along cautiously with native oppressors. After all, the natives outnumber them and may be convinced of their "divine" right to keep them in their place. Yet their seeming defeat becomes the source of their success. It necessitates so much compensation of their oppressed form potency that in the end they may outdo the natives in production and renown.

Gentle Strategies of Secret Compensation

If hidden compensation is the only way to exercise form potency, open firmness will be impossible. In this case, apparent gentleness may be both necessary and justifiable. To be sure, it would be more consonant if gentleness toward one's oppressors could be wholeheartedly felt. It takes a long time, however, for one to mature to the point of compassion with one's oppressors, to see them as victims of self-deception, of deforming accretions of their traditions, of insecurity, of blind compliance with unjust structures of their social institutions. Most oppressed people do not attain such compassion in a lifetime. But they cannot sit by idly while their sense of personal potency is destroyed. Compensation may require them to don the veil of apparent gentleness. While they cannot yet wholeheartedly feel gentle, they may will themselves to be gentle, not only to veil their compensatory actions but also to show compassion toward those who make them suffer. Eventually, when they realize that the perpetrators of injustice are also its victims, they may feel true compassion. Insofar as their apparent gentleness manifests at least the will to compassion, it can be called genuine. It is, so to speak, the not yet sufficiently incarnated will of people who are on the way.

We must always bear in mind that the oppressed themselves are affected by the pride-form. They, too, are tempted by violence, revenge, hatred and greed. The pride-form inclines them at times to see injustice, oppression, and diminishment of their form potency where there is little or none. The right to compensation may become an excuse to escape from open resistance or for greed and self-serving action. No one should engage in compensation lightly. One should consult with people of acknowledged integrity and wisdom before treading this path. One should be willing to bear the consequences if one is discovered.

For the same reason, one should not lightly believe everyone who complains about oppression. This complaint itself may be an injustice against those unfairly accused. By believing such remarks uncritically or by provoking them unwisely, we may promote the illness we want to cure.

Excessive Firmness Blocks Gentle Receptivity

When the disposition of firmness becomes excessive, gentleness fails to modulate its forcefulness. Excessive firmness often conceals an arrogant need to be in control. Fortitude is no longer guided by enlightened willing but by willfulness. It is nourished by illusions of the pride-form to attain perfect self-possession. Stubborn firmness replaces gentleness with a calculated facade of gentility. If excessive firmness prevails, we may lose our natural bent toward receptivity. Gentleness becomes a feat of self-mastery.

Firm discipline is necessary for formation, but it should not be the central event in our history of unfolding. Gentle receptivity to the mystery and its disclosures should be the primary source of our inspiration and of our discipline. Relaxed firmness and the flexible discipline that flows from it is both a protection and a preparation for the unique working of the mystery disclosed to us in gentle receptivity.

Our culture tends to applaud conquest and mastery, symbolized in modern technical and scientific advances. We are tempted to construe our personal formation in terms of the principles of management that allow us to gain dominance over nature. People who pursue excessive firmness exalt a perfect form of life to be gained by inflexible willfulness. Their functional minds operate like computers. They refuse to be distracted by sensitivity to others or by openness to mystery. They like to project the appearance of never losing control, even in the most trying situations. They fear anger that may lead to loss of poise and self-possession. Their gentleness is distorted in appearance. It seems more like impeccable politeness or straight-laced correctness than gracious receptivity. Being enslaved to exclusive fortitude, they display an unyielding angularity rooted in rigid training and painstaking self-control. Smooth comportment, not gentleness, serves their self-centered projects.

When the disposition of gentleness is suppressed by excessive firmness, one's emotional life suffers many deformities. It loses spontaneity, flexibility, and vivacity. Any feeling that conflicts with one's project of self-mastery is automatically put down. The refused or repudiated feelings cannot be appraised for what they are. One cannot use them as stepping-stones for growth in wisdom and consonance. This gentleness is only a facade; it does not flow forth from one's inmost center. One becomes a sick idolator of poise and perfect self-possession. Humanness is denied and maimed by perverted gentility.

Pseudogentility and the Paralysis of Vital Feeling

Not only anger but any vital feeling may be deadened in order to maintain this pseudogentle, straight-laced comportment. To prevent being surprised by any emotion, one distances oneself from all of them. Emotions that accompany aspirations are especially distrusted. One cannot let go in wonder, admiration, love, zeal, devotion and dedication. Signs of aliveness are subdued by a suspicion of spontaneous feelings. Emotionality no longer serves one's humanity. This emotional paralysis makes it impossible for one to empathize with others. A mask of pseudogentility may cover up the death of emotion, but it cannot do so lastingly. People soon sense a chill behind one's calculated expressions of concern.

Paralyzed feelings sink into one's infrafocal life, but they do not remain inert in that dark region of consciousness. They grow luxuriantly like mushrooms in murky caves. Somehow they will manifest their hidden presence. Because one bans them from the light of focal awareness, their indirect expression will be twisted and distorted. Indeed, it may be difficult to recognize them as manifestations of real feelings. They may be translated into physical ailments, like muscle spasms, headaches or digestive troubles. One may be perversely proud of maintaining a gentle smile in the face of such sufferings, not seeing that false gentility could be the source of a torment that is ultimately self-inflicted.

Contrived gentility also blocks the apprehension and appraisal of envy, jealousy, lust, pride, and arrogance. One refuses to own these emotions, to bear with them humbly while working patiently toward their reformation. It should not surprise us that the pseudopoliteness of such people is replaced by harsh cruelness against prisoners and opponents in times of war and turmoil.

Pseudogentility and Deformative Anxiety

Feelings that are refused due to paralyzed or pseudogentility may be twisted into deformative anxiety, which can be either crude or complex. Crude anxiety is manifested directly in our mind and body. We may feel somewhat fearful, or the anxiety may be so intense that we almost go to pieces. Our muscles cramp; our heart flutters; our stomach is upset; our back and neck stiffen in pain. Possibly we feel nauseated or shaky, alternately chilly and flushed. Deformative anxiety can evoke one or another of these symptoms or a mixture of them. Pseudogentle people are excessively concerned about maintaining their poise and polite comportment. They may suffer a sudden anxiety attack when emotions endanger their staid composure. Such attacks are linked to their identification with the mask of gentility. They feel that their life-form itself is threatened by a multiplicity of maladies and agitations. These may be passing or lasting, that is, in some cases they may accompany one's formation journey as a whole.

In the pseudogentle personality, complex anxiety may deform life with dispositions of rigid apprehension and appraisal, inflexible functioning, and unyielding patterns of behavior. Other symptoms include insomnia, phobias, depression, obsession, and so on. Smooth interformation with others is blocked by these deformities of lifestyle and appearance. The diffusion of complex anxiety diminishes its overwhelming power and pain, but it also obscures our focal awareness that anxiety as such is at the root of these deformities. Unfortunately, the dissonant lifestyle one develops evokes new anxieties. This stirring up is again diffused by an increase of deformative, seemingly unrelated symptoms. In this way anxiety and its translation in deformities increases like an endless spiral.

Pseudogentle people can break this vicious circle only by confronting their dissonant feelings and the deformative dispositions from which they emerge. Usually they need help from formation counselors. They are the most immediate experts available to the population at large when one is faced with formation problems that are still within the normal range of those suffered within a specific society. As long as one's symptoms do not lead to severe emotional illness, one can be helped by well-trained formation counselors. When the psychological or psychosomatic disorder is severe, the formation counselor may have to refer the person to other experts for long-term help.

Formation counselors should be aware that pseudogentility can occur in people who strive too anxiously to attain a spiritual life in accordance with some powerful religious or ideological form tradition. They should realize that this tense striving can breed deformative anxiety. Such excessive fear may evoke a multiplicity of dispositional deformities. These spawn in turn many dissonant emotions. Attention to dissonance assists formation counselors in recommending strategies that prevent the emergence of more serious disorders. Most people manifest only the initial symptoms of this type of deformation. They can be helped in time by expert formation counseling.

The same attentiveness enables formation counselors to spot severe disorders that may require intense treatment. They should refer such cases to the appropriate experts. Formation counselors have neither the training nor the time to engage in prolonged periods of treatment over many years. They must remain available to the population at large, forming, as it were, a first line of defense against the serious deformation of life. Their time, energy, and expertise should not be restricted to a small number of seriously afflicted people who need other specialists to attend to their maladies.

Pseudogentility and Deformative Transposition of Anger

Anxious striving to acquire a gentle disposition may lead people deeper into the quagmire of contrived gentility. Their apparent life-form seems gentle enough, while in reality their core and current forms are seething with rage. One way of prefocally handling their fury is by means of transposition. For example, a man might transpose his irritation from his supervisor, whose power frightens him, to his anxious wife when she makes a small error in the preparation of the evening meal. The family already knows from past experience of these irate moods and feelings that the man's gentle demeanor outside the family is a farce. Since he no longer has an image to lose in front of his family, his behavior at home is often gross compared to his conduct outside the home. Appearances are easy to keep up when we do not live with people day after day.

Pseudogentle persons may suddenly go wild with anger with no clear incitement. The pressure of unrelieved fury makes them take offense where no one else would. It triggers their dormant rage. Persons like this may have been mistreated by people or social institutions with whom they were compelled to be gentle because of their power over them. Injuries to one's dignity and to one's right to honest communication may have sedimented in a silent rage over the years. An angry, seething heart may be the result of many hurts borne in reticent rebellion. When it becomes too much to bear, one's anger is let loose on people who have nothing to do with the original offense or unfair treatment.

One may also transpose anger from its original object pole to a group of people one imagines will justify an unbridled release of fury. They may be the members of an opposing political party, the adherents of another form tradition, or people belonging to another culture, country, or formation segment. One lashes out at the "filthy" rich or the "lazy" poor, the "stupidity" of women or the "sleaziness" of men, the "foolishness" of youth, or the "vegetating" of the aged. While one may rightly object to certain actions or people, what betrays a hidden cesspool of anger is the ferocity of the crusade. One's gentle image seems forgotten or suspended. Some may spend a lifetime splattering the "derelicts" of society with the slush of old aggravations and hurt feelings.

One's deformative transposition of hidden rage may seek its object in oneself. Such victims develop a disposition of self-depreciation along with such subdispositions as false guilt, shame, self-punishment, and depreciative abandonment. All of this may be concealed under a veil of vulnerable gentleness. Often the transposition of anger to one's own life leads to depression. At times self-depreciation may be transposed outwardly to others. One begins to depreciate them without being aware that one is basically depreciating oneself.

Deformative transposition can become complex. Unable to admit one's anger, one may be equally unable to apprehend and appraise this disposition to depreciate self and others. Instead, one's deformative imagination twists the unadmitted anger into the persuasion that one is depreciated by others. This deformation could be called "reverse transposition." In this case, the original transposition of one's anger from its real object pole to a generalized self-depreciation is now transposed again to others. It seems as though the depreciation of oneself comes not from oneself but from others.

Milder manifestations of such deformative processes can be found in many people and may still fall within the normal range of deformation. As such they belong to the field of competence of the formation counselor.

Cases that lead to severe mental and emotional derangement may require hospitalization, medical treatment, or years of therapy. In this eventuality, the formation counselor again refers such persons who are no longer counselees, but patients to the appropriate experts.

True and Make-Believe Gentleness

Many people who strive for a consonant form of life develop both a true and a make-believe gentleness. True gentleness usually prevails, interrupted at moments by justified anger and its appropriate expression. Make-believe gentleness, alternated with inordinate expressions of rage and irritation, may interrupt this consonant lifestyle if one is under common strain. Make-believe gentleness can thus exist side by side with the gentle core and current forms of life. This pseudoform develops its own coherent structure of perceptions, apprehensions, appraisals, voluntary directives, memories, imaginations, and anticipations, together with the dispositions and feelings to which they give rise. The pseudoform lies in waiting, as it were, until the conditions for its inception prevail. Then it comes to the fore and threatens to dominate our actual form of life momentarily. Its insidious power is due to the formation energy we have invested in it prefocally, perhaps long ago under the pressure of anxiety. We may easily confuse this defensive version of gentility with real gentleness, which is motivated and guided by congeniality, compatibility and compassion.

Good formation counseling or direction can help us to become aware of such a secondary dormant form of make-believe gentility and its subtle manifestations. We grow more sensitive to its assertion in our actual life-form, especially in situations that threaten our form potency conviction. We should learn to cope with such threats through reapprehension and reappraisal of their meaning rather than by donning the mask of pseudo-gentle decorum. We should remain aware also that the main strategical tactic of the falsely gentle form of life is transposition. We transpose responsibility for our rational or irrational anger to others. We transpose it to imperfect people, events, and things, to institutions or movements about which we can feel indignant without losing our self-image of pious gentleness. Thus we can release our aggravation and feel justified in the process.

This make-believe life-form may lastingly dominate our actual life-form, subverting all hope of beneficial interformation and spawning inappropriate reactions and responses to people and situations. False gentleness always puts a great strain on our human relationships. Even if it hides our hostility well, some people will sense its presence under our composure, no matter how sweet or polite we seem. They will feel uncomfortable with us, even if they cannot pinpoint the cause of their unease. All of this spoils interformative appreciation and the possibility to express mutual empathy.

Pseudogentility and an Obsessively Preventive Life-Form

The formation of an obsessively preventive life-form usually starts early. It is fostered by fixation on deformative accretions of one's formation tradition by one's family, formation segment, or local culture. Insofar as a form tradition is rooted in a consonant faith tradition, the *foundations* of that tradition are beneficial. However, certain interpretations of these foundations may not be so beneficial. It is beyond the expertise and training of the formation scientist to correct these accretions. Theologians or philosophers of the religious or ideological faith tradition concerned are experts in the correct and beneficial interpretation of such traditions and their purification from dissonant accretions. Their work is of utmost importance for consonant life formation insofar as they influence our proximate form traditions in ultimate ways.

Form traditions, more often than faith traditions, may contain accretions that stress gentle appearance over inner formation. They may instill detrimental forms of false humility. These tend to deny the necessity of at least a minimum of form potency conviction. True humility means that one experiences one's form potency as a gift of the formation mystery. False accretions may suggest that one should negate, cripple, or depreciate any sense of form potency, as if its exertion were sheer arrogance.

According to this deforming vision, one must above all look good in the eyes of other adherents of the form tradition living in one's family, neighborhood, and community. One should uphold meek and gentle appearances, no matter how one really feels. In such surroundings, looking gentle is the way to gain acceptance. It allows one to unfold and exercise form potency without appearing too different from others. An original person, gifted with unusual form potency and creative ability, always feels threatened in such an atmosphere. The unusual kind of service one is called to render to humanity can be diminished or destroyed. One's display of humility, meekness, and gentleness could be suspect. Fanatic or anxious adherents of the same form tradition who are fixated on false accretions may find ample reason in this regard to level the original person whom they secretly distrust, fear, and envy. To prevent this destruction of originality, the creative person may develop many prefocal strategies of prevention, among them pseudogentility.

If this threat to one's form potency was experienced early in childhood and later protracted by followers of one's form tradition, the preventive life-form may become obsessive. Much of one's life is centered around real or imagined threats by pious or envious oppressors, who always seem to question one's humility. These threats to one's form potency and the enterprises that manifest its effectiveness begin to be anticipated on basis of what one remembers of past misunderstanding and ridicule. Such memories and anticipations are kept alive and often magnified by one's formative imagination. Continually anticipated threats lead one to assume an overly protective lifestyle. Perception, apprehension, appraisal, decision, memory, imagination, and anticipation are disposed to prevent suspicion and envy from being aroused in others. One builds an intricate web of obsessively protective dispositions. These dispose one to be overly vigilant, hypercautious, and suspicious. One always expects the worst to happen. One may feel compelled to display a meek gentility that veils one's original thought, imagination, action, and achievement. Such dispositions breed corresponding feelings of fear, aggravation, irritation, defiance, vulnerability, or active or passive aggressiveness. To hide these seething emotions under the mantle of meekness demands more and more energy.

Irrational emotions and exertions are accompanied by hormonal stimulation that prepares the body steadily for excessive approach or withdrawal. One has to quell such feelings to please fellow adherents of one's form tradition and to maintain one's freedom to pursue originality. Should one be predisposed by genetic inheritance to such chronic ailments as heart disease or diabetes, such hormonal stimulation may adversely affect one's condition. In some cases, it may aggravate the inherited condition so badly that it could be fatal.

People who develop such an obsessively preventive form of life, even if they succeed in surviving, may be hounded by a sense of the possible destruction of their accomplishments and their good name. They are always on the watch for potential threats to what they experience as their vulnerable victory. The pretense of gentility has to go on. Genuine gentleness is difficult to maintain when one is besieged by real or imaginary threats. One cannot feel spontaneously gentle toward real or imagined oppressors.

The dreams of people living an obsessively preventive life-form disclose the same deformative patterns. Their dreams are often populated by people, actions, movements, and words that threaten to destroy their opportunities for creative accomplishment, for recognition and confirmation of their form potency, for an honorable name. Accordingly, they may be busy devising sweet pretenses, clever excuses to justify their originality, polite facial expressions, ingratiating and gentle movements—whatever it takes to stall, prevent, avert, nip in the bud, ward off, sidetrack, neutralize, or render harmless potentially wrong impressions, suspicions, fears, or distrust in fellow adherents of the same form tradition.

In everyday life, a trusted friend may bring to one's attention an unfortunate piece of news or a problem that could point to a possible threat to the success and continuation of one's work. This friend would never take advantage of one's consequent angry explosion. Hence, one may drop the mask enforced by the form tradition and let the accumulated aggravation come out in a way disproportionate to the issue at hand. The same may happen during a meeting with a trusted formation counselor or director.

Not all adherents of the same form tradition, as it is onesidedly communicated in some dissonant period of formation history, will develop such an obsessively preventive form of life. They may be too compliant. Hence, their initiative and creativity may be severely limited. They may be somewhat deformed, yet they may not manifest the same serious symptoms. Ready targets for prevention-obsession are people who are unusually creative and original. They may be endowed with a refined and vulnerable sensitivity, a passionate and lively temperament. At the same time, they may deeply adhere to the foundations of their faith tradition and the form tradition implementing it. They are especially vulnerable if their parents were similarly afflicted or believed deeply in the deformative accretions of their form tradition. Such children have little chance of escaping this deformation, except by total rebellion and defection or by good formation counseling. If vital inheritance predisposes them to chronic illnesses later in life, illnesses that are adversely affected by such tensions, their deformation will be compounded by a worsening of their physical condition.

One should develop strategies of reformation that can help one gradually replace pseudogentility by real gentleness. This implies first of all being able to forgive those who have deformed one's life. Most of them were probably well-meaning. They themselves were the victims of the deformative accretions of their form traditions. One may be too old to eradicate totally the residues of an obsessive preventive form of life. However, mellowing, no matter how slight, means progress, liberation, a slight gain in consonance, and more room for joy and inner relaxation. If one's health is seriously affected, any mellowing may mean the difference between life and death. Mellowing of prevention anxiety, therefore, has a life-saving quality.

The first movement of an effective reformation strategy should be one of reapprehension and reappraisal of one's gentility and one's hidden aggravation. One should try in relaxed, gentle vigilance to reapprehend and reappraise any thoughts, feelings, dispositions, directives, or expressions that are somehow linked to one's obsessive preventive life-form. When one clearly apprehends it as such, one must begin to reappraise the excessive, exaggerated, or phobic form directives to which it gives rise in one's life. Such disclosures slowly affect one's decisions and actions after a long period of repeated appraisal.

A formation counselor may facilitate this process. So, too, may the keeping of a journal and the reading of texts relevant to this problem. The prevention-obsession deeply affects one's formation journey. It plays a crucial role in one's actual life-form. Therefore, one should not be surprised about the automatic activation of its dispositions. The slightest provocation may trigger the deformative process at the spur of the moment. Yet we must never be discouraged; we must believe in the just-noticeable improvements that show up over the years. Each of them is a step toward the joyous life of consonance and true gentleness. Every small advance is one link broken in the chain of deformation that has imprisoned one so cruelly from infancy on.

Pseudogentility and the Life of Depreciation

The pseudogentle life tends to be depreciative, whereas true gentleness engages one in the disposition of appreciation. Depreciation may be restricted to a skeptical, cynical, or negative outlook on life. It may also lead to despondency and depression that disable and paralyze the sufferer. In between these extremes, many variations of depreciation are possible. We cannot deal with the kind of depression that is rooted in physical causes and that should be treated by medical specialists. But we can deal with the depreciation and despondency that are caused by deformation and that clearly diminish joy, vitality, and heartfelt interest in people.

It is difficult to feel gentle when things are gloomy and life is disappointing. At the same time, depreciative people may feel compelled to manifest gentility to hide their negative attitude toward others in various situations. They know from experience that the display of depreciation diminishes their effectiveness in daily affairs. To receive at least some confirmation, they may exhibit a token gentility that conceals their dismal frame of mind. This polite stance hides their true somber, gloomy, downhearted disposition. At times a cynical, sarcastic wit betrays their depreciative point of view.

This problem is traceable to the primordial option between appreciative and depreciative abandonment, discussed at length in the first volume of this series. It may be fostered by deformative accretions of one's form traditions. These could paint the consonant life as inflexible, stilted, sustained by a grim denial of joy, creativity, graciousness, and aesthetic refinement.

Another cause of depreciation may be the bottling up of aggravation and irritation during a significant period of one's formation journey. This repudiation may give rise to anxiety and intense self-depreciation, leading to a lasting mood of gloom and despondency. The forced gentility of such morose people may ironically impress others. A dour disposition, when gently and pompously communicated, may be admired by those already predisposed to depreciation. The danger of contagion deepens when supporters of the gloomy, deformative accretions of form traditions are in a position of authority or formative leadership. They may not have passed through the kind of program that would have detected and helped to reform their harmful dispositions before they could pass the same deformation onto others. They may have been elected to such positions exactly because of their solemn negativity that paraded as gentle wisdom. Sadly, they may be people of obviously goodwill, with genuine conviction but without the faintest suspicion of their own deformation. This obvious goodness may enhance the impression they radiate of sedate, gentle wisdom. Their compulsively gentle looks, their sad and contrived smiles, their expressions of gloomy self-depreciation may be mistaken for humility, exceptional maturity, or saintliness.

As formation counselors or people in authority, they may unwittingly deform those entrusted to their care. Their counselees may spread the same gloom among those they meet, in some instances scorning even the pretense of gentleness. They proclaim a grim style of life as the sign and symbol of wisdom and maturity.

In many people, this abiding self-depreciation may be covered so artfully by pseudogentility that one rarely notices how much sadness there is under their cheerful platitudes. Self-depreciation may be manifested only in certain deformative modes of life that are not clearly and directly linked to this problem as such. People who are overweight, for example, may eat to the point of disgust. They may go on binges when the strain of emergent aggravation threatens their facade of jolly gentleness. People not deformed in this way would simply become anxious or aggravated, not ravenous. Such compulsive eaters may never discover the link between their need to be happy-go-lucky good fellows and the corresponding denial of their anxiety, aggravation, and depreciation of life. Nor can they see its relation to their voracious, self-destructive eating dispositions.

The same goes for opposite types of symptoms: some people turn their intense self-depreciation into starvation. They, too, hide their negative dispositions under the guise of pseudogentility. Because the underlying deformation is the same, a self-depreciative person may switch from one kind of self-destructive style of life to another.

Self-depreciation may be one cause of insomnia. How can one sleep when one is burned up by the irritation hidden so carefully during the day under gentle appearances? At night the gentle mask falls away. It is no longer necessary. One does not have to smile at oneself in the dark. The removal of the mask lowers one's resistance against the inner demons. Yet even then a lack of inner gentleness and peace may remain veiled from its victim. Such people sense only the agitation that, like lethal radiation, seeps into their wide-awake consciousness. They may feel perplexed by visual images of disasters befalling the people upon whom they lavish so much gentleness during the day. Little do they know that small aggravations, hidden under a blanket of feigned gentleness, can return as obsessive images at night. Meanwhile, other people who live in the same tense depreciation may try prefocally to evade the burden of their depreciative life by excessive sleep.

Some people punish themselves for the absence of gentleness by tortuously dwelling on past failures and misfortunes related to their unsolved aggravation and to their pervasive depreciation of life. Others punish themselves by endless, useless worry about the future. Constant brooding is another means to evade any focal awareness of the anger that threatens the maintenance of one's pseudogentility. As long as one dwells anxiously on the past or future, one does not have to face the denied depreciation of the present. Ceaseless mulling over real or imagined problems also serves as a strategy to diffuse the ever increasing pain of self-depreciation.

Accumulated anger cannot be fully dispersed by any of these strategies. It may appear in a disguised form in compulsive images and thoughts, in anxious concerns about friends and relatives, in dreams at night as well as during the day. Those toward whom one displays so much apparent gentleness are often pictured on the verge of tragedy, defeat, or physical debilitation. As a prefocal defense against such intrafocal wishes of harm to those one secretly hates, one may be obsessively preoccupied with casualties and catastrophes that may ruin their health or career. Deeply buried irritation over their failures or displeasing features seeks an outlet in such grotesque concerns. This type of other-centered anxiety may cover destructive desires for revenge or for other outlets for one's pernicious resentment. One does not dare to admit this dissonant facet into focal awareness. Yet it is only when one is able to acknowledge such anger or envy, either alone or with the help of a formation counselor, that one may be liberated from this obsession and led to a new appraisal of one's life, illumined by presence to the formation mystery.

Usually resentment and irritation that are repudiated do not result in such extreme forms of dissonance. Side by side with our life of gentle consonance, most of us develop some form of pseudogentility. It comes to the fore in times of excessive strain. Unexpected overwhelming opposition may loosen a wave of rage and resentment that bursts through in spite of our usually gentle disposition. At such moments irritations repudiated in the past and injustices overlooked earlier flood our memory, imagination, and anticipation. Less intense and pervasive than the fury felt by people who live in constant denial of anger, our outburst passes. It leaves behind only a trail of ruffled feelings that are not infrafocal but prefocal. They are near enough to the boundaries of our focal attentiveness that formative reflection can bring them to light. Even without the assistance of a formation counselor or director, we can appraise and reform the felt dissonance between pseudo- and authentic gentleness. We can find ways to express our irritation in a congenial, compatible, and compassionate fashion to ourselves, to trusted friends, and perhaps to those who irk us in the first place.

Growth in genuine gentleness leaves room for the dispositions of firmness, legitimate anger, justified indignation, and their consonant expression. It saves us from the dismal communications of morose individuals, who grimly denounce graciousness and joy in other people. We avoid the dark cloud cast by their dour dispositions and try to remain open to the joyful tidings of the formation mystery. Their despondent moods and anxious frowns, their sickly feelings of guilt, and their entrapment in the deformative accretions of form traditions no longer spoil our day. We simply avoid, whenever possible, being victimized by their buried rage, the depth of which they do not know. They need our compassion, not our condemnation.

Gentleness and the Effectiveness of Form Potency

Our conviction of form potency is facilitated by two main conditions. One is the experience of a firm yet gentle form effectiveness; the other is confirmation by significant others, assuring us of this effectiveness. To exercise form potency most effectively, three other conditions are necessary. They are: uniqueness in execution and result; adequate stimulation in our formation field; and a certain assurance and security in performance and outcome.

The effects of our form potency must be marked by some trace of our uniqueness if we are to experience what we do as our own accomplishment. Such personalization does not have to entail anything spectacular. It may be as simple as the inflection of our voice or the personal care we take when doing the dishes or when welcoming people into our home.

We feel invited to exercise our form potency fully only when it is appealed to or stimulated by some event in our formation field. This stimulation becomes distinctively human when we turn it freely into gentle human motivations that draw our dormant form potency into action. Finally, we should attain such calm certainty in the usual, effective activation of our potency that we can exercise it firmly yet gently, almost casually, without inner or outer violence.

Predisposition for Consonant Stimulation

The predisposition for uniqueness is primary in regard to form potency. Yet in terms of the process of actuation, the predisposition to be stimulated or to receive an animating form has priority. Without form reception, our form potency would not be activated at all. Hence, practically speaking, the reception of a stimulating form comes first. In other words, our form potency must be energized by the reception of formative stimulation within our formation field. Interwoven with our form potency is the predisposition to be receptively open to stimulations that can activate and energize it fully.

The absence of stimulation can be as deadly as the absence of confirmation. The more we advance in the consonant life, the more we are able to draw upon inner sources of stimulation. However, the fact remains that we are mostly dependent on the energy flow that is channelled through inter- and outer stimulation. Immature people always remain dependent on such extraneous stimuli because their fund of inner resources is low.

An analogy could be drawn with formation processes in the physical universe. Plants need the stimulation of sunlight, soil, and water to develop their best form. They receive formative stimulation by a process of vital assimilation, storing within what they need for mature growth. People assimilate physiological stimuli in similar ways. However, higher stimulation in the form of sociohistorical pulsations, vital-functional rewards and punishments, and transcendent aspirations and inspirations is assimilated in a distinctively human way. This input is carefully apprehended, appraised, and affirmed. It can be turned into formative motivations, which, once affirmed by the will, can push us toward full implementation.

We can give and receive form only by interformation with others and by interaction with the outer dimensions of our formation field. If we are not stimulated, challenged, or inspired by these sources, our abilities, along with their underlying unique form potency, are not activated. Soon we become bored and tired. Life loses its dynamism. This flaccid state can generate anxiety, emptiness, and despair, at times interspersed with sudden outbursts of rebellion and violence. Witness what happens in underprivileged neighborhoods when young people are without work, stripped of their dignity. Vandalism can be a dissonant explosion of the need for some stimulation of one's paralyzed form potency.

The absence of consonant stimulation alerts us instinctively that our life-form itself is in jeopardy. Animals need only biophysical stimulation for the exercise of their form potency. The stimulation of human potency, however, is dependent on the sociohistorical meanings provided by shared form traditions and objectified in cultural media, customs, monuments, and events. We need such stimulation to arouse our personal motivations. These awaken our form potency and the abilities it sustains. Think of the stimulating values offered to us by our form traditions. If we continually personalize them in our motivations, we will not lose the formation energy they generate.

The demons of apathy, tedium, and boredom would soon invade our lives were it not for this predisposition. But if we do not exercise it, it may lose its gentle and firm direction. Such loss could generate an anxious search for artificial and dissonant stimulation, symbolized by vicarious involvement in the personal lives of other people, achieved by prying. One becomes a Peeping Tom in the spiritual and psychological sense. One may seek stimulation in thrills like drugs, alcohol, riots, vandalism, crime, sexual promiscuity, bragging, torturing of animals or people, and in countless other dissonant ways. These represent dissonant transpositions of the craving of our form potency for consonant stimulation. The disposition of gentleness guards us against the temptation to substitute spasmodic thrills for consonant stimulation.

Form Potency and the Predisposition for Unique Self-Expression

The predisposition to receive consonant stimulation is the first one engendered by our unique form potency. We want to express this uniqueness in some recognizable way in our formation field. This is why humans shun total conformity or collectivism. Everyone wants to personalize his or her endeavors, at least in small but personal styles of presence and dedication to what we do.

This primary predisposition of our form potency for unique expression identifies us as individual laborers and professionals, friends and lovers, students and teachers, administrators and technicians. This bent toward uniqueness does not detract from our communal disposition. If anything, it deepens our capacity for gentle compatibility and compassion with others and our surroundings. It makes us counteract the tendency to turn the community into an anonymous crowd or collectivity. A relatively unique, responsible person does not succumb easily to programs devised by seductive leaders that would quell personal initiative. True community is gracious, gentle, and refined, full of reverence and respect for each one's personal contribution. It inspires us to personalize creatively the things we do in common. Most of all, it enables us to balance the communal and the privacy disposition, though one or the other may prevail in accordance with the disclosures of our foundational life-form. It follows from this reflection that we must avoid any violence that would mar the manifestation of the gift of our relative uniqueness.

Form Potency and the Predisposition for Secure Self-Exertion

Security of our form potency and its actualization is another predisposition for the development of a consonant life. This concern for secure self-exertion is strong, yet we may sacrifice it in favor of either the predisposition for stimulation or the predisposition for uniqueness. The readiness to put our security into the background explains the behavior of certain people. A soldier in battle may jeopardize his life, that is to say, he may risk the total destruction of his form potency, to prove to himself and his comrades his identity as a daring fighter. Firemen may risk their form potency in a similar way. In search of any stimulation that makes them feel as if their dormant potency is coming to life, some people may drive irresponsibly, engage in foolish duels, or taunt powerful officials who could destroy their effectiveness. Still others defy security by daring statements that may make headlines but may also endanger needlessly their position in the state, church, or company. Some may be so driven by their need to be noticed that they commit spectacular crimes. All may put their lives on the line to appear unique or to experience maximum stimulation of their form potency.

This primacy of our predispositions for unique and animated living does seem more attuned to effective form giving and receiving than does one's drive for security. However, security is a key factor. It should not be unwisely endangered, nor should it become our main life directive. While we should not be frantic about security, we should be gently concerned. We should try to organize life for ourselves and others in such a way that we can at least feel secure enough to exercise our form potency.

The powerful often oppress the powerless by taking away their security. Threatened by punishment, torture, and persecution many do not dare to be themselves. Their predisposition for sheer survival has been so overactivated by oppression that the predispositions for being themselves and for animating stimulation have been paralyzed. In their case, the hierarchy of form potency dispositions is radically reversed. The need for security, safety, and survival takes over totally. They may not even be aware that their oppressors have unjustly deprived them of their rights for unique formation and consonant stimulation.

The only way to reverse this process of dehumanization is to restore the original hierarchy of predispositions. Oppressed persons should be made aware of the social injustices they are suffering. They should be alert to the unjust infraformation their exploiters have built into the dissonant accretions of form traditions to which they blindly adhere. Unoppressed persons are obliged in conscience to help them become focally aware of the shared potency they have as a group of oppressed people. The time may come when they have to band together against their tormentors, who would entirely destroy their form potency and enslave them for the sake of enhancing their own wealth and power.

Powerless, oppressed people suffer from this continual diminishment of their striving for unique self-expression and consonant humane stimulation. The need for security obviously becomes prevalent when survival itself is at stake under oppressive regimes. But in those who do not have to face this ultimate threat from infancy to old age, an excessive preoccupation with security can become deformative. When the striving for it in unoppressed people loses gentle moderation, it may lead to an anxious overstructuring of one's life. The more such persons focus on their feelings of insecurity and danger, the more anxious they become about every potential threat in their formation field. They fear anything that might possibly infringe upon the safety structures they have so carefully erected to protect their lives and projects. Beneficial interformation becomes difficult. They feel suspicious about those who dare to risk being their unique selves. In their security system, each person is carefully placed in a well-delineated niche. One has to know exactly what one can expect so that one can be in control. As soon as people act differently than they should, according to this security scheme, they experience anxiety. They feel uncertain about whether they can manipulate people in a way that will insure their own position of safety and control.

This disposition for security is now likely to generate constant anxiety. Fearing the secure actualization of one's form potency, one may feel obliged to pry into the lives of others, even if this means transgressing the boundaries of their privacy. One may stall the loss of one's security by recording every change taking place in one's formation field. Immense amounts of energy are invested in checking any detail of behavior that may clue such persons in to changes that could threaten their own form effectiveness.

We should try to help such people to modulate gently their overanxious security dispositions. More energy would then be available to them to realize their true form potency more effectively. This would not only increase the quality of their presence; it would lead in turn to a natural and normal increase in the peripheral type of security they seem to need. To be sure, peripheral security is not as important as the foundational security that can only be gained if one grows in presence to the formation mystery in faith, hope, and consonance. It takes time to mature in this fundamental security.

Further Implications of Security That Lacks Gentleness

The tendency to overstructure one's life and formation field is a sign that security lacks gentle modulation. Rigid organization makes one feel safe, but at the same time it hampers the free and joyous realization of form potency. It makes one ward off many consonant stimulations that could keep this potency alive. Tight safety measures do protect us from some disapproval or misunderstanding, but the price one pays for such stringent measures may be the death of original potency and its spontaneous expression in daily life. One becomes anonymous, absorbed in a numbing collectivity, inordinately attached to safety directives. When traces of gentleness entirely disappear from one's obsessive striving for security, one may experience a pervasive disgust with life, combined with an aching need for selfhood and excitement.

In some people, these refused predispositions may suddenly burst forth and overwhelm their boring life. They try to assert at once their denied form potency and its feared uniqueness, leaving others to wonder how such sedate citizens could suddenly go on a rampage, look for thrills, break up their marriage, destroy their career, engage in sexual promiscuity, crime or sedition.

Another consequence of paralyzing absorption in security directives may be the birth of secret envy. People who have crippled their form potency may envy those who have escaped a similar paralysis. It pains them to see these people moving freely in their formation field. They are alive and energetic, renewed by motivations into which they freely translate the consonant stimulations they disclose in their surroundings. Joyously they can turn obstacles into opportunities. Observing such alive persons, obsessively secure people may painfully sense that in their eagerness to find and secure their lives they may have lost them. Their envious disposition is doubly aroused when they meet people who seem to have failed physically, economically, or popularly, yet who seem filled with joy and security. Such people experience their form potency, no matter how limited its expression, as a continual gift of the formation mystery. They are bound to be a reproach to anyone who has anxiously submerged him- or herself in the contagious moods, whims, and anonymity of crowd and collectivity. Their freedom and resiliency necessarily evoke envious, aggressive feelings in those who sold out.

Such persons, secure in their consonance, can expect to suffer some persecution as a result. Only outstanding power, wealth, or renown may shield them from the resentment of those who have betrayed their own form of life. Those who fear creative life formation cannot live in peace with this other kind of person. They are a constant reproach.

Bitterness, vindictiveness, and resentment are rooted partly in the deformative disposition to make everyone conform to one's own safe, predictable formation structures. Unique persons, who are vital, joyous, and open to the inspiration of the formation mystery and its epiphanies, cannot be totally predictable in all facets of life. Such annoying unpredictability irritates people who live by anxious control of everything that moves in their formation field. Their pain is aggravated by the fact that they experience at times their own hidden desire to be true to who they are rather than to sell themselves, their life directives and convictions, to please the crowd or collectivity where they hope to remain secure.

In this project of security that has lost gentle moderation, a final twist is the reversal of all consonant dispositions. What is dissonant is now labeled consonant. In other words, people who have sacrificed their life to gain guarantees may claim and believe that mediocrity is prudence; anxious anonymity is humility; betrayal of one's uniqueness is compatibility; cowardly refusal to commit oneself is wisdom; the frantic pursuit of popularity is charity.

In this perverted state, consonant dispositions of fidelity to the call of one's uniqueness in service of humanity are appraised as pride; dedication as self-centered exhibition; courage as foolish ambition. One's deformed mind generates a reversed world of appraisals and form directives. This web of perverted appraisals makes one feel righteous about one's destructive persecution of those who remain faithful to their call. If many people in a society are affected by this reversal of dispositions, communities deteriorate into leveling collectivities that promise absolute security to those who conform. These leveling infraforms of approval and disapproval are meant to insure the mediocrity of all.

To be faithful and secure in the fulfillment of one's unique call does not mean doing things in a peculiar way or doing only what one likes to do. The consonant, secure life is not only congenial; it is also compatible and compassionate. These latter dispositions foster gentleness in one's search for congeniality and security. A consonant society organizes itself around the principle of respectful promotion of each person's uniqueness. To assure congeniality for all, this principle is protected also by compatibility and compassion. These dispositions prevent whimsical individualism by generating laws, customs, and institutions that limit and discipline individualistic needs and desires. They aim at the maximum exertion of form potency for the maximum number of people with a minimum of suffering for all. They foster gentle respect for the unique potency of everyone, insofar as this is compatible with the personal appropriation of common laws and rules.

A consonant society forms people to commit themselves to common tasks with personal responsibility and dedication. Congenial, secure citizens can find meaning in the smallest social task by bringing to it their personal gifts of apprehension, appraisal, commitment, and increasing competence. Their engagement in social tasks as fully present persons will generate zeal, inventiveness, and quiet fidelity as one personally appropriates each task as an invitiation of the formation mystery in its social epiphany. The more a society becomes consonant, the more this atmosphere of gentle generosity will prevail.

Pulsations, Pulsions, Ambitions, and the Disposition of Gentleness

If pulsations, pulsions, and ambitions were to rule our life exclusively, they would soon generate a dissonant striving for pleasure, power, and possession. Anxious cravings would grip our hearts, muting their gentle modulation. The ephemeral gratification we might find would only leave us sad and unfulfilled. Agitated by the chase for pleasure, frantically clutching our attainments, worrying about their loss or decline—all this would smother gentleness while increasing our resentment when these things elude our grasp. As long as we seek fulfillment in passing possessions, gentleness cannot establish itself as an enduring disposition and we cannot find abiding peace.

Pulsations, pulsions, and ambitions have to be lifted into the light of transcendent appraisal. This illumination will mellow our striving. Its gentle influence will direct these lower dispositions in a distinctively human way, enabling us to apprehend what is truly consonant. Instead of endless disappointment, restlessness and tension, it becomes possible for us to be gently present to self and others, to the formation mystery, and to the events it allows to be.

Silence, Speech, and Gentleness

The disposition of gentleness affects our formation of inner and outer speech. When we speak loudly or too much at inappropriate times, without gentleness and discretion, our language is no longer formative. The gentle disposition inclines us to know when to speak and when to be silent. It prevents us from turning our formation field into a wasteland of hollow chatter, a swamp of coarse, useless talk. It teaches us how to soften our voices when they become shrill and strident. When the propitious time for speech announces itself to the sensitive heart, gentleness generates the right modulation of caring words and silent pauses.

Language is formed inwardly. Intraformative words sculpt the form of our life without our knowing it. These words can be consonant or dissonant. Consonant inner speech thrives in a climate of gentleness. Too many dissonant images, thoughts, or sounds can destroy the gentle ambience of consciousness. Inner words may be agitated, harsh, anxious, scrupulous, depreciative. Dissonant speech results in unrealistic apprehensions, appraisals, decisions. It shapes discordant images, exalted memories, excessive anticipations, and the turbulent affections that accompany them.

When inner words are depreciative, they flow into strident or deceptive conversation. Unless we can silence them wisely, without repudiation, they will become a breeding ground of agitation and manipulation. We are our language. Hence, we should be suspicious of words that exalt status, power, possession, vital pleasure, and functional performance above everything else. These products of the pride-form generate excessive self-preoccupation, fretfulness, and tense forebodings of the future. They may imprison our hearts in popular movements that we have not appraised in freedom, entwining us in exhausting schemes, tense rivalries, and endless frustrations. Such dissonant inner and outer words will drive us on relentlessly unless we live in gentleness and free ourselves from words that imperil distinctively human formation.

Acquired and Infused Gentility

An excessive desire to demonstrate our form potency can despoil gentility. Willfulness silences the gentle disposition because the attainment of calculated success becomes our paramount venture. Life is no longer anchored in the formation mystery, whose channels we are called to be. When we grow gentle and flexible enough to remain receptive to its creative presence, our journey toward consonance really begins.

We have to ready ourselves for this gift by the discipline of an acquired gentility that will dispose us to become channels of the mystery. This preparatory gentleness, which the mystery certainly helps us to acquire, does not have the abiding quality of infused gentility. This is a pure gift of the mystery, an undeserved endowment that completes and exceeds gratuitously our acquired disposition. It melts the lingering vestiges of self-will and violence. The forming mystery, that first kindled our yearning, begins to fulfill the deepest longings implanted in our soul.

Serious and Playful Coformants of the Gentle Disposition

Gentleness makes us playful. It mitigates stressful solemnity, takes the edge off anxious vigilance, and relieves the tediousness of life in a technocratic society. But gentleness is not merely playful. It is coformed by seriousness. Unmitigated gravity of mood and demeanor is as bad as constant frivolity. Playfulness frees us from a gravity that could freeze joyfulness and flexibility. Seriousness keeps our feet on the solid ground of wisdom. Gentleness is gracious and elegant as well as earnest and full of respect. In the transcendent dimension, the playful side of the gentle disposition attunes us to the dance of the mystery in history and humanity. This infused awareness makes us lighthearted, carefree, and serene. The mystery itself becomes the source of our playful seriousness, our gentle gravity.

Infused gentleness springs from the depths of our formation where the mystery dwells silently, even though in our formation field itself we may experience suffering. Social and personal factors may generate injustice, exploitation, failure, defeat, self-deception, frustration. Despite all of these limits, we experience the gentility of a caring mystery as the deeper ground of our formation field. This presence is more profound than any oppressive expressions of personal or social life. These deformed infrastructures are like hidden landmines, ready to explode at any moment. We should wisely tread the pathways of our formation field in an abiding faith that the mystery is at work in us in a benevolent way that encompasses space and time. We must try to welcome whatever the mystery sends into our lives, appraising people, events, and things as challenges to be met firmly yet gently. We cannot give back the freedom and responsibility the mystery has bestowed on us as humans. Abuse of this freedom may generate immense suffering, especially in those who are without defense.

Only the mystery knows the form potency of each player. What does any conservative or progressive movement accomplish in the strategy of a game that spans the aeons? What counts is that we play the game the mystery wants us to play, remaining open to its disclosures in every situation. We must take the game seriously, but not too seriously. We must never lose sight of the passing nature of our formation field. Otherwise the gentle disposition will elude us. We may feel sorrow, not despair, when familiar forms collapse around us. We may be stunned momentarily when cherished ways of life disappear in unexpected upheavals. Yet we cannot mourn forever when accretions of a tradition are shaken loose by the tempests of time. War may shatter whole populations, but life goes on. What counts is our response. However serious our troubles may be, we must never succumb to a humorless gravity that kills the creative, playful coformant of our gentle disposition. We must resist the kind of somberness that dampens spontaneity and the search for new opportunity.

Above all we should resist the temptations of the exalted pride-form with its destructive push to be popular at any cost or to surrender our freedom to a leveling collectivity. We should be content to play our small part in the game of life, remaining gently open to what the mystery wills for us on this passing trip through space and time. We should be courageous in spite of the pain inflicted by the powerful on those whose life and action are vulnerable. If we are faithful to our calling in freedom, we can echo the words of Gandhi, saying that, in the end, truth and goodness will prevail.

CHAPTER 8

Privacy Disposition

The privacy disposition is crucial for consonant human formation. It protects the intra- or intraformative sphere of our formation field. At the same time, it does not impede fluid interaction with the other spheres of this field. For instance, the richness of intraformative reflection on the meaning of my life is not destroyed but nourished by my experiences of what others go through or tell me. In turn I may share with them what I have learned inwardly, provided such exposition is congenial with my basic life call and compatible with my life formation at this moment. The science of formation identifies what happens here as either the consonant expansion or the consonant contraction of the intraformative sphere in relation to the interformative sphere.

The same expansion and contraction is possible in relation to the outer spheres of formation. My intraformative sphere is nourished not only by direct interformation with people but also by the symbols and formation events in my life situation and wider world. Books, architecture, music, paintings, sculptures, myths, rituals, and other situational expressions of form traditions may enhance the meaning of life and deepen my intraformative reflections. The intrasphere in turn may expand into these outer spheres by symbolic expression and formative action. The symbolic arrangement of my room, house, or garden, my clothes or choice of car, may express something of what is going on in my intrasphere.

Briefly, formation science emphasizes as ideal the relative consonance of the formation field in all its spheres. Hence, we shall consider some of the main formative structures developed by this science and relate them provisionally to the disposition of privacy.

Formation Field and the Privacy Disposition

One of the basic constructs of this science pertains to its positing of a unified formation field. Because we are part of this field, we participate in it and coform it. For the newborn infant the formation field may be initially indistinct. Soon, however, the never ending process of refining the formation field begins. The myriad nuances that later mark the unfolding field of each human life-form are of such a variety that we could not enumerate and describe them all. Initially, the basic or foundational nuances of the formation field are universal. These basic, universal nuances comprise the pre-, intra-, inter-, and outer spheres of the field. Often we call them formation *poles* to indicate that there exists a certain tension between these interrelated spheres of formation and their contracting and expanding influence on each other. This concept will be helpful in our discussion of the privacy disposition, for this disposition plays an important role in the contracting and expanding movements of the intrasphere.

Privacy and the Actualization of the Four Basic Life-Form Dimensions

Related to these spheres is our actualization of four basic life-form dimensions or form potencies, these being the socio-historical, vital, functional, and transcendent. To foster the consonant life, these potencies should be actualized in each sphere in such a way that their right hierarchy is maintained or restored. The transcendent should prevail, for instance, over the functional, vital, and sociohistorical dimensions without preempting the unique contribution of these subordinate dimensions.

For example, the privacy disposition enables us to contract the intrasphere when intrusions by the inter- and outer spheres threaten to strengthen subordinate dimensions at the expense of higher ones. Say that personal overinvolvement in sociohistorical pulsations or functional ambitions in the inter- and outer sphere begins to be reflected in my intraformative life. This onesided emphasis may make me lose my inner presence to the transcendent. In such an event, the privacy disposition disposes me to timely retreat into the intrasphere to regain my balance.

Privacy and the Four Integrative Life-Forms

The actualization of these four form potencies demands integration into the integrative life-forms that make them consonant with the disclosures of the formation mystery in my preformation and in my actual life situation. In the science of formation, we distinguish the integrative core, current, and apparent life-forms as well as the final actual life-form, blending the three former ones into our actual presence here and now at this moment of life.

These life-forms both influence and are influenced by the intrasphere. In regard to the core form, as explained in the first volume of this series, the relative constellation of any basic form disposition is coformed by the intraformative sphere. So are the dispositions of the current, apparent, and actual life-forms.

We may illustrate this fact by the example of a poetess. The main recurrent themes of her poetry flow from her heart. The formation of her heart is influenced by her intraformative sphere, by her inward musings. Her current poetic life is in part formed by the intraformative sphere insofar as her present poetry mirrors not only the lasting underlying themes of her heart but also current concerns, interests, crises, and dreams. Her apparent life-form, her attempt to appear somewhat compatible with her less poetic colleagues, family members, and neighbors, is also formed in part by her intraformative reflections on her predicament in a functional society. The same can be said of her actual form of presence. Intraformative intuitions or considerations preceded and accompanied the prefocal integration of her total here-and-now presence in her formation field as a poetess at heart, absorbing current impressions, trying to survive in a functional culture.

The disposition of privacy protects this formative integration every time it threatens to become dissonant because of too much contraction within one's intrasphere or too much expansion in one's inter- and outer spheres. From the foregoing, it may already be evident that the privacy disposition, if effective, is a refined and nuanced disposition in need of a lifetime of formation for its full unfolding.

Foundational Life-Form and the Privacy Disposition

The first volume of this series introduced another basic construct of the science, that of the foundational life-form and the fact that we are preformed in a unique direction. Underlying our whole formation is a basic orientation that is exclusive for each of us. This unparalleled pattern is only gradually and in part disclosed to us during our ongoing dialogue with the successive formation fields within which our life unfolds. This disclosure of our uniqueness takes place mainly in our intrasphere. Within that sphere it makes its abode. There it is primarily maintained, elaborated, apprehended, appraised, affirmed, and applied to life. Such ongoing disclosure and elaboration in the intrasphere can progress only in dialogical interaction with the inter- and outer spheres of formation. The danger is that in this dialogical process we may be tempted to allow the other spheres to take over. If we let this happen, we lose fidelity to our life call in its uniqueness. Our life becomes uncongenial with who and what we are most deeply called to be. Our service of humanity and world in the light of the mystery loses its distinctiveness. We become alienated from our original life-form instead of making our home there.

For example, part of the preformed life project of a high-school student may be an unusual sensitivity for classical music. Her companions may loathe this kind of composition. To make her life compatible with others in the interformative sphere, she develops an apparent life-form that cautiously keeps a low profile in this area. In the process she may allow too much room for dissonant interformative influences to enter into her life. In that case she may repudiate and deny to herself her personal musical preference. This will lead to some dissonance and deformation due to the fact that in this region of life she uncritically fused the intra- with the interformative sphere. Encounter between these spheres deteriorated into fusion. The inter- and outer poles were allowed to intrude upon, invade, and overwhelm the intraformative. This made it impossible for the intrasphere to exercise its distinctive function in her history, that is, to maintain, restore, and expand the influence of her unique foundational life-form in her overall emergence. The science of formation refers to the above movement as the congeniality function, for its purpose is to make our life increasingly congenial with our original call and its ongoing disclosures. The compatibility function of the intraformative sphere should remain subordinate to the congeniality function as obedient to the objective disclosures of the mystery. The privacy disposition disposes us to a form donation and reception that is in tune with this obedient congeniality function at the root of our intraformative processes.

Encounter versus Fusion

What is the distinction between encounter and fusion in our interformative relationships? The disposition of privacy is clearly meant to foster encounter, not fusion. What constitutes fusion is a total identification between the intra- and interspheres in our formation field. In a sense we no longer know who we are. Other persons or sociohistorical pulsations direct our life without our personal apprehension, appraisal, and affirmation of their influences and of their congeniality with who we are called to be. We lose the capacity to counter inwardly what may be uncongenial for us in others' views or projects.

The privacy disposition replaces fusion with encounter. Our society tends to homogenize people so that they can be used indiscriminately for its functional projects. Such leveling stills the voice of intraformation and of one's obedience to its inner call. In the light of this leveling process, the word *encounter* may become for many synonymous with sympathetic fusion with others and with social pulsations.

Our task as formation scientists is to restore the word encounter to its original meaning. In its origins the word implied some kind of confrontation. People would face or encounter each other in debate or contestation. Something similar would apply to whole groups. For example, the troops of a king would encounter those of rebellious landlords. The deeper meaning of the word is found in reflection on its etymology, for it is composed of two elements with distinct roots, *en* and *counter*. They come from the French words *en* and *contre*. *En* is derived from the Latin *in* and refers to interformation insofar as it implies that one allows one's intrasphere to enter the interformative one. *Contre* is derived from the Latin *contra*, which has the opposite meaning of the "in" aspect of interformation. It refers to interformation insofar as it implies that one maintains a certain distinction and reservation. One allows one's intrasphere and its unique core to set itself over against interformative influences that would be uncongenial with the will of the transcendent for us. The privacy disposition disposes us to maintain a flexible polarity between such "in" and "counter" aspects of a truly consonant process of interformation. Both are necessary if these spheres of the formation field are to maintain their integrity.

The disposition of privacy means that I am disposed to respect in awe the call of the mystery at the root of my life; to acknowledge that both I and others, in our foundational life-form, are unique orientations in the evolvement of humanity, so unique that it will be impossible ever to fuse perfectly with others. Interformation can never totally replace intraformation. Intraformation is nourished not only by the inter- and outer spheres of our life but first and foremost by the disclosures of our preformation where the mystery speaks its unique word for us to be received in awe.

The privacy disposition is based on the insight that interformation can go only so far, that other persons and social pulsations should never violate this sacred realm of human life, that the interformative sphere should be marked by awe, respect, and fear of offending this most inner sanctuary in our own life and that of others. No matter how deep the empathy between ourselves and others, neither they nor we can ever totally know or fuse with this radical spring of each one's life formation.

This insight is the source of the counterformation that asserts itself through the privacy disposition when the interformative sphere threatens to desecrate the disclosures of the life call in our intraformative sphere. As long as we are not sure of this mutual respect for who we are, we will be unable to relate to one another freely and to interform with community and society without anxiety. When awe is absent, pseudointerformation takes over: one's intraformative sphere may be absorbed into that of somebody else's or into a faceless collectivity. Mature men and women face each other as unique and, therefore, at times contrary centers of apprehension, appraisal, and affirmation.

The privacy disposition is thus based on the awe-filled intuition that I am a mystery for myself and for others. To protect this mystery, I am disposed to contract or expand my intraformative sphere in flexible adaptation to any opportunity for life formation that is obediently congenial and compatible. Because I am always a dialogue with the inter- and outer spheres of my formation field, my intraformative sphere can and does overlap with that of others. Briefly, my formation field contains spheres where I encounter others, but my intraformative sphere is at least to some degree proper to me alone.

Formative Privacy

The privacy disposition disposes me to create periods of privacy in my life. These are pauses from inter- and outer formation, moments of homecoming in my intrasphere. The moments of privacy represent a temporary contraction and a relative closure of my intraformative sphere; they provide a passing release from focal interaction with the inter- and outer spheres. I grant myself some space and time to assimilate congenially what may have influenced my ongoing life formation during this interaction. Inwardly I seek for some consonance. I want to place all inter- and outer influences in the perspective of my life call as disclosed and evolved so far by my intrasphere and made available to me at least to some degree by a kind of private life.

In some way I am always my whole formation field. Hence, the inter- and outer spheres are never totally absent, even at moments of deepest privacy, but they have become prefocal instead of focal. In the privacy moment, the focus of my presence is my intrasphere and the private kind of life it engenders. The inter- and outer spheres become blurred and indistinct; they recede in the background. They are waiting, as it were, in my prefocal consciousness to become focal again as soon as I shift from privacy to my usual interactions with the world.

Remnants of former inter- and outer interactions that are incorporated in my memory, imagination, and anticipation can be alive in my intrasphere. I may also organize the intrasphere around books, music, art, or nature, carefully selected mainly in terms of my own private interest at the moment.

Before we proceed farther, it is necessary to distinguish formative from deformative privacy. The five main modes of deformative privacy are: imposed, evasive, depreciative, paranoid, and schizoid. Because of their potentially deformative impact on our lives, each of them deserves to be discussed in turn.

Imposed Privacy

During successive periods of privacy, I form a kind of private life out of preferred excerpts from my intraformative processes. I consider this particular private life to be characteristic of me. In a moment of privacy, I return first of all to this already existing private life within my intrasphere. I keep it available to my focal awareness for moments of retreat or strategic withdrawal from the world. This private life has been selectively formed by me during my formation history in interaction with all the processes in my intraformative sphere. It is a chosen private life, distinct but not separate from the inter- and outer spheres of my life as a whole. To restore balance, to retain personal motivation, to rediscover myself, I retreat from time to time in this private realm.

Imposed privacy, on the contrary, is the kind of private life forced upon me by others. It is deformative. It is not constituted by me in dialogue with my intraformative sphere and its intimacy with my unique preformation. Therefore, it cannot approach what I am really called to be. The obedient congeniality of my life as a whole is threatened by such an imposition. I am thrown back by powerful others, usually during childhood and early adolescence, on a private life I did not choose. The freedom of relaxed fluid intraformation should keep pulsing through the ongoing unfolding of my private life. This, of course, becomes impossible when I am boxed in, as it were, in a certain frame imposed on me by others.

What is supposed to be my specific private life did not emerge from my spontaneous intraformative sphere with its wavelike contractions and expansions. It is a make-believe image of my interiority imposed on me by the appraisal of others. Children may be inclined to resign themselves inwardly to the fixed private life that parents or other adults invented for them. Making it their own, they forget who they really are.

For example, some children may have taken over from their parents the depreciative appraisal that they are preformed to be a failure in life, that form impotence marks their private life basically, no matter how effective they may appear to be to others. They may believe so deeply in this imposed negative image of their privacy that they return to it regularly in moments of aloneness in later life.

Retreating into this private conviction may mean that any confirmation of their form potency received from others and from objective success in the world will simply be ignored or denied. This kind of privacy is deformative. In no way is it congenial with one's preformation or one's real form potency. In its rigidity it misses the flexibility and fluidity of ongoing interaction with the total realm of one's intraformative sphere and its consonant openness to the inter- and outer spheres of formation.

Evasive Privacy

Effective presence in our formation field demands a firmness of discipline, transcendence of inertia, availability to service, a spirit of responsibility. Inertia is due to the tendency of all forms in the cosmos to sink back into their formative energy field so as to make room for the emergence of new forms. This tendency affects also the human life-form. It engenders the negative disposition of evasion of discipline and industriousness, of dedication and responsibility. This depreciative disposition makes us look for ways of escaping or evading responsibility. We may substitute charm for effective service, verbosity for production, coffee klatches for sustained labor in solitude, endless committee meetings for the pain of personal reflection, sweet compliance for responsible direction.

Privacy can be one of the countless ways we devise to evade the discipline of effective life formation in the midst of our labor. Of course, when the demands of the inter- and outer spheres of formation become unmanageable, it may be wise to withdraw temporarily in one's private life. There the sense of equilibrium can be restored. Recuperated and refreshed, restored to a renewed sense of self-possession, one can be more firm and effective in one's specific life of service. Such retreat, however, becomes evasion if it is used constantly to escape the responsibilities of life.

Evasive privacy is a form of inertia, a mode of escape from ordinary living, a cloak for irresponsibility. It is no longer privacy in the true formative sense. Its fruit is not consonance but dissonance with the inter- and outer spheres of our field and the call of the mystery to firm and gentle service of humanity and its unfolding. Consonant life formation implies vigilance in regard to the motivation of one's search for periods of privacy. Is it responsible self-restoration that we seek? Or is it evasion of our task in the world, of compatible service, of the struggle for social justice, peace, and mercy? Is it a veiled manifestation of the prefocal bent to inertia, to absorption of our demanding human form in the cosmic energy field? We may discover that our life has become more evasive than desirable for its consonant formation. Perhaps formative direction or counseling in private or in common could help us to identify the ramifications of our evasive disposition and to find the right means of reformation.

Depreciative Privacy

The private life engendered by the intrasphere is sustained and animated by somewhat insular apprehensions, appreciations, affirmations, memories, imaginations, and anticipations. These may be appreciative, filled with faith and hope in the formation mystery and the form potency we share with that mystery, or they may be depreciative. In the latter case our private life may be dominated by self-depreciation, lack of faith in the form potency we received from the mystery, and depreciation of the formative possibilities and opportunities in our formation field.

The intraformative sphere, with the private life built into it, is not only contractive but expansive. It affects the inter- and outer spheres of our field prefocally or focally. Because we are bodily beings, our vital life is modulated by the appreciative or depreciative orientation of our private life.

A depreciative interior life is harmful for our vital, functional, and transcendent effectiveness in our formation field. We should, therefore, try to reform our interiority if it is depreciative. First of all, positive abandonment to the mystery, as described in the first volume of this series, is the ground of an appreciative inner life. Secondary means of reformation entail the development of some of the major ways of interior appreciation that can influence our well-being and render our impact on life and world more beneficial. These additional ways are meant to supplement, not to replace, other basic means of beneficial life formation. Examples would be wise nutrition, meditation, regular exercise, proper rest, medical care, study, observation, reading, and reflection.

We should not be discouraged if we do not see the immediate reformation of the kinds of problems that resulted from depreciative interiority. It takes time for any depreciative disposition to build such problems into our life. It may take even more time to solve them by the reformation of our interiority. Initially, we may have to be satisfied with just-noticeable improvements.

The first and simplest act of reform is to look at our private beliefs about these problematic areas of health and life and about our potency to improve them. Do I expect things to get better or worse? Do I worry constantly about my health, my personality, my work, the people for whom I care? Do I have confidence in the means I use to better myself and my situation? Do my fears often come true?

There are strong connections between such private feelings and musings and what happens in our body and in the inter- and outer spheres of our life. A main factor in our depreciative private life may be our memory of a past trauma. For example, we may have been misunderstood as children. Later on in moments of privacy we may consistently experience an anxious anticipation of misunderstanding. When our private life extends itself again in the other spheres, this predisposing anticipation may indeed effect such misunderstanding.

If we get in touch with and release the interior feelings left over from such memories, the result may be amazing in terms of a more joyful and effective form of life and physical improvement. One rule for reformation of a depreciative inner life is to let go of our worries. Our private fears and anxieties only agitate our mind and body and make reform and recovery more difficult. If we are ill, we must make sure that we receive necessary medical care. Yet we should also watch the tendency of our private life to let every symptom or turn of events upset us. This may be a sign of a depreciative inner life orientation that lacks trust in the innate formative powers of the body.

If we notice that we are worrying habitually about our health or effectiveness, or if we are inwardly anticipating problems, we ought to say simply "Cease!" or "Stop!" to that depreciative thought and feeling. We should renew our faith that our form potency, granted by the formation mystery, can initiate a different appreciative disposition. We should try to replace the depreciative thought with an appreciative one. For instance, in moments of privacy, we can actually repeat to ourselves a few sentences like, "I am full of energy and radiant health"; "I can do this job effectively here and now"; "I can communicate with this person pleasantly and convincingly"; "I am joyful and resilient in this situation"; or "The mystery loves me as I am."

We should fill our private moments with sayings like these until we feel appreciative of our form potencies and filled with confidence. We ought always to say inwardly what we want, not what we don't want. It is wise to avoid depreciatively phrased thoughts, such as "I do not feel fatigued"; "I have no worries"; "I am not rejected or punished by the mystery"; "I will not fail," for in that case our private mind and imagination will still picture that we have a problem. We should keep such inner sayings in the present tense, as though the result has already happened or is happening presently. Don't say "I *will* get better"; "I *will* improve my communications"; "I *will* be more outgoing." That way of phrasing always postpones reform. Say instead, "I *am* getting better," and so on.

Appreciative, trusting phrases are not instances of self-deception. We should utilize moments of privacy during the day to foster positive inner dispositions. We thereby form a powerful private life that will definitely transform our presence in the formation field.

Reversing the Depreciative Privacy Disposition

Another means to reform a problematic depreciative disposition is to use moments of privacy to imagine concretely that we are doing well in the area affected. First, we can imagine that the area of affliction, illness, doubt, fear, bad communication, or whatever, is glowing with the transforming and soothing light of the formation mystery. We try to see every aspect of our situation bathed in its radiance. Then we imagine as concretely as possible the affected organ, act, or situation being transformed pleasantly and fully. We finish by picturing ourselves totally relaxed and content, happily engaged in work and play as a result of a complete transformation of this problem. It is best to seek such moments of reformative privacy just before or after sleep or during a period of relaxation.

We should use our private pauses during the day to encourage and reassure ourselves, to talk inwardly to ourselves in a light and upbeat way. We must not abuse such precious moments of privacy to undermine our health and happiness by dwelling morosely on our emotional conflicts, tensions, and general stresses. Often we will find that in certain stubborn conflicts things finally do get well only after we learn not to fill our private moments with depreciative memories, thoughts, images, and endless analyses of the problems concerned.

The pause of privacy should not be used for becoming upset about conflicts with family members, friends, colleagues, or neighbors. The moment of privacy should be one of reinvigoration, not of blaming ourselves for each conflict that may emerge in our surroundings. If we often feel upset, unhappy, or depressed, we should try to notice whether it is the content of our private life, as elaborated in moments of privacy, that gives rise to such negative moods. We can seek help, if we feel we need it, and do what we can to understand what is fueling such obsessive dwelling on our problems. Though we cannot eliminate all stress from life (nor would it be good formation policy to do so), we should try to minimize it.

We must avoid becoming dependent on so-called "side benefits" of depreciative private thinking and feeling. Such dependency may lead to physical and psychological symptoms that gain us excessive attention and sympathy. The pattern is relatively predictable. Fueled by private musings on our miserable condition, we may display subtly a minor symptom or two, which attracts attention. Persons sympathetic to our plight make a fuss over us. We feel reassured by their acceptance. The problem is that we gained this reassurance by displaying symptoms and becoming ill.

People who attract attention in this way may worsen their condition. They unwittingly use their private time to think and feel negatively because depreciation gives rise to the symptoms that gain them the attention they crave. Once we see this pattern, we can learn to deal with moments of privacy in a positive fashion and begin to relinquish the emotional "benefits" of self-depreciation. We can learn to love ourselves as unique epiphanies of the mystery, a far cry from coddling ourselves excessively the instant we feel unwell.

The way we fill our moments of privacy not only *can* but *does* affect our inter- and outer formation and our vital well-being. Understanding this prevents us from feeling like an impotent bystander in the process of deformation. Fostering the appreciative disposition during periods of privacy enables us to affirm again our own form potency. We are able spontaneously to tap into the strength stored up during these periods to support consonant formation.

Paranoid Privacy

Another mode of deformative privacy is motivated and sustained by an excessive fear and suspicion that other people are against us. The term *paranoid privacy* does not mean that we link this kind of deformative privacy with the psychotic illness of paranoia. The adjective *paranoid* is used to describe certain traits in normal people that remind us of the far more serious distortions that are manifested in that illness.

Paranoid deformation in otherwise healthy persons means that they are oversensitive to any sign of opposition, misunderstanding, and rejection. They are inclined to generalize that attitude to many more people than actually exhibit these expressions. Gradually they develop an overall suspicion that people are against them. They do not recognize and appreciate the consonant aspects of their life. One consequence of this disposition is that they seek refuge from these real and imagined opponents in increasingly lengthy periods of privacy. Their private life begins to evolve around these suspicions and the anxious analysis of what some persons may do or say against them. They wallow in frustration over lack of recognition for their qualities, which may appear greater in their private appraisal than they really are.

While not too many of us go as far as paranoid privacy, we may have a slight tinge of it. We must honestly ask ourselves if our private ponderings and feelings are in some measure animated by anxious forebodings about the possible harm others may do to us. Are we engaged excessively in distrustful analysis of their behavior and personality in relation to us. If so, we ought to question the motivation for our search for privacy.

To reform the anxious processes of our private life, we must engage other intraformative forces. These may have been left untapped during the fashioning of our private life out of selective excerpts from the events that fill our intrasphere. Furthermore, the suggestions made earlier in regard to the reformation of the contents of the depreciative private life can be applied to the reformation of the paranoid private life. A formation director or counselor in a one-to-one session or through direction in common can be of great help here. In serious cases the person may have to be referred to other experts for professional assistance.

Schizoid Privacy

We are not using the term *schizoid* to indicate any connection between this deformation, which falls within the normal range of the formation problems many of us share, and the psychosis called schizophrenia. Schizoid privacy implies a certain split or separation between one's intrasphere, with the private life it engenders, and the inter- and outer spheres of one's formation field. It may accompany and aggravate the symptoms of the imposed, evasive, depreciative, and paranoid privacy described above.

Sometimes the cause may be found in dissonant accretions of spiritual formation traditions. In certain periods some adherents may overemphasize the interior private life in intimacy with the transcendent as symbolized in their tradition. They contrast the dangers of the inter- and outer spheres of the formation field with the eminence of inner visions and voices, of powers of miraculous physical healing and exorcisms, of speaking in a tongue so private no one else can understand it.

If such unusual aspects of the spiritual life are stressed and pursued to excess, the person may more and more retreat in a private life anxiously walled off from the inter- and outer spheres. If they enter these spheres at all, they do so primarily as form givers, meaning that they try to give form to others and the world out of their closed-off private life. They are far less concerned with form reception in relation to the object poles in the inter- and outer spheres. The world outside their realm of private musings becomes so distrusted that they cut themselves off from the corrective formation this world and others could give them as a counterbalance against their schizoid, pious interiority. They cherish their "interior life" above everything else.

The formation director or counselor may have to open their eyes gradually to the dissonant accretions of their form traditions, accretions that led to this separation between the spheres of their formation field. Only then may they be able to regain the natural rhythm of contraction and expansion of the intraformative sphere and its private life and to engage in both form donation and form reception in all spheres at the appropriate time.

Differences in Privacy Dispositions

Consider again the modes of deficient privacy we have just described. What strikes us is that their deficiency is not directly related to the amount of time spent in the intrasphere. Nor is it primarily the style of privacy which renders these modes deformative. Rather, the criterion of their formative or deformative orientation must be sought in their underlying motivation. If this motivation is the result of encapsulation in a private life imposed on us by others, if it is escape from social responsibility, retreat in depreciative appraisals, paranoid suspicion of people around us, or schizoid enclosure in a fantastic interiority, then privacy is deformative. It seems important to keep this criterion in mind because the role the privacy disposition plays in the lives of different people and the style of its expression can be dissimilar without being unwholesome.

The intensity of one's privacy disposition influences the time dimension of privacy. Obviously, thinkers, poets, painters, mystics, and inventive scientists spend more time alone and immerse themselves more deeply in their inner resources than do people who are inherently less reflective and creative. This does not mean that their privacy disposition is deformative. Orlo Strunk's book on privacy, *Privacy: Experience, Understanding, Expression*, focuses on this difference. In the preface, the author ends with an emphasis on this difference between himself and his wife Mary:

> ... it has been Mary, more than anyone else, who has been willing to more than simply tolerate my propensity and appreciation for privacy. Because she herself is not at heart a private person, this willingness takes on an even greater amazement. For over thirty years she has sensed at a profound level that my privacy is an important and essential quality of my personhood and has honored that reality even when the full understanding of it was not possible. This, it seems to me, falls only slightly short of being a modern miracle.

In chapter 2, entitled "Sharings of Others," the author quotes at length communications of some reflective people about their privacy experience. Because these passages highlight the intensity and unique expression of privacy, they are enlightening for formation scientists and practitioners. Here are some salient sentences:

> A thirty-year-old man writes: "When I invite others into my home for social occasions, it means an offer of great intimacy to me and is not a casual event to be taken lightly. My possessions and living area are private to me—that is, very personal. I feel offended when I find someone has been handling them or looking at them without invitation."
> A twenty-six-year-old homemaker writes: "Even in close relationships, especially those which entail a great deal of risk, I am reserved about what I reveal of my inner feelings and thoughts. I dislike very loud and aggressive persons.... Persons are important to me—and I am by no means a loner ... yet I do value and enjoy my solitude and privacy. It doesn't usually bother me to eat alone or pursue other activities by myself. I enjoy myself and my own company. I am not afraid to wrestle with myself alone, although I do value and need outside feedback and support along with my private wrestlings."
> A fifty-year-old Roman Catholic priest writes: "In saying that I am a private person I mean that I share depth feelings about myself or anyone else with very few people. I have a few close friends who know me intimately; but to other people I'm a warm and friendly person— yet I don't let them into my world to any more than a superficial degree. I keep secrets as though they went into the grave, and I don't ask probing questions of others...."
> A seventy-two-year-old woman writes: "All my life I have enjoyed being alone. At first I thought I was 'different' or 'odd.' This fright-

ened me for a time. Once my father said, 'You've got to mix or you'll always be unhappy.' I remember how this scared me; and I tried hard to be a good mixer. But it was a foolish attempt.

"Later, in college, I talked to my philosophy teacher about this, and he assured me that it was quite all right to want to be alone, especially to study and read.

"But I think I was nearly thirty years old before I really came to believe that wanting to be alone could be a good thing.

"But this is the first time in my life I've been asked to think about this. I guess I came to see that solitude was an essential part of me— and that's all there's to it.

"My husband and children never seemed to worry about my desires to be alone. I remember them saying, 'That's just Mama's way.' They weren't like that; but they seemed to understand how important privacy was for me. It still is."

Another revealing quote on the first page of this book is from Henry David Thoreau, who said, "I find it wholesome to be alone the greater part of the time. To be in company, even the best, is soon wearisome and dissipating. I love to be alone."

These quotes demonstrate that the privacy disposition, or the intrasphere with its private life, is of greater intensity in certain persons than in others; yet it can be quite wholesome and in no way a flight from people or from one's daily task. Part of the distinctiveness of each human formation field is the unique, mutually complementary proportion of the pre-, intra-, inter- and outer spheres. Their relationship with one another varies from person to person. Formation becomes deformation if we do not respect the unique proportion of spheres that is potentially given in the ongoing preformation of each person.

Formative Disposition of Privacy: A Recapitulation

We can now recapitulate the main features of the formative disposition of privacy that have emerged thus far.

This disposition inclines us to retreat periodically into the private life that has been formed by us within the intrasphere of our formation field. In periods of privacy we distance ourselves from the pressures of inter- and outer formation. We are motivated not by an anxious need for isolation but by the aspiration to foster consonance in our formation field as a whole. This aspiration makes retreat formative instead of deformative, even if such consonance is only minimally attained or still eludes us.

The moment of privacy is a creative opportunity for the disclosure of our foundational form of life, which is somehow concealed in our ongoing preformation by the mystery. By the same token, it is an opportunity for transcendent presence to that mystery itself. It also facilitates creative reflection on our functional, vital, and sociohistorical formation from the viewpoint of our personal call by the mystery. This call is increasingly disclosed and elaborated in our private life, as we allow this life to emerge from our intraformative processes.

Periodic retreats in privacy enable us to mark off our call from the call of others. They help us to restore the intraform of our life when it has been lost in an interform that has deteriorated into mindless fusion. We see more clearly how we can be wholeheartedly "in" with others without losing the contours, or "counters," that are uniquely ours. Such insight readies us for true human encounter.

The privacy disposition must remain operative during our whole life, creating for us ever new moments of restorative solitude. The reason is that our original foundational life-form is only gradually disclosed to us, and, even then, never fully. This disclosure takes place through dialogue with the successive formation events that occur in the inter- and outer spheres of our field. Our unfolding intrasphere, with its emergent private life, is the personal partner in this dialogue; it is the locus of disclosure.

The inter- and outer spheres of our formation field do not vanish when we contract our attention mainly into the intrasphere. They remain pre-focally present, but they are adumbrated or put into brackets, as it were, while we are focusing on our private life. Because of their enduring presence in the background, we are warned in time if events in the inter- or outer spheres of life demand that we shift our focal attention to them. Hence, we can recollect ourselves within our private life in the midst of a busy world without losing sufficient contact with its realities, demands, and dangers. In privacy we do not explicitly interact with people or events on their own terms. During our private retreats, we allow others to touch us only insofar as they affect our intraformative disclosures.

CHAPTER 9

Embodiment of Privacy

The disposition of privacy inclines us to reserve a life for ourselves within the intrasphere. When we retreat into our private life, we create some distance between this sphere and the inter- and outer ones. This distance is first of all a creation of the human spirit. As such it cannot be measured, weighed, or calculated. Nonetheless, we are always *embodied* spirits in a formation field that manifests itself to us in corporeal appearances. Our spiritual privacy disposition, as embodied, inclines us to symbolize the distancing of privacy by the creation of an actual and observable distance in relation to the world. This observable sphere of distance facilitates the maintenance of our intrasphere against intrusion. Timely retreat into our private life contains and nourishes this sphere continually.

The observable sphere of distance around us symbolizes for ourselves and others the inner distance we wish to preserve. All people shield this inner, private sphere with a certain vigilance. They feel and may even manifest annoyance if anybody violates their symbolic space. People sense prefocally the fences they erect between each other. We can usually sense whether others are closed or open, though we are not always able to pinpoint exactly the signs and symbols they use to communicate how much distance they want to preserve. We simply know we can go so far and no farther.

The symbolic distance we create around us depends more or less on the nature of our relationships. Relationships with people are intimate to the degree that we allow others to share our private life. In other words, our inner distance to those with whom we are more intimate is less than toward others. Accordingly, the observable symbolic distance we keep between them and us will be far less than the one we maintain with others.

Lovers, married couples, parents and children, and close friends usually have more access to each other's intrasphere. Hence, their symbolic observable distance may be minimal. The symbolic distance mirrors the intraformative movement of contraction and expansion described in the previous chapter. In our daily encounters with different persons who exhibit various degrees of closeness and affinity to our intrasphere, we spontaneously contract or expand the observable symbolic distance between us.

As in every other aspect of formation, so, too, in this one: influence by our form tradition is always a factor. A form tradition may carry the message that certain persons deserve special deference because of their position in society. This deference implies that the external symbolic position of such persons is more important for the community than the communication of their inner life. An exposition of their intrasphere could manifest vulnerabilities that would belie and destroy the power and perfection attributed to them as leaders and authorities. This enhanced symbolic distance is almost ritually maintained between certain communities and their leaders in accordance with their form traditions.

Every culture is a mixture of form tradition in which one or more religious or ideological traditions may be dominant. The actual final form tradition that is the result of such blending tells its adherents how to symbolize distance and nearness. It may seem as though some cultures do not respect privacy at all, but a closer look reveals that this impression is deceptive. The need for privacy and distance is universally felt. Its protection and symbolization in a variety of form traditions is so diverse that it may seem to be totally absent to casual observers. Yet careful observation may reveal, for instance, subtle forms of aloofness and formality that come spontaneously into play when one goes too far.

For instance, in English cultures there may be less need to make one's private room with its closed door the symbol of privacy than is the case in Germanic cultures. Yet an English person can masterfully withdraw and give any violator of privacy the silent treatment, maintaining a facade of formal propriety that seems impeccable.

Development of symbolic distance directives depends largely on sociohistorical factors, such as population density. Within a culture as a whole, and within a form tradition, certain creative persons may invent more modes and symbols of physical distance than others who are more conventional. Communities that force upon their members too much togetherness are interesting places to observe. It is often amazing how ingenious the more original members are in finding ways to protect their privacy.

Symbolic observable distance is more important to preserve today than perhaps at any previous time in the formation history of humanity. The functional society tends to herd people into leveling masses where symbols of privacy and distance are frowned upon. The absence of such symbols seriously affects the intrasphere of human life and its fragile capacity for generating a privacy that mirrors the unique preformation of each person.

A well-formed private life serves society uniquely when it expands itself into the inter- and outer spheres. The more the unique life call of each person is respected, the more one can make one's best contribution to the unfolding formation of humanity. If symbols of distance die, awe may die with them, and without awe human life loses its mystery. Already in infancy parents should foster the awakening of the intrasphere in their children. The dawning intrasphere, with its potency for privacy, should be cultivated by the cultivation of respect for the symbols of perceptible privacy proper to children. Children should have, for instance, some space of their own—a corner, a drawer. Others should not be allowed freely to use a child's little treasures, as if they were not entrusted to the child personally.

Privacy Disposition and Direction Disclosures

The privacy disposition disposes us to a consonant movement of contraction and expansion of the intrasphere. In expansion we expose our private life to enrichment through form reception from the inter- and outer spheres. In contraction we retreat into our private life to ensure its obedient congeniality with the unique life direction speaking in our ongoing preformation.

In the science of formation, we envision life's formation as a series of decisive direction disclosures. Each disclosure is limited; none reveals the total direction of our life, only an approximation of this direction. Each disclosure may be consonant or dissonant; it may give rise to formative or deformative life directives, or to both. Part of the search for our unique direction is to uncover the dissonant directives that lead us astray and to purify or bypass them, as the case may require.

Such disclosures are usually occasioned by formation events in our inter- or outer spheres. They can only become affirmed directives for our life in the privacy of our intrasphere. Having received tentative forms of life direction during the expansion of our interiority in the inter- and outer spheres, we retreat into the privacy of our now contracting intrasphere.

There we apprehend, appraise, affirm, or reject the tentative directions proposed to us. A *tentative* direction disclosure only becomes an *affirmed* disclosure if we assent to it inwardly.

A succession of affirmed direction disclosures should not be seen as one straight line. It is not the case that one disclosure after the other is worked through and finished off in the privacy of our interiority, never to return in any shape or form. Each significant disclosure crystalizes itself around a decisive turning point in our formation. Such turning points are not left behind. They are interiorized in our private life. Intraformation refines, deepens, and widens the direction disclosure continuously. This inwardly, constantly enriched direction gives rise to actual directives that keep co-forming the core, current, apparent, and actual forms of our life.

An affirmed direction disclosure does not remain totally encapsulated in our private interiority. During the moment of expansion of our intrasphere, the disclosure of direction may give rise to a global reorganization not only of the intra- but also of the inter- and outer spheres of our formation field. This restructuring by new life directives, affirmed interiorily, affects our relations to the mystery of formation and to people, events, and things that emerge in our field. For example, our adult life is still in some measure characterized by directives that resulted from our inter-formative relationships with our parents.

Briefly, affirmed direction disclosures in our private interiority are not incidental and passing. Some aspects of our emergent life-forms may be structured lastingly by such directives.

Privacy and the Phase of a Shared Intrasphere

Infants are totally helpless and, therefore, dependent on their mothers. Without maternal care they could not survive. Scarcely able to master their motor behavior, they cannot yet experience and designate themselves as a vital unity differentiated from the life-form of their mothers. Privacy is at a minimum during this early stage. Infants live in an atmosphere of overwhelming at-oneness with the caring mother. Their life is interwoven with hers. They feel immanent in her private intrasphere insofar as this sphere is manifested in her interformative presence. They float, as it were, within a motherly space that is almost a prolongation of life in the womb. This absorption of infants in the mother's intrasphere does not leave room for self-awareness. No differentiation is yet possible between their own intrasphere and the inter- and outer sphere in which the appearance of the mother dominates. They experience the phase of a shared intrasphere, a life of unquestioned blind participation in the mother's life. She is experienced as all-powerful and all-nourishing. Nor does the infant differentiate her from the outer sphere and its mysterious ground. At this stage, life is probably experienced as a vital at-oneness with all that is, as fullness and omnipotence. However, the emergence of the privacy experience will mean an expulsion from this paradise.

What is the direction disclosure to which this phase may later give rise in one's inward life? It can lead to the vague private feeling that it would be desirable in some way to regain trusting rootedness in the goodness of all that is, once represented by the nurturing and sustaining mother. Later in life this memory may inspire a search for an all-embracing mystery.

Privacy and a First Glimpse of Transcendence

Our human spirit is, among other things, our ability to be open to all that is, to the whole that transcends incidental and isolated appearances of people, events, and things. This transcendent dimension of the human form is partly, but not totally, dormant in children. At a certain moment in their formation history, a pristine gleam of the transcendent dimension seems to touch them briefly, passingly. It gives them a vague glimpse of the unknown beyond, of mystery. This awareness may evoke an overwhelming feeling of powerlessness; it may call forth dread, accompanied by another related experience, formation anxiety.

The transcendent dimension also includes the distinctively human ability to become aware of one's call to uniqueness. As children grow, they feel tempted by the first vague intimations of the call of their uniqueness to look beyond the safe niche of parental protection. This first invitation to privacy is threatening. Once again the great unknown that looms beyond mother and father frightens them even more, now that it may have to be faced privately. To obliterate this first taste of privacy and the fear it evokes, children begin to develop a protective lifestyle that helps them to elude the call of their transcendent dimension to evolve a private life.

The first intimation of this call evokes in them a feeling of lostness, impotence, and vulnerability. Hence, an encapsulating lifestyle is construed as a system of protections against the implicit call to privacy. Children try defensively to get lost again in the inter- and outer sphere of their formation field, in the family, their playmates, the neighborhood, the nursery.

Because the system of protective directives is imperfect at first, the refused anxiety keeps seeping through. It comes out in the dreams of infants, in their terror of being alone in the vast darkness that seems to engulf them, in their need for hair-raising fairy tales, replete with witches and malicious animals. They need the concreteness of the horror story to focus their free-floating anxiety on some recognizable object. To a degree, infants can manage their fear of what is depicted concretely better than their vague anxiety about the transcendent vastness to which this dimension of life opens them.

It is difficult for children to come to terms with the formation anxiety inspired by this implicit and tentative awakening to the great beyond, to the "more than" and the call to privacy. Without their protective armor, they might be torn to pieces by anxiety. Hence, we should respect their reluctance to differentiate their own intrasphere too hastily from the inter- and outer ones. We should not push them into privacy before they are ready. We may find out later in life that we flee privacy and interiority because we have not resolved the formation anxiety of infancy. We may still be tempted to lose ourselves in the inter- and outer spheres and to ignore our rootedness in the mystery of preformation. As long as this anxiety is not solved, the privacy disposition cannot develop in strength and flexibility.

Privacy and the Phase of Differentiation of the Intrasphere

At a certain period of their formation history, children go beyond the phase of interformation with the mother and of the intrasphere they share with her. They begin to experience the stirrings of their own intrasphere, of a private inner life formation. This differentiation of the intrasphere implies a first vague experience of an "I," a private person apart from mother. This experience becomes increasingly articulated. It signals the beginning of the possibility of becoming a person with one's own direction, one's inner private life.

Like all the spheres of one's formation field, so too the intrasphere has a transcendent, functional, vital, and sociohistorical dimension. At this early stage the vital dimension prevails. This may be manifested by the tendency in many children to symbolize privacy by wanting to be alone when going to the bathroom, when taking a bath, and so on. Children may become fixated on their newly discovered and differentiated intrasphere. They could close in upon themselves in fascination with this inner world. In that case, the former shared intrasphere with the mother (insofar as it is manifested by the mother) is replaced by a solitary private world of their own that misses sufficient timely expansion in the inter- and outer world.

Onesided fascination with their private sphere of thought, feeling, imagination, memory, and anticipation, if not overcome in time, may lead to deformative disturbances later in life. This fascination must cease if consonant life is to be born. For the consonant life implies a balanced openness to all spheres of our formation field and to the mystery disclosing our life direction by means of them.

Privacy and Interformation with Formation Models

From about the third year on, children differentiate between the various models of life that appear in their interformative sphere. They do not seek indiscriminately interformation with all the human forms they meet. They choose those with whom they want interformation. This private choice is still another factor leading to the differentiation of the intrasphere.

Initially, the choice one makes is not independent of the mother. Choosing a model for interformation is directed by the appreciation children themselves receive from their mothers. Their faith, hope, and love called their children forth to become admirable individuals in their own right. This appreciative experience lays the ground for a later experience of the call to become one's unique and best self before the mystery.

Children cannot yet grasp or live the deeper meaning of this phase that, like all other phases, prepares them for the structures and dynamics of consonant intra-, inter-, and outer formation. Children have to live this ultimate hidden meaning in indirect ways. They seek interformation with formation models that seem to promise confirmation of their own form potency. Their interformative imitation of a baseball star, a nurse, a teacher, or Superman implies practicing a role that may give them approval and applause. Their imitation is an attempt to become as important as the models who give form so magnificently to their lives. By imitating them children anticipate that they will attract appreciation of their form potency by significant adults. Since they feel that these adults transcend them immensely, their approval and appreciation is of decisive value.

This kind of choice is only a weak manifestation of a just-emerging intraformative imagination, memory, and anticipation. Yet it is one of the many beginnings of the private life of the child. Also the transcendent dimension of this intraform of life is primitive. What children at this age experience as transcending them are parents and other impressive grownups. Theirs is by no means an explicit awareness of the transcendent mystery: children of this age are not yet able to seek the unique private significance of their life as dignified by the call and confirmation of the mystery. This confirmation is often subsumed by the applause children share imaginatively with their heroes. They interform symbolically not only with the life-form of a cowboy, clergyman, acrobat, nurse, princess, fashion model, movie hero or heroine, doctor, or teacher; they also share imaginatively in the applause they envision people showering on those who perform great feats superbly.

The forms of life, with which children interform symbolically, show various features. In this respect, the first emergence of the intrasphere enables children to select some of the features that they will turn into directives in a prefocal attempt to approach their own life direction. Most of these directives drop out later, but some of them may linger on in one's private life. They may interfere with later directives that more truly approximate the unique direction of the person.

Privacy, Real Life, and Form Directives

The differentiation of the intrasphere from other spheres enables children to experience for the first time a divergence between what they inwardly would like to be and what they really are. Failed form directives that emerged from the child's imagination and anticipation tell them what they are not yet. At the same time, such experiences of failure can deepen and strengthen the private life. For such failed directives prompt children inwardly to become different from what they already are. They begin to feel prefocally that they should become more truly themselves and choose directives that are congenial with their own form potency. They come more in touch with their preformation by the mystery as implicitly disclosed in their deepening interiority. Yet this in-touchness with preformation is intermittent and tenuous. The impact of their chosen interformative models still prevails in their emergent intrasphere.

To be sure, when a selected formation model has no immediate contact with a child, we cannot speak of an interformation that takes place directly between the child and the image of the model. Children are formed by the image of the model and that image in turn is reformed by the children. Theirs may thus be mainly a symbolic interformation. An example would be the models offered by the media.

As we have seen, children devise in an earlier phase a protective, uncongenial lifestyle. This style still influences the choice and affirmation of their interformative models and the form directives derived from them. They will be inclined to select as models whoever assures them a popular, immediate appreciation. They cannot yet choose models that could expose them to the great beyond, which the transcendent dimension evokes as its appropriate horizon.

Once form directives enter the intrasphere, they may become absolutized, as though they already fully represented the unique direction that alone can give ultimate meaning to a person's life. When children grow older, they may begin to idolize the formation model they would like to imitate in accordance with such interiorized directives.

People may not open up in adolescence or adulthood to the preformative direction of their life insofar as it is disclosed in the privacy of their intrasphere. The idolized directives of their models may become their ultimate horizon. These directives tend to become grandiose when the person who cherishes them gets older. Otherwise they could not keep functioning as substitutes for the transcendent horizon of their life. This development can cause extreme tension between the inter- and outer spheres of one's formation field and the exalted directives after which one strives in private life.

The danger of alienation from one's preformative direction may increase with the increase in interformative relationships later in life. When children grow up, the number of these relationships in which they become involved tends to expand. The new persons they experience as significant in their environment may function for them as implicit directors. They may look at them to find out what direction they should take instead of trusting the deeper experience of their own private life. Rather than rooting themselves in preformation by the mystery, they begin to trust exclusively the expectations of others. They fill their private life with the directives of strangers, trying to live up to what others think they should be like or to exhibit the feelings, attitudes, and dispositions others would like them to have.

Interiorizing such alien directives prostitutes one's interiority. My life direction is no longer congenial with the ongoing, unique preformation by the mystery; it is a matter of conformity to alien directives. I begin to live an "as-if life," even within the intrasphere. In the inter- and outer sphere, I may show the forced or affected style of a person imprisoned in an artificial structure of form directives that happen to be "in" at this moment among the people to whom I would like to conform. In such cases, the first task of the formation director or counselor, in private sessions or in common, is to liberate people from this encapsulation of their life by foreign directives.

Privacy and Mediation

We have seen so far that from early infancy on no real growth or emergence of a private life can happen without actual or symbolic interformation. We have also discovered the danger that one may get lost in the form directives of others, thereby losing the link between one's intrasphere and the mystery of preformation. This brings us to the question of what is the right way of interformation?

The key notion of the science applicable here is *formative mediation.* Form directives manifested in the life formation of other people should not be the goal of our interformation. They are only a means to disclose which of these directives may be congenial with our preformation. The same is true of appreciation by others. At times we need these confirmations to accept ourselves and our own form potency. Such confirmation in and by itself should not be our ultimate goal. It is only a means to facilitate appraisal, appreciation, and affirmation of our own life direction and of our corresponding form potency. In other words, people who function as formal or informal formation directors in our life, often without knowing it, are transitional mediators of our awareness of what our right direction may be.

No one can grow by private experience alone. Everyone needs feedback from the inter- and outer spheres. Emergence of the private life takes place by means of formative mediation and transitional directors. We find directors and directives even in the language we learn to speak, and in the faith and form traditions we inherit. People pass on directives by the way in which they develop language and culture. Without this tradition people could not approximate an effective compatibility between their unique preformed life direction and the best overall directives their formation field has to offer.

We can only express our direction in its incarnated concreteness by means of participation in language, tradition, and culture and in the lives of others. We must discover in them directives that may be congenial to us. We then have to appropriate these uniquely in awe for the formation mystery at the root of our privacy.

Similarly, people cannot approximate their unique direction without interformation with relevant others as *possible* models for some aspects of their life. The way to the disclosure and structuring of one's concrete direction in everyday life is an indirect path. Others have to function as mediators in this process of becoming who and what one is called to be, first in the privacy of one's heart, then in one's concrete emergence in the inter- and outer spheres of life. The problem is to distinguish in the influence of others that which hampers from that which helps the approximation of our true direction.

Family Formation and Privacy Disposition

The formation of one's privacy disposition depends partly on one's family. Families may be prevalently either intradirected or inter- and outer directed. Such family orientations are influenced by the cultural form traditions of the society to which they belong.

Families that are almost exclusively inter- and outer directed are not marked by mutual awe for each other's privacy. Families that are respectfully intradirected in a wholesome way tend to see each family and its home territory as a sanctuary not easily to be intruded upon. The same awe moves them to compatibility and compassion with other families. Awe fosters among them a climate of gracious accommodation without degeneration into mutual compliance.

In certain dissonant cases, the inward orientation of a family may not be rooted in awe for the unique call and responsibility of each member. Its source may be anxiety, possessiveness, competition, envy, anger, and suspicion. Compatibility and compassion are lacking. The family becomes closed in upon itself. There is no consonant rhythm of intra- and interformation between their own and other families.

Lack of Privacy in Inter- and Outer-Directed Families

Families that are mainly inter- and outer directed tend to neglect the timely contraction of their intrasphere. Family privacy is eroded or depleted. They are inclined to divulge so much of what goes on within the family that its intrasphere becomes almost absorbed in the inter- and outer spheres. This tendency leaves them wide open to pressures for compliance.

A society where the inter- and outer family form prevails is usually a leveling society. The contemporary trend toward functionalism clears the way for homogenization of all families. In totalitarian states, children may even be encouraged to betray their family secrets to the authorities, particularly those words and actions that threaten the power of the state. From the totalitarian perspective, no family should cultivate the sacredness and reserve of its own intimate life and traditions. It should simply mirror the appraisals and form traditions initiated or propagated by the state. In this view, privacy is the enemy of "the people."

Privacy in the Intradirected Family

The philosophy of the family that appreciates privacy is quite the opposite. Its style of inwardness is rooted in awe for its own mission in the light of the mystery. In reverence for its own task in the world, it guards jealously its own faith and form traditions and their unique shared embodiment in the family circle. Such a family tries to purify dissonant accretions of these traditions added by preceding generations. Yet it adds consonant accretions of its own. These make sense, at least for the period of the formation history in which this family finds itself and in view of the specific traits and functions of its members.

The intrasphere of such a family gives rise to a specific type of family privacy. This can only be maintained when certain limits are set in regard to how far the inter- and outer forming forces in society are allowed to intrude on the sacredness of home and family life. The same limitations are respected in regard to other families. A refined sensitivity guards against intrusion in one's own or others' familial sphere.

Privacy Formation in Childhood

The intraoriented family facilitates the formation of the privacy disposition in children. Children share the faith and form traditions of parents and grandparents. They carry these with them when they leave their home for school, play, or occupation. They begin to feel inwardly responsible for such familial directives. They become part of their emergent conscience. Their formation is deepened when they experience in our pluralistic society divergent faith and form traditions. At times they may meet with misunderstanding, opposition, or ridicule for the form directives their families instilled in them.

In their struggle to remain compatible and compassionate without falling into blind compliance, the children's own intrasphere and private life light up for them. Initially this inner life is much like that of their family's. Gradually, however, they develop traits of their own. The specific situations they face in society, their own ongoing preformation, are different from those of other members of the family. Hence, their specific concretizations of the private life of the family marks the birth of their own private life.

Privacy Formation and the Formation of Firmness and Gentleness

The intradirected family and its children need to be formed in the disposition of firmness in the face of pressures for compliance. These may come either from a leveling society or from opposing faith and form traditions. Hence, the formation of the privacy disposition within the family fosters indirectly the formation of firmness, another basic disposition. The formation of reasonable compatibility and compassion with other families and their members calls for the formation of gentleness, which wisely balances firmness in the consonant human form. It is another expression of awe for what the formation mystery allows to be.

In contrast the inter- and outer-oriented family is less conducive to the formation of firmness and gentleness. Their children are not given something profound and worthwhile, with deep roots in family history; nor are they made to feel the need for gentle reluctance to intrude unnecessarily in the privacy sphere of others.

Parents in intraoriented families may by contrast undermine the firmness and the personal privacy disposition of their children. This happens when they try to form their children more in the mere personal accretions of their form traditions than in its foundations. When parental awe for the mystery embraces the unique preformation of each child, parents will be less inclined to impose on children the traits of their own preformation.

Privacy Formation in Adolescence

The formation of a child's interiority beyond that of its family accelerates in adolescence. Adolescents need room to engage in their own discoveries, self-disclosures, and appraisals. This voyage of disclosure into one's intrasphere may be symbolized by words and actions, dress and manners that are at odds with those of the family, especially when the family insists too strongly that the adolescent assume the mere personal, parental accretions of faith and form traditions.

A certain forbearance is recommended in this state of adolescent disclosure of one's own form of life. Mistakes by adolescents are probably unavoidable. They are part of the painful way of formation of an inner life of apprehension, appraisal, and affirmation, with corresponding personal feelings, tastes, and emerging dispositions. It is mainly in this way that one of the treasures of the inner life forms itself, namely, the sense of personal responsibility with its corresponding dispositions of formative guilt, repentance, and reformation. If the family becomes too intrusive in this emergent stage of one's private life, personal responsibility for one's actions may not develop sufficiently.

Privacy and the Personalized Functional Dimension

Our personal private life thus emerges out of our family life. This formation of interiority does not cease at any point in our formation history. For the purposes of this chapter, we traced the process as far as the adolescent formation of privacy. In fact the search for one's personal intrasphere is ongoing. So, too, is the search for balance between this sphere and the other spheres of our formation field, between compatibility and compliance, between inwardness and outwardness. Such is the lifelong story of our quest for consonant presence to the mystery and its epiphanies in self, others, and society as a whole.

Our private life expands into the inter- and outer zones of formation. When it gives form concretely to these spheres, it does so through the managing or functional dimension of our life-form. Our incarnating spirit propels us through our inspired interiority to embody our private aspirations in the world of people, events, and things. Hence we can differentiate a *hidden* intrasphere from the totality of our formation field. Were this sphere only a *concealed* individuality, known to nobody else and without visible effect on our appearance and surroundings, we would be recognizable only as a physically distinct organism, with a vital individuality. This kind of individuality is observable in animal life, too. What is distinctively human is our unique spiritual personhood, which, through the functional dimension, can be embodied in our appearance and action, in our form giving to life and world. Human formation as such thus transcends both vital and functional individuality.

There is a correlation between the consonant contraction and expansion of our intrasphere and the formation of a personalized functional dimension of the life-form. The functional dimension becomes personalized under the influence of our growing intrasphere. Open to the disclosures of our private inner life, we begin to experiment with setting limits in relation to the forming influence it allows the inter- and outer spheres to attain.

The initiation of this process can be observed already in the child's passing through the "no" phase. A child's arbitrary and emphatic refusal to go along with what he or she is asked to do at this stage is their expression of a newly awakening sense of an intrasphere. They discover that it can be asserted over against the other spheres in their formation field. This awakening is accompanied by the fascinating discovery of the functional form potency to make their own inner wishes concrete in their surroundings. Children are eager to see how this newfound potency really works. Of course, all of this usually happens on a prefocal level of awareness.

Illusion of the Autonomous Self

A typical deformation in functionalistic societies is the isolation of the functional form dimension. Isolation replaces differentiation. It gives rise to the illusion of an autonomous self, in no way dependent on the formation field and its mysterious source. If people try to organize their life as a whole around this illusory exalted selfhood, a curious reversal takes place. The intrasphere is no longer emerging from its spiritual ground as disclosed in its ongoing preformation. It has lost awareness in awe of its unique relation to the formation mystery. It no longer uses the personalized functional dimension as merely a bridge to the inter- and outer spheres, as an instrument of embodiment. Instead the autonomous functional dimension feeds the intrasphere with its own illusions of grandeur and independence, with anything exalted in the inter- and outer spheres, anything that seems to promise the realization of such fantasies.

Because this idealized functional self is an illusion, its victims become alienated from their true interiority. Losing rootedness in the mystery of preformation through one's spirit, life becomes excessively vulnerable. One's whole project is built on sand, as it were. There is a hidden feeling that the illusion may be unmasked or exposed at any moment. Hence, a secret anxiety eats away at one's heart. Death, illness, failure in one's enterprises, loss of a loved one, economic disaster, anything that shows up the precariousness of life may lead to the collapse of the spurious confidence one places in one's autonomous self-structure and its illusions. As long as the differentiated intrasphere and its private life are not purified from the illusion of autonomous selfhood, we cannot find peace and consonance.

Symbolic Extensions of the Private Life

The embodiment of one's privacy is not only manifest in one's words and behavior, as in the "no" phase of the young child. The expansion of one's intrasphere is especially apparent in the incorporation within one's private life of various things appearing in the outer spheres. They become symbolic extensions of one's personal life. A kind of identification happens between such acquired symbols of privacy and one's inner person. They become an intimate part of our personality. We surround them with the same limits as our interiority. We resent any intrusion in their regard with the same outrage as violations of our personal life. Already in children this resentment can be observed when we presume to take their favorite toy away without asking them or when we intrude in the private space of a locker or drawer assigned to them as their own.

In similar ways we incorporate our own room, purse, briefcase, personal drawer, or locker into our privacy sphere. Transgression of the limits we assign to them symbolically evokes our indignation.

Privacy and the Heart or Core Form of Life

The formation of the intrasphere thus implies setting not only inner but also outer limits. These provide us with the kind of seclusion necessary for ongoing intraformation. Intraformation is the ground of the core form or heart of our life. The heart is the privileged shrine of privacy. The heart can flourish only within the protection of privacy limits. It is nourished on solitude. Only within the intrasphere can we cordially apprehend, appraise, and affirm who we are called to be as servants of the mystery. Although the sense of this call is not set in principle against the inter- and outer spheres of our formation field, the differentiation of the intrasphere includes the necessity to set oneself over against them *when necessary*.

Privacy of the heart creates a kind of inviolate inner sanctum. It prevents us from being wholly outer directed, from becoming like public billboards quickly read in passing, people of empty chatter, filled with gossip and insatiable curiosity. Privacy of the heart grants us the refined taste for discretion and reserve that symbolizes our awe for the unique mystery within.

Present-Day Obstacles to the Private Life

Present-day living arrangements do not facilitate our quest for the limits within which privacy thrives. Solitude is difficult to come by. In this culture full of distractions, we do not easily find soul companions with whom to share our intimate musings and feelings. Once we meet such friends, the contemporary lifestyle makes it difficult to find sufficient time and solitary spaces for communication in depth without interruption. The inter- and outer spheres of our formation fields are suffused with disturbing noises, advertisements, blaring propaganda, and countless other unsolicited intrusions. The eyes of the other always seem to be upon us, filled with curiosity and indiscrete surveillance. We, too, may police others in the same deforming fashion. These are not the eyes of gentle awe, compatibility, consideration, and compassion. Even the pretense of care, consideration, and loving concern may be used to force our way into another's intrasphere and its secrets. Countless ways can be devised in which we violate each other's privacy.

The human form needs an inviolate interiority to unfold its distinctive humanness, a private sphere no one is allowed to enter without invitation. Awe for the unique call of each person is the only powerful antidote against the germ of manipulation of others that lies dormant in all of us. This awe is the source of genuine encounter in mutual respect and love. When the sense of awe dies, we begin to tread the dehumanizing path of subtle or gross manipulation of others. We begin to oppress our spouses, children, acquaintances, friends, employees, and others over whom we have some influence or authority. Ironically, we do not allow them their dignity while we may be sharing enthusiastically in protest movements against social injustice in society and world. So prone are we to self-deception in our immediate dealings with others that we fail to realize the influence we have on others, no matter how slight and subtle it may be. As soon as we are aware of this power to manipulate others, we should renew in ourselves a deep sense of awe for their inmost mystery, questioning whether we encroach in any way on this most personal zone.

Temptation to Violate the Privacy of Insecure People

One way to rob people of their private dignity and responsibility is to make ourselves indispensable to them, even with the best of intentions. By making them powerless and overdependent, we break into their intrasphere. No longer is personal privacy the fertile soil of their own formation. Instead our "imperial suggestions," uttered with a certainty that does not invite personal doubt and deliberation, become the source of their life direction. We should never allow another person to lean wholly on us. This is the great temptation therapists, physicians, spiritual directors, gurus, clergy, parents, and educators have to deal with. The more admired, learned, gracious, popular, attractive, clever, and prestigious they are, the greater is this temptation. Many deny their admirers and followers, their counselees and directees, the freedom and self-respect that is their due. They prevent growth in responsibility for their own life in personal apprehension, appraisal, and affirmation.

In the presence of the "great" man or woman, no breathing space may be left to these dependents. True greatness implies awe for each person's dignity and privacy, awe that allows them to grow by their own trials and errors on the path of consonance. This does not exclude advice and a pointing out of the dangers on the road. The great art is to give counsel in such a way that people can work through the meaning for themselves. They should be allowed to adapt admiration as well as admonition to their own situation.

The temptation to intrude is intensified by the precarious nature of modern life. Many are plagued by self-doubt, insecurity, and faint-heartedness in the face of pending disaster. These feelings render them susceptible to any implicit invitation to surrender the initiative of their life to seemingly all-knowing others. They are easy prey for any needy therapist, counselor, teacher, healer, guru, or "deliverer" who knows how to exude personal interest in them combined with absolute certitude of judgment about how people should live their life. Feeling vulnerable and defenseless, they may be seduced by pleasing, dominant persons who leave no doubt about having all the answers. They are relieved and delighted to surrender their intrasphere to anyone who seems able to care for them, diffident and unsteady as they are.

Persons who live in awe for the inviolate center of one's intrasphere know when and how to dim their outgoing manifestations of interest and sympathy. They know how to play down their expertise when they meet vulnerable people in search of some omniscient guide who will take over their life. They have trained themselves in creating a certain respectful distance, in maintaining a quiet reserve when they are faced with those whom they could easily overwhelm with personal magnetism and unfailing certitude. Anyone who does not practice a similar respectful reserve will attract persons who are basically insecure, who are only too ready to surrender their initiative.

Paradoxically, persons who really care for one's growth in responsibility by maintaining loving, respectful reserve, may become unpopular. Others may accuse them of being "standoffish" in comparison with mesmerizing seducers, who wittingly or unwittingly destroy one's freedom of formation. Such seductive patterns betray awe and violate the privacy of vulnerable people.

Privacy and Life as a Dynamic Formation Project

Human life is always in ongoing formation. This unique life-form involves a precommitment to form reception and donation, which has to be translated into concrete commitment dispositions to be disclosed and deepened during our formation history. In short, the human form is basically never a finished structure but always a dynamic formation project.

As such, it is called to become what it is not yet. It is precisely the intra-sphere that enables people to give many possible formative meanings and directions inwardly to the people, events, and things that coform their successive life situations. Such inner directives may grow to be inner commitments that are to be embodied in turn in effective dispositions and actions.

The power of self-reliant form donation and reception grows by meeting head on the obstacles and resistances that block our way. By caring too much for others, by taking over their responsibilities and initiatives, we may smother their own intraformative potencies. By smoothing their way, we may smash their ability to transform obstacles into formation opportunities. The gifts of hardship and discipline liberate people for the obstacle course of life. They help us to grow in a resilient privacy of responsible apprehension, appraisal, affirmation, and action.

CHAPTER 10

Commonality and Privacy
of Our Human Formation Field

The human form of life shares its field of formation with others. Hence, this field is marked by commonality as well as privacy. The aspect of commonality resides in the inter- and outer spheres; the aspect of privacy resides in the intrasphere. A formation field is not only that which I have in common with others; it is also that which is mine. Therefore, I disclose in it the formation directives I share with many others as well as those that are unique to me. Moreover, the common directives I welcome inwardly are somehow filtered through the private ones that are already mine. In turn, my private form directives affect in some way the common directives I assimilate. We have already described this process as one of wavelike contraction and expansion of the intrasphere within the whole of one's formation field.

There is thus a polarity between the intrasphere of the formation field and its inter- and outer aspects. The intrasphere at times resists or opposes certain directives that make themselves felt in the inter- and outer spheres. If this happens, my "privacy" form functions as a "counter" form. In other situations I allow my intrasphere to be "in" with those whose directives I appreciate as congenial and compatible. This does not mean that I surrender privacy or give up the directives that are mine. Rather, I try to maintain the necessary "counters" or limits of my private life while at the same time allowing some aspect of it to be "in" with others. At such moments I truly experience an "encounter," that is, an integration without fusion or confusion of the "en" (intra) and the "counter" (inter- and outer) spheres of my life. There is no dichotomy between these spheres since they are meant to complement one another in dialogical interaction. The beneficial effect of this ongoing dialogue is at times creative distance and at other times creative encounter. Both modes give

161

a form to life that should be congenial and compatible. They ensure that we never lose ourselves in others, but instead become an original presence to them.

This dynamic is a source of human culture and civilization. When it is lost—as, for instance, in a frenzied crowd or mob—the effects will be dehumanizing, perhaps disastrous. Distinctive humanness (or spirituality) resides in the intrasphere as personally touched by the formation mystery in its ongoing and unique preformation of each human life. Human culture and its underlying form traditions can be maintained only by an appeal to this enlightened intrasphere. Human encounter, too, is possible only through a mutual appeal of enlightened intraspheres. Without this touch of illumined privacy the inter- and outer spheres lose their humanness. Frantic sexual promiscuity, for instance, can be a symptom of a desperate search to enter the intrasphere of others and to share one's own interiority, which has been repudiated or closed off in anxiety, hostility, or frustration.

Moments of Full Privacy

In the case of consonant dialogue between the intra- and interspheres, the moment of full privacy is one of reassertion of the limits or counter aspects of my interiority. In relation to my inter- and outer spheres, I am no longer engaged in one or another specific encounter or involvement. In full privacy, I am a waiting, relaxed openness to reality as a whole and to the mystery that permeates it. It follows that the meditative or contemplative stance is at the same time one of total privacy and of total openness to the mystery and its epiphanies. This moment of full privacy and openness has a profoundly relaxing effect on our entire embodied form of life.

The concrete, manifold engagements of the intrasphere in daily endeavors bind and absorb our formation energy. The neuromuscular channels utilized to embody formation become tense and strained. Released from these particular engagements in a moment of privacy, we may regain for a while the state of intraformative receptivity and openness to the mystery as a whole. Such receptivity uses a minimum of formation energy. Neuromuscular agitation is also at a low ebb, thus having a restorative effect on a tense, tired organism.

Dissonant Privacy

Privacy can be formative or deformative. Moments of deformative privacy are common to all human forms. Affected as we are by a principle of radical dissonance, we are bound to lose the right direction from time to time. Our main concern in the following is to address an enduring condition of deformative privacy that may lastingly mar our own life or that of others.

Dissonance of Excessive Private Control

The intrasphere of the human formation field is endowed with limited freedom. Operating out of my intrasphere enables me to exercise a modest, always limited control over the inter- and outer spheres. I may, for instance, advise my children about certain dangers, but I have no guarantee that they will heed my admonitions. Because human life includes by its nature both inter- and outer spheres, the scope of freedom is relative. The absence of absolute control means that any exposition of my interiority implies a risk. I cannot control what others will do with it. What I expose may be betrayed, abused, ridiculed, rejected, or used against me.

The art of proximate living includes, therefore, a disposition of wise appreciation of the appropriate times and circumstances of congenial, compatible, and compassionate disclosure. Yet even the wisest appraisal cannot always avoid risk. Risk is rooted in the structure of our human field of formation, which includes inter- and outer spheres that are not under our command.

If we are generally unsure about our potency to receive and give form in life, we may anxiously try the impossible, namely, to control totally our inter- and outer spheres. When we experience that this is in fact impossible, we may withdraw into a closed-off interiority rather than face the risks of failure, rejection, ridicule, misunderstanding, and betrayal of trusting communication.

How sure I am about my form potency depends largely on my interformative experiences in the past. If my parents were appreciative, if they confirmed my attempts to exercise my form potency in my own consonant way, this initial confirmation will be part of my formative memory, imagination, and anticipation. Hence, I will be more inclined to risk the expansion of the intra- into the inter- and outer spheres. I do not feel as alone when facing communication with unsympathetic strangers. My intrasphere is filled with confirming interformative memories of the past. If an encounter fails, it will not destroy the faith and hope built in me by my experiences as a child. The same confirmative experience in childhood enables me to be at ease when alone and to feel quietly at home in my private sphere.

Initial Formation and At-Homeness in Privacy

It may be threatening for children to be left alone by their mothers. However, if the mother's presence radiates faith, hope, and love, gently and consistently expressed in appreciation and confirmation of the child's form potency, confidence is rapidly gained. This experience is germinal to the child's trusting disclosure of his or her own form potency and intraspheric life. A first manifestation of such confident disclosure and inner at-homeness would be the child's ability to pay little or no attention to the mother's presence. She is there, but the child has already discovered that one does not lose her when absorbed in private play or explorations.

Because of former appreciative experiences, children feel less alone inwardly and consequently less dependent on the actual presence of their mothers. On this basis they can grow to the experience of being alone with their private musings and doings without fear, even when their mothers are no longer physically around them. They develop a growing sense of their own intrasphere and its functional potency to give form concretely to their observable life and surroundings. They become peacefully at home in their own interiority, filled as it is by confirmative experiences of the past. They can then relate in faith, hope, and love to their unfolding inner life.

Such children are increasingly able to bear with solitude. Since their intrasphere has been enriched by confirming interformation, they seldom feel emotionally alone within themselves. Later in life, they will not easily be overcome by feelings of dejection if a privacy disclosure of theirs is brushed off or sneered at. Their intrasphere is too rich to suffer easily such destruction. They feel free either to interact with others or to enjoy solitude. In some sense they are never alone, even in the midst of an indifferent or hostile crowd. Certain religious form traditions deepen this experience of inner richness by fostering experiences of intimacy with the confirmative mystery within one's own deepest interiority.

Conversely, if our overall experience in childhood has been that of depreciation, if we did not experience warm and spontaneous confirmation of our form potency, then naturally, we will be inclined to wall off our inner life. Every new appearance in our inter- and outer sphere will pose a threat to our privacy. We cannot help but be fearful and wary. This distrust is even more intense when we are exposed to suspicious, prying parents and other formative authorities who may betray our secrets. The consequent deformative memories of the past should be reformed or transformed. Otherwise they will negatively coform our apprehension and appraisal of others. To protect ourselves against others as potential invaders of our threatened interiority, we form compulsive, anxious, suspicious safety directives that may solidify into excessive security dispositions. We lose the natural rhythm between distance and encounter.

When defensive distance prevails, it precludes a full and spontaneous dialogue between our inner and outer spheres. We withdraw in anxious inwardness. Solitude is replaced first by loneliness, then by isolation. The isolation of our intrasphere excludes free form reception and donation in relation to our inter- and outer spheres. Loneliness is different; there are still hesitant attempts to interformative presence, combined with the painful feeling that we are not succeeding. This experience is common to all of us at certain moments of life. It is an especially widespread experience in our functionalistic society.

Aloneness, on the other hand, can either be an extreme experience of isolation or one of rich, creative solitude. If we are blessed with an interiority filled with remnants of appreciative and confirmative events of past or present interformation, aloneness can be enjoyed as nourishing solitude. This explains the peace and joy of hermits whose solitude is filled with the memories of the interwovenness of their intrasphere with the confirming presence of the Holy. Inwardly such hermits, if their life formation happens to be consonant, are not alone but intimately in touch with the Wholly Other.

If people are basically not at home in their intrasphere, if it is empty of confirmative memories, if they have lost all formative potency in regard to their inter- and outer spheres, their fate is one of extreme isolation. All appearances in their inter- and outer spheres become increasingly unreal. Because these spheres are essential to human life, and hence indesctructible, they will be filled by necessity with illusions and fantasies.

Pride-Form and Isolated Privacy

The isolated privacy of mental illness is quite different from the privacy that is a consequence of the pride-form of life. We all suffer in various degrees from this latter kind of isolation. In a number of people, it becomes a lasting disposition. The science of formation holds that the human life-form, while striving for consonance, suffers from a radical dissonance. This dissonance and its consequences have been observed by experts in various human sciences. Many religious and ideological faith and form traditions provide their own basic explanation of this phenomenon. Their faith explanations can be neither proved nor disproved by formation science. Some formation experts, however, specialize in articulation research. They try to articulate the findings of the science in terms of one or the other of these traditions. They respect the basic tenets of the tradition concerned without betraying scientific facts and findings.

Many observations seem to point indeed to a radical dissonance. There seems to be a tendency in the human form to set itself apart in a kind of arrogant self-sufficiency from the rest of the cosmos, from humanity and history and their mysterious ground. This breeds the illusion of a fully autonomous selfhood. Of course, the resistance of reality to such illusions compels people to adapt themselves in their daily actions to the inescapable preformation of their life as well as to its inter- and outer formation. Yet they remain inclined to cherish the illusion of total autonomy. They try to realize it without doing too much harm to their health, status, and wealth. This tendency gives rise to the pride-form of life, which in turn fosters the isolation of an arrogant privacy. This cuts us off from many formative sources contained in our preformative roots and in our intra-, inter, and outer spheres. It makes us strangers in the cosmos, alienated from the all-embracing mystery of formation, forlorn in a sterile, closed off interiority that tries desperately to control people, events, and things.

In the measure that the inter- and outer spheres of our formation field seem to threaten privacy, anxiety is evoked. We will be tempted to withdraw in a dissonant way into our intrasphere. Such moments of withdrawal in a world of fantasy, daydreaming, loneliness, and secrecy are a normal part of everyone's life. When such withdrawal becomes an enduring, dominant disposition, there is cause for concern.

How to maintain or regain the right rhythm between contraction and expansion of our intrasphere may be a question that emerges in many life situations. As long as the dialogue between the spheres is not completely cut off, the consonant spheric rhythm is easier to restore. If we do not find the path of return, we may become victims of a disintegrative and increasingly dissonant loneliness or isolation.

Functional Form Traditions and Privacy
The disposition of privacy, like all dispositions, depends on form traditions that play a role in one's society. Ideological, functional traditions that emerged more recently in our formation history are less favorable to privacy than the classical ones. Capitalist and socialist form traditions, if they are still collectivistic, stress outer more than inner formation. They are rooted in faith traditions that hold that human life is valuable either

for the state or for private enterprises to the degree that it functions effectively within the framework of an often leveling organization. Form traditions are incorporated by means of symbols in the interconsciousness of a people. The science of formation, as we indicated in the first volume of this series, distinguishes between a personal consciousness and an interconsciousness. Both of these can be focal, prefocal, infrafocal, or transfocal. Our present-day functional interconsciousness remains *prefocal* in most people. This means that they are usually not *focally* aware of the impact of this interconsciousness on their life formation. In other people the pervasive influence of interconscious functionalism may be *infrafocal*, meaning that this modification of their consciousness is, in principle, not available to their focal attention and awareness. Interconscious functionalism can be *prefocal* in the sense that it can be made available to awareness without extraordinary means, such as, for instance, psychoanalytic treatment or formation counseling in depth.

The functional form tradition is reductionistic; it shrinks the human form mainly to one of its dimensions: the functional. It does not take into account the intrasphere of people or the preformation of human life, its congeniality, its transcendent dimension, its openness to mystery. Both the socialist state and the conglomeration of private enterprises in the capitalistic one, if they are still collectivistic, resemble more and more giant computers. Functional form traditions encourage people to conform to computerized life at the expense of their private life and their congeniality. Computers, to be sure, are superb inventions to be utilized in the best way possible for the advancement of humanity. They should, however, serve, not enslave, the intrasphere of human life.

Techniques of homogenization foster the functional interconsciousness that marks the present-day existence of large masses of people. Deformative manipulation by means of the media and impersonal bureaucracies tends to reduce persons to mere functionaries. They are dealt with as though they had no interiority but only a functional psyche, as this word is understood by certain reductionistic psychologies.

Personal Freedom, Functional Freedom, and Privacy

Personal freedom is rooted in one's intrasphere. The denial of this sphere is the denial of the primary human right to be oneself. It cannot be replaced by external freedom alone. One's private life is unjustly invaded by a functional interconsciousnes that is spread and strengthened, often unwittingly, by the media, pragmatic education, technocracy, organizations of employers and employees, massive political parties, and even religious organizations. The functional form tradition minimizes the opportunities for personal apprehension, appraisal, and affirmation. These central human potencies of knowledge and decision are dominated by the outer spheres of one's formation field, which are in turn victimized by the functional interconsciousness that tends to absorb personal consciousness.

On the scale of form directives of the functional tradition, what matters is not one's inner life so much as one's popularity, power, possessions, practical effectiveness, and precise slot in the computerized society. The human form is appraised not by fidelity to its uniqueness, its creativity and the richness of its interiority, but by the fame of its titles and the value of its stocks, bonds, salaries, and fringe benefits. Valued most is not what one is inwardly, but externally—not what one experiences in depth or creates in quality, but what one produces in quantity.

Functional form traditions foster a conspiracy of silence in regard to the formation mystery. They substitute technology for mystery. Hence, the private life of people becomes increasingly absorbed in the vast emptiness of a functional interconsciousness. Personal inner apprehension, appraisal, and affirmation are easily abdicated in such an atmosphere. The functional interconsciousness, from which we borrow our appraisals, is without transcendent reflection. Technique is excellent as an extension of the functional capacities of humanity. What is deformative is to substitute for the mystery an idolized technocracy and the worship of an autonomous functional dimension that takes the place of the spiritual person as a whole. This emphasis spells the death of privacy.

Shift of Concern from Inner Freedom to Outer Freedom

The functionalization of the human form by ideological form traditions implies a shift from concern for inner to outer freedom. People become more free, independent, self-reliant, and critical in the functional dimension of their consciousness and in the inter- and outer spheres of their formation field. The same ideological traditions make them less concerned about the freedom of the intrasphere of their life. Unfortunately, the demise of inwardness makes them impotent as distinctively human forms of life. No matter how powerful and important they may be in their inter- and outer spheres, deep down they feel insignificant. Many may experience this emptiness in a prefocal way. Their personal transfocal consciousness has gone unacknowledged due to the exclusively functional type of interconsciousness promoted by certain ideological form traditions. Yet their transfocal dimension may not as yet be totally identified with this interconscious refusal. Their transcendent potency may stir up feelings of lost freedom, of unease and dissatisfaction in the prefocal dimension of their consciousness. If these experiences can be made available to focal awareness, they may initiate a restoration of interiority in the midst of an externalized, distracting society. Outward freedom may be complemented by the far more basic inner freedom that should sustain it.

What happens when identification with the interconscious refusal of respectful concern for inner liberty becomes total? Not only is the transcendent sphere of consciousness refused, but the subsequent feelings of loss and dissatisfaction are relegated to the infrafocal dimension of consciousness. Hence, such warning signs are no longer available to people in an ordinary way. Extraordinary means, such as therapy or formation counseling in private or in common, may still be able to restore some sense of inner liberty.

Modes of Paralysis of Inner Freedom

Functional ideological form traditions paralyze the awareness of our aspiration for inner liberty in many ways. A most effective way is to concentrate our attention exclusively on the fight for freedom in the inter- and outer spheres. Many of these traditions will focus exclusively on freedom from observable restraints in the external expressions of sexual encounter, of contractual work relationships, of discrimination due to class, creed, color, or gender. Many effects of this focus are to be lauded. Increased freedom in the inter- and outer spheres of the human formation field may be a facilitating or even a necessary condition for an increase in inner freedom. Often, however, a desirable release from unjust external bondage may feed the illusion that victory of freedom in the outer sphere automatically implies inward freedom. This illusion overlooks the fact that the same ideological form traditions burden people with new inner restraints that block the full unfolding of the deepest inner freedom.

We are made to believe, for instance, that freedom of sexual encounter is one of the great gains for people today. It may be in some way, if it is consonant. But adherents of the same ideological traditions risk losing the inner capacity and freedom to live in the human love and fidelity that is at the heart of a meaningful sexual encounter between married persons. These new restraints placed on their inner life make people lonely and isolated in the midst of their recently gained independence in the inter- and outer spheres of life.

The problem is that many ideological form traditions overrate the importance of the struggle for freedom in our inter- and outer spheres. We become myopic in regard to the interiorized, interconscious pulsations, pulsions, compulsions, and fears that paralyze the free unfolding of a congenial private life. This inner numbness vitiates our ability to profit fully from our gains in outer freedom. Social liberty should serve spiritual liberation. Otherwise both forms of freedom will be destroyed. The struggle for social freedom is initiated and nourished by the spiritual aspirations of humanity. This struggle will cease with the death of inner freedom and its consequent inspirations and aspirations.

Mutual Complementarity of the Sciences of the Inner and Outer Life

We may become oblivious of the formative powers that anonymously pervade our inter- and outer spheres. Among them may be the tradition of scientism and, in its wake, that of technocracy. There is a polarity between the distinctively human sciences, which serve primarily the unfolding of our intrasphere, and the positive or exact sciences, which serve mainly the formation of our inter- and outer spheres under their functional aspect. Each type of science has its own kind of rigor in research methodology, its own mode of certitude, its rules of validation attainable within its sphere of probability. The sciences of the intrasphere, along with their distinctively human directives and dynamics, cannot pursue their specific investigations with the exact quantifying methods of the sciences of the functional inter- and outer sphere.

Scientism is a powerful form tradition whose popularity is based on the success of the exact sciences of the outer sphere; it claims that the sciences of the inner sphere should follow the methodology of the physical sciences, thereby abdicating their own scope and identity. Scientism claims that what cannot be measured in the inner life is unavailable to intellectual understanding.

The science of formation holds that both types of scientific approaches are valid and mutually complementary. The sciences of the outer spheres should serve those of the inner by providing useful information about the functional aspects of the pre-, intra-, inter-, and outer dimensions. The sciences of the distinctively human aspects of the inner sphere should utilize this information to improve conditions for consonant formation. In turn, they should communicate their findings and insights to the sciences of the outer sphere. Some of these insights may stimulate further research into the functional conditions pertinent to all the spheres. In this way, the exact sciences may help to provide optimal conditions for the distinctively human unfolding of the maximum number and variety of people. They in turn can better serve social justice, peace, and mercy.

Consonant formation can only be fostered by a balanced exposure to both kinds of science. A society dominated by scientistic, positivistic, and technocratic traditions is not interested in the distinctively human directives of the intrasphere and the richness or poverty of the private life it engenders. The faith tradition underlying such functional form traditions makes us believe that humanity's way to happiness, success, and security can only be gained by the control of physical and biopsychological processes. In accordance with this tradition, it is assumed that people should develop a strong, willful functional dimension, isolated from the "useless" distractions of the inner life with which the classical form traditions and the sciences of the intrasphere were "naively" concerned.

The science of formation holds, on the contrary, that awe-filled cultivation of the intrasphere of life is the most valuable contribution made by the classical form traditions of both the East and West. It is this treasure of humanity, this precious fruit of generations, that is threatened by recent ideological form traditions.

Unsolved Restlessness of the Functional Form of Life

When life is exclusively formed in accordance with the form traditions of scientism and positivism, one may be overcome by a sense of loneliness and isolation. This is the price we pay for severing ourselves from the intrasphere and from its rootedness in the unique preforming mystery in its cosmic, human, and transhuman epiphanies. Usually this experience of isolation is repudiated and denied to such a degree that it becomes infrafocal, meaning that it is no longer available to formative reflection. Repudiation of this kind cannot prevent feelings of uneasiness from seeping into prefocal and focal dimensions of consciousness. Because the source of this uneasiness is relegated to the infrafocal realm of life, we often cannot understand or resolve this vague feeling of restlessness. We may seek the solution in further absorption in the positivistic interconsciousness mediated by the ideological form traditions and their symbolic sources of deformation. The greater this absorption, the more we tend to distrust our own apprehension, appraisal, and affirmation. We live more and more as isolated functionaries who manage to survive with some margin of measurable success in those capitalist or Marxist societies that have not yet overcome collectivism. Yet despite all our efforts, our restlessness may never be solved totally. It may keep seeping through the boundaries of our prefocal consciousness.

The ideological faith and form traditions that have emerged in the last several centuries of our formation history were not primarily concerned with the *concrete* human form, that is, with its personal intraspheric form potencies, its distinctive humanness, its openness to the mystery, its unique call to the service of humanity, and the treasures of its private life. Their concern was above all for generalized abstractions of the human form. They spoke about "the employer," "the employee," "the woman," "the black," "the Hispanic," "the poor." Undeniably, this concern has vastly improved external conditions for dignity and freedom. Yet the same improvements may have suppressed in many instances the private life of outwardly liberated people. Their powers of inner appraisal may be imprisoned by the homogenizing interconsciousness of positivist movements and the societies they so meticulously structure. The human spirit may be suffocated by these collectivizing attempts insofar as they tend to invade the privacy of people's personal lives and to shrink the boundaries of their interior freedom.

This critique by no means implies that we ought to discontinue the struggle for social justice in the inner as well as in the outer spheres of human life. If anything, this struggle should be intensified and complemented by genuine concern for the overall liberation and growth of people. However, we believe that social justice in regard to the external conditions of human freedom should be subordinated to social justice in regard to the basic, inner freedom of all people.

Loss of Formative Intradirectives

Classical formation traditions, insofar as they are consonant, have provided people with effective directives for the formation of their inner life. Ideological form traditions have tended to replace these directives mainly with external functional ones. As a result, the directives that should guide one's inner unfolding in the light of the mystery became lost, vague, or ambiguous. People who are caught in the main by functional interconsciousness can no longer fall back upon the directives developed over the centuries by classical form traditions. Functional form directives are by their nature more dependent on changes in the external situation, demanding opportunistic adaptation in service of measurable success and vital gratification. Hence, these directives change rapidly. The same opportunism makes it necessary to keep them sufficiently vague and flexible in order to facilitate fast adjustment to changing external opportunities, to new hypothetical visions of the sciences of the outer sphere, and/or to mood swings in popular interconsciousness. These directives are thus far less stable and dependable than those emerging from the classical traditions.

Universal inner form directives, on the contrary, when personally assimilated in dialogue with a classical form tradition, relate each person's formation to all of humanity and its millennia of formation history, its sense of mystery, its place in the cosmos. When such directives are taken away, people feel insecure, unrelated, and unidentified in their intrasphere of life. As long as the choices they have to make are merely functional or vital, ideological directives may prove sufficient. As soon as deeper meanings of life and world are involved, such as issues of congeniality and fidelity to one's unique call to serve humanity, people feel lost and anxious. Functional interconsciousness does not provide directives that resonate in their own intraspheric experience since they have lost touch for the most part with the age-old formation wisdom of humanity. By themselves alone people cannot find the directives that persuasively counter the suggestions of mere functional form traditions. A lifetime is too short to test them all. There is little wonder that the disposition for privacy diminishes.

To live in the realm of private responsibility and decision becomes intolerable when one is not supported by the formation wisdom of revered predecessors who have lived through the same quandaries and whose wisdom is sedimented in classical form traditions. To be sure, this wisdom has to be purified of many accretions that today can no longer direct life. New consonant accretions have to be created, but the basic directives will hold true in the human intrasphere, for they are timeless and universal.

Fusion and the Loss of Privacy

The loss of genuine interiority makes intimate interformation with others impossible. As distinguished from functional interformation, that which is intimate presupposes a sharing of our spirit-illumined private life. Intimate interformation happens through encounters in which, unlike in fusion, two or more persons are "with" one another without losing themselves "in" one another. They maintain the "counters" or "limits" of their uniqueness in service of their togetherness. The absence of privacy-boundaries thus implies the impossibility of intimate interformation. The death of the *disposition* of privacy does not, however, destroy the human *predisposition* to privacy, which keeps on generating, among other things, longings for shared privacy or intimacy. If the possibility of fulfilling this desire remains absent, it leads to a hunger for its substitute: deformative fusion. To fill the void between them, merely functional people seek desperately some substitute for intimacy, some sign of belonging. They try, therefore, to fuse their lives with others, with groups or movements.

Fusion is the opposite of encounter. It means being swallowed up by the emotional interconsciousness of a group that shares similar needs. Togetherness of this sort may grant a moment of forgetfulness of one's isolation. When the experience of fusion is over, one may feel more lonesome than before in the realization that there was no real communion in depth, that the hunger evoked by the predisposition for intimacy is still there, gnawing away at one's lonely heart.

The togetherness of fusion is not a mode of genuine intimacy but a desperate attempt to relieve isolated lives. In true encounter I appeal to the intrasphere of others and I confirm their private life, its mystery and unique potency. In this confirmation, I likewise affirm my own intrasphere as unique, mysterious, and not totally communicable to others; I also affirm my own form potency as an inalienable epiphany of the mystery. Through such appeal to the mystery of the privacy of each other, we may truly encounter one another. We invite each other to transcend our immanence in the functional-vital interconsciousness imposed by functionalistic form traditions. We transcend our embeddedness in an everydayness not illumined by the mystery. We summon each other to be faithful to our own form potencies. This marks the beginning of interformative intimacy and community.

In fusion, there is really no unique interiority experiencing in awe the mystery of another inwardness. There are only isolated functionaries desperately trying to escape their imprisonment by melting into one another. Symptoms of this attempt would be the cult of instant sexual unity, leaving nothing to the imagination, or the "therapeutic" attempt to force the emergence of instantaneous intimacy in certain "encounter" groups. Nothing remains awesome, personal, or private. If all fails, people may resort in anger, frustration, and despair to sadistic and masochistic cruelty. They may do anything to squeeze the inner secret out of self and others, to take revenge for the emptiness of everything.

The age of loneliness leads to the age of violence. Pseudorelationships cannot prevent physical abuse, even of one's partner and children, for they aggravate our sense of isolation and frustration. This movement of immersion in one another prevents the birth of privacy. Frustration inevitably follows the idle attempt to fusion. It deepens peoples' isolation while alienating them from their own intrasphere.

Privacy and the Idealized Form of Life

Formation science hold that one of the basic dynamics of life's unfolding is consonant ideal formation. The human life-form is what it is not yet; it is a going ahead of itself, a reaching for the unique image of the mystery it is called to be. The disclosure of this original image over a lifetime is served in many ways. One of them is that of ideal formation. We form an idea or ideal of what we feel we are called to be. If this is congenial with the hidden image in our soul and compatible with our unique life situations, if it is attuned to the foundations of the form traditions to which we are committed, we call it a consonant ideal. If not, it is dissonant and has to be corrected, complemented, or replaced. In our attempt to live up to the ideal, we disclose its consonance or dissonance. This disclosure enables us indirectly to gain some awareness of our original image or foundational life-form. The lifelong attempt to approximate our own epiphany of the mystery goes through a succession of both consonant and dissonant ideal images of what we may be called to be.

There is an intimate link between privacy and ideal formation. The more our ideals approximate what we are called to be, the more they will be in tune with the mysterious preformation at the root of our intrasphere and the private life it engenders. At-homeness in this sphere increases the probability that we may form consonant ideals. When confirmed in everyday life as really congenial and compatible, these ideals in turn illumine our private awareness of who we are called to be.

Idealized Forms of Life

One mode of dissonant idealism is idealizing. Idealizing means that we make into a formative ideal what cannot in fact form us congenially and compatibly. The idealized form of life is alien to our intrasphere and its preforming source. It is not only uncongenial but also incompatible with the deeper personal meaning of the situations we meet in the inter- and outer spheres of our formation field. When privacy dies, so, too, does the source of consonant ideals. To forget the wisdom of classical form traditions is to rob this already diminished privacy of inspiring ideals. This is unfortunate because ideals handed over (without their dissonant accretions) bear formative power for many generations. They make available a universal treasure to be personalized by each unique interiority.

While consonant ideals have died out in many people, the process of ideal formation cannot be discarded so easily. This process is inherent in the human form of life. Hence, a wayward mode of dissonant idealizing will usurp the power of consonant ideal formation. Functional form traditions fill the interconsciousness of their adherents with idealized functionalistic and vitalistic forms of life. These are not the fruit of private meditation and personal assimilation through trial and error. They are pale reflections of what the collectivistic form traditions identify as success, self-actualization, or "making it," regardless of whether this type of idealizing is in tune with one's interiority. Such idealizing is kept alive in the interconsciousness of the public through the mass media. Those who live by these idealized life-forms are driven by the universal need to prove form potency to self and others. A problem arises when one seeks confirmation of one's form potency by trying anxiously to measure up to popular idealized forms of functional living.

To force ourselves to conform to such dissonant ideals requires a persistent violence to our own and others' intrasphere. Instead of fostering a relaxed transcendent self-presence, we engage in harsh introspection—a characteristic of the isolated functional dimension that has lost its openness to inner inspiration and has become subservient to inter- and outer spheres dominated by a functional interconsciousness. The sense of who we are called to be in confident self-affirmation is no longer sought for in our interiority but in the public consciousness. We apprehend, appraise, and affirm our life in terms of what "they" think of us. We do not appreciate our life in its interiority, enlightened by the wisdom of generations. Anxiously self-observant, we engage focally or prefocally in an interminable questioning of how we measure up to the idealized life-forms the impersonal public exalts. We look at ourselves through the reproachful eyes of others. Not at home in our inner sphere, powerlessly delivered over to exalted life-forms foreign to our deepest call, we cannot experience privacy in any true sense of the word. Conformity to functionalistic form traditions begins to drain us; we become one more cog in the wheel of collective organizations.

Apparent Life-Form and the Disposition of Privacy Protection

The science of formation describes the differentiation of the human life-form in its sociohistorical, vital, functional, and transcendent form potencies. It accounts for the observable integration of the dispositions formed by these potencies by positing the integrative forms of life: these are, respectively, the core, current, apparent, and actual life-forms. In relation to the privacy disposition, we should be especially attentive to the apparent form of life.

The disposition of privacy implies, like most other dispositions, related subdispositions. Perhaps most noticeable among them is the disposition of privacy protection. It is noticeable because it gives rise to various observable ways of life that protect our privacy against intrusion. Such external safeguards are more visible than the private life they protect. Hence, the term privacy is often analogously applied to these zones of protection themselves. People may speak of the privacy of their diary, mail, purse, locker, drawer, room, home, or family life.

One of the important functions of our apparent life-form itself is to safeguard our privacy. The human form is not imprisoned or concealed within its intrasphere. Being an embodied form of life, it both forms and manifests itself in and through its bodily presence in the inter- and outer spheres of its formation field. One may try to be more or less present in these spheres or, as we observed earlier, one can contract or expand the intrasphere. One can never be totally absent from the inter- and outer spheres, for they coform our life due to its embodiment. Our form is always incarnated and incarnating. Even if we live in seclusion or absolute silence, we are still accessible to others. We cannot escape the disclosure of our interiority, even if few may be able to read our bodily signs and symbols.

Apparent Life-Form as Privacy Protection

In childhood we may be like an open book, easily read by others. Soon life teaches us that what others read may be used against us or misunderstood. We also become aware that such openness enables others to intrude in the delicate story of our inner unfolding, to disturb its slowly developing thread.

The apparent life-form can function as a protection of this vulnerability. It can help to diminish the public accessibility of our intrasphere. Through our appearance, we can veil our thoughts and feelings. We have no control over all aspects of the way we appear. The basic incarnational nature of the human form makes such control impossible. Still, human life shapes many features of its embodied presence. Unlike animal forms, we are able in some measure to form our appearance so that it conceals the facets of our inner life that we do not want to reveal. We can, therefore, modulate the expressivity of our incarnating body. This ability is already present in childhood. Children feel initially that people can see right through them.

A great moment of incipient intraformation occurs when they realize that they can keep a secret that adults cannot discover so long as they keep up the proper appearances.

This secret marks the first awakening of our intrasphere, a private life that is really ours and that we can defend ingeniously against invaders by means of an apparent life-form that integrates many modes of privacy protection. For example, well-integrated people have learned when and how to be reserved in word, gesture, and facial expression without appearing secretive, stiff, or anxious. They have formed themselves in the art of not revealing prematurely what should remain hidden.

Another protection is their enjoyment of intimacy with trusted friends to whom they can divulge more of their inner life than to others. Such intimacy acts like a safety valve. Letting off steam with a few trustworthy people makes it less likely that they will lose their composure in public or with those who might use such frankness against them.

A functional type of appearance is another protection we can use to prevent disclosures of our inner feelings that could harm ourselves or others. When we visit a beloved person in a sickroom and are inwardly overcome by their symptoms of deterioration, we may hide our grief and forebodings by cheerfully engaging in such functions as arranging the flowers, pouring water, or preparing a food tray.

The formation history of the not-too-distant past shows that during the Victorian period people favored the apparent form of life in its veiling capacity rather than using it as a screen that allowed their intrasphere to shine through. At present the pendulum seems to have swung in the opposite direction. The apparent form has become a kind of transparent screen through which one reveals as much as possible. One's appearance has to be casual, open, more disclosing than concealing. It is beneficial that a certain hypersensitivity in regard to unnecessary secrets (like hiding a serious ailment from one's family) has been overcome. However, excessive openness hinders the subtle unfolding of the intrasphere. The present vulgarization of communication may be due in part to the absence of a meaningful private life in many people. They may not have much to hide to begin with.

Private Appraisals and Public Appearance

Formation science teaches that, like all the spheres of human life, so, too, the intrasphere is stuctured by our form dimensions. Our private life is coformed by the sociohistorical, vital, functional, and transcendent dimensions. It manifests a wide range of feelings, strivings, and dispositions that correspond with these dimensions. Hence, our intrasphere is filled with sociohistorical pulsations, vital pulsions, functional ambitions, and transcendent aspirations and inspirations. Meeting others, we may be inwardly moved by any of these feelings and strivings. Some of them may be acceptable while the expression of others is not tolerated in society. While all should be present, not all of them should be apparent. Formation science also distinguishes between dimensional strivings that are personal, prepersonal, and impersonal. They are personal when they have been apprehended, appraised, and affirmed by us as relatively free and insightful persons; prepersonal if this is not the case; impersonal if they have been personalized earlier but have now become routine dispositions.

A special problem for our apparent life-form is our prepersonal likes and dislikes. They may be activated when we meet people who sometimes by their sheer appearance elicit a spontaneous sympathy or antipathy in us. This prepersonal appraisal will be communicated through our body, our tone of voice, and our eyes without us being aware of it. While we cannot immediately correct our inner feelings, we can improve our apparent life-form so that it sufficiently conceals our bias. This presupposes, however, a minimum of personalization of such prepersonal dispositions. First of all, we must try to be aware of how our apparent form of life might affect others. When we grow in sensitivity to their reactions, responses, and unguarded body language, we become more aware that something in our own apparent form of presence strikes them in the wrong way. Repeated, relaxed reflection and consultation with friends or formation counselors may enable us to disclose what kind of inner feeling communicates itself in and through our body in a dissonant fashion. We should then try to apprehend and appraise our dislike of the other, especially if we have repudiated and therewith enclosed in our infrafocal awareness our own spontaneous antipathy.

A first step toward personalization is to bring this feeling into focus, to befriend it, to converse with it, to ask ourselves how it affects our appearance. It may take a long time before we are able to change such deeply rooted emotions. In the meantime what we can change to some degree is how these emotions are expressed in our apparent form of life. This is not necessarily a pretense or deception. We can honestly *will* the well-being of others and respect them as called uniquely by the formation mystery, in spite of the fact that privately we cannot feel at ease with them and may not like their style of thought and action. Our personal center of free appraisal, illumined by our spirit, can tell us in what deeper sense we can experience appreciation for those we impulsively dislike. This also holds true of liking people prepersonally. Often our like is rooted in our impulsive apprehension and appraisal of certain aspects of people that confirm our wishes, prejudices, fantasies, and expectations. Here, too, the process of personalization can enable us to *will* their good as unique epiphanies of the mystery.

Formal Structures of the Apparent Life-Form

On the personal level of our intrasphere, we should refuse to allow pulsations, pulsions, or ambitions to dominate our apparent form exclusively. In many instances these prepersonal feelings are so persistent that our attempt to personalize them is not sufficient to create the ideal appearance. It is for this reason that we often have to rely on the formal structures of right appearance that have been handed over by form traditions. Again there is no pretense and deception involved as long as we honestly *will* them for the benefit of the other. Our formative will can be far ahead of our formative feeling. Unfortunately, such feeling is more readily expressed in our bodily appearance. Yet formal structures of compatible and compassionate appearance, expressing our genuine will to be pleasant, can veil the unintentional expression of our depreciative emotions.

Such traditional structures of consonant appearance are, for example, the common conventions of politeness, tact, gentleness, respect rooted in awe, and consideration and care as embodied in customs, language symbols, and bodily expressions. These are shared and understood by the average person in a culture or subculture that has been formed in part by such traditions. They can guide our usual expressions of respect and sympathy. They shape our apparent form while protecting us against the intrusion of private feelings and dispositions uncalled for in the situation.

These traditional structures that comprise a compatible apparent form have been developed by generations of people who experienced the destructive impact of indiscriminate exhibition of one's private thoughts and feelings. By ourselves alone, we could not easily invent these structures of a respectful apparent form. Ways of appropriate public appearance refine human togetherness. They teach us how to move, dress, and speak in varied social situations. Life would become impossible if each one of us had to invent personally and anew the acceptable structures of appearance in the usual situations we all share in a common culture or subculture.

Personalization of Formal Structures

Initially, inherited structures of appearance may be formal, only slightly pervaded by our personal presence. They could become deadening if they stayed that way. We should try to reform our interiority itself in the light of appearances sanctioned by consonant form traditions. When we succeed increasingly in such reformation of our intrasphere, we can grow toward graciousness.

Graciousness manifests itself when the sphere of privacy and the traditional structures of respectful public appearance become so deeply interwoven that the personal becomes to some degree structural and the structural becomes personal. The apparent form is no longer merely an armor that shields us from unwarranted public expressions of prepersonal pulsations, pulsions, ambitions, and exalted aspirations in our intrasphere. It also lets our personal respect come through; it manifests those formerly prepersonal feelings and dispositions that have now been transformed in the light of traditional appearance structures.

The same respect protects us against the power of one another's uniqueness by means of the apparent form and the formal structures of appearance that we now embody graciously. In some way they have become a part of us; they prevent us from overimposing on one another. Some of them will now become impersonal at many moments of our life. This means that we are able to live personalized directives in a prefocal gracious fashion without giving them our full personal attention at every moment.

Everyday Rituals of Privacy Protection

Common structures of the apparent form, personalized or not, protect our privacy. Sharing in the same form traditions, we recognize in each other the signs of a request for privacy. We perceive the contraction of the intrasphere in tone of voice, change of posture, gesture, or facial expression. Withholding may be communicated by changing the subject, addressing somebody else, excusing oneself to go to the salad bar or rest room, concentrating on food or drink. The same holds for the intimacy of shared privacy. Signs are exchanged that announce the contraction of one's privacy in reference to those with whom one shares it. Examples of such ritual signs, connoting a certain intimacy in our cultural form traditions, are private hints, allusions, smiles, frowns, and winks, all of which exclude others who are present.

Privacy contraction rituals are commonly known and accepted within specific form traditions. They provide us with a protective commonality that leaves us free to be ourselves apart from others. Such commonality in appearance makes us look and behave like everyone else. We do not stand out and give others the chance to analyze and scrutinize our private life. Commonality of apparent life-form secures a timely anonymity that enables us to grow inwardly, unencumbered by the pressure to share our growth prematurely with others.

There are facets of our unfolding intrasphere that we do not yet fully understand ourselves. During our formation history, we slowly disclose the form directives such inner events imply or demand. Then we give consonant form to them in the light of our growing apprehension, appraisal, and affirmation. Before the process of inner formation has sufficiently clarified such inner features, it could be disastrous to expose them to others who may not be able to share our inner struggle or respect our search for our unique call to the service of humanity.

Limits of Privacy Protection by Means of Our Apparent Life-Form

Formation scientists believe that the apparent form is an indispensable facet of human existence. Being but one facet, it should never substitute for our actual human form as a whole. The apparent form should serve, not eliminate, the foundational, core, and current forms of human presence. We may become so identified with our apparent form that we lose touch with our inwardness and its interwovenness with the other life-forms. In that case, instead of safeguarding our privacy, it isolates and paralyzes our inwardness. We not only succeed in concealing our intrasphere from others; we also conceal it from ourselves. Too much privacy protection can be as deformative as too little.

All of us to some degree engage at times in such overprotection. We know so little about the dynamics of our intrasphere; we may feel so insecure in this mysterious realm, so threatened by seemingly confident people who emerge in our inter- and outer spheres, that we succumb to a mere apparent life in utter conformity to others.

Our search for the unique form we are called to be moves between two poles. At times we try to disclose our calling by means of identification of our apparent form with that of others. At other times we seek disclosures by presence to our intrasphere and its preforming roots. Both modes of disclosure can be effective if they complement each other consonantly. Through successive identifications of our apparent form with those of others, we disclose possibilities for concrete formation we would not have known otherwise. In inward disclosure we become aware of whether the apparent forms we adopted tentatively are congenial. Without an alive intrasphere, utilizing dialogically both modes of disclosure, there could be no such thing as a personal form of life. There would only be form-types shared with similar people.

If we are never alone with our private appraisals and inmost dispositions, how can we come to know who we are? Absorbed in our apparent form we lose our interiority. Thus the external safeguards of privacy should never take over. They are meant not only to protect the outer conditions for privacy but also to give us the space we need to disclose ourselves inwardly to ourselves.

Restoration of Inwardness

Human life can sustain its apparent form only for reasonable periods of time. There have to be pauses during which the intrasphere can reassert itself fully. During such moments of restoration of inwardness, human life should take leave, so to speak, from its concentration on its appearances in the inter- and outer spheres. During this respite, we should celebrate our intraspheric life. We can do so by ourselves alone or in intimacy with those who share key aspects of our interiority by affinity, empathy, and confirming appreciation.

At times the intrasphere calls us back to creative solitude by experiences of emptiness, of feeling drained or dissipated, tense and irritable. We feel the need for withdrawal in external conditions of privacy so that our inner life may be renewed in presence to the preforming mystery in our interiority.

In certain periods of our formation history, a momentary turn inward in total privacy seems mandatory for consonant formation. These moments occur during decisive formation events, such as the loss of a loved one, serious illness, marital crisis, or the transcendence crisis of moving from one current form of life to another. At such junctures of our formation history, the energy invested in the apparent form may be withdrawn as much as possible and directed toward inner formation. This explains why people bearing the agony of the loss of a child or spouse, or facing a transcendence crisis, are temporarily, as we say, "not really with it" in the outer spheres of their daily existence.

CHAPTER 11

Privacy and the Polarity of Intraformation and Interformation

I ntra- and interformation are complementary movements of life's consonant unfolding. There is a time for intraformation in solitude and for interformation in togetherness. It is a question of prominence. When we live prominently in the intrasphere we feel in due course the need for communion with others and for involvement in the inter- and outer spheres. Conversely, when we are prominently engaged in the inter- and outer spheres, sooner or later a need for privacy may announce itself. The point of return to such inwardness is the movement of formative reflection.

Formative and Informative Reflection

In formative reflection we distance ourselves both from our immediate involvement and from the kind of reflection that is merely informative. Informative reflection, too, implies a break with our immediate engagements, but this break is not total. The reflection restricts itself to an exclusive appraisal of useful information gained in the outer sphere in order to apply it to specific situations themselves in practical ways. The purpose of informative reflection is to improve as directly as possible one's effective handling of inter- and outer situations.

Formative reflection, on the contrary, breaks with the inter- and outer spheres in their immediacy. We ask ourselves what an experience means in terms of in-depth formation of our inner sphere. We may question whether we should be involved in this or that project, in view of our unique calling to serve humanity in some way.

Formative reflection is as necessary as informative. One should complement the other. Without formative reflection we cannot restore centeredness. To remain centered, we must integrate congenially the differentiations of our outer sphere into our inner life and its preformative roots. We should remember here that our life of consonant formation is a rhythm of intraspheric integration and inter- and outer-spheric differentiation. The integrative potency of the intrasphere increases with its ingathering of the pulsations, pulsions, ambitions, aspirations, and inspirations that are alive in this sphere. Such integration facilitates further integration of new outer differentiations of our life-form.

No matter how profound the integration of both intra- and outer coformants may be, we always sense inside a certain aloneness. In contrast to the sphere of interformation, in this inner domain we are not in immediate contact with others. Hence, we feel joyful when we meet another human being in whom we sense respect, affinity, empathy, and confirmation. We enjoy a feeling of shared privacy in this meeting of intraspheres.

In our attempts to disclose to each other certain aspects of our private life, we ourselves become more clear about what moves us inwardly. Attempts to articulate it for others delineate its features more distinctly for us. Disclosure also makes us more aware of the ultimate mystery of our intrasphere. We realize that we cannot completely articulate for others what we are. We can sense, but we do not exhaustively know, our mystery. We can only point to that in us which cannot be put into words, even for ourselves.

Formation Theory and Creative Polarity
of Intraformation and Interformation

Why does consonant human formation imply that we communicate at the appropriate time to trustworthy others some of our private feelings and appraisals?

To understand the necessity of communication, we have to return to the formation theory of human unfolding. Our life does not form itself and the outer spheres of its formation field in the same way as animals, plants, and minerals are formed. Nonhuman formation is always the result of anonymous formative processes and forces whose meaning and direction fall outside the subject's awareness and control. Unlike these other kinds of life, human life receives and gives form in relative freedom. To be sure, the form reception and donation of the human form is also conditioned. A vast variety of formative determinants impinge upon its emergence. Because of these determinants human beings are limited in their freedom.

Formation freedom in humans does not reside primarily in outer control but in an inner, distinctively human potency rooted in the intrasphere. Ours is a relatively free form potency, one which enables us to give formative direction inwardly to the determinations influencing us during our life history. Within these limits, humans are the architects of their own formation. Ours is thus a relatively free form potency responsible for its own apprehension, appraisal, and affirmation of formation directives.

The human form does not find itself alone in its formation field in a solipsistic manner. It is always a project of this field in relation to others who are also projects of their field. This fact opens out the dimension of interformation, which again limits our personal freedom. Each human inhabits a different formation field because of each person's unique preformation, intraformation, and formation history. At the same time we share this field with others. Humans can never totally "do their own thing." Some mode of interformation is always operative in every choice. A choice is never absolutely independent from interformative influences. Conversely, any choice made by one human form of life affects to some degree the formation freedom of others.

Risk of Disclosure of Our Intrasphere

There is always a chance that what we disclose of our intrasphere will be misinterpreted, rejected, betrayed, or frustrated. In other words, to move from the intra- into the intersphere of one's formation field implies at least a minimum of risk. Without taking this risk, we would remain imprisoned in the sterile process of a closed-off intraformation. We would refuse to acknowledge that our sources of growth include not only pre- and intraformation but also inter- and outer formation. Consonant living implies a creative polarity between intra- and interformation, between private and public life. This polarity is usually latent and mainly prefocal. It becomes manifest and focal when we have to make a decision. Every decision implies a risk. We have no absolute certitude, only probabilities about what may transpire in the inter- and outer spheres of our formation field as a result of our decisions and how such happenings may affect our lives. In addition, we realize with some fear that we have to live up to the responsibility of our choices and all their consequences. This explains, for example, the crisis people go through before deciding to marry, initiate a friendship, start a new job, or choose where to study.

People may try to avoid the tension of consonant living in the totality of their formation field. They may hide in an engulfing privacy sphere, becoming secretive, unresponsive, and exclusive. They live sphinxlike lives, lonely, suspicious, and uncommunicative. Intraformation necessarily becomes stilted when all dialogue with the inter- and outer spheres is silenced. The disclosures of preformation itself are withheld from the intrasphere if it is not in dialogue with inter- and outer formation. This dialogue awakens the intrasphere to what one might become in service of humanity.

The opposite way of escape from the intra-inter tension of consonant formation is to deny one's inner life. We forsake privacy, abdicate a life of personal responsibility, and cease to engage in free apprehension, appraisal, and affirmation. Life is lived in blind conformity to a popular interconsciousness promoted by one or another mainly functional form traditions.

Formative Responsibility
and Overprotection or Underprotection of Privacy

Formative responsibility is the ability as well as the readiness to respond in free form reception and donation to the consonant challenges of our basic preformation *and* to those of our inter- and outer spheres. To hear these challenges, we must avoid the extremes of over- and underprotection of our privacy. When we are too fearful of the risk of expanding our intrasphere communicatively into the intersphere, we fall into the trap of overprotection of privacy. This anxious protectiveness somehow communicates itself to others, for we always coform each other. This prefocal communication of our embodied protectiveness will necessarily breed protectiveness in the other. If both of us are on guard anxiously, the human quality of our interformative togetherness will be low, perhaps almost nonexistent. If we remain politely enclosed in our intrasphere, our ability and readiness to respond freely and spontaneously cannot be exercised.

Conversely, underprotection of our privacy, the abdication of any caution and reserve, is potentially deformative, too. In this case we try to respond exclusively to the challenges of interformation. We close ourselves off from our own unique preformation and its particular disclosures to our intra-sphere during and through our dialogue with the challenges posed by the inter- and outer spheres. We neglect to respond to the demands of congeniality. We lose our inner freedom the minute our formation becomes exclusively directed by others.

When the creative polarity of an interformative relationship between two people is lost, the dominant party may initially relish his or her power. In the long run, mutual resentment is the result. True communion can only unfold between two self-aware, freely embodied intraspheres. Hence, a marriage may not last if one partner depletes his or her intrasphere because of total subjection to the direction of the other. The dominating partner becomes dissatisfied, often unwittingly, and may seek for other outside partners with whom one can "really talk." Timely solitude fostering the recentering of one's interiority is the basis of consonant interformation in depth between people. Friendship and love are a meeting between two solitudes.

Appropriate Closure and Disclosure of One's Intrasphere

Consonant life formation implies the art and discipline of congenial, compatible, and compassionate closure and disclosure of one's intrasphere. We are formed in this by trial and error. Some experiences of interformation are rewarding; others are disappointing. Our growth in this art also depends on our growth in consonance, in intraformative freedom, in firmness and gentleness, in wise apprehension and appraisal. Unlike animal forms of life, the human form can opt for the right moment of response. We are not bound to the reflexes and consequent immediate reactions of animal interformation. We can delay our response as long as we appraise that such delay is appropriate, that it is in service of a distinctively human interformation marked by congeniality, compatibility, and compassion.

Interformation that is based on the mutual sharing of one's private life can reach intimacy in some cases. Yet even the deepest intimacy cannot disclose to ourselves or others the ultimate mystery of who we are. Moments of disappointment in one another are bound to occur. The deeper the intimacy, the more severe the shock of disappointment. In such a crisis of failed expectations, we are thrust back momentarily on our own interiority. It was this private life with its aspiration after communion that inspired us in the first place to meet the other in intimacy. Wounded, we now return to this center. We dwell there to restore ourselves. When we are restored and centered again, the same rhythm of formation will awaken in our contracted intrasphere the aspiration to expand again in interformation and intimacy. This ongoing rhythm of the alternating prominence of intra- and interformation will be with us during our entire life history.

Intimacy makes us vulnerable. Our intrasphere becomes a shelter in times of failed interformation. Initially, interformation disappoints us because of the illusion that it might totally relieve the loneliness of our intrasphere. There are secret longings in all of us for the past careless absorption of the intrasphere into that of our mothers. This prompts our exalted anticipations of intimate interformation.

Formation History of the Intrasphere

Our intrasphere is at first absorbed in our inter- and outer spheres, in people, events, and things emerging in our formation field. Life is prepersonal, prefocal, careless, and irresponsible. Gradually, however, our distinctively human form potency awakens us to formative reflection. It draws us into our intrasphere. There we begin to disclose the roots of our ongoing preformation by the mystery and their effect on our unique, inner, silent dialogue with the formative influences in our inter- and outer spheres of life. We experience that this disclosure and dialogue generate a private life that no one can penetrate in its depth. We alone are the responsible shepherds of this unfolding interiority. The moment we acknowledge this inner mysterious sphere we find ourselves alone.

Our latent formation anxiety is awakened by this experience of solitary responsibility for the disclosure and implementation of a unique inner form of life that begins to announce itself. This is the birth cry of the intrasphere. To discover the call of our uniqueness is to suffer solitude. We realize that we alone can make our home in our own interiority. Yet we have to venture out in compatible and compassionate inter- and outer formation. We have to make our peace with strangers who can never wholly share that inner home in which we feel exiled from the chattering multitudes.

We can, therefore, expand the limits of our privacy, but we can never transmit all of it, even in deepest intimacy. It may be initially frightening, even agonizing, to become aware of an intrasphere that is ours alone. For we realize that it can never be shared wholly with anyone else, that the paradise of infancy is over. Our new awareness, born from formative reflection, is like the angel with the flaming sword making it impossible to enter the Eden of a totally shared intimacy ever again. No wonder people try to escape this burden by identification with a public interconsciousness that is functional and forgetful of inwardness. Hence, many are attracted to functional faith and form traditions that help them escape from freedom and responsibility, especially from the pain of solitude.

The price people pay for this escape is high. If we do not risk the solitary stance with all its initial anxiety, misery, and loneliness, we will never achieve interformation in depth with others and fruitful interaction with things and events in our formation field. Trying too anxiously to gain and maintain exclusively a public life means the loss of our privacy. Our true inner form of life can only disclose itself when we escape a merely public life by personal formative reflection. The path to integral living is painful but the mystery of formation will come to meet us when we signal our readiness by entering this narrow road. In the end, it will reveal itself as the royal road of liberation.

Once we are at home in our interiority, we acknowledge the inviolable uniqueness and the ultimate unknowability of the formation story of others, too. This prepares us for a solid commitment to social justice, compatibility, consideration, and compassion, nourished by awe for the formation mystery enlightening all of us in unpredictable ways. We realize more and more that it would not profit us to win the friendship of people in the inter- and outer spheres of our formation field if that meant losing our intrasphere and the animating preformation that gives form to it uniquely.

Privacy as Basis of Universal Interformation

The solitude of privacy should contract our intrasphere enough to protect it, when necessary, against absorption and distraction by our inter- and outer spheres. Privacy makes possible formative reflection, which discloses ways in which to implement in our empirical everyday existence our preempirical foundational life-form. This fundamental form, which is pointed to in our preformation, slowly reveals itself first in our intrasphere under the influence of formative reflection on the events taking place in our inter- and outer spheres. Reflective concentration in the inner sphere may initially take us away from what is going on in the inter- and outer spheres. Gradually we may discover in our interiority formation dynamics that are foundational; we become aware of a universal formation mystery that fills us with awe. In this way, solitude yields its ultimate treasure.

The discovery of the formation mystery as the foundation of our unique life formation and that of all others is awesome. Awe-filled presence to the mystery and its epiphanies in self, others, and world enables us at the same time to be faithful to its original epiphany in us and to participate in the awe others are called to cultivate in regard to their own epiphany of the mystery. It is this shared awe that binds us lovingly together as unique centers of generosity in this world. It unites us also with the cosmos as another reflection of the mystery. Though we are unique, we share the same origin. We are called to revere each other in the Wholly Other.

Stages of Formative Differentiation of the Intrasphere

The intrasphere of the human form has to be differentiated from its inter- and outer spheres. Consonant life formation fosters this differentiation, but it does not happen at once. This differentiation of the intrasphere is never finished. Maturation means that we grow less dependent on the intrasphere of others while gradually enlarging our own intrasphere in its relative independence. In other words, at different times during our personal formation history we are challenged to transcend formerly shared aspects of the intrasphere of others and to come into our own.

The formation history of people is marked by periods of decisive transcendence from a past current intrasphere to a new current one. We will consider here only three of these transcendence periods: childhood, adolescence, and, more specifically, young adulthood. The latter will be the object of special attention because it marks the period of a definite transcendence of the intrasphere we shared with our family and with the particular version of the form traditions to which they adhered.

Intraspheric Differentiation in Childhood

We referred previously to the differentiation of the intrasphere of the child from that of the mother. For a long time after birth, children share the intrasphere of their mothers. Because they are not yet aware of their own intrasphere, they feel compelled to share everything with her. That children share the intrasphere of their mother, as if it were their own, is manifested in the fact that they tell her things they would tell no one else. The ongoing dynamics of human formation, however, move children gradually to differentiate their own intrasphere from that of their mothers. A first disclosure of their intrasphere occurs in the surprising realization that they can have thoughts, feelings, and images no one else can know or suspect. Children experience for the first time the possibility of an inner life that escapes intrusion by their parents. They become aware of a sphere that is exclusively their own. This differentiation of their interiority makes them aware that they are distinct from their parents as well as from anything or anyone else appearing in their inter- and outer spheres. To have private thoughts, feelings, and fantasies; to know how to conceal them from others; and to let others in only by one's own decision, are first steps in the formation of an intrasphere and a private life of one's own.

Children not only hide their private knowledge; they also like to tell about it. In this communication they want to show and verify for themselves that they have an interiority, an inner space of their own. In addition, by divulging something of their private knowledge, they show that they can freely decide to open their own intrasphere to people in whom they themselves choose to confide. By playing with knowledge, feelings, and fantasies of their own, inaccessible to others, their intrasphere and private life begin to form. Then, by allowing others into that intrasphere, freely and by choice, they affirm the reality of this new intraformative potency and elicit its confirmation by others.

If this early differentiation fails, one may later be faced with the deformation of becoming a person who can never bear to keep anything to himself or herself, who always has to tell everything to somebody in authority. This may be an infantile attempt to restore the fusion of one's own, never well-differentiated intrasphere with that of another. Certain immature or power-hungry authorities, insufficiently prepared spiritual directors, gurus, and counselors may abuse and foster such infantile tendencies in their admirers.

Intraspheric Differentiation in Young Adulthood

Over the years this differentiation deepens and expands. More specifically, adolescence is a period in which young people begin to live increasingly a life of their own that mirrors their attempt to expand their own intrasphere and their privacy. In present-day culture, the period of intraspheric differentiation occurs for many in young adulthood, mostly in the early and sometimes in the later twenties. In this formation phase, the human form tries to transcend the adolescent intrasphere, which is still too embedded in the family.

In my book *The Transcendent Self*, I stressed that, from the viewpoint of the science of formation, crises of transcendence happen not only in adolescence or in middle life; they recur all through one's formation history when a current life-form has to be transcended by another current form because of the dynamic of transcendence typical of human life. These are normal formation crises that do not necessarily require psychotherapeutic or psychiatric treatment as do psychoses and serious neuroses. If help is needed, it can best be given by a formation counselor or director who is especially trained to help people with normal formation problems and crises.

Such transcendence crises, though not primarily the field of the psychotherapist or psychiatrist but of the formation specialist, are unsettling and often perilous. To people not conversant with formation science, they may look like an indication of psychopathology. If the symptoms appear that way, it usually means that the normal transcendence of aspects of the familial intrasphere was not sufficiently facilitated at the appropriate time by family formation or that it was even condemned, resented, or ridiculed. These families themselves may have been formed personally or communally by dissonant accretions of their form traditions. These may have fostered in turn the belief that any gain in one's independent intrasphere is a sign of pride or self-centeredness, manifesting a lack of family or community spirit, and so on.

Temporary Distancing from Familial Intrasphere

Young adults are entitled to a private inner life of their own. They have a right to the protection of privacy that the fullness of personal interiority demands. The process of differentiation of an adult intrasphere implies some distancing from one's inter- and outer spheres insofar as they mirror uncritically the intrasphere of one's family. The human life-form at this stage must be stripped of uncritically absorbed intrafamilial dispositions. This may lead to a painful state in young adults. Their own intrasphere is not yet sufficiently deepened, amplified, and adapted in its distinctiveness to make them feel sure about how to give form to their life. Intrafamilial form directives, as expressed in their inter- and outer spheres, are suspended by them, at least for the time being. They are in a kind of limbo, in the midst of a transcendence crisis, not yet knowing to what they are transcending. This transcendence phase ends when these young adults find their amplified intrasphere, rooted in the disclosures of their unique preformation and compatible with the adult life they now enter not merely as representatives of their family but as responsible persons with an intrasphere that is fully their own.

The science of formation refers to these three stages as pretranscendent, transcendent, and posttranscendent in relation to the current intraform of life. Because this specific type of transcendence crisis can also be called a differentiation crisis, its phases are also named predifferential, acute differential, and postdifferential. Formation scientists emphasize the ordinary and necessary character of such crises of increasing differentiation of one's formation field. They are formative in a creative way, for they make possible the reformation and amplification of our intrasphere and our private life.

The intrafamilial sphere resembles in a significant way the form traditions and accretions to which the family adheres. These traditions and their dissonant accretions have been objectified in certain segments of a functionally organized society. Hence, distancing from the intrafamilial life directives, as objectified in the inter- and outer spheres, often implies taking distance from similar objectifications of the familial traditions and accretions in society at large. Such distancing does not take away the human yearning for intimacy and communion. Hence, we notice the inclination in certain young adults during this phase of transcendence to find communion with others on the basis of a similar search for a deepened, more personal interiority, temporarily separated from the traditional structures of family and society.

A certain idealistic longing may be awakened for a deeper communion with people who share awe for the mystery that appears as a unique epiphany in each human life and in the whole of creation. This explains a newly emerging interest during this transcendence period in the spiritual or even mystical aspect of religious faith and form traditions and temporarily less interest in the study of the organizational and technical-theological aspects of the same. It explains also the attraction of cults during this period of transition.

Prevalence of Form Receptivity

When young people are in such a crisis of differentiation, form receptivity prevails over form giving. They suspend their usual way of giving form to their parentally shared intrasphere. Up to this period, form donation occurred in the image of familial dispositions. Young people do not yet know how to give form uniquely to their own intrasphere and with it to their life-form as a whole. Hence, they are more receptive to the unique life formation the mystery may inspire through its presence in the preformation at the root of their intrasphere. Their need to suspend intrafamilial directives of formation may make them turn to the formative powers within themselves. They may sense that these are greater than those that dominate functionally the everyday structures of their usual surroundings. They may also seek for spiritual guidance outside the family in those fundamental writings and representatives of form traditions that claim to point the way to the interior life.

In tribal form traditions elaborate initiation rituals dramatized these changes. The post-tribal classical form traditions of the West have less contact with these formative phases in the intrasphere of people. They offer fewer traditional rituals to help them through this crisis. Ideological form traditions, especially the predominantly functional ones, produce no ritual at all that is relevant to the intrasphere. Their preoccupation with functional-vital formation leaves people directionless when faced with critical phases of further differentiation of their inner life. The result is that one's intraspheric crisis is frequently not acknowledged or appreciated. Often there are no experienced adults available to direct one through the dark, empty tunnel of such a period. One may be left on one's own to seek support and enlightenment where one can. Original form receptivity to the mystery, awakened at such moments, deteriorates easily into indiscriminate passivity, gullibility, and submissiveness in regard to any fascinating leader or movement promising a way of life that goes beyond intrafamilial and functional-social directives.

Loss of the shared intrasphere of the family is painful and shocking for many. They may feel guilty or angry about it, gloomy or depressed; at other times they may feel the elation of liberation. Until a fuller intrasphere of their own is disclosed, they may be tempted to refuse to share wholeheartedly in the usual routines of life in their surroundings. Having lost their rootedness in their own interiority, their sense of responsibility may be suspended until they can give social routines a new meaning on the basis of their private convictions. Gradually they realize that their inner life is not isolated from the inter- and outer spheres of their concrete formation field. They learn by trial and error that the disclosure of their preformative life direction, also in their fully personal intrasphere, depends on interformative dialogue with this concrete field and its underlying form traditions. This leads to the emergence of a congenial intraformative sphere, fully their own yet obedient to the mystery and compatible and compassionate with people, events, and things in their inter- and outer spheres. The differentiation crisis is over until new formation events coincide to evoke a new crisis. Differentiation crises are part of the ordinary formation process. To understand this process is already an immense relief: one is normal! The process can also be facilitated by formation counselors enlightened by the study of this science.

Duration of a Differentiation Crisis

We cannot predict how much time a specific crisis of differentiation may take. Its duration depends partly on the biogenetic and transcendent preformation of people, as modulated by initial formation, and on the related conformity or compatibility dispositions they have developed before the onset of the differentiation crisis. Traumas experienced during one's preceding formation history also influence the duration and intensity of the differentiation process. In addition, the period can be lengthened or shortened by favorable or unfavorable conditions in one's environment and the availability or unavailability of formal or informal formation counselors or directors. The process can be unduly prolonged if it is misunderstood as a symptom of severe neurosis or latent psychosis and treated as such over the long term by specialists from fields other than formation. This is not to deny that latent neurotic or psychotic symptoms may manifest themselves on the occasion of a differentiation crisis. In such an event, the cooperation of experts from other fields should be sought by the formation counselor or director. Since it is dependent on all of these factors, the time to work through this crisis may take from a few months to a year or more.

Differentiation Anxiety

The first task of the formation counselor or director is to clarify for people that what they experience as unusual or aberrant thoughts, feelings, and actions are an ordinary and necessary acceleration of the formation process of their life. The unrest they feel is ordinary differentiation anxiety, one of the many forms formation anxiety can take in our life. It is evoked by a newly emerging awareness—the prefocal, pressing insight that one's intrasphere must differentiate itself more definitely from the inter- and outer spheres.

We feel challenged to make our inner life more distinct from that of others. We sense the need to become more fully responsible for our own intraformation and therewith for its personal expansion into the outer spheres. Because the differentiation of our intrasphere is never totally finished, because it is always open to contestation, differentiation crises of varied intensity may emerge at any time in life. The dynamics of differentiation anxiety during young adulthood are grounded in the fear of what may happen to us if we lose the familial support we have been leaning on securely and unquestioningly until this moment of inner appeal to complete the differentiation of our intrasphere.

In the transcendence from a less to a more differentiated intrasphere, people are figuratively dying to a familial formation field that was, up to that moment, most supportive to them. They sense the radical loss of a still partially shared intraformation that previously gave direction to their life. A formation counselor or director should provide insight into the differentiation crisis, showing how it can be a basis for understanding the complexities and controversial feelings and dispositions to which a person in crisis and those with whom they live are exposed.

Predifferential, Acute Differential, and Postdifferential Phases of Crisis

Indeed, formation counseling or direction may be beneficial also for the people who have to live with those who are in a differentiation crisis. To them it may look like a sudden change of formation dynamics demanding medical treatment instead of ordinary formation counseling or direction. It should be explained to them that this sudden manifestation has its roots in a far longer preparatory differentiation process during which prefocal doubts accumulated in regard to one's overdependency on the intrasphere of the family. The sudden change in formation dynamics is only the tip of the iceberg. The predifferentiation phase of the crisis has been forming prefocally for a long time. A seemingly sudden change is the outward manifestation of entrance into the acute differentiation phase of the crisis.

When the deeper and more ample differentiation of one's own intrasphere has taken place, it will be followed by a postdifferential phase. Postdifferentiation is marked by a gradual reintegration of past and present form directives in the reformed current intrasphere. The predifferentiation phase leads up to the acute differentiation crisis. This phase is usually *prefocal*. This lack of awareness does not prepare people for the jolt they may experience when they suddenly become *focally* aware that they have been drifting away from the shelter and safety of the familial intrasphere. This experience can be traumatic, leading to a continuing perplexity during the beginning stages of the acute crisis and causing a somewhat spaced-out look in the eyes of the surprised sufferer. Although all of this is still within the range of ordinary crises of people's inner formation history, we should not underestimate the severity of this jolt.

The loss of inner form direction, the emotional suspension of intrafamilial directives, and the disorientation of the appraisal capacity may be felt for months after this shock has abated. Family members may exacerbate the crisis by expressing scorn about a seeming rejection of certain familial appraisals. These were cherished by persons when their intrasphere was still imbued by and identified with the familial intrasphere. For example, the family appraisal of blacks or other minorities may have been unwittingly discriminatory. Young adults may no longer feel the way their parents did in this regard. Their own intrasphere seems to form a different social sensitivity.

People in search of a more distinctive differentiation of their intrasphere are ambivalent. They may love their family, but at the same time inner formation dynamics compel them to create room for the unfolding of still vulnerable, initially hesitant, more distinct interior appraisals of their own. Meeting or expecting silent or open resistance, some may feel frustrated, angry, or hostile. A stance of cold distance or irritation, and even offensive words, acts, and appearance, are nourished partly by the prefocal fear that any milder way of presence to the family will draw them back again into the familial intrasphere and prevent, perhaps forever, the emergence of a definitely distinct, fully intraformative life of their own.

Surrender to Spiritual Guides and the Danger of Excessive Form Receptivity

While distancing themselves from parental and parent-related authority, young adults feel the need for a kind of authority that is expert in pointing the way to the inner life. They momentarily feel less need for intimate interaction with those authorities who are mainly responsible for functional administration and organization, or scholarly authorities who specialize in theoretical issues. Lost for the time being in their search for interiority, they look for experiential enlightenment about the art of living and the mystery of their inner life. They may find such guides during the acute crisis of intraspheric differentiation. Rightly or wrongly they ascribe to them penetrating powers of apprehension and appraisal of their predicament and its solution. They may surrender to them in their anxious quest, ready to listen with the fullness of their form receptivity, which, as we have seen, is at this moment onesidedly dominant in their formation process, silencing form donation.

The hazard of this middle phase of the crisis is in fact excessive form receptivity. Such excess tends to exclude even the necessary minimum of inner critical form donation in regard to the apprehension, appraisal, and affirmation of the claims and counsels of such guides. Unscrupulous, power-hungry directors, who have an exalted vision of their own wisdom, who are poorly prepared for this precarious task, and who are insufficiently rooted in classical faith and form traditions, may take advantage of young people in their desperate search for an interior life of their own, yet one that is rooted in a mystery that transcends their familial and functional society.

For one thing, such directors may prolong unnecessarily the state of overdependent form receptivity and delay the postdifferentiation phase of active reintegration into society. We want to stress again that the state of somewhat onesided form receptivity and subsequent dependency is not necessarily abnormal in this formation phase. Usually it can be handled by a well-prepared formation counselor or director without recourse to medical treatment.

Ascetic Aspect of Differentiation Crisis

The need to differentiate an intrasphere that is more fully one's own may lead temporarily to certain ascetic and sacrificial practices that may be somewhat excessive. One harbors a vague suspicion that one has failed to find an inner life of one's own due to participation in certain functional self-centered life directives that were prominent in the familial and social intrasphere. To attain as fast as possible a purer interiority of one's own, one may accept any discipline without question if it seems to promise liberation from functionalistic and vitalistic self-centeredness.

Such ascetic distancing from one's family should be carefully appraised. Emotional appeals to return to the previous intrafamilial sphere may be apprehended as a dangerous temptation. One may feel compelled to resist them at all costs, even if it means leaving one's home and neighborhood. Once a current form of life has lost its persuasive power, one cannot return uncritically to its dispositions. Consonant formation demands that one travel through the desert of no-form in search of a new current form of life that is more wisely rooted in the foundations of a consonant form tradition. A formation crisis is resolved in its own time. It cannot be terminated at will. Premature closure of the process leaves the main issues unresolved and can lead to depresssion, passivity, asocial behavior, and other deviations.

Temporary Suspension of Functional Vigor

The quest for a differentiation of one's intrasphere in depth, the suspension of certain functional accomplishments in the intrafamilial sphere, and the prevalence of form receptivity may lead to a temporary reduction, if not a suspension, of the functional dimension of the human life-form. When one is no longer sure which inner form directives should be embodied in the inter- and outer spheres through one's functional potency, the functional dimension will be exercised less emphatically. The seeming paralysis of functional vigor is only passing. Once a fuller differentiation of one's inner life is achieved, rootedness in preformation, in the foundations of a consonant form tradition, and in the formation mystery will inspire new aspirations, ambitions, and dispositions that are congenial and vigorous. These in turn will stimulate one's functional potency to a new incarnation form giving in the inter- and outer spheres, in acts and projects of social justice, peace, and mercy.

In other words, the temporary suspension of pronounced functioning makes possible a far more effective and determined functioning when the differentiation crisis is over. The same applies to the functional mind. Most people in this crisis are temporarily less fascinated by ideological, philosophical, theological, and abstract theoretical issues. Critical interest in formal logic is replaced by fascination with inner experience, its truths and dynamics. Logical treatises on abstract systems of thought give way to poetry, novels, writings of spiritual masters and mystics, books on meditation, journals of experience—any writing that might illumine the inner quest. Once the differentiation has occurred, the functional mind may be stimulated to find rational justification, correction, completion, and integration of the newly developed interior directives. Inner experience is thus complemented by functional reason.

Initial Family Formation and Persistent Receptivity Dominance

Some people never seem to reach the postdifferential phase of the differentiation crisis. Nor does life allow them to return fully to the intrasphere of the family. Being adults, they have to take their place in society. Yet they have not developed an intrasphere that is fully their own. They remain onesidedly form receptive without the balance of creative and responsible form donation. They are in search of the intrasphere through fusion with some movement or group in which they can share as they once did as children in the family.

The source of such exclusive, debilitating form receptivity can usually be found in initial family formation. As children, they did not receive sufficient manifestations of the foundational formation triad of faith, hope, and love expressed in appreciation and confirmation of their own form giving potencies. Consequently they were not able to develop a consonant core form of life and the beginnings of a confident intrasphere with a private life of its own. As a result, they were not inwardly stimulated to fortify the functional dimension by form giving to their life and surroundings.

Often it is only when they have to leave home for study or work that they are faced with the task of separating themselves finally from the intrasphere of the family. They can no longer deny the challenge to form an intrasphere of their own. They experience the stress of losing their *shared* intrasphere only to find an emptiness where their *own* intrasphere should be. Yet the situation within which the symptoms of such stress manifest themselves is not their fault. At fault is the lack of initial formation in independence. Their parents may not have instilled confidence in the formation mystery and in their own life call, which may be different from that of other family members.

Intradifferentiation and Familial Formation Field

The science of formation has developed an extensive subtheory of form traditions. Accordingly it is concerned about the dynamics of family formation, since the family is the prime agent of transmission of form traditions. In the course of these investigations, a distinction was made between consonant and dissonant family formation. This distinction and its underlying formation dynamics can enlighten us about the success or failure of later differentiation crises. It is a basic intuition of the science that personal unfolding should always be understood in terms of a formation field. Applying this insight to children means that we can understand their formation or deformation only as an exponent, at least in part, of the familial formation field. If something goes wrong in the child's formation, the familial formation field as whole contributes to it in some way.

For example, a child whose behavior looks dissonant may make other family members prefocally feel much better because of the contrast between him and them. Hence, in prefocal ways, they may be less eager to help this child overcome unsympathetic behavior. What if parents feel needed by overdependent children? Then their excessive need to be needed may keep children in that role. A recalcitrant child may offer an occasion to vent one's anger and to feel justified in doing so. These are only a few examples of the numerous formation dynamics by means of which a seemingly consonant family can aggravate in a child a perhaps preformed inclination to dissonance. This negative influence leads necessarily to under- or overprotection of privacy in already dissonant children.

Because children share in the complex intrasphere of the family, one should not ascribe their problems merely to their own intrasphere and its private life. While this may be true of adults who more fully differentiated their own intrasphere, the same cannot be said of children, adolescents, and young adults who have not yet achieved such differentiation. Children do not apprehend, appraise, and affirm themselves independently from intrafamilial apprehension, appraisal, and affirmation. This appraisal is based partly on an implicit and prefocal consensus as to what formative role, consonant or dissonant, the child should play in the familial formation field. The formation counselor or director may enable the family to appraise focally the total structure of its formation field and its impact on the differentiation crisis of the person in question.

The same appraisal would apply to small, familylike communities that are fostered by certain faith and form traditions. It is often remarkable how one's seemingly "innate" dissonant life changes when the formation field changes. It is no longer necessary to maintain the dissonant role as a means of feeling holier or more needed as a defender of the true form tradition or of stepping into a higher position of trust in the community.

Accommodating Familial Formation Field

The structure of the familial formation field becomes especially important when it has to change its main function from formation protection to facilitation of personal intradifferentiation. At this crucial moment of full intraspheric formation, the familial field should lovingly accommodate this process. The family should facilitate the emergent fullness of a private life. It should promote the painful process of differentiating one's own interiority from that of the family.

Only the establishment of a personal intrasphere will enable young adults to cope effectively with the inter- and outer spheres outside the family field. Once this process of intradifferentiation is complete, one's consonant human form will resume normal interformative relationships with its family field, though now on an adult basis.

Oppressive Familial Formation Field

In certain families or familylike communities, the process of intradifferentiation may be experienced as a threat. People are forced into a dilemma. Should they remain absorbed in the intrasphere of the family or the familylike community? Should they risk painful rejection, isolation, or silent condemnation by those who remain absorbed in the shared intrasphere? Such secret or open disapproval may be more intense if the personal intradifferentiation of a member of the family or community is prefocally appraised as a threatening reminder of the lack of firmness in others who hesitate to face up to their own neglected task of intradifferentiation. They continue to remain absorbed in the familial or communal intrasphere, allowing their life formation to be basically bland and dependent on their need for total parental confirmation of any thought, disposition, feeling, or desire they develop.

When such children grow up, they may insist on living with their parents or at least staying in the old neighborhood. Typically their parents are likely to look upon this failure of intradifferentiation as normal, perhaps even as ideal. On the focal level they may express the desire for more initiative and independence in their grown-up children, but prefocally they seem blissfully unaware that their family formation field has effectively dampened any strong desire to develop such traits.

Another response to an absorbing familial intrasphere is an explosion of protest. The shared intrasphere, its apprehensions and appraisals, are increasingly challenged, often in an aggressive and offensive fashion. The family may respond by finally giving up on such offensive children, who then go their own way for better or worse. Then, too, the family may oppress by force any attempt at intradifferentiation. Their children may decide that the only way to assert some intrasphere of their own is dissonant and possibly deformative action. They may even resort to drastic separation measures, such as joining a radical political or religious movement, enlisting in the military, running away from home, getting pregnant, or entering into a premature marriage with a person who represents the opposite of the family's form ideals. To deny the intrasphere of the family may lead them to join a fanatic religious movement, if, for example, the familial intrasphere happens to be secularist. If the family is pious, the child's revolt against real or imagined oppression may express itself in the opposite way, namely, in aggressive secularity.

Concern with Underlying Formation Dynamics

What can formation science advise when a young-adult son or daughter, a directee, counselee, or student, engages in dissonant behavior as a response to the delayed or oppressed opportunity for personal intraformation? First of all, our attention should not be fixated on the dissonant behavior itself. Rather, we should be concerned in an empathic way with the formation dynamics behind it. What is the formative purpose of this action, separation, withdrawal, or aggression? Is it possibly a desperate attempt to free oneself from a shared intrafamilial or intracommunal sphere that is experienced, rightly or wrongly, as lethal for one's own intraformation? If this is the case, it is surely not an appropriate time for intimidation or recrimination. Such a response would be misunderstood and only serve to reinforce the underlying formation anxiety about being sucked back into the shared intrasphere and possibly paralyzed in one's own personal life formation. If parents or other significant formation personnel have not in the past warmly welcomed and shown profound respect for privacy, present admonitions will not be trusted. Instead we ought to manifest gently and consistently that the lines of a new respectful interformation are now available and will be kept open, no matter what.

We ought not to expect fast results. The disposition of distrust formed over years of discouragement of privacy cannot be reformed in a few weeks or months. People beginning to reclaim their own intraformation will take our outstretched hands only when they feel sure we will introject no new oppression of their inner initiatives. Restoration of trust takes time, lots of time. While waiting in patience, we must try increasingly to perceive and understand the deeper meaning of their seemingly aberrant behavior. We should realize that they may be convinced that we are not even ready to discuss with them the behavior of which we disapprove. If they are young adults, we should not necessarily agree with their way, but we should show that we respect their attempts to find their own intrasphere, independent of ours. We should not be misled by their bravado. Young adults, not yet able confidently to form a private inner life of their own, are deep down more in despair than they show, despite the victorious self-assurance they may feign to themselves and others. They easily appraise their lack of a sufficiently independent intrasphere as failure. Any depreciation of even their most obnoxious attempts to escape what they refer to as the suffocating intrasphere of the family may be more harmful than helpful.

We have acknowledged previously the importance of form images that are consonant, or that are at least more positive than negative. Young adults suffering a crisis of differentiation may have a weak set of formative images to begin with because of their discovery of this lack of a sufficient intrasphere of their own. This explains their differentiation crisis. Telling them how unwise, stupid, disgusting, or disappointing their attempts to privacy are, is a sign of negative and destructive interformation. It will serve only to strengthen and augment their already negative images, memories, and anticipations and weaken the few vulnerable, positive ones they have. Instead, we should show them our faith that they will find their own intraformative life and that they will learn by trial and error to appraise how to make this intrasphere not only congenial but also compatible, compassionate, competent, and effective. We should renew our faith and hope in the formation mystery's grant to every human life of the necessary resources it needs to reach its own unique destiny, no matter how wayward the road may temporarily be. In this faith we can find the equanimity that is quietly confirmative and reassuring to others.

It is impossible to live in consonant interformation with people who upset and disappoint us if we are not aware of the many conflicting dispositions and corresponding feelings they evoke. These may consist of disappointment and affection, frustrated love and shame for what others say, anger and guilt. These emotions should be sorted out, if necessary, with a formation counselor or director. Only when they are apprehended and appraised can we come to some equanimity and inner order. Otherwise we may discharge wildly unappraised dispositions and emotions. In the family, both we as parents and our children are left bewildered and disturbed, with less chance for restoring interformation. To grow in compassion with ourselves and our children, we should try to learn more about the plight of people in a differentiation crisis. This knowledge of formation will protect us against simplistic solutions and deformative misinformation.

Intrasphere and the Transcendent Dimension of the Human Life-Form

Not only the intrasphere but also the inter- and outer spheres of our life foster transcendent experiences. People may feel uplifted in mutual respect and love. The beauty of order in the cosmos carries for many a transcendent meaning. In the cultural sphere, artistic creations may elevate the mind to higher regions. Yet ultimately such experiences touch the intrasphere of people who are moved inwardly by signs and symbols. The transcendent dimension, while evoked by these outer manifestations, has its primary roots in our intrasphere.

The depths of our private life are a mystery both to ourselves and others. We can never fully fathom who we are. The roots of privacy reach deep into our preformation. It is the hidden realm from which we constantly emerge and which we never know exhaustively. This preformation in turn is grounded in the mystery of formation itself. Because of this depth, the human life-form is not hemmed in by its immediate surroundings; it is a longing to go beyond the boundaries of self and world. It points us to a realm beyond our appearance in space and time.

When this awareness breaks through, it may shatter our naive trust in our skills and achievements, in our power, status, and possessions. If we cultivate this awareness, it may grow even more deeply enlightened. The exaltation we feel over our petty projects crumbles. Negatively, our longing for a transcendent healing power discloses itself in our awareness of incompleteness, brokenness, and dissonance crying out for completion, wholeness, and consonance.

When the formation mystery lights up our intrasphere, our life stands etched in its limitations against this inner luminosity. We pierce the veil that hides the human form from its inner nobility. Our finitude begins to share in the fullness of this Presence. Consonant faith and form traditions appeal to this obscure sensitivity, overshadowed by our ignorance. They are meant to liberate us from the pain of idle craving, fomented by the denial of our deepest longing.

Our intrasphere, therefore, not only has historical, vital, and functional dimensions, but also a transcendent one. This is the potential openness of our interior life to the manifestations of the Divine. When the veil of this inner presence is lifted, we can see people, events, and things as they are in their own luminous meaning.

CHAPTER 12

Privacy, Solitude, Intrusion, and Sharing

The life of privacy stems from our preformation, which is grounded in turn in the formation mystery. This mystery marks the human form *preformatively* with potential uniqueness and privacy. The process begins already in the mother's womb, which is the formation field of the unborn child. This field is in tune with the primal cosmic field provided by the forming mystery for all emergent forms in nature, humanity, and history. The unborn child is touched profoundly by this omnipresent care. From the beginning, each human life is substantially united with this sacred power of formation.

When children are born and begin to mature, this original union beckons them to a union of consonance with the mystery. They sense this appeal prefocally. Later in life the remnants of this vital memory remain in the depths of our intrasphere, where we experience a secret longing to regain this lost consonance. It is this aspiration of the spirit that grants our life its distinctive humanness. It is this feature that no computer can ever duplicate.

Formative Participation and Distancing in Children

When the human person leaves its first formation field in the mother's womb, it must form a field of its own. Children receive and give form by formative participation in people, events, and things and in the traditions that permeate their surroundings. They reach out for a field of life that is pervaded and vitalized by a loving, caring presence. Anything the infant comes in touch with—a human finger, a shiny toy, a doll, or a teddy bear —is spontaneously endowed with an epiphanic warmth and radiance. The child searches first of all for vital intimacy, which kindles prefocally the latent aspiration for consonance. At this stage the promise of union is experienced in a seminal fashion.

Later, longing for intimacy is balanced by the need for distancing. Initial interformation in early childhood is necessarily dominated by identification with others, an identification that is almost prepersonal. The art of distancing liberates children for a more personal form reception and donation. It enables them to differentiate their formation field and their own presence in it more critically. They become able to engage in personal encounter. This means that they can be "in" with others while maintaining some "counter" features of their own. Formative distance thus complements formative participation.

Consonance with the Mystery

At privileged moments children may awaken to a consonance with the mystery that shines forth uniquely in people, events, and things. In infancy they tend to imagine that the caring presence that surrounds them is identical with the care of their parents. Later they may sense prefocally that a deeper mystery goes beyond the immediacy of their parents. They begin to long for consonance with that underlying presence that manifests itself in all of these appearances. Their human predisposition for consonance with the source of all that is is thus aroused. This moment of intimation awakens the awareness that they are already a prepresence to the epiphanic ground of the sacred.

Universal Human Yearning for Intimacy with the Sacred

A secret yearning for intimacy with the sacred pervades the human lifeform. When the mystery enables us to participate in its rhythm in the universe, our isolation is lessened. Every encounter begins to be appreciated in awe as related to this harmonious presence. Our participation in this great harmony is experienced most deeply in our intrasphere, in the abyss of our private life. There the mystery is nearer to us than we are to ourselves.

Our entire journey is a search in light and darkness for this epiphany at the root of our privacy. Its concealment is due partly to our bodiliness. We are enfleshed spirits. Our concrete life is embodied in this world; it is vital, sensate, pulsing, and ambitious in its need for concrete survival and self-assertion. Such worldly concerns can be distracting. They may veil for us the unique epiphany of the holy we are deep down. Because of our bodiliness, we are not wholly transparent to ourselves. We are a veiled existence, a hidden privacy. The depths of our intrasphere conceal themselves from our restless quest. Hence, we fall easily into illusions in our search for the sacred source that calls us forth. Such illusions are intensified and expanded by the exalting pride-form of life. It is perilous to seek the path without the support of consonant traditions and their enlightened representatives.

Prepresence to the Mystery

Let us reflect on the prepresence we always already are to the mystery. At birth, human life is set adrift in a foreign ambience out of which it has to fashion its own field of formation. We are no longer at home in the womb, symbolizing as it does the primal undifferentiated field of cosmic formation in its embrace by the mystery. Expelled from "paradise," the burden and beauty of formative dialogue is upon us, accompanying us until the end of our journey. In the course of this odyssey, an intrasphere of our own unfolds itself. In wavelike contraction and expansion, this sphere permeates the simultaneously unfolding inter- and outer spheres of our life.

Our spirit, through our intrasphere, illumines our presence in the world. In its light we may open ourselves receptively to the sacredness of people, events, and things in their deepest reality. Transcendent openness is the hidden source of stillness, equanimity, peace, and wholeness in our life. It helps us to center ourselves inwardly in the mystery.

Specification of Our Prepresence

Our bodiliness simultaneously conceals and unconceals our intrasphere. Our body betrays feelings and dispositions we would like to hide. Posture, movement, and facial expression announce what we may deny in speech. Our body is an exposition of our intrasphere. At the same time it limits and specifies how much can be revealed of what moves us inwardly. What totally transcends bodiliness cannot be adequately manifested by corporeal appearance.

Our bodiliness limits also our spiritual access to the presence of the holy in this world. Our senses specify the way in which we grasp people, events, and things as epiphanies of the sacred. Initially we experience the mystery in and through disclosures that are particular and, thus, attuned to our limited grasp. Many of these specific manifestations take place in the transcendent dimension of our intrasphere. Others appear in the outside world, yet they touch us inwardly. Examples of the latter are the love of a spouse or friend, the genuine respect of a student, the smile of a child, the peace and spontaneity of a consonant person, the beauty of a sunset, the fragrance of a flower in early spring, the mellowness of a sip of wine, the smell and taste of freshly baked bread. Each can be experienced as a trace of the all-forming mystery, which discloses something while concealing much more. Each disclosure is but a glimpse of the ineffability of the great presence that fills the universe, a glimpse that is at the same time a moment of discovery and of closure.

Epiphanic Intimations

Inner enlightenment, the song of the bird, the scent of a flower, the love of people who really care, are "epiphanic intimations." Each. of them grants a specific form to our predisposition to receive the universal mystery in our particularizing awareness. Such formative intimations should be experienced as feeble pointers to the ineffable they symbolize.

One or the other particular appearance may stand out for us as an epiphanic symbol of the holy that speaks to our heart. In this case, our aspiration for the ineffable may focus on that appearance. We give it our own meaning while assimilating it in our intrasphere. Where does that meaning come from? It emerges from the whole of our life as represented in our intrasphere. Our private life is filled with vitally affective memories, imaginations, and anticipations. Having become ours during our history of formation, they affect the transcendent meaning we give to each particular appearance.

For example, what a beautiful tree in blossom means to us depends on our past perceptions of trees; the role they played in our personal history; how they were presented to us in the symbols, pictures, and stories of our form tradition; the quality of our innate potency for vital sensitivity and expressivity; the power and liveliness of our imagination; and like factors. All of this pertains to the rich diversity of symbols and metaphors used by various poets to express the same spiritual experiences and aspirations.

A glimpse of the ineffable, via a symbolizing experience, is partly shared in interconsciousness with others, partly privatized because of the private aspects of our intrasphere through which our symbolizing search for the mystery has to pass. This makes the presence to the mystery of each human life-form personal and private while still in some way communal and shared with others. It is perilous to formation if we lose the sense of the symbol as pointing beyond itself to what cannot be spoken, even inwardly. There is so much of our own story in these symbols that we are tempted to make them and the larger intermediate wholes of which they are a part—such as nature, the cosmos, the wonder of formative evolution, the ideal of social justice—into *the* whole itself; *the* mystery of formation; *the* primordial truth, goodness, and beauty. These particulars and intermediate wholes may become too exclusive in our lives; they may assume for us the absolute markings of the mystery itself, which cannot be marked. In this way, we make idols out of symbols. We become fixated on something that expresses our personal history and vital pulsions, losing sight of the mystery that surpasses them infinitely.

We are especially inclined to identify the vital-functional dimension of our intrasphere as the ultimate source of formation. This leads to separateness and introspectionism. We put ourselves over against the formation field, manipulating it to suit our projects. An illusory private life arranges itself around this exalted functional dimension. It becomes a caricature of what we are called to be. Our heart swells up, full of itself. The functional dimension loses its meaning as a humble bridge between our interiority and exteriority.

To make the bridge by itself the center of our ambitions is to make it a substitute for the mystery. Vital pulsions, functional ambitions, and interiorized pulsations become our central concern. We suffer estrangement from the inmost source of our life, which is our ongoing preformation by the mystery.

This inner split is the root of self-deception, anxiety, pain, and suffering. Formation is no longer a mystery to be lived but a problem to be solved. The density of accumulated layers of vital-functional apprehensions, appraisals, memories, imaginations, and anticipations have *coiled* our intrasphere. They clamor for attention and obscure the transcendent awareness of our life call and its gradual disclosures. Transcendent reformation of our private sphere implies *uncoiling* in the light of a consonant tradition, which should be listened to in solitude.

Periodic Distancing in Service of Transcendence

Solitude seems mandatory for privacy since it fosters the growth of our inner life. Solitude frees us from functionalism; it readies us to meet the mystery. Unfortunately, solitude can lead to isolation. This happens when we deny our inter- and outer spheres, which are also manifestations of the mystery. An isolated interiority can never disclose all relevant form directives. Locked within a prison of privacy, we tend to shrivel up, like plants without water. It is equally true that interaction with the inter- and outer spheres can nourish our formation only when we digest this dialogue in the privacy of recollection.

Periodic distancing in service of transcendence is necessary for privacy. In such moments of stillness, we find ourselves at the center of things, where we share the transhuman life of the formation mystery and experience its epiphany in our own life. Who we are becomes a response to this transcendent call. We rise beyond formation ignorance, drawn by a distant glimmer of light. We are reborn in a place of repose where we can admit our flaws and face our vulnerability. We may even experience for a moment the ultimate simplicity of formation.

Shared Privacy

Imagine that you are a student in a foreign land. Among fellow students from your country are a number of friends with whom you talk about things at home. You enter wholeheartedly into the feelings you share. What the language means for each of you personally comes to life in animated words. You share images and dispositions alive in your intrasphere. You sense the mutual affinity of your private lives. Similar feelings are reflected in your eyes, facial features, gestures, bodily movements, and posture. Your show of appreciation confirms your friends in their disclosure of personal thoughts and feelings. Conversely, you feel confirmed in your own disclosures by their appreciation. Their flowing with you enables you to suspend your apparent form of life. You are able to be yourselves in one another's presence. In spontaneous interformation, you create a world filled with meaning for each of you. Your intrasphere extends accordingly as you experience the fruits of shared privacy.

The possibility of sharing our privacy may be limited for obvious reasons. People may be at home with each other in special realms, like those of aesthetic taste, religious aspiration, political ideals, concern for peace and justice, or love of nature. Their shared privacy will be shaped by the specificity of their affinity. Certain customs and rituals of form traditions may foster interformative intimacy in the realm of religious and ideological experience.

Shared Privacy and Integrative Forms of Life

The core, current, apparent, and actual forms of human presence represent the basic modes of human integration. Each of them has its own measure of privacy.

Our core form can be perceived as an inner region surrounded by three larger regions that represent, respectively, the current, apparent, and actual forms of life. The inner region shelters our deepest form dispositions with their attendant feelings and motivations. We may share them with the people closest to us, such as a spouse, an intimate friend, or a respectful formation counselor or director. Paradoxically, we may share these moments with strangers who cannot harm us and whom we may never meet again. This explains why people often communicate intimately with strangers they meet by chance seated beside them on an airplane.

The region of our current form is open to certain comrades, colleagues, and acquaintances close enough to be trusted. We may not tell them our deepest aspirations, but we do feel at ease talking with them about private cares and projects relevant to our family, profession, or similar situations that concern us currently.

The realm of the apparent form of life is sustained in its effectiveness by directives we would not want to disclose to everyone, lest we lose our surface appeal. Some of these may be communicated to trusted companions in spite of the fact that they do not belong to the circle comprising our more intimate friends and colleagues.

Finally, in terms of the actual life-form, we may engage in casual conversation with many people we meet in everyday surroundings. What and how much we share pertinent to any one of these regions of privacy depends on our appraisal. We alone can judge what seems congenial, compatible, and compassionate in regard to any disclosure of our private life on these levels of presence.

Social Injustice of Intrusion into Privacy

The dignity and effectiveness of our formation would be threatened if others could infiltrate the privacy of our heart, if intruders could spy, so to speak, on our intimate directives and experiences. The abuse of religious, emotional, physical, economic, chemical, psychological, or other means to penetrate this region is a violation of social justice. A shell of security directives shields this sanctuary. It should not be pierced by force or such deceit as making a pretense of understanding care and love. Violators may use our personal directives against us. Naked and vulnerable, we are open to blackmail, ridicule, shame, and exposure. Hence, any life-form that approximates consonance, and with it concern for social justice, ought to respond in revulsion and protest when anyone's privacy is threatened this way.

A subtle, sympathetic play on religious feelings of devotion, anxiety, guilt, humility, and surrender is another means to force oneself into the intrasphere of unsuspecting people. Certain representatives of religion may be obsessed, either prefocally or infrafocally, by a deep-seated need for power and control that eludes them in other areas of life. As a result, they may be tempted to engage in this sordid kind of injustice.

Sensitivity to Uninvited Intrusion into One's Privacy

The necessity for privacy explains our sensitivity to uninvited intrusions that may reveal how we are or how we feel. Since we are unable to control this revelation, we may fiercely resent it when someone bursts in unannounced. We feel at a loss in a situation that discloses how we feel privately. For instance, we may not want people to see us half-dressed, with uncombed hair or an unwashed face. We do not want them to spot the unmade bed, the dishes in the sink, the disorder on our desk, a controversial book we are reading, the unpaid bills on the coffee table, the open medicine bottle on the sink in our bathroom.

When people call before visiting us, we feel differently. They give us a chance to remain in charge of our surroundings which participate so obviously in our apparent form of life. But the more we sense mastery eluding us, the more we feel irritation or even downright anger, and rightly so, for our formation freedom itself is at stake.

Formation of Respect for Privacy in Children

Formation of respect for privacy in children should be encouraged by our own respect for *their* privacy. We should allow them the privacy that is possible without damage to them at their young age. It is also necessary to teach them not to intrude on our adult privacy or on the privacy of their siblings or other people they meet. The same disposition should extend itself to private drawers, notes, books, letters, clothes, toys, and other things entrusted to them or to their brothers, sisters, friends, or playmates. To form them in respect for what belongs privately to self or others is a fine preparation for justice. At the same time they should be formed in the complementary dispositions of generosity, compatibility, and compassion, which dispose them to give *freely* to others their personal possessions or to allow others to share some of their toys, books, or candy.

Intersphere and Private Life

Privacy calls for a congenial and compatible rhythm of sharing and withholding. Withholding preserves congeniality. Sharing preserves compatibility. Both foster consonance. Withholding maintains space for attunement to the epiphany within, sharing to the epiphany without.

The finitude of life makes it impossible for us to share our privacy equally with all those for whom we feel affinity. For one thing our energy for personal interformation is limited. We cannot be equally involved with very many people. Affinity is a gift that cannot be experienced in the same measure toward each person. Its potential varies among different relationships. The depth of intimacy we can attain is not the same with all our friends. The opportunities they offer for sharing privacy are conditioned by affinity, respect, compassion, and confidentiality. Respect in this regard is the disposition never to use shared secrets for the manipulation of others. Compassion disposes us to empathize with others' vulnerability. Confidentiality makes us the reliable recipients of their secrets. They can feel at ease, knowing that their confidences are safe with us, no matter what.

These conditions form a necessary context for intimate sharing of important aspects of our intrasphere. Such sharing relieves the tension of unnecessary withholding, the pressure of shame, guilt, or anxiety, or of an excess of inner joy and excitement that we could not share with anyone else. Sharing grants us an opportunity to receive confirmation and correction by trusted others. The blessing of such confidential companionship enables us to share the facets of our intrasphere in which we experience a mutual empathic compatibility.

Recall the example of intimate conversation about a homeland left behind: Someone who does not share your affinity may enter the conversation, speak the same words, and point to the same features of the country you and your friends share. Yet there is a difference. Something is missing. The words of the newcomer do not evoke the same resonance in your interiority. Lacking are the subtle overtones of empathic communication that only affinity and intimacy can engender.

The more unique a life-form is, the more difficult it is to find empathic affinity. Such a life may only find relief in intimacy with the mystery itself. Companions for empathic participation may be absent because of one's unusual intrasphere. This may explain the despair and loneliness that may overwhelm innovative artists, thinkers, and mystics. They are burdened and blessed with uncommon powers of sensitivity and vision. They deserve respect and compassion, not rejection and ridicule born of the arrogance or ignorance of a bourgeois mediocrity. Such cruel social injustice against the minority of these abandoned souls can only deepen the tragedy of their lonely, oversensitive existence.

Friendship and Empathic Affinity

Sharing facets of our private life creates a special bond. It predisposes us to expand the boundaries of our interiority; to allow a special other in; to share directives, feelings, and motives we do not have to share with anyone else. By granting each other access to some hidden regions of our intrasphere we lay the ground for friendship and love.

The intimacy of friendship does not necessarily unfold into the deeper intimacy of love. Friendship knows many gradations of shared privacy. How we modulate the hierarchy of our various friendships depends on such conditions as our preformation; our resources of affinity, emotionality, and expressivity; our life direction; our form-giving memories, images, and anticipations; our moods and feelings and their availability to focal attention; and, of course, the time and energy we have at our disposal. The cultivation of friendship demands both time and the convenience of private space for intimate communication. Wise modulation of intimate contacts on basis of such conditions leads necessarily to a certain prefocal hierarchy of friendships.

Conditions of Sharing and Withholding

Our actual life-form as a whole; its formation history; its trans-, infra-, prefocal, and focal retentions; its prepersonal, personal, and impersonal modulations; its realized and not-yet-realized formation potentials—all play a role in the wavelike rhythm of withholding and participation of our intrasphere. For this reason, the sharing of our private life happens spontaneously on certain occasions or with certain people. Meeting one another, we may experience consonance immediately. Or, on other occasions, a spontaneous antagonism or inner distance may make itself felt from the beginning and nothing will prevent the protective closure of our threatened interiority.

What should remain private varies for each human form of life in accordance with its potential and actual uniqueness. It may vary from moment to moment and from setting to setting. The disposition of social justice demands that we respect each other's right to appraise and affirm in any particular situation how many of our inner directives we will share with one or more people. There will always be a tension between our need to share and our fear of the consequences. We are afraid that our sharing may tempt confidants to abuse this disclosure to manipulate our life direction. Frequently we make tentative moves in the direction of intimate sharing, only to withdraw into the security of our apparent form of life when the initial response of others makes us doubt their empathic affinity or sincerity.

We need, therefore, to form dispositions of effective appraisal of what a consonant rhythm of flexible sharing and withholding entails. The result of such appraisal will usually be a wise compromise between isolation and excessive disclosure. Both would be dissonant and deformative. Isolation would paralyze compatibility and compassion; excessive disclosure would do the same to congeniality, peace, and equanimity.

Even if disclosure seems congenial, we still have to ask ourselves if such communication is compatible and compassionate in regard to others. We have no right to burden people unnecessarily with our private visions, feelings, and worries. They may be unable to comprehend them or to bear with them at this moment of their own history and according to their vulnerability.

Art of Gracious Sharing and Withholding

Withholding when necessary should be exercised in a way that is least offensive. The art of gracious reserve is helpful here. One should never arouse false anticipations by a show of accessibility that one cannot live up to realistically. When, finally, a line must be drawn it is much resented because of the earlier suggestion of limitless access to one's intrasphere. A certain moderate and natural reserve can be a gracious sign of quiet self-respect that should be shared by others. To be gracious, such relaxed reserve should be accompanied by warmth, sympathy, and the spontaneous sharing of what really can be shared.

One must resist the temptation of the pride-form to look important by being mysterious about things that could be commonly known or readily divulged. Withholding should be unobvious, indirect, almost playful in its natural ease. It should not deteriorate into secretiveness, unresponsiveness, or demonstrative exclusivity. Public displays of secret understanding between insiders should be especially avoided. They are odious and are naturally resented by those who are made to feel outsiders by knowing winks or whispers between friends, colleagues, or acquaintances.

Above all, our style of withholding should be genuine, not pretentious. Genuine privacy is the basis of honest interformation. Knowing when to share and not to share is truly an art. Like all arts it is learned by trial and error. Much depends on the maturity of our apprehension and appraisal dispositions, which imply the effective assessment of right timing. Human appraisal, unlike the prehuman reflexes of animal life, implies the ability to choose the right moment for sharing, to wait for such an opportunity with equanimity, to respect the need for dignified silence in self and others. The art of gracious sharing thus complements that of wise withholding.

A final caution: intimate interformation will sooner or later acquaint us with one another's defects and weaknesses. The more we have romanticized each other's intrasphere, the greater the shock of disappointment will be. Resentments may flare. We may withdraw as wounded people in the lair of an isolated intrasphere. Healed there from romanticism by wise reflection, we may be able to restore the flow of intimacy with kindred spirits. We will now share our private life on basis of a more realistic mutual apprehension and appreciation that includes compassion for each other's frailties and failures.

Limits of Privacy Sharing

The embodied human form imposes on us intra- as well as inter- and outer spheres of formation. This imposition makes human life paradoxically the most open and closed life on this planet. At birth, our human form is set adrift in a world that is only partly accessible to the restricted range of our senses and of our limited cortical and subcortical brain powers. Consequently, we have to unfold our formation field out of a foreign ambience that we can grasp only in a limited fashion. This means a struggle for each newborn life after it is separated from the blissful warmth and security of the initial field of formation that the womb of the mother provides. The breadth and depth of each life's unfolding field will determine in part its potency for empathic participation.

Fortunately, the formation wisdom of the human race, embodied in consonant formation traditions, awaits us as newborn children. It supports our efforts from the beginning. Our initial steps are facilitated by our sharing in the intrasphere of our mother. Soon we are ejected from this secondary womb and born anew to our own intrasphere. But the memory of that lost "paradise" never leaves us. This is one reason why we seek so eagerly at least a partial sharing in the intrasphere of people to whom we feel an affinity. Such sharing is always partial and intermittent and can never attain the identification we experienced with the intrasphere of our mother. Our sharing is always limited by the limits of our personal field of empathy, affinity, and expertise.

From the moment when our own intrasphere emerges, our life is a constant justaposition of sharing and withholding. At times we suffer because we see nothing but the walls of withholding between ourselves and others.

We feel as if all people are locked in their own cell of isolation. Then, at other times, we discover a kindred spirit; the walls crumble; we share our inwardness and relive some of the intimacy of our infancy. The joy of this encounter is rooted in an experience of "in-being" so figural that the pain of exclusive "counter-being" is relieved. Yet in such a relationship of growing intimacy we also become more aware of each other's mystery. We realize that we can never completely communicate our intrasphere. Every moment of revealing conceals it at the same time. In some way we always remain strangers to ourselves and others.

Recapitulation

Human life is, first of all, a primordial at-oneness, a substantial union with the mystery. However, the mystery calls us forth out of this mere transconscious union to a union of likeness with it. This call leaves us free to acknowledge or not to acknowledge the disclosures of the substantial union we already are, to cultivate or to spurn the ongoing work of consonant formation.

At birth a vital separation takes place where formerly there was a sense of oneness. Initially the infant shares the intrasphere of the mother. Then a second birth of "life as independently functional" is experienced. A capacity emerges to experience one's intrasphere as distinct from that of the mother. The birth of the intrasphere implies the potency to give formative meaning personally to people, events, and things and to form one's own formation field. Children begin to apprehend themselves prefocally as persons with a formation field of their own. They learn this by first relating formatively to the appearances in their emergent field, which have now become separate forms of life and world. This power of forming presence is expressive of their primordial participation in the supreme principle that lies dormant under their sensate bodily involvement in the inter- and outer spheres of their emergent world.

Our entire spiritual formation entails making explicit our original transconscious union with the mystery while growing in consonance with its disclosures in our life. This explicitness is first of all a disclosure of the unique epiphany of this supreme principle at the root of our intrasphere.

The peripheral regions of our privacy are filled with protective directives imposed on us by our sensate bodily interaction with a threatening world. Because of these daily-operative safety directives, we may "play hide-and-seek" with our deeper interiority. It is easy to get caught in this play that modulates our apparent form of life. Often we ourselves or others may mistake apearances, and their underlying, private dimension, for our life as a whole. We fall in the trap of self-deception, clinging to our exaltation of passing performance and appearance. Still we may be prefocally pained by our alienation from the sacred roots of our interiority.

At the same time and on another level, infra- and prefocal memories of our pristine at-oneness with the intrasphere of our mother fill us with a secret longing for what can never be again. Idle attempts to restore this "lost paradise" may confuse our love relationships, imposing on spouse, child, friend, or lover secret demands that we do not fully understand and that they cannot possibly fulfill. Only the mystery itself can satisfy us totally.

CHAPTER 13

Intraspheric Depth of Privacy and Its Corporeal Manifestation

P articipative union with the mystery is truly a gift. Readiness for its reception presupposes the purification of our fixations on passing forms. This must be complemented by a subsequent illumination of our intrasphere. Inner purification and illumination are served by moments of recollection. In recollection we may spiral into the depth of our private life. Spiraling down means descending the convoluted stairways of our privacy protections. They are like the distracting passageways of a pyramid protecting the treasure chamber at its center from invaders. Such protective directives have been proliferating on the periphery of our intrasphere. They serve our safe and effective interaction with a threatening world. The problem is that we may no longer know the difference between our private self and our privacy protectives. The latter sustain our apparent form of life. Instead of pointing to the deeper regions of our interiority, privacy protectives may serve only to obscure them.

Spiraling down thus implies breaking through the facade of a merely apparent form. Only in recollection may we overcome our ignorance of formation in depth. Various form traditions refer to this breakthrough into the depths of the intrasphere in striking symbols, such as enlightenment, conversion, rebirth. These symbols point to a radically new vision in which everything appears in the light of participation in the mystery and its epiphanies.

Spiraling down into one's intrasphere is not an easy venture. Thrust out of the complacency of everyday routines, we are exposed to the disclosures of the unique form of the mystery within. We face radical aloneness and the dread of our ultimate unique responsibility and its ambiguities. This sphere can be shared with no one, and yet it is only in the loneliness of utmost privacy that we may be compelled to disclose a calling we would not have known otherwise.

Corporeal Exposure of Our Recollected Intrasphere

All human formation, inner and outer, is essentially embodied; hence, it is somehow exposed to the world. We may illustrate this point by reflecting on a famous creation of the French sculptor Rodin, entitled *Le Penseur* ("The Thinker").

Rodin captured in marble the human embodiment of recollection. The seated, concentrated body speaks to us of withdrawal, inwardness, absorption in a world of reflection. The statue professes that the shouting multiplicity of the surrounding world has lost its hold on *The Thinker*. The absence of outer engagement highlights inner presence. We are overwhelmed by the mystery of interiorization, announcing yet concealing itself in every line of this sculpture. We cannot escape the impression of an inwardly absorbing world, immune to the murmurs of the crowd and the tensions of comparison, envy, and competition. *The Thinker* is the image of a life-form no longer dispersed in the inter- and outer spheres. At the same time, it embodies in posture and features an inner presence that celebrates the freedom of the spirit. It is a hymn in stone to the mystery of interiority, a celebration of the human power to invest itself freely in the sanctuary of its privacy.

As long as a life-form engages itself fully in the inter- and outer spheres, we can, on the basis of observation, functionally categorize what this life-form seems to be about at this moment of its interaction. Although the recollected form does not expose itself in this fashion, its corporeal expression manifests unwittingly a forming human presence dwelling in a mysterious intrasphere in ways we can neither fathom nor categorize.

Rodin's sculpture captures a moment of recollection and its distinctive manifestation in human bodiliness. This is a moment of immanence, of interiorized power. It remains *in* the world of inter- and outer spheres without being *of* this world. Not to be of this world means neither giving form to it actively at this moment nor being subjected passively to other outer forms imposed aggressively or seductively. Recollection is the privileged state in which the human form experiences that it has meaning in and of itself, a meaning nothing in the inter- and outer world can disturb.

Recollection and Contemplation

The Thinker of Rodin is the embodiment of one mode of recollected inner presence, that of reflection. The highest mode of recollection is silent contemplation. We dwell in the deepest realm of our intrasphere where it touches the entrance to and the epiphany of the formation mystery. Here there is only receptivity and gratuitous unfolding. This apex of infused recollection stills our life awhile, renewing its innocence. Like the lilies of the field, we do not labor nor are we burdened by strife or care. We radiate peace without concern for the morrow, when our worldly splendor may be absorbed in the forming matrix of the cosmos.

In recollection each human form can restore the ineffable unique epiphany it is called to be in the world. This distinctive mark of human spirituality conveys the message that one is filled with an inner world of meaning evolving around a still point of the intrasphere where the image of the mystery silently enters one's formation history.

Rodin's creation conveys the idea that the secret of one's interiority cannot be fully veiled by bodily appearance. This applies also to the life of contemplation. The more inward our life becomes, the more it will give form to our vital and functional expressions. Our modes of interformation with others, of interaction with the world, will point increasingly to the epiphany lighting up in the core of our centered life. The paradoxical disposition, "to care and not to care," bears testimony to this inner fullness and freedom. One is in the world yet beyond its worldliness, beyond excessive concern for success and status, for rank, power, possession, or glamorous appearance.

Carefree presence, rooted in abandonment to our epiphany, disposes us to a generous yet congenial availability to others and to the work of justice, peace, and mercy in this world. Obedient congeniality prevents us from succumbing to the self-destructive illusion of limitless generosity, erratic heroism, or ministerial hysteria. The latter responses are rooted in the exalted pride-form, the former in the humility of dwelling constantly in the truth of the limits of one's epiphany and the modest modes of generosity that flow from it congenially.

Recollection, Loneliness, and Solitude

Initially, awareness of our oneness in recollection makes us experience loneliness. This may tempt us to seek fusion with others, to shun privacy, silence, and solitude. Hunger for fusion is the vital reverberation of our aspiration for union with the mystery and its epiphanies. The more we realize this, the more loneliness may be transformed into solitude. Solitude is not isolation, for we may experience it in intimacy with others. Deep friendship is a meeting of solitudes. We may feel most at one and most alone in togetherness. Solitude grants us the silent dignity of an unspeakable interiority. What we most deeply are cannot be communicated to others; it can only be shared wordlessly with the mystery that is its secret source.

The solitude of the human heart shines out through our inner and outer spheres. It is a silent radiation of the hidden treasure of our private life. Each of us is a secret of the mystery. Solitude preserves the secret that we are. Solitary receptivity facilitates some of its inner disclosures. We have not chosen the mystery; it has chosen us. Our intrasphere is called to a covenant with the sacred that will outlast time. The unfolding of this life implies an emptying of excessive functional concern, of blind vital desire. It demands the disposition to maintain flexible privacy protections in space and time.

Profanation and Consecration of the Formation Field

Recollection makes us sensitive to the wavelike movement of our intrasphere that affects our formation field as a whole. The intrasphere represents, as do the other spheres, the potency dimensions of human life, namely, the sociohistorical, vital, functional, and transcendent. When transcendent intraformation prevails, our field is illumined by presence to the mystery. It is consecrated or transformed by this presence. Functional-vital intraformation, on the contrary, if not subordinated to the transcendent, profanes the field or fixates it in its mere functional-vital meanings. In that case, our field of action is not seen in the perspective of the cosmos as a sanctuary of the sacred.

The word *profane* comes from the Latin *pro*, which means "in front of," and *fanum*, which means "sanctuary" or "temple." Hence, it literally means that which is outside the temple or sanctuary, which is not sacred or consecrated, not elevated or transformed into a spiritually meaningful place pervaded by the mystery. The word *consecrate* comes from the Latin *cum*, meaning "thoroughly" or "through and through," and *sacrare*, meaning "to treat as sacred," "to make holy," "to bestow a sacred meaning upon." In this context, it implies that we acknowledge the mystery dimension that pervades and transforms our profane formation field through and through.

Consecration-Profanation Conflict

Usually the predispositions to profane and to consecrate affect in some measure our formation; they vie with each other for ascendancy. The outcome of each consecration-profanation conflict is decided upon in our intrasphere. If we grow in intimacy with the mystery, our disposition of consecration is strengthened. If not, our autarchic pride-form takes over; it swells our feelings of functional-vital importance; it profanes our field by fashioning it in isolation from the mystery; it turns this field into a self-enclosed, self-sufficient unit. Autarchic comes from the Greek *autarkeia*, meaning "sufficiency"; it is composed of the terms *auto* ("self") and *arkein* ("to suffice"). The profaned formation field is autarchic in the sense that it is apprehended, appraised, and affirmed as sufficient in itself. We do not envision it as nourished, maintained, and illumined by the all-embracing mystery of the sacred. We choose to believe that it finds its resources in itself alone. (*Autarchic* is similarly employed by economists to describe an economically independent area that does not have to rely on any outside resources.)

Briefly, consecrating our field means linking it to the formation mystery; profaning it means separating it from this perspective. Given our dissonant human condition, our efforts to consecrate will always be interfered with by our tendency to profane. Hence, we may unwittingly separate our life from the sacred in spite of our best focal intentions.

Consecrating the formation field presupposes first of all that we are in touch with the transcendent dimension of our interiority. In that depth of privacy, we are disclosed as forms or images of the mystery. Our isolating pride-form exercises a powerful urge to usurp the role of this self-disclosure. It wants to disclose to us how successful and fulfilled we can be merely by doing what we will, exclusively on the basis of either personal or shared power.

Our pride-form urges us to appraise our formation field as the ultimate measure of life, to deny its transcendent horizon. We live no longer in the disposition of gratitude for what the mystery allows into our life. Any endowment, opportunity, or fortuitous event is apprehended as either a mere stroke of good fortune or an effect of human effort alone. Even if we adhere to a religious form tradition, the profane appraisal of our field may come first, the invocation of the mystery as an afterthought. Our innate pride manifests itself in the duplicity of consecrating our formation field and at the same time profaning it.

Profanation of the Formation Field and the
Historical Dimension of the Intrasphere

The intrasphere is affected by the sociohistorical dimension of the human life-form. This dimension comprises the interconsciousness of humanity, which is communicated to us in turn by symbols established by people who share the same history, society, and social pulsations.

In Western culture, the periods of the Renaissance, the Enlightenment, and the Industrial Revolution formed this interconsciousness increasingly in terms of nontranscendence. These movements fostered isolating individualism and extolled functional rationalization. They promoted a preference for specialization insufficiently balanced by the holistic aspirations of the human spirit. This dissonant interconsciousness, of course, affected our intraconsciousness. The formation field of people became autarchic, cut off from the sacred source and its flow of epiphanies in nature, humanity, and history.

Human fields of meaning began to lose their symphonic coherence with the mystery. People felt lonely and isolated in their disjointed societies. Their intrasphere was like a void. Transcendent identity rooted in one's unique at-homeness in the sacred was never disclosed to them. A sparse functional identity was substituted for in-depth formation. This meager sense of self was culled mostly from functionalistic and vitalistic confirmations by others, from popular pulsations, and from one's definition by bureaucratic structures, status symbols, and possessions.

The ignored intrasphere, the repudiated life of privacy, begins to protest under these circumstances. Unfulfilled longings explode in desperate revolt against structures that are mistakenly identified as the only and ultimate cause of the loss of privacy. Groups and individuals rise up in rebellion, resentful of any structural or institutional authority. Not rooted in the spirit, people easily become victims of romantic, cultic, vitalistic, or fanatic militant functionalism. Their revolt itself, no matter how well-intentioned, becomes an alternate manifestation of the problem, not its solution.

Vulnerability and Vacillation of the Profaned Life

Many people thus lack transcendent roots of identity. Their sense of self is merely functional, profane, vital. Their spiritual conscience is replaced by one that is mainly at the mercy of vital pulsions and social pulsations popularized by the media. Lacking a firm, well-defined sense of distinctively human life, they are thus vacillating, vulnerable, and restless. The emptiness of their intrasphere makes them insensitive to the need for privacy. It makes it impossible for them to relate in true inwardness to others. Platitudes, gossip, and witticisms take the place of the communication of wisdom and experience.

Craving for Fusion

The pain of functional isolation generates the urge for vital fusion. Such fusion can link only the outer shells of human life. Disappointment is unavoidable. It is followed by despair or by a frantic hunt for new occasions of fusion. Promiscuity, confusion, and anxious ambiguity surround such desperate relationships. People's forced attempts to open up to one another fail to fill the void. Because of their impoverished interiority, there is not much substance to communicate, not much that reverberates in depth. Their frenzied or half-hearted efforts to build community, intimacy, and mutual understanding may compel them indiscriminately to spill out vital feelings and functional information about their confused existence. Such an explosive and unbridled release of emotion may give a momentary feeling of relief; it may even create a passing illusion of true community. Ultimately, however, it only compounds the sense of despair over one's shared emptiness and confusion. This apparent expansiveness hides a secret sense of isolation.

This is the problem Sigmund Koch seems to refer to in his well-known article "The Image of Man in Encounter Groups":

> The principal toll [of such encounter groups] is in the reducing and simplifying impact upon the personalities and sensibilities of those who emerge from the group experience with an enthusiastic commitment to its values.... [the group movement] is the most extreme excursion thus far of man's talent for reducing, distorting, evading, and vulgarizing his own reality. It is also the most poignant exercise of that talent, for it seeks and promises to do the very reverse. It is adept at the image-making maneuver of evading human reality in the very process of seeking to discover and enhance it. It seeks to court spontaneity and authenticity by artifice; to combat instrumentalism instrumentally; to provide access to experience by reducing it to a packaged commodity; to engineer autonomy by group pressure; to liberate individuality by group sharing. Within the lexicon of its concepts and methods, openness becomes transparency; love, caring, and sharing become a barter of "reinforcements" or perhaps mutual ego-titillation; aesthetic receptivity or immediacy becomes "sensory awareness." It can provide only a grotesque simulacrum of every noble quality it courts. It provides, in effect, a convenient psychic whorehouse for the purchase of a gamut of well-advertised existential "goodies": authenticity, freedom, wholeness, flexibility, community, love, joy. One enters for such liberating consummations but settles for psychic striptease.

While his analysis may appear excessive, while it does not apply necessarily to every encounter group, yet formation scientists and practitioners know not only from experience but also from years of studying the great formation traditions that such experiential "goodies" can only be approximated after many years of ascetical reformation of dispositions and meditative reflection in the light of the formation mystery. In the domain of spiritual growth, no shortcuts are available. Ultimately the mystery itself has to grant a final transformation of these humanly reformed dispositions.

The inner and outer fragmentation of contemporary humanity can only be overcome by a homecoming in the intrasphere and by the gentle disclosure of its sacred roots via the great formation traditions. Without this birth of a spiritual identity in its uniqueness and in its intimate interwovenness with the whole and holy in nature, humanity, and history, our search for clarity and intimacy will be in vain. We will continue to suffer famine in the deserts of autarchic, profaned formation fields.

CHAPTER 14

Consciousness and Privacy

W e cannot bring our considerations of privacy to closure without asking the question of the relationship of consciousness to privacy. Our intrasphere is also a mode of consciousness. How does intraspheric consciousness relate to the other modes of consciousness? When we engage in intraspheric consciousness, does it necessarily exclude all consciousness of the inter- and outer spheres. Does it totally separate us from people, events, and things?

Privacy and Fundamental Consciousness

Turning inward to our intraspheric consciousness does not necessarily imply that we are removed or remote from people and other animate or nonanimate forms in the universe. We may meet others at such moments in their most fundamental consciousness. In a sense, we can be more at one with them in our fundamental consciousness than in our social inter-consciousness. The latter is the consciousness we share with others as a result of historical and contemporary processes of interformation. The fundamental human consciousness in which we all participate is prior to this interconsciousness. To understand the mystery of the fundamental human unity of consciousness, even in utmost privacy, we have to ask ourselves what formation science means by its concept of fundamental consciousness.

Formation Theory of Consciousness

Formation science continually updates its theory of consciousness. The science is concerned with the formation of human life as an unfolding integral whole during the formation history of humanity. Hence, it must do justice to all formationally relevant disclosures about human consciousness that appear in the course of this history. In this process, it should consult not only the differential arts and sciences but also the rich variety of human form traditions and historical formation events. In the light of these sources, formative consciousness is disclosed first of all as an *embodied* consciousness. This means that it can be distinguished but not separated from our vital, functional, and sociohistorical life with its sensory, imaginative, and neuromuscular and hormonal processes. Nor can formative consciousness be severed from any aspect of our formation field.

Our consciousness is the power of human awareness as actualizing itself within our interwovenness with successive or simultaneous formation fields. We can explain in this vein the derivation of the term *consciousness* from the Latin *scire* and *cum*, literally meaning "to know with." Human consciousness is not the autarchic knowing of an isolated intelligence; it is a knowing that unfolds within the manifold modes of awareness of our formation field. Yet this is not all that can be said of the marvel of human consciousness, for it also transcends the formation field in a pure intuition of the spirit. It can receive from the forming mystery the potency to open up to the universal consciousness that marks the all-embracing presence of the mystery. It is within this penetrating consciousness that particular modes of consciousness are rooted.

Our consciousness—like all manifestations of the forming consciousness in the universe, even in our most private moments—is a reflection of this universal consciousness, which is the formation mystery itself. We may experience privileged moments of pure transcendence. At such times, vital sense impressions and functional categories are kept in suspension, as it were. Our human consciousness experiences blissful union with the universal consciousness.

Human Form: Source of Common Fundamental Consciousness

The term *fundamental consciousness* refers to an awareness-potential we share with all persons, simply on the basis of the common structuration of our human form of life. This form is fundamentally structured in its potencies in the same way in all people. Consequently, fundamental potential consciousness, when actualized, gives rise to the same *seminal* human awareness. An example would be the seminal awareness of awe, wonder, and marvel of which all people seem capable, given the right conditions.

Imagine that we discover on other planets intelligent forms structured differently in an organismic way from intelligent forms on this planet. In that case, we could not be sure whether or how they potentially share our basic human experiences. Their consciousness might not be rooted in the same kind of brain, nervous system, or sensory, hormonal, and neuro-muscular structures and processes typical of the human form on Planet Earth.

Participation in Universal Consciousness:
Source of Common Fundamental Consciousness

Another source of the sameness of fundamental consciousness is its transcendent capacity. We are called in the depths of our interiority to participate in the universal consciousness that is the formation mystery. To hear that call, we must recollect ourselves in the abyss of our intra-sphere where we may intuit the source of our consciousness, which is the limitless consciousness that pervades the cosmos formatively.

United with that ground, we experience an overwhelming oneness with other human forms of consciousness in their basic mirroring of the same infinite consciousness from which they, too, emerge. We may experience this shared mode of emergence of our fundamental human consciousness in moments of deepest privacy.

Solitude and Community

We emphasized the potential, as well as the seminal nature, of our fun-damental consciousness. One means to actualize this potency is solitude, silence, and privacy. Silent recollection in intraspheric consciousness may bring us into intimate contact with the emergent humanness in our fellow human beings. Paradoxically, we may become more intimately at home with them at such periods of diminishment of our external rela-tions with them. This is one of the reasons why busy people of the an-cient Greek and Roman cities sought so eagerly the insight and inspira-tion of lonely hermits in the desert. They realized that these men and women of silence and solitude were most in touch with the aspirations potentially alive in all of us. Solitude, therefore, is a source of deepest human communion.

Privacy and Interconsciousness

Our fundamental consciousness is actualized in a differential way. Fun-damental consciousness is first of all differentiated into two subordinated kinds of consciousness: an interconsciousness and an intraconsciousness.

This differentiation is the result of our interaction with others, which actualizes and specifies our fundamental consciousness. They are the people with whom we share sociohistorical formation fields. This differential actualization gives rise to specific sensory perceptions, apprehensions, images, memories, anticipations, pulsations, pulsions, ambitions, and aspirations. These acquisitions are maintained in the interconscious realm of form-traditional signs and symbols. They become part of our intraconsciousness insofar as it has appropriated this realm.

Accordingly, we distinguish from fundamental consciousness our differentiated interconsciousness and intraconsciousness. Both are differentiations of seminal fundamental consciousness.

Mutual Interaction on Interconsciousness and Intraconsciousness

Interconsciousness and intraconsciousness influence each other formatively. For instance, the actualization of the fundamental consciousness of children, with their basic human predispositions, happens through interconscious form directives. Such directives are embedded in the form traditions disclosed to them by significant people, events, and things in their formation field. During their formation journey, children appropriate and increasingly personalize such form directives in their own intraconsciousness. Such unique intraconscious appropriation enables them in turn to influence or enhance interconscious experience.

For instance, people may participate as a community in the ritual of a form tradition. The participants may execute merely functionally or aesthetically the interconscious ritual directives of their traditions. Ritualism replaces the heartfelt celebration of ritual. On other occasions, however, they may spontaneously infuse their participation in the ceremony with an intraconsciously elaborated conviction of the forming value and experience of these form directives. Their heart is in it, which, of course, makes a profound difference.

Because their intraconscious life is embodied, the body will expose some of this inner conviction, even in its private concealing. Such radiation of inner conviction infuses the celebrating community with interconscious vibrations that enliven and enhance formatively the experience of ritual. Hence, periods of privacy, silence, solitude, and inner deepening are a source not only of human community based on the fundamental consciousness all humans share but also of form-traditional interconsciousness.

Infra-, Trans-, Pre-, and Focal Consciousness:
Their Vocal Implications

Fundamental, inter- and intraconsciousness refine themselves into four main modes of consciousness. In the first volume of this series and in my book *In Search of Spiritual Identity* I explained more extensively the distinction between infra-, trans-, pre-, and focal consciousness. The limits of our topic in this volume do not allow us to repeat these considerations. We shall only mention them here to remind the reader that each of these distinctive modes of consciousness applies to fundamental consciousness as well as to inter- and intraconsciousness.

As a closing remark, we may note that in recent reflections we have at times used the word *focal* in connection with the word *vocal*. *Focal* refers to the focusing of our consciousness. *Vocal* refers to the verbalization, inwardly or outwardly, of what we are conscious of. Only what is somehow verbalized, even if only by symbolic pointers, becomes focal; what is available to verbalization is prefocal or prevocal; what cannot yet be verbalized or linguistically symbolized in any way is infra- or transfocal or, what is the same, infra- or transvocal.

Review

This discussion of privacy and consciousness brings to an end our considerations of the privacy disposition. Before passing on to the communal disposition, which complements that of privacy, we would like to review the main insights discussed in the chapters on privacy.

The privacy disposition is a basic mode of presence of the human heart. It is an avenue to our intrasphere; an openness to its disclosures of the form that should animate our life; an access to the depths of our inwardness where this form is in substantial union with the all-embracing mystery from which it emerges.

Yet, as we have seen, privacy is also a preparation for encounter. Respectful encounter between unique persons will only happen insofar as our intrasphere permeates the inter- and outer spheres within which we interact with others. Our privacy disposition is a protection as well as an expression of our personal formation and the sense of identity it implies.

The privacy disposition is closely connected with the radical freedom of our transcendent will. Responsible privacy implies a free response of participation in the mystery. This mystery in its personal givenness defies rational lucidity, yet it is nearer to us in direct apprehension than anything that can be deduced logically or measured with exact precision. This reverence of privacy extends itself to the same mystery as uniquely operative in others.

The privacy disposition is, then, a primer for self-disclosure to others in vital-functional bodily presence; it is also a source of wise concealment. Hence, it is the basis of communion as well as of solitude. The privacy of solitude is that of periodic diminishment of vital-functional expressivity. Timely withdrawal in inwardness is mandatory if we are to maintain a sense of personal calling in the midst of the hubris of our social and functional involvements. The formal structures of social roles can be protectively utilized by our privacy disposition to preserve a certain distance between inwardness and polite outwardness. To be sure, certain facets of our intrasphere can be shared more intimately with those with whom we experience a deeper affinity. With them we may create a zone of shared privacy in regard to special apprehensions and appreciations. This does not diminish the need for a deeper personal privacy. On the contrary, it evokes and confirms it.

The privacy disposition is disclosed only in human life. The distinctively human form of embodied freedom is both the most open and the most closed of all forms known to us. Human life receives and gives form in openness to humanity, history, and world. At the same time this form, because of its relative freedom of uniqueness, needs to withdraw periodically in solitude. Otherwise it might lose its relative freedom of formation in the material and social processes in which it necessarily shares because of its bodily determinants.

The intrasphere preserved by the privacy disposition is not only a presence to the disclosures of our basic form of life. It contains also the memories, images, and anticipations, the feelings and strivings, that are the residues of the formation events that mark our journey. Constantly interacting with one another and with the disclosure of our unique life-form, they take on a personal shape and emotional tone. Such personalization of the intrasphere explains why no two persons ever apprehend a shared formation field in quite the same fashion. They apprehend the same reality under different objective and subjective facets.

Our apprehension privatizes to some degree our formation field. This personalized field reinforces our privacy disposition, which gave rise to its personal sense in the first place. This is true even if the facets of the field personally preferred are in themselves objective and universal. The consonance or dissonance of our formation depends for a great part on the quality of this apprehension and appreciation. If we experience our formation field—on the basis of previous apprehensions and appraisals—as threatening, we are prone to develop a guarded, suspicious, anxious privacy disposition. Such a dissonant disposition will give rise to insecurity, secretiveness, oversensitivity, loneliness, suspicious, and painful alienation.

We have pointed out that not all facets of our private sphere are equally available to our focal consciousness. Infra-, trans-, and prefocal facets interfere with our intentional interactions. Farthest removed from insight and choice are infra- and transfocal feelings and strivings. Hence, these aspects of our intrasphere cannot yet play a role in our free and insightful formation. They may come out indirectly. For example, an avowed materialistic atheist may betray unwittingly a transfocal longing for the transcendent mystery. Conversely, a religiously committed person may be infrafocally controlled by resentment of the deity he or she exalts focally. We conclude that the privacy disposition by itself alone does not assure us of perfect control of our inner or outer life. This disposition, however, creates space and time to become reflectively aware of our interiority. We can expose its disclosures and apprehensions increasingly to our own free apprehension, appreciation, and affirmation. These enable us to bestow a personal form on our life.

Despite this partial manifestation of its inspired originality, the free uniqueness of our life can never be fully apprehended, appreciated, and affirmed by anyone else. In this sense, others can only confirm, not affirm, our uniqueness. Affirmation comes from within, confirmation from without. The latter is more an expression of loving trust than of full understanding.

Through transcendent self-presence in privacy, we sense what areas of our intrasphere can be shared in what measure and with whom. We come to appreciate ourselves as a secret of the mystery of formation. We feel called to ascend from one current form of life to another. This unfolding happens in a simultaneous movement of self-disclosure and concealment within the formation fields we share with others. We experience a secret invitation to become that self we most deeply are, hidden in the mystery as the protoform of our life.

Taking personal responsibility for our formation is thus not an isolated, arbitrary option. It should be an increasingly free and insightful affirmation of what is gradually disclosed to us as the mystery's silent inspiration. This disclosure of our private destiny happens to us in our concrete life situations. They form us uniquely, provided we meditate upon them in privacy and in dialogue with the inner disclosures of the protoform of our life, which announces itself more and more in our unfolding intrasphere.

CHAPTER 15

Communal Disposition

Consonance is the criterion of effective life formation. In service of consonance, our privacy disposition must be balanced by one that is communal. Fortunately, our human form is predisposed to community and communication. Already our reflections on the privacy disposition in the preceding chapters evidenced this feature. We addressed continually the necessity of interaction between our intrasphere and our intersphere, where we meet with others.

All people have a communal predisposition. When they live together in society, this disposition gives rise to various groups of social interaction. Some of these groups are remote; others offer a proximate occasion for communion between participants in them. The forms such social groups assume vary greatly. Formation science distinguishes three main different types of socially formative groups of people: consociations, associations, and communities. Each of them presents in different measure an opportunity for formative communion between their participants. This opportunity is greatest in communities, less so in associations, and least in consociations. Formative communion between people is the highest achievement of our communal disposition. Hence, before discussing the three social types of togetherness and their relation to communion, we must first consider formative communion itself.

Formative Communion

We know from our reflections thus far on the intrasphere that we are free to share or not to share our intimate sphere with others. If two or more people freely share this sphere in mutual understanding and empathy, they experience communion. We have seen that it would be impossible to communicate our whole intrasphere. Our ultimate uniqueness cannot be fully expressed to anyone else. But we can share significant

237

aspects of our interiority. They may be more or less central, but they should at least be significant if we want to experience meaningful intimacy with other people.

Mutual understanding and empathy is only possible when there exists a certain affinity between the aspects of our interior life we want to share. When we try to communicate such facets of our personal concerns and interests, we soon sense whether this affinity is present in the other. If it is not, we may try to communicate other aspects with which the other may resonate. For example, somebody may be unable to empathize with our delight in classical music but may share our interest in spirituality or our concern for children and their initial formation. A certain affinity is thus a necessary condition for the experience of communion. If this affinity is totally absent, we may withdraw in peripheral communications, empty chatter, or deadening silence.

Not every form of human life has the same radius of affinity in regard to other people. Lack of affinity may be caused by either an excessive poverty or an excessive richness in one's intrasphere. Some may have neglected their interior growth, settling for a rather superficial life. They may not be much more than pleasant mouthpieces of the vital-functional interconsciousness of the population to which they belong. They have nothing personal to share. While they may be popular, intimacy with them is almost impossible.

Others cannot reach communion because of the depth and uniqueness of their intrasphere. They are exceptional people. It is difficult for them to find a matching affinity, especially when their sociohistorical formation field is limited. This can be the fate of a deeply sensitive child, artistically gifted, living in a small secluded mining town. Such children may not find anyone in their neighborhood they can really commune with on an intimate level.

Indeed, the more special one's life call and form potency are, the more difficult it will be to find communion in depth with others. The number of potential people with whom one can communicate, whose intrasphere resonates spontaneously with one's own interiority, may be exceedingly small. In some cases, it may only be possible to find intimate communion with one or two friends. They must not only manifest affinity but an ability and a readiness to enter into a relationship of mutually formative communion. Some exceptional people may be destined to a lonely life. However, if their loneliness can be transformed into creative solitude, in intimacy with the mystery, it may become a source of quiet joy and fruitfulness.

Most people are not so exceptional. In their given intrasphere they can find some resonance of affinity with many others. Therefore, they can experience formative communion with a number of people.

The communion that results from our communal disposition, combined with a certain affinity, affects our life situation. It coforms in a special way our everyday world. For this reason, we designate it *formative* communnion. It creates a bond that grants us a certain degree of spontaneous intimacy with people who share like concerns. Usually this intimacy does not go beyond those facets of our intrasphere that gave rise to this specific communion in the first place.

Communion can be neither forced nor planned. It springs up spontaneously and thrives in a shared history. Within the warmth of communion, we rise beyond the anonymity of the everyday routines we share with others in our society and in the various social groups in which we are inserted by choice or by destiny. Let us now turn to those groups that may facilitate the experience of formative communion.

Consociations, Associations, and Communities

The term *association* is more familiar to us than the term *consociation*. The latter refers to an appreciated and affirmed bond existing between all members of a specific formation segment of a population. Consociates identify with the general style and interests of that segment. Examples are the citizens of a country or city; members of labor unions; the middle class; artists; intellectuals; medical doctors; or adherents of an organized religion. Such groups constitute consociations in society if they appreciate and affirm the formation segments to which they belong. In the latter respect, they differ from the same group constituted as a mere formation segment. Not all people who belong to a specific segment of the population appreciate and affirm it. A Jew may reject Jewishness; a child of aristocrats may dislike aristocracy; a black person may deny his or her ethnicity and refuse to participate in the concern for racial justice, and so on. In all such cases, they still belong factually to their segment and are identified as such, but they refuse to experience it as a consociation. To feel, appreciate, and affirm a certain informal bond with the various formation segments to which we (usually implicitly) belong is the minimal effect of our communal disposition.

A higher manifestation of this disposition can be found in the formation of associations. Not only is an association more freely chosen than a consociation; it can also be wider in membership. People belonging to different consociations and their underlying formation segments may form together an association. For example, an association of parents of school children may have members of different consociations—the middle class, blue-collar workers, the urban poor, or members of various churches—who happen to have children in the same public school and hence may form the same association of parents of these school children.

An association is a structured organization initiated and chosen by its members for well-delir·ated, practical purposes. It is more restricted than a consociation because it chooses its own members on basis of freely established criteria. To join such associations and remain in them enlists our communal disposition in a more deliberate apprehension, appraisal, and affirmation than do consociations. However, the communality of an association is less than that of a community; it offers far less of an opportunity for the deeply formative intimacy of communion. A mere association misses the intimacy, spontaneity, and concern for the unique yet compatible unfolding of its members that are characteristic of a community.

In a formative community, we share convictions, dispositions, motivations, and problems in regard to specific ideals. These more intimate shared concerns of communities could play an important role, at least indirectly, in the consociations and associations within which such communities are often formed. They may nourish life and invigorate the corresponding routine dispositions we have to maintain in our consocial life or in our associations.

Communities that foster spiritual deepening among members of a church consociation may have an inspirational influence in the ecclesiastical consociation to which they belong. A freely established formative community of professionals may disclose and foster transcendent motivations for professional dedication. This may deepen the routine dispositions of polite dignified service of the public, claimed and promoted by the professional associations out of which such communities emerged. Such sharing with other professionals within a freely formed community is life giving and rejuvenating. It diminishes professional loneliness. It offers an extra protection against the danger of the erosion of one's faith in the unique form potency the mystery has granted one as a professional.

Community and Mutual Confirmation

Community creates time and space for mutual confirmation. It deepens and restores our conviction that we can do what we are called to do. It renews our esteem for our unique calling, so necessary when the public at large or certain authorities seem to ignore or underestimate our work. As community members, we seek together effective means to implement our ideals in a partly shared formation field.

We have already seen that communion, unlike a community, can only emerge spontaneously, that it can never be planned, forced, or made. Many communities claim that they foster communion among their members. Realistically, this can only mean that one of their primary purposes is to provide the ideal conditions for the development of the communal disposition. Conversely, some organizations that start out as mere associations, not calling themselves communities, may in time grow into communities in this same secondary sense. Such associations prepare the way for the eventual emergence of the community experience among their members. This in turn may facilitate the emergence of communion among those members who are endowed with the necessary mutual trust, spontaneous resonance, and affinity.

The establishment of certain conditions to facilitate the emergence of the community experience, not to speak of the communion experience, does not mean that all of these conditions are absolutely necessary for the maintenance of the community spirit. Some conditions may militate against this experience in certain types of persons. For instance, living under one roof, sharing all meals, being subjected to one rule of life, are not essential to the community experience as such, though these things can facilitate the emergence of this experience for a great number of people lastingly or during one or another formation phase of their life.

Formation Theory of Society

To gain more insight into the communal disposition, let us look at some aspects of the formation theory of society developed by the science of formation. Its social theory provides a basis for our understanding of the specific formative power of community and its source, the communal disposition.

Human societies are composed of various consociations, each consisting of people who have something in common because they belong to the same formation segment of the population. They form a consociation insofar as they appreciate and affirm their rootedness in such segments and face similar formation challenges and opportunities. They have to form life and world under similar professional, economic, educational, spiritual, functional, vital, or sociohistorical conditions.

Formation scientists apply to the emergence and endurance of such segments and consociations the same laws of formation they observe in the physical universe and its formative evolution as a whole. Namely, the epiphanies of the formation mystery in the subhuman world tend toward diversification, not homogenization. This law has been amply demonstrated by the theory of formative evolution based on numerous observations. A complementary law is that the diverse forms resulting from the differentiating processes of formation in the universe tend toward consonance. This law has been confirmed by the observations and theoretical elaborations of quantum physics.

Both laws can be applied to the human epiphany of the formation mystery in society. One aspect of that human epiphany is the emergence of formation segments and subsequent formation consociations. Formative consociations will keep evolving and differentiating, yet they must at the same time strive after consonance with one another and with the formation mystery that is their common ground. These consociations evolve because of the specific challenges people share. Those facing similar formation demands can respond more effectively to such common situations if they share their experiences and responses. Together they can develop adaptive formation styles, which, at least in part, can be handed down from generation to generation.

Such styles usually consist of workable sets of routine dispositions, applicable to different consociations of people. Ballet dancers and bartenders, undertakers and clowns, executives and street cleaners, all face different formation challenges and situations. They do not dress, behave, talk, and recreate in the same fashion. They feel the need to seek confirmation of their own specific formation by consociates who share their preferences. Hence, they tend to form different consociations that are informal and accidental, based on nothing more than a vague, implicit general affirmation of their belonging to the formation segment concerned. A number of consociates may form more explicit, freely structured associations. Consociates display similarities in certain routine dispositions that form their life. So do associates, albeit in a more freely affirmed and explicitly structured fashion.

Consocial and Associational Routine Dispositions
and Distinctively Human Community Dispositions

Ideally, routine dispositions of consociates and associates should be related to the distinctively human dispositions from which they originated. The persons who adopt them should personalize them. No matter how much one identifies with a consociation or association, one should live the common dispositions, however slightly, in a unique way.

Take the example of scholars who are faced with the question of how to labor in relative solitude without neglecting the critical, sustaining support of their colleagues. Over the centuries scholars develop certain consocial or associational routine dispositions to form such contacts and to share a style of life that facilitates their efforts in service of society. Examples of such routines would be their participation in congresses, symposia, and scholarly associations. One can engage routinely in this style of scholarly interaction, maintaining a matter-of-fact anonymity in dress, conversation, and behavior. Under the cover of consocial or associational anonymity, one does not have to reveal one's private opinions or passionate convictions regarding a scholarly commitment. This kind of interaction appropriately protects the smooth flow of a consociation or of an association.

However, some people may experience the need to transcend the efficient, rather anonymous workings of both consociations and associations. They want to replace anonymity by intimacy. Everything in human relations that goes beyond routine dispositions and actions represents a sharing of intraspheric dispositions that is no longer anonymous but intimate. Such intimacy can take on inexhaustible shades of meaning and expression. It is the intimacy between certain adherents of consociations or associations that can lead to the emergence of a formative community.

We could describe formative community as a free association of people who want to share more intimately certain aspects of their formation journey and corresponding intrasphere, which they may already share routinely. Such formative communities may range from family relationships raised beyond routines of everyday interaction, or from friendships between two or more persons, to extensive formative groups guided by rules and regulations. For example, a number of professionals may join together to form a community that fosters in an intimate way the appraisal of certain aspects of their shared professional situation insofar as they enlist their personal intrasphere. In relative mutual intimacy, they may try to develop effective ways to form their professional life on basis of their intraspheric convictions and appraisals. They allow their feelings, thoughts, and opinions to shine through their communications within the trusted ambience of this freely chosen community.

One can belong to various communities at the same time. The professionals just mentioned may also be members of a familial, social, charitable, religious, or athletic community. One's main concern should be to join only those communities that prove to be congenial, compatible, and compassionate in regard to one's unique life-form and position in a formation field.

Main Consociations of Society

The main consociations that coform a society are, respectively, the sociohistorical, vital, functional, and transcendent consociations. Through focal, pre-, infra-, and transfocal interformation or its withholding, they give form to society in countless ways. These consociations can be studied from various perspectives, our chosen one being the formative. We may question the influence of these consociations on the formation of a society and its members. How does any consociation participate in the ways in which the society, of which it is a part, gives form to the wider world? How is it formed in turn by the wider world through this society?

We may clarify the formative social function of various consociations by way of an example. The formative climate, style, and tone of North American society differs, of course, from that of the Japanese. This difference is the end result of the interaction of the various consociations that coform each society uniquely. The deepest powers of these consociations are vested in the transcendent informal or formal communities that evolve within one or more of them. To illustrate this point, let us consider the main kinds of consociations that give shape to the formative climate of North America.

An example of sociohistorical consociations in North America would be blue- or white-collar workers, farmers, industrialists, the middle class, intellectuals, artists, or routinized religious or ideological constituencies. Such consociations are called sociohistorical because they nuance in some measure the historical unfolding of a pluriform society. They coform it as such with other consociations. Children are born into consociations to which their parents belong. A significant number of these children tend to maintain certain facets of the formation traditions they assimilated during their initial formation in their original consociations. This may remain the case in some who, later on in life, join other consociations. This disposition tends to maintain the influence of such consociations on the pluriform formation field of present-day society. Consociations are the guardians of pluriformity. Formation science refers to these sociohistorical consociations as the formation segments of our pluriform formation field. Particular attention is paid to the formative segmental language customs of such consociations.

Examples of functionally formative consociations would be companies, mills, and factories; armies, postal services, and shopping centers; labor unions, political parties, and lobbying groups. They bestow a certain functional form on our society. Without their specific style, North American society would look and act differently.

Vitally formative consociations would be medical, health, ecological, and consumer consociations. The way in which they pursue their objectives has a formative impact on the lifestyle of their adherents, on their immediate environment and on their society as a whole.

Such consociations instill certain routine dispositions that their participants implicitly share, such as style of dress and language. Clearly blue-collar workers differ in these traits from artists, fashion models, movie stars, industrialists, or surgeons.

Original Roots of Routine Dispositions

The roots of the anonymous dispositions shared by various segments and their consociations go deeper than these peripheral expressions. They emerge from certain distinctive human dispositions, convictions, or feelings that are neither anonymous nor routine or peripheral. On the contrary, they are intimate, personal, and centered in the human heart.

These underlying dispositions of the heart can be restored to life by communal intimacy. Such restoration is crucial for the beneficial, dynamic formation of a society. Here freely formed and structured communities come into play. If we do not cultivate these sustaining dispositions of the heart, routine dispositions lose their formative power. Their ability to inspire people evaporates. Consequently, the formative depth and intensity of a country or culture is eroded and eventually depleted.

Community and the Restoration of the Roots of Routine Dispositions

The restoration of the formative roots of routine dispositions is served by freely initiated communities, in which people confirm one another in their fidelity to these roots. They disclose and cultivate together the more personal and intimate dispositions in which routine dispositions originated prior to becoming routinized. It is difficult, if not impossible, for a single individual to succeed in this humanization process: from the viewpoint of distinctively human formation, each person should belong to one or more of these formative communities. Without them one could hardly hope to keep this deeper ground alive and active in one's life.

We can participate in such communities only if we develop a communal disposition to search for appropriate congenial, compatible, and compassionate communities in which we can disclose and celebrate with like-minded people the inner sources of the formation routines we already live in our various consociations and associations.

Community as a Facilitating Condition for Communion

Communities cannot *guarantee* their members the experience of communion. Communion is a gift that cannot be compelled. Communities can only function as a facilitating condition for communion. That is to say, their claim can only be to foster optimal conditions for the emergence of communion among those members who share a certain intraspheric affinity. Not every kind of community is effective for everyone in this regard. What is an optimal condition for one may be a deterrent for another. To live under one roof, sharing the same detailed rule of life, may be wearisome for some and delightful for others. Much depends on the predispositions instilled by one's preformation or acquired during one's initial formation.

We should carefully choose a community that is sufficiently congenial, compatible, and compassionate. Only then can it nourish and satisfy our unique communal disposition. If we choose wrongly and cannot change our affiliation, we may have to make the best of it. If possible, we should try to find a complementary source of communion with friends outside the chosen community.

Communion and the development of the communal disposition are basic for the life of consonance—so basic that we cannot neglect the search for conditions that favor its unfolding. In some cases this may mean that the ideal conditions for communion for us will be found mainly with a few like-minded friends. Even the hermit has a communal disposition. Though it may be dormant, he still needs to experience and celebrate the epiphany of the holy in humanity. Hence, the hermit, too, needs a minimum of communion with certain compatible people.

Some communities may nourish the exalted expectation that they can provide communion for each member in the primary sense of the word. This pretense may betray itself in expressions such as "making community" or "building community" that are misleadingly meant to imply communion experiences in depth. Some facilitating conditions for such experiences can be met by means of routine meetings, celebrations, and regulations. However, these cannot "make" community happen in the sense of real communion.

We repeat, communion is a gift. It cannot be built, fashioned, made, feigned, or forced. Such a parody of communion would destroy the possibility of real spontaneous communion. It could be harmful to persons whose preformation belies affinity with buoyant community-makers. The more blatantly we mouth community slogans, as if we were speaking about the communion experience in depth, the more surely we prevent its spontaneous emergence. The shaping of a community that offers opportunities for moments of communion in depth should be a concern of all members. The emergence of intimate communion at certain times between certain members should be left to the history of their formation and, above all, to the mystery that guides it.

Communities as Sources of Spiritual Survival

Attempts by communities to facilitate moments of communion between their participants can be and are effective to some degree. Therefore, communities are also sources of spiritual survival. They revitalize consociations and associations insofar as the latter are always in danger of losing their inspiration. Without the experience of communion, their members may succumb to mere routine dispositions.

Consider a family that receives the gift of true communion. Its members strive to cultivate the right conditional routines and, by going at times beyond them, to reach communion. These moments of intimacy enable them to vent their frustrations, to communicate their aspirations, to celebrate the form traditions they share, to confirm each other wholeheartedly. Such families are a source of strength and inspiration. Renewed by moments of communion, the members return to their jobs and other consociations, associations, and communities with restored vigor and dedication. The same can be said of any community that becomes an occasion for moments of communion.

Not every family can be a source of communion for its members. The relative uniqueness of some members may be preformed in such a way that their communal disposition can be awakened only by intimate interformation with persons outside the family with whom they experience spontaneous affinity. This should not be frowned upon but fostered, provided the choice is potentially consonant.

The right to awaken and deepen one's communal disposition by finding a congenial community with compatible people is one of the primary human rights bestowed on us by the formation mystery. No one should be forced to live a life of mere routine dispositions in the realm of human relations. A minimum of human community is the birthright of all human beings, no matter how unique their preformation may be.

Conditional Constituent of the Communal Disposition

An essential constituent of the communal disposition is that one be disposed first of all to create favorable conditions for the birth of intimacy in its many gradations. We say gradations because community seldom attains the overwhelming experience of oneness conjured up by an exalted imagination or suggested by romantic films and novels. Even moments of moderate intimacy are not common in everyday life.

The communal disposition disposes us to prepare ourselves for the possible emergence of communion by promoting genuine communication or expressions of courtesy, empathy, and concern that may be partly routine. At propitious moments, the communal disposition may suffuse routine manifestations with the kind of symbolic nuances that pave the way for a spontaneous sharing of intraspheric facets of our life. One could say that distinctively human interformation is marked by a rhythm of community and communion, of symbolic invitation and gratuitous response, of partly routine preparation and the spontaneous emergence of intraspheric mutuality.

Spontaneous Emergence of Communion in Everydayness

Communion may happen when people share their intimate feelings, needs, joys, and sufferings. A unit of soldiers battling common enemies, farmers toiling in a small village, painters struggling for self-expression, friends inspired by the same ideals—such persons begin to share a history of formation. They grow in the affinity initiated by their shared formation field, often developing similar intraspheric dispositions of labor and leisure, of language and celebration, of shared meals and devotion, of neighborly interest and concern. These commonalities begin to pervade their life, creating a kind of communal intraspheric identity. Many surface routines are linked to such deeper dispositions to which they point symbolically.

Moments of communion and intimacy flow from the spontaneous experience of the symbolic meanings that pervade the routines of eating and drinking, working the earth, braving dangers, resisting the intrusion of prying strangers, sharing the joy of nuptials, soothing the suffering of sickness, and offering aid and relief in countless ways. One feels carried by the communal flow of life and the consonance it entails.

Once a consociation or association becomes a community, its common dispositions differ slightly in each member. Though the same in appearance, these dispositions carry the signature of each participant's uniqueness. They are creatively appropriated without losing their commonality of intention and expression. Shared communal dispositions are interformative. They affect one's own apparent form of life as well as giving form to the expectations of others. To disappoint that expectation is to risk dissonance. Thus communal dispositions and moments of communion become a stabilizing force of human consonance in a community.

Deepening of Routine Communal Dispositions

When we discover their symbolic meaning, routine dispositions become distinctively human ones. For instance, when a woman puts candles on the table in preparation for a leisurely meal with a colleague, the meaning of this act is not merely to illumine the plates and glasses. Her gesture is an invitation to communion, to a mode of togetherness that goes beyond their everyday interaction in the company where they work.

The more a community grows, the more these simple routines begin to manifest a significance far more intimate than what is initially evident. They transcend mere peripheral conformity and rise to favorable conditions for a moment of communion. They tap the deeper communal dispositions latent in each human form. No longer is the fulfillment of these conditions restricted to the vital and functional dimensions only. They begin to draw forth the transcendent. Routines of sympathetic interaction are transformed into expressions of distinctively human presence. The merely functional facets of life recede at moments of communion, when the transcendent dimension, longing silently for consonance, comes to the fore.

Experiences of human consonance cannot be reduced to words. Transcendent interformation is ultimately inexpressible. We feel simply more consonant inside ourselves, with each other, and with the formation mystery. We pass almost unnoticeably from vital and functional community to transcendent communion in which the communal disposition finds a moment of fulfillment.

This shared sense of consonance is usually conditioned by our vital and functional modes of sympathetic togetherness. They set us free for this moment of communion. Sensing and doing things together in sympathy can deepen the experience of being together in transcendent consonance. The communal disposition disposes us to transcend vital and functional togetherness. We celebrate in silence our uniqueness and simultaneously our deepest consonance in the light of the formation mystery, which is the source of both uniqueness and communion.

We cannot always live on the heights of this experience, for routine dispositions of sympathetic togetherness have to guide most of our daily interactions. No one can live constantly in the vivid experience of full human consonance. Routine dispositions temper the intensity of full human presence without diminishing sympathetic collaboration. The best we may hope for is a relaxed polarity between the full blossoming of the communal disposition at privileged moments and its preliminary expression in conditional routines that enhance the possibility of communion at the propitious time and place.

To try to live in only one or the other dimension of the communal disposition would lead to frustration. We cannot eliminate either facet. This disposition is a blend of routine modes of simple communication *and* relaxed readiness to enjoy the experience of full human consonance when it comes as a gift. Both experiences carry their own inherent values. Hence, we must give form to them in relaxed freedom of mind and heart. In cherishing, but not holding onto, the ease of routine communication or the joy of communion in depth, we will find the more embracing consonance of life as a whole in all its mystery and commonality, in its quiet functionality and fulfilling transcendence.

Formation Field and the Communal Disposition

The communal disposition, like other dispositions, is directed in its particular expression by the formation field within which it manifests and unfolds itself. Communality and intimacy can be lived in many equally human and respectful ways. Its expressions are simply different in the diverse situations we meet in our formation field. This difference is also influenced by our preformation and our intraformative history.

The communal disposition varies throughout its expression in relationships between husband and wife, employer and employee, salesperson and buyer, formation director and directee. Teammates, close friends, people collaborating in common projects—all illustrate the inexhaustible variety of relationships in communal life.

The same can be said regarding the pre-, intra-, and interformative influences that form each mode of communication and communion. These, too, are responsible for the rich variety of expressions in the human community. For example, a husband does not greet his wife as he does the waiter in his favorite bar. An employer addresses her employees differently than she does the friends with whom she plans to dine in the evening. Each of these encounters is modulated further by the personalities of the participants.

Being a person-in-formation means living in a dynamic, creative, ever more nuanced field of formation. A full description of any disposition has to take this field into account. In short, we can never speak about a specific expression of the communal disposition without considering the momentary configuration of the formation field in which it emerges. A true encounter implies attending to those aspects that are peculiar to each of us.

For instance, a respectful relationship between employers and employees takes into account their mutual commitment to serve the production of the best possible goods for their clients. Their shared formation field inclines them to seek profits to benefit the company, to improve its means of production, and to provide reasonable standards of living for employers, employees, shareholders, and their families. Communality between employers and employees thus implies that neither thwart the inner coherence of their shared formation field. While respecting each one's needs and talents, they should not let the intimacy strivings of the communal disposition prevail over its functional-sympathetic expression.

If intimacy strivings were to prevail, effective productivity is likely to decrease. Specific functional dimensions of the field would lose their meaning; the enterprise could then fail. It would be a violation of the formation field concerned if employees lost hours on the job telling their bosses about the personal problems upsetting them and employers felt obliged to encourage them to express their moods and concerns. Such a company would soon be transformed into an amateur counseling center, dealing with the intimacy needs of each one's personal formation field. The company could hardly compete with other firms appropriately enlisting their time and energy in the production of marketable goods. Ideally, the communal disposition should exert some beneficial influence on the interactions between company personnel. A moderate activation of this disposition will foster the easy flow of sympathetic human collaboration.

The functional-sympathetic facet of the communal disposition should remain in the foreground, the intimacy facet in the background. The latter is not repressed or denied, but one does not allow it to interfere with the primary purpose of an industrial formation field.

The opposite would be true in a field that evokes primarily the intimacy facet of the communal disposition. Imagine the meeting of two young people, ardently in love. Even when the intimacy aspect prevails, the functional-sympathetic aspect is not totally absent. The prevalence of intimacy accords with the special configuration of the shared formation field. The field of an engaged couple is quite different from that of an employer and employee. The purpose of engagement is growth in intraspheric intimacy. The meaning and structure of the love situation would be distorted if the couple were merely to meet functionally. Their encounters should not be restricted to computing the cost of furniture and cooking utensils for the efficient organization of their future home. Still, the functional-sympathetic aspect of these practical matters cannot be neglected, for this would render their communality unrealistic. Their future family can only be supported through the concrete means our society provides. A discussion of items to be bought for their home is only one of many routines involved in marriage. Even the couple's expression of the communal disposition of mutual love must at times be sustained by routine signs developed by the social form traditions they share. They cannot always experience and express the summit of intimacy and intraspheric sharing.

The couple naturally conforms to certain customary expressions of their communal disposition, such as kissing, in Western populations, or nose rubbing, among Eskimos. The lovers themselves do not institute such signs of communality. They adopt them spontaneously from their form traditions and personalize them in tune with their own temperament, history, and phase of intimacy. While they do not necessarily become the primary or dominant element in their communion, they do provide a significant, sustaining tradition for the expression of intimacy.

Later, perhaps after years of marriage, it may happen that functional-sympathetic routine expressions of their marital communion prevail over the experience and expression of intimacy. At these moments, the traditional kiss may no longer be mainly an embodiment of felt intimacy. It has become a sustaining expression of the communal disposition one repeats morning and evening. Were this routine expression to take over totally, the marriage community would no longer be what it ideally should be. Routines would no longer be remote reminders of intimacy. They would no longer express intraspheric sharing and affinity; rather, they would have become ends in themselves.

CHAPTER 16

Consonant Intraformation and Interformation and the Communal Disposition

T he science of formation distinquishes among intra-, inter-, and outer formation. Intraformation refers to the relatively unique, usually concealed inner formation of our apprehensions, appreciations, affirmations, imaginations, memories, anticipations, and their corresponding feelings. We do not expose to everyone indiscriminately what is going on inside us. Yet community between two or more persons can grow to intimacy only if some exposure of interiority happens to them. They share some of their intraformation. This may be the beginning of a community of interformation in depth.

Disposition to Consonant Intraexposure

Interformation can be beneficial only when it is consonant. Overexposure or underexposure of one's intrasphere would lead to dissonance. What constitutes over- or underexposure depends on the particular situation; on the phase of intimacy people have reached; on their mutual affinity and confirmation; on their consonance with the formation mystery; and on similar factors pertaining to their development.

The communal disposition does dispose people toward consonant intraexposure. When the situation seems appropriate, it activates this disposition in them. Intraexposure, or exposure of one's interiority, facilitates the formation and maintenance of an enduring community between people. It fosters intimate formative relationships. Thus, consonant exposure of our interiority is interformative, meaning that it has some forming influence on the people involved.

Intraexposure becomes interexposure when two or more persons reveal something of their inner life to one another. If this is done in a consonant way, their interexposure will be beneficial. One must constantly apprehend, appraise, and decide whether intraexposure is the congenial, compatible, and compassionate thing to do in a certain situation. Should we expose our appreciations, thoughts, and feelings, our formative affirmations, images, memories, and anticipations, to another person? How far should we go in these exposures? What are the situations that make it consonant to disclose our inner life to others? Might this be the beginning of some kind of communion and community with those with whom we share an insight into our inner life? Would they respond in turn, or would they reject our overtures?

The apprehensions, appraisals, and affirmations we form concerning intraexposure will have a formative impact on our lives. They will determine the number and quality of the intimate communities to which we give form and from which we receive form. This sharing will deepen our knowledge of our own inner formation as well as that of others who expose their interiority to us.

Some people may live or work together for years without experiencing communion in the deeper sense. They may come no farther than the conditional courtesy of general sympathy that marks decent human relationships. Children may have the feeling that their parents never pay real attention when they try to expose to them how they feel. Parents may sense that they cannot get through to their children. Men working together for years in the same company may wonder why they cannot get along. Women may spend hours in coffee klatches because they find no sympathetic hearing for their inner life within their own home.

The disposition to intraexposure is natural. Its lack of fulfillment is typical of our functionalistic society, which abounds in consociations and associations, but manifests a scarcity of communities that foster interformation in depth. Our effectiveness in the formation field is enhanced by consonant, mutual interexposure. We begin to understand better what moves us and others in this field. Such insight facilitates our consonant appraisal of the situation and our subsequent appropriate response.

Levels of Intraexposure

Because we live our lives in different dimensions, our intraexposure can correspondingly take place on the sociohistorical, vital, functional, and transcendent levels. For instance, we can expose some aspects of these levels that affect our intraformation. Such exposure may be extensive but not necessarily intensive. We tell people a great deal about the superficial things that touch us in these various dimensions, but we do not communicate what really moves us deeply. We may tell someone, for instance, that the middle-class mentality has some bearing on our outlook; that our vitality makes us prone to physical exercise; that we are inclined to favor science and technology over music and poetry; that, transcendentally speaking, we are interested in Buddhist art.

Such extensive information exposes certain aspects of our intraformation, but it does not grant others a deep insight into what gives form intensely and dynamically to our inner life, our dreams and disappointments, our fears and expectations, our failures and hopes. We have not yet experienced intimate intraexposure in depth.

Deeper exposure carries the unspoken message that we really want to communicate with those in whom we confide. We experience faith, hope, and consonance in regard to these others and hope they will show the same dispositions toward us. Exposure of this sort makes us vulnerable. We could be hurt by those who know our inner secrets. These revelations could be used against us. Implicitly our exposure is an appeal to form a community of silence around what has been communicated in confidence. It is also a silent appeal to seal that community by a similar degree of intraexposure wherein the other people become vulnerable, too. This shared vulnerability serves to strengthen the community through supportive reserve and privacy.

The gradual formation of intimate communion through mutual intraexposure usually has to pass through three stages: purification, illumination, and consonance. Purification has to occur in our apparent life-form insofar as we try to hide or distort what our apprehensions, appreciations, affirmations, and corresponding feelings really are. Illumination enables us to bring to light how we feel. After sufficient purification and illumination, we may experience consonance with one another in shared intraformation.

While these three phases are not absolutely separated from one another, they do not necessarily follow in strict logical sequence. Every new instance of bringing to light some facet of our interiority may demand a purification of corresponding dispositions of concealment peculiar to our apparent life-form. Our momentary experience of consonance may be diminished or lost when we become aware of another concealment that is an obstacle to deeper consonance; this, too, needs purification, followed by illumination of the concealed sector. In the end, we become aware that our uniqueness and solitude can only be shared by the formation mystery itself in the center of our being. Still, a high degree of sharing is possible before we touch this quiet center of the soul.

Intraexposure happens not only through language. The way in which we give form to our gestures, facial expressions, and voice inflections communicates on a prefocal basis much of our intraformative feelings, thoughts, and dispositions. This vital substructure often exposes more of our emotional dispositions than words can expose.

Communal Disposition and Intraisolation

Why is exposure of our thoughts and feelings so basic for the awakening of the communal disposition? Why do we feel so isolated in our intraformation? Undoubtedly isolation is a central problem in the contemporary formation fields of humanity. The dormancy of the communal disposition is not an exceptional, curious incident. Lack of community and communion, of interformation in depth, is closely linked to the deformative forces of dissonance in our public formation field. The functionalistic organization of labor and leisure makes it difficult, if not impossible, for many people to experience themselves as personal participants in the processes that give form to their world. They experience these formation processes as happening to them, as out of their control. They do not feel that they can make things happen together with others, nor do they feel called to offer a unique contribution.

Many experience the public formation field as a vast game in which they are moved around indifferently. Since there is little or no appeal to their communal disposition, they close themselves up in their own intraformative history. Such intraisolation may give rise to symptoms of an overexalted fantasy life. When this reaches extreme proportions, persons may act in bizarre ways; they may even be declared psychotic. In many, a lack of communion leads to withdrawal from the inter- and outer aspects of the formation field. Their communal disposition seems almost nonexistent. They live lives of sedate despondency, polite but empty. Desires for intimacy are muted.

Many events in the recent formation history of humanity have contributed to this paralysis of the communal disposition. To mention only a few: the lack of opportunity to make a real difference in the midst of gigantic political systems and bureaucracies; an industrial production process that makes it impossible to experience one's own distinctive form-giving to the products that leave the factory; the mobility of families, which prevents the creation of stable fields of time and space conducive to the slow process of giving and receiving in interformative communion with people and places that become familiar; the decline of the extended family as a significant, reliable center of formation whose members live within a short distance from one another; urban forms of life that lead to segmentation instead of communication between residents in adjacent apartments, shoppers in supermarkets, commuters in trains or buses or cars; a technological form giving that makes personal participation a disturbing interference with the smooth, computerized processes it has established.

Humanity cannot find the consonant life when its fundamental communal disposition is suppressed. Modern styles of production, organization, and technology are unavoidable events in our formation history. We cannot deny or destroy them, nor can we turn back the clock. We must integrate them in the consonant totality of a fully responsible human life.

It is our hope that the rise of formative spirituality will create new forms of appeal to our communal disposition. Spiritual formation in communion with others must balance our awesome technical and scientific formation. Otherwise we could all become the joyless captives of our isolated intraformative prisons.

The Pride-Form, the Foundational Triad, and the Communal Disposition

Spiritual formation will have another beneficial effect in regard to our communal disposition and its awakening. The sociohistorical factors mentioned above do have an adverse impact on the actualization of this disposition. Yet there is another more profound force deep within us that counteracts community formation: the exalting autarchic pride-form. Its force of exaltation makes us falsify our apparent form of life. We try to appear grander than we are. This play of pretensions is another obstacle to the kind of frank exposure that could create communion between us and our friends and relatives.

Another obstacle to communion may be the realistic observation that, because of our innate finiteness and vulnerability, no human form can be totally trusted. People deserve only limited trust, not necessarily because of bad will on their part but because of their inherent human weakness and fallibility.

Spiritual formation in communion is centered ultimately in the formation mystery. Such communion fosters faith, hope, and consonance in relation to this mystery and its epiphanies, especially the human. It enables us to develop faith, hope, and consonance toward people as beneficiaries of the mystery residing in their inmost center. This triad is the ultimate basis of enduring human community and communion. It overcomes the realistic distrust that everyone should feel in regard to human relationships isolated from the mystery.

Learning this lesson starts at home, especially when parents are able to admit that they cannot always be perfect tutors and guardians. Paradoxically, it is this gift of distrust of self that opens the way to faith, hope, and consonance. A certain distrust of the merely human, developed in childhood, should be revived in adult life, insofar as it is a realistic distrust. It should not be magnified in an unwholesome fashion, lest it threaten the emergence of our communal disposition. It is the task of spiritual formation to restore the triad of faith, hope, and consonance as a main source of both community and communion.

Interformative Penetration and Parallel Exposure

Intimate interformative communion usually develops through a process of interformative penetration. This means that friends expose to one another more and more of their intraformation. As time passes, these exposures may gradually increase. Such interformative mutuality is essential if the development of communion is to take place. If one person exposes more intraformative feelings and dispositions, the other does likewise. The communal disposition inclines them to correlate their levels of self-exposure. These two processes of interformative penetration and parallel exposure deepen the experience of really feeling understood by one another. This experience affects in turn the growth of faith, hope, and consonance, with their attendant dispositions of mutual sustenance, cordiality, and receptivity.

Real communion advances only as long as it is interformative and not merely conformative. The unique epiphany of the formation mystery in one another is exposed increasingly in free and frank communion. Interformation in depth means precisely to sustain one another in obedience to each person's unique life call. It excludes mere conformity and excessive dependency.

Exposure of our inner life tends to expand our own apprehension of our interiority. We need more time by ourselves to appraise what has emerged in our awareness during experienced moments of communion. This private appraisal may give rise in turn to more self-exposure when communion is resumed. Paradoxically, communion leads to solitude, solitude to communion. This rhythm of solitude and communion is most noticeable in the consonant life.

Wise, limited exposure at the right time to the right person is a mark of consonance and a means of growth toward the fully consonant life. If we cannot be close to at least one or a few persons in openness and honesty, our formation will be blocked. We cannot fulfill our form potency if we lack appreciative abandonment to the formation mystery as it manifests itself in true communion.

One cannot say a priori that intraexposure is either consonant or dissonant. If it is consonant, it tends to activate the communal disposition in others and to foster communion. If it is dissonant, it turns others away and others feel inclined to retreat from communication and communion. We have all experienced such negative feelings when people unexpectedly inundate us with intimate details of their personal life and feelings. We are often secretly repelled by such revelations, even if we pretend to go along with them. We fear looking smug and selfish if we do not indulge in the same kind of sharing.

Consonant and Dissonant Exposures

The consonant life manifests itself in intraexposure that is congenial, compatible, and compassionate. It is congenial if it is in tune with who the exposer really is without divulging private dispositions in such a way that they harm one's formation. It is compatible when all relevant aspects of the formation field—such as the time, the occasion, and the relationship between the exposer and the listener—are respected. Exposure is compassionate if it takes into account what others can bear at this moment of their formation history and in view of their unique preformation.

Parents, for instance, do not expose their sexual problems to small children; scholars do not expose their highly speculative and unconfirmed inner doubts to simple defenseless people without much education; we do not impose our inner anxieties on people who we know are already over-anxious. Such actions manifest a lack of consonance in the exposures of our inner life. A dissonant life tends to give rise to inappropriate exposures.

Intraformative revelations can be too intimate or not intimate enough in view of the circumstances. Consonant exposure has to be in tune with prevalent form traditions not only in their foundations but even in their periodic accretions (if these accretions are not at odds with what is truly foundational). Public exposures that are unnecessarily at variance with the prevailing form traditions of the period in which we live foster division, not communion. It may be necessary in exceptional cases to counter certain popular accretions of form traditions; to do so may be an expression of higher consonance with the formation mystery, reforming and transforming human history. However, if average persons completely disregard their form traditions in regard to intraexposure, one may suspect that their life has not yet attained sufficient consonance.

The communal disposition inclines us to expose to trustworthy others relevant facets of our intraformative life. If we hide these inner apprehensions, appraisals, affirmations, and dispositions, no one can help us to clarify and correct them. To be unique does not mean that it is impossible for others to commune with us. There are persons who can in some measure appraise the forms we give to our life and world. People share the same potential human thoughts and feelings; uniqueness means that these thoughts and feelings carry a personal nuance and signature. They are, moreover, coordinated in a distinctive fashion within our particular life call, formation field, and history. If we meet people with the necessary affinity as well as the willingness and readiness for interformative encounter, communion may happen.

We can commune meaningfully with people to whom we have an affinity. While no two people experience precisely the same configuration of meanings, sensitive people can empathize with us. Others have experienced similar feelings in analogous settings. If not, they can creatively imagine such situations. Imagined formation fields can activate in them the potential universal human feelings evoked by such images. Gradually formative empathy enables them to enter into our own story. They begin to approximate increasingly, if not perfectly, what we are going through. This universal human potency for empathic formation of similar imaginary formation fields is basic to the communal disposition and typical of human life.

Relief of Intraisolation and Expansion of Appraisal

Mutual communion relieves the illusion of inner isolation. We are not alone with our feelings of awe and reverence, sensuality and ambitiousness, love and hate, fear and doubt, anger and resentment, envy and jealousy, guilt and shame. Our confidential exposure of these feelings may be paralleled by similar exposures from an empathic listener. In this way communion helps us to gain not only in apprehension and appraisal of our own motivations and emotions but also in those of others. Such mutual refinement of insight into what moves us inwardly generalizes itself to a better appraisal of the inner dynamics shared by the people we meet.

An ever growing, nuanced appreciation of our formation field and its inner dynamism is a critical condition for consonant life formation. It is difficult to grow in such sensitivity without at least a minimum of mutual communion about our thoughts and feelings. The problem is that the illusions of the pride-form obscure our appraisals through subtle distortions and deceptions. Classical spiritual form traditions contend that people cannot pierce the cloud of self-illusion without exposing their appraisals to other people. Hence, they emphasize the need for community, communion, and formative direction in private or in common. When people have been able to expose their inner leanings to empathic listeners, they learn how to get in touch with their real feelings. This access facilitates the disclosure of their own life direction.

Refusal of the Communal Disposition and the Apparent Life-Form

We may refuse to listen to the stirrings of our communal disposition. Instead of communing with one or more persons, we conceal ourselves from people. To succeed in such concealment, we have to form and maintain deceptive appearances. Unguarded or excessive exposure of our foundational, core, and current forms of life would be as dissonant as an excessive withholding of communication. Hence, we need to develop an appropriate appearance in daily life, one that both conceals and reveals our interiority without deception. Consonant appearances take into account the directives of our life call, of the situations in which we find ourselves, of the sensitivities of others, and of the form traditions to which we are committed.

The apparent life-form can be consonant or dissonant. It is consonant when it lets what is appropriate under the circumstances shine through without denial or distortion of who we are. It is dissonant when we live in anxious and excessive vigilance about our appearance, lest any aspect of who we are manifest itself, no matter how appropriate and beneficial. In that case, the apparent life-form is no longer a screen but a facade. To maintain that facade demands much energy, usually on the pre- or infra-focal levels of attention.

The formation energy available to us is limited. The energy we use for the dissonant formation of deceptive appearances is no longer at our disposal for consonant life formation. Hiding our intraformation totally from others is an exhausting diversion that taxes all our form potencies and energies.

Fear may cause one to develop an apparent life-form that refuses to make room for the expression of one's communal disposition. Will others accept my communication? Will it be used against me when I reveal it to others? Will I be laughed at? Rather than risk such threats, we may make our apparent life-form an impenetrable wall or shield. We keep improving on this camouflage of our interiority. Much of our formative energy becomes absorbed in the extension of such fortifications and protective appearances. Finally, we ourselves may no longer know where our real life-form ends and the apparent one begins.

This effort may become excessively stressful. One who continually refuses the communal disposition may eventually manifest psychosomatic symptoms. Problems get bottled up and find no outlet in confidential communion. Many marriage relationships fail due to this inability or unwillingness to commune with one another beyond appearances. For example, irritation with each others' routine dispositions should not be disguised but frankly discussed. Otherwise the denied feelings keep festering and may suddenly explode in an irrational vehemence that can destroy the marriage community.

Initial Formation of the Communal Disposition and Its Expression

Children learn to respect, activate, and cherish their communal disposition by what we could call "situational osmosis." Usually they adopt the patterns of exposure they experience in their parents and peers. When parents are outgoing and communicative, children will probably imitate their warm expressiveness. When they are secretive, evasive, and reticent, children may distrust their own communicative tendencies. Then, too, parents may ask their children to expose themselves more than is necessary or desirable. This may lead to closure on the part of the children, thus inaugurating a lifelong tendency in their patterns of communication and communion.

Communal Disposition and Form Traditions

Most influential for initial formation are the form traditions that prevail in one's family and formation segment of society. In some competitive segments of a population, children may be imbued with excessively vigilant dispositions in regard to people, lest others take advantage of them. In such segments, exposure of one's interior life is minimal. People become almost paranoid about their intraformative feelings and motives. Everyone is made to believe that it is clever to maintain an advantage over others by tricking them into divulging personal feelings that can eventually be used against them in competitive situations. If the form tradition of an entire formation segment tends to foster relentless competition for success, people are likely to be excessively secretive behind a front of camaraderie and cheerful sociability that substitutes for communion and community.

Other form traditions, especially spiritual ones, foster the communal disposition and its expression in compatibility and compassion. The consonant life lived in the light of the mystery is a life together. The gift of the communal disposition is by its nature a transpersonal endowment. It is a disposition granted to all people, representing their original oneness in the mystery. It excludes conceit and unfair competition.

Spiritual form traditions create conditional communities. They constantly inspire the participants in such communities to communion, mutual aid, and service of the needs of humanity. These traditions try to overcome the inclination of the autarchic pride-form. They do not foster erratic spiritual heroism or individualistic exaltation. Rather, they inspire a new way of living in compatibility and compassion.

The more the participants in such form traditions enter into these transforming aspirations, the more they experience each other as people journeying along the same road of formation in the light of the mystery. They begin to share intimately the faith, hope, and consonance that coforms them within their spiritual form tradition. Such classical spiritual traditions touch directly on what is most intimate in human life. They can effect, therefore, an intimate communion between all those who allow their hearts to be moved by similar inspirations.

The great spiritual classics foster universal communion between humans through the inspiration and example of those adherents who have grown in mutual communion. Such traditions are a source of compassion for humanity in its pain and suffering. Adherents should refuse to withdraw to a small world of their own when the human community is weighed down by oppression, conflict, and nuclear threat. Nonetheless, communion with one another within the restricted community of the shared tradition remains important. Spiritual love and experience is revitalized by prayerful reflection on the teachings of one's form tradition. This contact is necessary if one is to remain faithful to the wider ideal of selfless communion with suffering humanity. Together with others we should become a gentle epiphany of the mystery in the midst of a broken world.

Spiritual form traditions counsel adherents not to depend on their own limited communal disposition but on the communal disposition of the forming mystery always at work in the world. Wherever such communities spring up, communion happens in human history. People let go of the old, anxious ways of the autarchic pride-form. They find each other in the forming mystery and its compassion. They transcend their own formation fields and enter into the limitless field of the mystery in which all people are reconciled, cared for, and revered.

Spiritual Community and Universal Care

Spiritual communities in this sense are a response to our finiteness. The life of the spirit inspires us to relieve poverty and injustice everywhere in the world, in all segments of society. We suffer our finitude most when we realize that we as individuals cannot realistically aspire to do this. Our life call, as embodied in our talents, needs, and limitations, restricts our congenial possibilities for effective service. As a community, however, we can find and foster congenial service for many different adherents. Some will work well with laborers, others with spiritually deprived professionals, others with people who need entertainment or aesthetic beauty to illumine their life, and still others with people suffering in urban or rural poverty.

No matter how inspired and compassionate we are, we cannot be everything to everyone. Our communal disposition makes us sense, however, that the same disposition is present as a potency in all people of goodwill. They are all called to commune with others in compatible and compassionate service. We no longer feel alone, but realize that this disposition will dispose many of us to relieve an immense variety of poverties. Together with like-minded others, we may give form in compassion to a suffering society.

The communal disposition disposes us to establish small associations of spiritual inspiration. These will sustain our commitment and expand and deepen our obedient listening to the mystery in our lives. We will remain more attentive to anything that is a serious threat to honest congeniality, compatibility, and compassion in the particular kind of service to which we have been called uniquely.

Above all, we should realize that community does not necessarily mean the sharing of one roof, though this can be an excellent condition for it. One may even live alone and experience deep communion with others. In that case community in the conditional sense is minimal; communion in the primary sense is maximal.

It is difficult to remain committed to the service of humanity without the support of some community in the primary sense. If one's conditional community, like one's family does not succeed in creating communion one should never be bitter about that. No conditional community can compel communion. One should understand this failure of communion and respond with compassion, while trying to establish intimacy with friends or coworkers who manifest the necessary affinity. In the last analysis, we have to belong somewhere to prevent numbness and anger from overtaking our life of service and compassion.

CHAPTER 17

Communal Disposition in
Religious Faith and Form Traditions

T he science of formation refers often to the formation mystery.
This term points to the hidden source of all formation. Formative
evolution of the universe implies such a source. More recently, in terms
of the aeons of evolution, this hidden source has manifested itself in the
emergence and in the brief formation history of the human race. This
race is endowed with a receptive potency to acknowledge an underlying
mystery. To be sure, we cannot by our own light penetrate its nature and
meaning. Yet we have to assume its reality. Without this form directive
force, it becomes impossible to make any coherent sense of the inter-
weaving formation events increasingly disclosed to human experience,
scholarship, and scientific investigation.

For some formation scientists, the idea of a formation mystery is only
a working hypothesis or a hypothetical construct. For others it assumes a
more personal meaning. This is especially evident in religious faith and
form traditions.

Religious Faith and Form Traditions and the
Self-Disclosure of the Mystery

Take, for example, the Christian faith and form tradition, in which we
see a distinction between the formation mystery as disclosed in its cosmic
operations and the mystery as supereminent or as absolutely transcendent. The Christian tradition, as understood in articulation research,
holds that an absolutely transcendent mystery can in no way be included
in or subordinated to the formation mystery as cosmic manifestation. It
infinitely transcends the cosmic formation force and its implied orientations. Both may be called formation mystery but only in an analogous
way. The supereminent formation mystery is the ultimate source of the

cosmic mystery of formation. It makes the cosmic mystery be; it sustains it, empowers it, and appears in it. Hence, we may call it the cosmic epiphany of the absolutely transcendent formation mystery.

No scientist in this field can conclusively disprove the possibility that such a supereminent mystery of formation exists, or that it may disclose itself to humanity during its formation journey. Religious faith and form traditions are rooted in this possibility. A number of formation scientists are engaged in articulation research of such traditions. In view of their interest, it may be helpful to consider the relationships between such a possible self-disclosure of the mystery and the human community, as well as the communal disposition that unfolds within such a community.

Highly developed religious traditions personalize the supereminent formation mystery. They believe that it seeks out the human race as it makes its journey through history. For these higher traditions, revelation is the disclosure of the all-embracing love of this radical mystery for humankind as it travels through history. It journeys not as a collection of isolated individuals but in consociations, associations, and communities formed under the inspiration of humanity's communal disposition.

The expression "formation history of a faith and formation community" is central for an understanding of their vision. It includes their formation history as well as the formative evolution that is its providential prelude and biophysical setting. For these believers, it is a story of formative love. They believe that the supereminent formation mystery lovingly inscribes its forming power in the unfolding of the cosmos and humanity. Personal and communal formation histories are considered consonant insofar as they are in free coformation with that forming love. By this coformative response, communities allow the forming mystery to enter human life and history.

For these traditions the supereminent formation mystery is God himself. They celebrate him as Creator and Form Giver via the cosmic epiphany of the divine formation mystery. Many visible effects, mutations, and processes of this forming power can be observed by formation scientists who do not adhere to such traditions or who do not believe in such an absolutely transcendent source of formation.

Christian Community and Self-Disclosure of the Formation Mystery
The Christian tradition extols the history of Jesus of Nazareth as the decisive central moment of the formation history of cosmos and human-

ity. It believes that in his life story the divine formation mystery and human history become one.

In their faith vision, Christians apprehend the Christ form as calling the human race to a new appraisal and affirmation of the formation events that mark its adventure in the universe. This appeal for new appreciation radiates from his life, his teachings, his parables. In this light, all human formation events are to be seen, they believe, as disclosures of a divine mystery that he reveals as Father, Son, and Spirit. Christians believe that people are challenged by Jesus of Nazareth to appraise human formation events as invitations to participate in the eternal divine formation Event. (For an analogous elaboration of this term, see my book *The Mystery of Transforming Love.*)

Christians claim that the self-disclosure of the radical mystery is crystallized in the historical reality of Jesus of Nazareth. They believe that this disclosure is dynamic, open, and ongoing in time and space, that it will continue in an eminent way in eternity. They profess that the self-communication of the radical mystery in the Christ form is not something that happened only long ago. For them it is not merely a fact and date of the past filed away in archives buried in a dusty cabinet. They live in the faith that the Christ form and formation are alive in a community that in an eminent way can fulfill the communal disposition of humanity.

The disclosure of this life in Palestine gave rise to a number of truths that were later expressed in systematic theological propositions. Believers claim their assent to these, knowing they are declared authentic by the leaders of their community. But if these propositions were all, there would not be a living community. Believers could not aspire to mutual communion in the Christ form. Nor could they believe in an ongoing, formative, divine self-disclosure in and through their community. There would be no actual effect on their lives here and now. The disclosure in the past would lose its vibrancy. It would have only marginal importance to people today. It could not create living communion among them by a believed affinity to the Christ form uniquely alive in the intrasphere of each committed adherent of this tradition.

To be actually formative, such original disclosure cannot remain encapsulated in its basic manifestation, either in biblical history or past events. Nor are theological propositions sufficient to fulfill the deepest aspirations of the communal disposition of people: they do not as a rule touch people's lives in a formative fashion. To remain actually formative for people and their faith communities, this disclosure must be happening in some way in all formation events and throughout history. Such communities and their adherents must be able to apprehend, appraise, and affirm with their heart what happens in their everyday life in the light of that central event in Palestine and the truths and propositions that flow from it. Any event that makes them potentially aware of a new and deeper meaning in their life should be included in this living appreciation. In the light of the original event of the Christ form, they should see each formation event as a disclosure of this mystery. Sharing an intraspheric faith formation in their lives, they experience communion as the fruit of both their graced transcendent disposition and their graced communal disposition.

Community and Higher Faith and Form Traditions

The example of some aspects of the Christian tradition helps us to relate the communal disposition and its effect, communion, to the communities of all higher faith and form traditions. Such communities believe that the self-disclosure of the mystery usually happens within a community of people and its formation history. They admit that individual members of such communities may be singled out as special carriers of the message of the mystery. Yet they are affirmed as carriers of the message only when there is some basic continuation, in spite of innovation, of the foundational form of the community. Compatibility with its foundations is a basic criterion. Such prophets are not seen as isolated from the community but as its graced and gifted representatives.

The originators of a new faith and form tradition present a different case. Yet even they are not totally unrelated to the consociation, association, or community from which they emerge. Articulation research always discovers influences from their cultures.

When the originators of new religious traditions succeed, the unusual formation events marking their life, combined with their spoken or written message, give rise to a specific faith community that forms itself around these words and events. The communal disposition of the human heart becomes focused on this "togetherness-with-others" in the light of these revealing words and events. This disposition is deepened by the transcendent human aspiration and hunger for the mystery and its disclosure. Consequently, such a community reflects together in awe on these events and sayings of the originator of their incipient tradition. These formative reflections are recorded in oral or written traditions, or in both.

The growing collections of such traditions are distillations and crystallizations of the community's awe-filled contemplation. The community's contemplation of these formative events and words give rise to its concrete existence and continuation. Such contemplation is filled with wonder and awe. The events contemplated are believed to be self-disclosures of the divine formation mystery. Thus formed, community believes itself to be a chosen recipient and guardian of a privileged record of the self-disclosure of the mystery to humanity. Members use this record as a light projected on all formation events in the past, present, and future. They believe that this communal treasure allows them to decipher more easily and with greater certainty the message of the mystery hidden in all formation events.

Such records are not intended to give an exact and detailed account of the events contemplated in awe. The community representatives do not write them down as a professional historian would record the events in the life of people. Their primary intent is not historical detail but the communication of the formative meaning of the event, its awe-evoking impact as a definite self-disclosure of the mystery. In the light of this shattering sense of the event, minor details sink into the background. The believer sees them as the incidental historical matter used by the mystery to give visible and audible form to its self-disclosure. The founding tradition is primarily a record of the awe-filled faith of the community as it apprehends, appraises, affirms, celebrates, and implements the meaning of its formation history. What matters for such a community of faith is awe-filled apprehension of its history as a privileged disclosure of the formation mystery. Both the transcendent aspiration disposition and the communal disposition of its adherents find their deepest fulfillment in this sharing of the record of faith and in the celebration and sacramental participation in the events it announces in awe.

Formation Scientists and Articulation Research of Religious Faith and Form Traditions

In the light of the former considerations, formation scientists do not focus mainly on the role of the individual authors of such records of the faith and form tradition of a community. They are more concerned with the role of the community whose faith orientation of their communal disposition such records reflect. The records are usually the product of a culture that is geographically and historically far removed from that of the researcher. To apprehend and appraise what was meant originally demands a special approach. Formation science calls this preliminary approach of its articulation research the method of *empathic coformation*. It is a cautious effort to enter into the formation experience of the original faith community out of whose reflection and contemplation this orientation of their transcendent and communal disposition emerged. Researchers try by empathy to accompany the early recording community on the original formation journey that generated their records. It is an attempt to foster experiential and imaginary coformation with their founding formation efforts.

Such empathic coformation should be complemented, corrected, and corroborated by objective data from other formation sources. Articulation research must take into account the relevant contributions of auxiliary sciences such as archeology, the science of literary forms, exegesis, cultural history, anthropology, and comparative religion. These subjects can throw light on the objective conditions of a faith and form community in its decisive founding stages. Only then can the researcher try to reinterpret the result of all these findings in terms of present-day formation science. Such research usually discovers that the self-disclosure of the mystery and its circumstances are less exotic than may appear at first sight. It shows how such disclosures happened in the midst of concrete human formation events and experiences whose deeper meaning for the community was later celebrated in poetic and mythical description and ritual.

Facilitated by the objective data of auxiliary sciences and clarified by the conceptual framework of formation theory, empathic coformation fashions the dynamic and concrete approach of this type of articulation research. In this respect, formation science differs from the rather abstract and intellectualistic methodology that marks many of its auxiliary sciences. Formation science utilizes gratefully their findings. It integrates the validated results of these approaches in the perspective opened up by its own holistic procedures.

Such research reveals that the self-disclosure of the mystery is experienced by these communities as a gradual process taking place in the midst of human formation events. This process is believed in some way to continue during the whole formation history of the community. This ongoing unfolding of the formation tradition is always appraised in terms of the founding faith tradition. The community returns to its beginnings for "re-sourcing" when its animation begins to falter. It does the same when faced with the necessity to reformulate its form tradition in the light of new historical formation events. The expansion of validated human experiences and knowledge may pose another challenge, demanding a return to the foundations.

Private and Communal Formation History

A similar process of ongoing reformation marks the dynamism of the private formation history of each adherent of a community of faith. Each is faced with unique formation events and situations. These may demand a private accommodation that cannot be covered or is not yet covered by the general customs of the community. Their privacy disposition compels them to make this unique adaptation. Their communal disposition, however, appeals to them to keep contact with the foundational traditions of their faith community, if not with all of the traditions' accretions. Without this bond their privacy disposition could lead to encapsulation. They could lose touch with the objective criteria of their faith community. They could be caught in isolating subjectivistic interpretations of the formation events in their private life. This might tempt them to justify individualistic experiences by selective and distorted fragments of their traditions. Such distortions may seem to them to sustain their dissonant subjectivism.

Forming Power of Faith and Form Communities

The actual forming power of faith and form communities is intense and pervasive. This is not simply due to an intellectual assent of their adherents to theological or traditional propositions. Such assent is only one indispensable aspect of the formative influence of such communities on their members.

Living faith in the actual self-disclosure of the formation mystery is the primary source of this forming power. Theological or traditional formulations are the secondary fruits. They are the result of the faith apprehension of the community. This apprehension comes first; it is irreplaceable as a source of formative power. Theological verbalization or poetic expression of what this apprehension means for the community comes after. The faith experience of the ongoing self-disclosure of the mystery is more formative than theological reflection on it. Yet the indispensable role of precise theological statement cannot be denied or neglected.

Briefly, the sense of an absolute formation mystery disclosing itself continually, both in the faith community and its adherents, is the deepest source of their actual formation, reformation, and transformation.

Underestimation of the Sense of Mystery in Communal Formation

Certain auxiliary sciences have been inclined to overlook the founding sense of mystery while scrutinizing faith and form traditions and their communal conditions. These sciences tended toward a somewhat sterile rationalism and positivism in their research. This made it impossible for them to appraise such traditions in depth. The prestige of a positivist methodology and its undeniable results may have led even scholarly adherents of these traditions to gravitate to a rationalist and/or positivist perspective. It might have veiled for them the mysterious heart of their own traditions. The dynamic, holistic, and empathic approach of formation science should complement the necessarily fragmented approaches of its auxiliary sciences in this regard.

Traditional Communal Forms of Life and Their Relation to Doctrine

Religious traditions proclaim faith as a gift, an inner light infused by the mystery illuminating its epiphanies in our human formation field. This gift of light enables the faithful to commit themselves to a special way of form reception and donation. Each enlightened way generates its own fundamental form of life, such as the Jewish, Christian, Islamic, Buddhist, Taoist, or tribal religious forms of existence. Each of these forms of life colors the concrete unfolding of both the privacy and the communal dispositions of believers.

The teachings of faith communities define and clarify what adherents should believe, what their commitment concretely entails. Assent of mind to these teachings is a necessary condition for believers' consonant realization of their faith within the boundaries of their field of formation and its horizons.

Articulation research in formation science discloses that it is not the teachings in isolation from the mystery to which the faithful fundamentally give their assent. Their assent is to the primordial truth of the Radical Formation Mystery itself. Mature adherents of the various traditions seem to affirm implicitly that this truth lies beneath and beyond all the propositional expressions of truth to which they mentally assent.

Articulation research discloses that faith communities manifest an impressive potency to form community in depth. A community rooted in a religious faith tradition seems more apt than secular communities to fulfill the communal dispositions and aspirations of members. Even the community-forming powers of the family seem to be enhanced considerably when family life is rooted in a religious faith and form tradition, sustained by a community of believers.

The magnitude of the potency for community formation differs in different traditions. It reaches a summit in the type of tradition that teaches that the mystery discloses itself as a transpersonal center of love and generosity. This vision seems to challenge its beholders to enter into loving and creative interformation with one another and with people outside their particular faith community. Their faith vision appears to function as an ongoing invitation to appreciate and affirm all people as embraced by the same loving mystery.

Formative Faith Apprehension, Word, and Event

Behind every genuine word spoken by the community lies a formative faith apprehension. This apprehension cannot fully manifest itself in any word. Words are but limping, halting metaphors compared to the faith they try to communicate. Words are the crutches of the experience, not the experience itself.

Faith traditions may claim that the transcosmic mystery itself has spoken to their founders or originating communities. They may realize, however, that even this transcendent mystery has to use inadequate, faltering human words to communicate with the limited human form and its historical communities. This is one of the reasons that the great religious traditions point beyond words to decisive formation events in which they believe the mystery disclosed itself to their community. They invite their adherents to enter into the key formation events around which the community formed itself in the first place. For them formative words come after formation events. They consider such words formative only to the extent they facilitate the participation of the faithful in those originating events themselves. Words about such events grow out of enlightened contemplation by the community and its subsequent theological reflection. Such words are always open to deeper understanding. Hence, a certain reformulation of expressions of the faith of a community is to be expected in the course of its history.

Originating formation events and the necessity of their variable expression over the centuries seems to spark a special formation dynamic in enduring faith communities. They experience a dynamic of ongoing contemplation and reflection, of increasing disclosure of new and rich facets of the mystery of formation as apprehended in the tradition concerned. Often this leads to passionate dialogue between proponents of old and new formulations. By means of this formative dynamism, the originating events penetrate the passage of a community through successive periods of its formation history. Briefly, religious traditions appear to believe that an ineffable reality lies behind their formulas about the primordial formation mystery and its epiphanies.

Communal Verbalization of Religious Formative Apprehensions

Our communal disposition unfolds by means of formative language. Such language is intimately related to the triad of human apprehensions, appreciations and affirmations, which it tries to express. Words can have no forming meaning for the members of a community if they cannot relate them in some way to their experiences. Words as formative are not things in themselves, like meaningless syllables may be. They are forming tools by which community members try to give form to what they think and feel in such a fashion that others can share in their experience. As we already know from formation science, language cannot give adequate form to what people experience. Formative experience always surpasses formation language. This limitation of language is especially evident in religious communication, which refers by its nature to an already elusive apprehension of the disclosures of what remains ultimately a mystery. Hence, such communication can become dissonant and deformative. This happens when the communicator or listeners substitute the words they use for the reality to which they point.

Religious words become consonant and formative within a faith community when they evoke a loving apprehension and appreciation of the disclosure of the mystery to which they refer. Such disclosures are not neutral in regard to the lives of the members of the community. They are pregnant with directives for the formation of their life and world. The members of the community cannot speak about such disclosures in a meaningful fashion if they are not in some way open to the form directives they entail. For instance, if the disclosures imply directives of justice, peace, and mercy, and we close our hearts to them, we falsify the disclosures by a conspiration of silence about such directives.

Formation science holds that words by themselves alone are not formative. They only become formative in context, be it in the context of a sentence, a culture, a book, a science, an art, a practical project or enterprise. Similarly, the language of a religious tradition has formative meaning only in the context of the believing community. The faith-illumined communal disposition opens the members of a believing community to the formative meaning of the community's religious language. Their eyes of faith behold behind and through all communal language the disclosure of the mystery. Formative religious words must refer to the personal apprehension of the epiphanies of the mystery by members of the community. The implicit communication of one's own ongoing life formation in the light of such disclosures is the animating soul of formative religious language.

The language of religious faith and form traditions shows an affinity to the formative language of poetry and to other kinds of formative human expression, such as visual art, music, song, symbols, silence. These modes of expression celebrate a transcendent presence at the heart of the cosmos, history, and humanity. They are a call to reformation insofar as they expose the pettiness and shallowness of a merely functional or vital existence lived outside the light of the mystery.

Religious Faith Community, Interformation, and Transformation

One basic way in which our communal disposition can find fulfillment in a faith community is by interformation. The communal disposition inclines people to go beyond their own apprehensions. They are disposed to reach out in an attempt to share in the experiences of others. They enrich one another by interformation through such means as shared actions and projects, formative dialogue, and mutual assistance.

In faith communities, interformation can become transformation. Adherents believe that the forming mystery uses their interformation as one of the means for its acts of sacred transformation. Formative obedience or openness is the readiness, engendered by the communal disposition, to learn from others, to share their interests and concerns, to join them in prayer.

Ecumenical Extension of the Communal Disposition

Ideally, this openness should extend itself also to other faith and form traditions. This expansion may lead to ecumenical interformation in areas of consonant foundations.

All interformation is a fruit of the communal disposition. This disposition is deepened and illumined by the faith that the mystery is formatively present in all people. It is possible that mature members of one faith tradition can be formed in some significant way by certain form directives of another faith tradition when these are translated in terms of their own wisdom and practice. They may justify this openness to possible interformation by the conviction that the seeds of consonant formation have been planted by the formation mystery throughout the world among all peoples and traditions. The communal disposition finds its full flowering in a serene and nonjudgmental approach to people, in an ability to bear with ambiguity in regard to their beliefs and lifestyles.

Formative spirituality includes a willingness to engage in responsible interformation with others. We can receive form through the insights and feelings of others. Conversely, we can give form to their life by sharing with them our own experiences. This presupposes that the communal disposition is transformed by a transcendent openness to the formation mystery as a mystery of loving kindness that engulfs all human forms of life. Only then can we be fully committed to respectful interformation. Ecumenical interformation is based on our contemplation of this all-pervading mystery. Without contemplation, interformation decays rapidly into mere intellectual discussions, idle chatter, or superficial and pragmatic relations.

The formative mystery acts formatively in every heart in secret and silent ways. It enables people of various traditions to engage in loving interformation, even if this is never explicitly known or expressed by them. Their willingness to interformation is the result of the secret and universal action of the formation mystery. By this action the mystery discloses itself in, among other areas, the communal disposition and aspiration of all human forms of life. It gives itself to each of them in mysterious ways known only to itself.

Enlightened Communal Disposition and Ecumenical Interformation

This universal self-disclosure of the mystery in communities of faith enables our communal disposition to extend itself respectfully with interest and affection to various religious traditions, such as the American Indian traditions; the tribal religious traditions in Africa; or the Hindu, Buddhist, Confucian, Taoist, and Shinto traditions in Asia. The reality and depth of transcendent formative directives hidden in every human heart and community should be approached with respect and gratitude. Such inner directives and inspirations may not be clearly understood by certain communities themselves. They may be wrongly expressed by them. Nevertheless, they may point, however imperfectly, to the loving action of the mystery within their respective formation fields.

The ecumenical communal disposition makes us seek out the consonant life directives in any community. Even if communities are on the verge of extinction, we should not allow their consonant form directives to disappear with them, as has happened to the traditions of various American-Indian tribes.

Adherents of all faith communities should rise above the long-standing prejudices that are rooted in dissonant accretions. Intolerance and bigotry has turned many faith communities into agents of war and fanatic persecution instead of sources of communion. The communal disposition, if consonant, inclines us to be inclusive, not exclusive, of others, regardless of their race, color, creed, sex, or culture. When this disposition attains its full unfolding, we welcome all people and we are ready for interformation with them within the possibilities of our obedient congeniality, compatibility, compassion, and competence. Interformation becomes for us the sacrament of communion with the formation mystery and with its actual or potential epiphanies in people.

Communal Disposition and Universal, Congenial Openness

The communal disposition forms our hearts in openness to the manifestations of the presence and action of the mystery in our formation field. Everywhere we may surmise the possible disclosure of the Sacred. Congenial and compatible openness is not easily maintained in the midst of prejudices that may be rampant in the interconsciousness of our consociations, associations, or communities. It may mean ceaseless conversion. This openness, even within the wise boundaries of congeniality and compatibility, is a demanding and at times a disturbing challenge. We sense this challenge once we awaken to the call of our communal predisposition. When we allow the communal call to expand itself, it becomes a thirst for communion with others insofar as reality allows this thirst to be fulfilled. The most exquisite fruit of the communal disposition is a search for universal interformation, for universal brotherhood and sisterhood, at least in intention if this is not totally possible in action. This universality of communion is limited by our actual formation field and its horizons. The search for communion is at the same time a search for the formation mystery disclosing or concealing itself in people and in communities appearing in our field of life. The science of foundational formative spirituality, because of its universal transcendent orientation, can facilitate our intention to keep our interformation as universal as possible within the limits of congeniality, compatibility, and competence.

Communal Disposition and Sensitivity for Formative Symbols

To grow in the art of communal and ecumenical interformation, we must realize that formative symbols are the best way people know to articulate transcendent apprehension and appreciation. Because the formation mystery is mysterious, it can be expressed only through formative symbolism. Everything that exists can be turned into a formative symbol, a "sacrament," whose form communicates what it signifies.

The core of a faith and form tradition is a universe of formative symbols.

The science of formation distinguishes these symbols from informative ones, such as mathematical, technical, functional, and pragmatic-linguistic symbols. Formative symbols emerge from the communal and creative apprehension, appreciation, and affirmation of a community, its founders, its formation field, its faith and form tradition, its formation history, its celebrations. Each community uses formative symbols to give transcendent form to its communal life in the light of the mystery. Interformation demands that we become sensitive to the formative symbols of other segments and communities. This empathy for formative symbols and the transcendent treasures they conceal can open us to what they mean to other communities, meanings that initially may have been alien to our way of life and appreciation. Sharing their symbolic intent, we touch the marrow of their traditions. We begin to sense what their symbols mean to them. These symbols may point to the same foundations of distinctively human formation that guide our own unfolding. Interformation in this regard may then take place spontaneously.

We can empathize with the apprehension and appreciation of symbols of others without necessarily affirming them personally. Empathic entrance into the symbolic universe of others is a highway to interformation appreciation. It can thrust our communal disposition toward unexpected heights.

CHAPTER 18

Disposition of Social Presence

Consonant life is marked by social presence, a concern that should be rooted in transcendence. The social awareness of Martin Luther King was illumined by a transcendent aspiration for justice for the underprivileged. The remarkable secretary-general of the United Nations Dag Hammarskjöld and his successor, the Buddhist U Thant, manifested the same transcendent ground in their concern for people. Such men, or a woman like Mother Teresa of Calcutta, evidence a disposition of reverence for a mystery that endows each person and each population with unique nobility. They care deeply for any segment of humanity that tries to live in the light of its own dignity. Consonant people stand up for the human rights this potential splendor demands. Their presence is marked by a personal respect for each person they meet. Therefore it emits a powerful appeal, evoking the best in others. Many feel uplifted by them.

Social presence is coformed by various dispositions. Their felicitous blend into a harmonious unity yields a pleasing, compassionate style of concern that is firm, effective, and evocative. Such dispositions are not a modification of the mind only. They may begin in the mind, but they end as inclinations of the heart. Our heart, as anchored by awe in the formation mystery, is the source of social presence. This implies that the basic movements of the heart—sensibility and responsibility—have attained a certain actualization and integration. They complement and modulate each other flexibly.

For example, U Thant was sensibly moved by the plight of humanity. Yet this sensitivity did not onesidedly dominate his responsible action. The feelings of his heart did not obstruct his administrative duties at the United Nations. Conversely, this responsible dedication did not paralyze the sensitivity of his heart.

Beyond this harmony, the heart must be moved by inclinations of care, which coform our committed presence. The truly concerned heart inspires a presence that is reverential, communal, personal, and evocative. Ideally these dispositions permeate each other. They form a benign and balanced blend. Such a mixture makes social presence appealing and powerful: it is similar to a delicious dinner prepared by a caring person. We delight in its taste and flavor. The different aromas and spices are subtly fused. We do not recognize them in their singularity. Yet each of them contributes to the final taste of the meal prepared for us with loving care.

The same applies to social concern. Various dispositions of the heart combine to create a presence that warms and illumines the lives of others. Social presence enhances life either on a large scale, as in our example of the United Nations, or on the more common scenes of family life, neighborhood, or place of leisure or labor. Hence, we need to dwell on this disposition. We ought to reflect also on the heart itself, for it is the heart that sustains and carries the disposition of social presence.

Socially Sensible Heart

The heart is socially sensible when it is both affable and effective. For instance, the Samaritan who took care of the man along the road who was wounded by robbers showed the right kind of sensitivity. He dealt with this wounded Jew as a companion. He was affable to him. For him the man was more than a member of a group that lived in enmity with the Samaritans. His heart was moved by what happened to the Jew as a fellow human being. He manifested sympathy for this victim. Above all, his companionship and affability were effective. They were translated into action. He brought the man to an inn and made sure he would be cared for. He arranged with the innkeeper to pay for all costs when he returned to the inn.

A socially sensible heart allows itself to be moved by human needs—not once or twice but over and over again. Its social sensitivity is a disposition to apprehend, appraise, and affirm human indigence. This concern emerges time and again. Finally, it becomes an enduring disposition of human sensitivity. The corresponding feelings are repeated, too. After sufficient reiteration, they become spontaneous appreciative dispositions. They sink from the appraising mind and affirming will into the heart. They endow the heart with enduring affective appreciations and orientations. The heart has integrated and keeps on integrating these social appreciative inclinations.

In a consonant existence, the dispositions of the heart illumine our empirical form of life. They touch all of its dimensions and structures. For example, a sensitive wife and mother exhibits this social presence in her functional cooking and cleaning; in her vital love making; in her current adaptation to the teenage phase of her children's lives; in her attractive, pleasing appearance; in her actual handling of each formation event in family life.

Socially Responsible Heart

Our heart is socially responsible when it is disposed to remain faithful to our responsibility for social needs, no matter what one's subjective feelings are. We can imagine that the Samaritan may have had an unpleasant trip when he returned to the inn to pay the bill for the nursing of his unfortunate neighbor. Perhaps his business did not go well, or perhaps he lost a lot of money. Certainly he was tired from the journey. His mood was low. Worried about many things, he may have felt less inspired by the enhanced sensitivity of heart that made him care for the wounded Jew in the first place. His heart was still endowed with the disposition of sensitivity, but, because of these many personal cares, it did not acutalize itself at this specific moment in the same spontaneous way. Nonetheless, he paid the bill as promised. He kept up a concerned appearance. Here the other characteristic of the heart comes into play: responsibility, which is the disposition to hold oneself responsible for the needs of one's neighbor and to act accordingly, no matter how one may be feeling.

The disposition of social responsibility in the spiritual person is rooted in transcendence. The formation mystery inspires us to give form to aspirations for justice, peace, and mercy in response to the needs of people. It is the mystery itself that makes us feel responsible for those needs we can relieve congenially, compatibly, and effectively.

Responsibility of the heart gives steadiness and solidity to our concern. At times the liveliness of social feeling may be low or absent. Yet our heart remains faithful to its commitments. It cultivates dispositions of responsibility in obedience to transcendent inspirations and aspirations. These dispositions permeate and strengthen the appreciative dispositions of our heart. From this illustration, we can see again that the consonant heart is a sensible-responsible unity.

Social-Reverential Disposition of the Heart

Mother Teresa of Calcutta treats with tender reverence the poor, sick, and dying in the streets of a teeming city. She does not ask them about their faith, background, moral standards, education, criminality, or personal righteousness. She reveres in each of them the preforming love of the mystery in which she believes with her whole heart. For her, each of these wretched bodies is like a muddied shrine of the Sacred.

A radical disposition of reverence for the all-embracing mystery of ongoing preformation should suffuse our social commitments. It grants our presence both depth and radiance. This disposition is grounded in the faith vision that the formation mystery does indeed embrace all societies, countries, minorities, majorities, races, traditions, formation segments, families, communities, and individuals. We are called to share in this benevolent availability of the mystery. Hence, we cultivate reverence for the people we can reach within the limits of our congeniality and compatibility. The hidden nobility of their mysterious preformation lights up in the eyes of faith. We believe in the founding and forming mystery that remains substantially united with their very being, even if they have not yet personally accepted and actualized the gift of their own preformation in the empirical form of their life.

Social-Communal Disposition of the Heart

Martin Luther King traveled and spoke tirelessly throughout the United States. His main audiences were communities of black people. Together they tried to facilitate consonant formation of the underprivileged. Not only did they revere the call of the Sacred at the center of each human being; they did something about it. They formed associations of communities of resistance against social evil and deformation. They realized under the inspiration of King that improvement can often be attained more effectively through community action. Hence, effective social presence implies a disposition to participate in social actions of communities of committed people, provided that such participation is congenial, compatible, and effective for the participant.

Social-Personal Disposition of the Heart

The disposition of social presence directs itself also to the unique, personal formation of people. It generates a delicate respect for any form of human life in its uniqueness. It opposes social injustice that inhibits distinctively human evolvement. It demands compassion for those who falter on their journey. It consoles and fortifies those who are wounded by a leveling society.

Social-Evocative Disposition of the Heart

This final component of the disposition of social presence awakens and kindles the slumbering powers of formation in people and communities. The evocative mode appeals to what is best in others. It invites them to bring to life potentialities they may not as yet have fully appreciated. It nourishes in others a gentle yet firm striving for the kind of excellence to which they are personally called. Fostering appreciation and "opportunity thinking", it combats any condition in society that discourages people by an unjust or merciless repudiation or depreciation of their gifts. The continuing disclosure and realization of consonant formation potencies are the fruit of this evocative presence.

These four dispositions of the heart are intertwined. Mutually complementary, they feed into an effective approach to the ills of societies. Together they help us to protect and promote the formative powers and dispositions that are to be found in consonant formation traditions, segments, and communities.

Media and Social Dispositions

Today's communications media play a significant role in formation. They extend our awareness beyond our immediate life situation. This extension affects the structure of our social consciousness, of our conscience, and of our dispositional life. We have explained elsewhere the five dimensions that coform our formation field. Among them we counted the two poles of outer formation, namely, the world pole and the pole of the immediate life situation in which we find ourselves. The influence of the media has changed the relationship between these two areas. In the past the immediate life situation was almost uncontested in its formative power. Today it is rivaled by the world pole. The media make us increasingly aware of social needs that stretch far beyond our surroundings.

This extension of awareness should serve the balanced formation of our life. It should steadily deepen our disposition to experience and exercise compassion and mercy worldwide. Such concern should remain congenial with the mysterious preformation of our own existence. It should be modulated by our consonant intraformation. Our wider engagement should remain compatible, moreover, with the compassion we are called to live and exercise in our own surroundings. We should do justice first of all to the interformation that exists between us and those whose daily journey we share.

Our exposure to the media can unfortunately have a deformative impact. This deformation is not necessarily due to the media themselves. Its source may be a lack of discipline in those who expose themselves to the media. When we are insufficiently aware of our human vulnerability, we may expose ourselves limitlessly to the media's message. This may lead to an overextension of our social consciousness. What happens in turn is that our social conscience is overtaxed. This may give rise to the development of deformative dispositions. In extreme cases, our overworked conscience may become destructive, depressing, and paralyzing. It may awaken latent hysteria and fanaticism. Psychosomatic symptoms may be indicators of such inner dissonance.

The tyranny of false guilt may impose on us an acute and excessive agitation. This is self-destructive insofar as it is incompatible with the burdens already implied in our immediate social situation and formation phase, burdens that may already be taxing us to the limits of our capacities. Our immediate task, with its sufferings and demands, may take up all our energy. For example, it would be unwise for a missionary, exhausting himself day and night to help victims of war, famine, and disease in a ravaged region of this planet, to agonize daily about the religious, sexual, and psychological problems of college students in Paris, Berlin, New York, and London as communicated by the media. This could be too much for anyone to bear.

Sources of Inordinate Deformative World Involvement

The main sources of an inordinate preoccupation with world problems are of great variety. We shall focus on some of them. As already mentioned, excessive pressure on our social consciousness and conscience can be caused by undisciplined self-exposure to social appeals. These can come in the form of well-intentioned speakers, preachers, demonstrators, or commentators who express overwhelming social sentiments. They awaken our concern by a stark presentation of undeniable suffering and injustice everywhere in the world. This kind of presentation may be necessary for people whose complacency in the face of global suffering is appalling.

However, the same strong presentation can be disastrous for sensitive people already involved in justice, peace, and mercy to the limit of their abilities. For those impressionable, socially committed persons, such emotional accounts should be balanced by some warnings. They should not allow themselves to be swept beyond the limits imposed on them by the formation mystery. They should be cautious about the absorbing and inundating power of weighty historical pulsations for world reform, especially when these pulsations are inflated by fanatical or hysterical promotions by highly excitable individuals.

Some of us may have a predisposition to hysteria, fanaticism, or willful heroism. These tendencies may trick us into blind service to a cause, as happens often in movements that demand a kind of cultic self-negation. If we become aware of this predisposition, we should avoid prolonged contact with cults, especially if they demand blind surrender of our freedom and reason in the service of world salvation.

Another source of excess can be our quasi-foundational pride-form. Pride is always subtly seducing us. It may push us beyond our limited possibilities. Willfulness replaces gentle yet firm participation in the reformation of unjust situations. A certain harshness enters our life. What can be healing if this happens is an abandonment in faith, hope, and consonance to the formation mystery. Abandonment helps us to believe in the ultimate transformation of humanity, even though this belief can never be an excuse not to do what we reasonably *can* do for its reformation here and now. Only a deep trust in the hidden mystery of consonant world formation can protect us from deformative social guilt.

Another source of inordinate world involvement is the latent disposition toward romantic adolescent idealism. Romanticism refuses to resign itself to the pedestrian everyday social duties that often go unadmired and unapplauded. This kind of idealism seduces us away from the silent heroism of tedious care in and through our daily task. Fantasies, dreams, and projects that are unrealistic take over. Meanwhile, we may not cultivate the dispositions that foster the less glamorous social services we could realistically render. We become less disposed to the gentle pursuit of excellence in our everyday occupation, profession, or family life.

Each formation tradition may contain dissonant accretions conducive to deformative social guilt. We shall restrict ourselves at this point to an example from the Christian form tradition. Latent traces of Jansenism and Puritanism in our historical Christian consciousness may masquerade as social world concern. These accretions of the Christian form tradition disposed people to disdain the enjoyment and celebration of the gifts of creation granted in one's family and social situation. We are called to delight in goods in a gracious, nonpossessive way. They are symbolic pointers to the transcendent splendor and generosity of the formation mystery. The rejection of all such pointers in our life would not directly alleviate the needs of the world. To disdain such gifts may harm unnecessarily the consonant unfolding of our own life and the lives of those entrusted to our care. Under the guise of world concern, persistent Jansenistic and Puritanical accretions may revive the anxious obsessive lifestyle of certain Christian believers in the past.

Foundational Disposition of Deformative Social Guilt

Our considerations of social concern have enabled us to identify the disposition of deformative social guilt. As a foundational disposition, it generates a persistent slush fund of guilt. We cannot manage this feeling rationally. Sometimes this guilt may be focused consciously on one or another aspect of life. For instance, we may feel personally guilty because we cannot relieve famine in a far away country. Usually this mood of guiltiness is vague and either pre- or infrafocal.

An irrational guilt disposition interferes with our ability to function optimally in everyday social situations. There is a disproportion between the excessive guilt disposition and the realistic, limited responsibilities that reside primarily in our immediate life situation and extend secondarily to the world situation insofar as it can reasonably be served by our restricted formation potencies.

One sign of an excessive guilt disposition is its bad effect on our health. Another sign is that its directives are incompatible with the reasonable demands of others directly dependent on our social care.

How can we reform a deformative social guilt disposition? One way is to seek formation counseling in private or in common. In severe and persistent cases the formation counselor may have to enlist therapeutic assistance. During the time of reformation of an excessive guilt disposition, it may be necessary to avoid exposure to communications that could excite further false guilt feelings.

One should engage in a guided reflection on related sociohistorical pulsations, deformative memories, and the dispositions of the pride-form. One should try also to disclose and appraise the trends in the culture that may initiate or increase an oversensitive social disposition. The same holds for memories bearing on this vulnerability, which may stem from one's cultural, personal, and familial history. When and where did this faulty disposition emerge? In some instances the history of one's country, family, or formation segment may give a clue. For example, if we appraise that our family's behavior was asocial, we may inaugurate as an overreaction an irrational social guilt disposition. This may incline us to bear personally the guilt of a whole history, of humanity as such, of an entire generation or family. The same faulty appraisal may breed other deformative dispositions, such as a "world savior complex."

As we have mentioned, another source of false social guilt is our hidden pride-form. Is there an overwhelming need in us to be *in* with what is current in society or in the formation segments of the population in which we participate? Is that need motivated by our pride-form? Do we want to be lauded at any price by contemporaries? Is our disposition to overinvolvement in public social causes motivated by their popularity in certain segments of the culture? Did this pride disposition become dominant? Has it bred its own excessive guilt dispositions?

On the positive side, we should deepen the foundational triad of faith, hope, and consonance and the ensuing disposition of abandonment to the formation mystery. A deepened disposition of abandonment will restore our peace in regard to what we cannot change in this world without pushing beyond the limited call of the mystery in our lives.

Another help will be found in an enduring appreciation for our everyday social participation in realistic means to improve the world. A gentle pursuit of the limited excellence possible for us within our own family, profession, task, or position does contribute to the social improvement of humanity and its formation field. People should do the best they can within the limits of their own possibilities to foster social presence. If many did so, the formation field of humanity would be blessed beyond recognition. Yet this truth does not excuse us from going beyond our everyday situation to participate in world concerns to the extent of our abilities.

Historical Dimension of Formative Social Presence

The dispositions of formative social consciousness and conscience are historical. They are formed not only by our apprehensions and appraisals of present pulsations. Past and anticipated future historical pulsations play a role in the ongoing formation of social dispositions. These are developed mainly by means of interformation, which is the privileged field of expression of the dispositions of social consciousness and conscience. This applies not only to the present but also to the past interformation of social dispositions. Hence, the science of formation distinguishes between a horizontal and a vertical or historical interformation of social dispositions.

Horizontal interformation takes place in social interaction with those we encounter directly or indirectly in the present. For example, the currentfeelings of one's friends and colleagues about legal or illegal foreign immigrants may coform one's appreciative or depreciative dispositions in regard to them.

Interformation of social dispositions evolves vertically or historically in our interaction with the forming pulsations expressed in the monuments, events, and praxis of generations who lived their formation history before us. For instance, the historical English disposition for fair play may still influence English players today in the formation of their social dispositions as sportsmen and sportswomen. The same applies to deforming pulsations of the past. The historical pulsations in the West to undervalue blacks deformed the social appraisal and appreciation dispositions of many generations of whites. They were partly the victims of deformative social dispositions in past ages.

We interact also with the generations who will come after us. We anticipate imaginatively their probable conditions of life. This anticipation is based on our formation awareness of the present and our memory of the past. This historical anticipation may influence our present formation of social dispositions. For instance, our anticipation of diminished availability of natural resources for coming generations on this planet may coform social dispositions to save existing resources for those who will come after us.

Certain ideological and religious form traditions focus in a special way on this coformation by anticipation of social dispositions. For example, the Marxist formation tradition emphasizes its anticipation of the equality and brotherhood of all workers in the world. Hence, its adherents are socially disposed to make sacrifices in anticipation of this global ideal. Certain religious form traditions go even farther. Anticipating the purification of deformative dispositions in an afterlife prompts them to reform more intensely self-centered, antisocial dispositions in this life.

CHAPTER 19

Hierarchy of Dispositions, Formation Segments, and Social Presence

The aspiration after consonance does not equally affect each dimension and disposition of human life formation due to the fact that form dimensions and dispositions are subordinated to one another in a hierarchy. The higher ones give direction to the lower ones. This hierarchy applies as well to our personal practice of social presence.

We may illustrate this point with an example of justice in academic life. A talented author and university professor may aspire after social justice in regard to her colleagues, students, and readers. She appraises that she can enrich their lives with more scientific insights if she is willing to sacrifice the fulfillment of many dispositions that distract her from research, class preparation, and publication. She decides that dispositions which foster the pursuit of academic excellence must take their place. This pursuit will enhance her ability to relieve humanity's poverty of knowledge.

To make her life more consonant with this aspiration, she limits the expressions of her compatibility and compassion dispositions in time-consuming social contacts that may inhibit her chosen responsibility. She appraises that she must find sufficient hours in the day for study, reflection, research, and writing so that her students can receive the material they need in her courses and her readers can derive the most from her publications. The call of social justice compels her to keep up with the literature in her field and makes her sacrifice some of the *congenial* enjoyment she experiences when she socializes with colleagues. The *congruent* expression of her functional-individual dispositions, in such skills as dancing, sewing, horseback riding, and music, is tempered too by the unique form of social justice her transcendent dispositions seem to suggest to her. Also modified is her congenial aspiration for a leisurely life of quiet contemplation and poetic beauty, uninterrupted by the rigors of study. This whole social form of her life may be reformed again when chronic illness or age demands such reformation.

Inspirations do not usually come to us out of an isolated interiority. More commonly they emerge from the traditions to which we belong. The formation mystery may wisely and gently speak in them to our emergent humanity. The moment of personal inspiration is usually one of enlightened understanding of the inspirations contained in our tradition. These private interpretations have to be dealt with cautiously, for they are easily contaminated when a lively imagination is perverted by the pride-form.

Formation Segments of the Population and Social Presence

Social presence is inspired by social justice. This calls us to create a more ideal ambience for the unfolding of human life on Planet Earth. It opposes conditions that lessen the possibility for people to be faithful to their calling. One main obstruction of people's right to congeniality is homogenization, or the tendency to level and collectivize all forms of human life. This injustice strikes at the root of humanity, for what makes us distinctively human cannot be leveled or collectivized. Leveling foments a struggle for survival between the various formation segments of the world population. Each one is inclined to level the other by imposition of its own form of life. Leveling belies the laws of formation. These basic form directives point the universe, humanity, and history toward unity through diversification, not homogenization.

Leveling destroys formative social justice, which is devoted to creating the facilitating conditions that enable the maximum number of people to follow their life call. People seek to develop diverse dispositions and traditions in service of distinct formation tasks. They share projects of life with specific groups inspired by similar responsibilities. Individualistic desires, ambitions, dispositions, and opportunities must be transcended, that is to say, they must be subjected to the formation design the mystery of formation wants for each person's life. Usually one is inspired to live this commitment within a consociation, association, or community of people. In this way informal groups emerge, such as those of scholars, artists, executives, laborers, writers, professionals, athletes. Such formation segments develop similar dispositions and traditions. They sustain a shared fidelity to a common formation responsibility in the history of humanity.

Fear or lethargy may tempt people to leveling submission. They may try to lose themselves in an anonymous world order, crowd, collectivity, state, or ideology. People may betray the call of the formation mystery to follow the unique direction of their life within a freely chosen or ratified formation segment of the population. Instead of fostering free, unique coformation with such segments, they may sabotage this call by evasion, meaning that they evade the responsibility to be compatible companions with unique others on the same formation journey. The leveling mentality takes over.

Social justice, peace, and mercy mean that we transcend the tendencies that threaten the congenial unfolding of self and others: An example is the tendency of certain formation segments to foster a collective and exclusive segment-centeredness. This tendency undermines their commitment to social justice in regard to other segments. The diverse social circles of society should not see themselves primarily as interest groups. They should not lobby exclusively for the increase and maintenance of privileged avenues to power, pleasure, and possession. Such an exclusive self-definition would be deformative and destructive because it would foster dispositions and traditions of social injustice, divisiveness, and competition. It would mark the death of compassion as people would vie endlessly to dominate one another and the diverse segments of society different from their own.

Not "Classes" but "Formation Segments"

The science of formation sees the diverse circles of society not as "classes" but as "formation segments." Their deepest meaning is to facilitate the congenial life formation of the people who belong to them by fostering beneficial dispositions and traditions. At some period in their formation history, these people happen to be similarly situated socially. Hence, they are challenged by their shared formation field to form their lives in similar ways. They strive to respond consonantly to the life situations they share. They assist each other interformatively.

The science of formation insists that each segment of society has the same dignity as any other. The dignity of people radiates in proportion to their fidelity to their life call. It is neither style nor status nor measurable accomplishment that grant this deepest human dignity. It rests in the congeniality, compatibility, compassion, and competence with which they follow their life direction. It resides in their faithfulness to the formation mystery as they make their way through life with companions who share the same field of action.

This position of the science is rooted in the related tenet that human life is formed through a series of successive life-forms. These current life-forms disclose increasingly one's foundational life-form. Each person is called to express this foundational form empirically in concrete ways of living. The succession of current life-forms that marks one's journey is partly a response to a succession of changing social situations. Each of them evokes a congenial, compatible, compassionate, and competent adaptation.

For many people during their whole lifetime, successive social situations and corresponding current life-forms may have much in common with those of a definite formation segment of the population. One and the same segment of society may accommodate and facilitate by its dispositions and traditions one's life formation during the whole of one's history. For example, blue-collar workers employed in the same mining industry in the same small town may share for a lifetime the same formation segment of the population, especially when they also share the same church.

The opposite may be true, too. People may experience drastic changes in their life situation. The dispositions and traditions of the formation segment to which they belong fail to accommodate them in their changing formation field. Hence, they have to change from one formation segment to another in their society. For instance, a gifted child of one of these miners may have to go to college in a city far away and become a successful lawyer.

Principle of "Social Formation Flow"

To facilitate change from one formation segment to another, the science of formation formulates and upholds the principle of "social formation flow," which should be one of the coforming dispositions of our social presence.

This principle pertains to the consonant structuring of society. It holds that societies should be structured in regard to dispositions and traditions in such a way that there is a reasonable flow of formation between the segments that coform that society. One main means to foster this formation flow is the opportunity for people to change from one segment to another when their ongoing formation makes such a change desirable and possible.

This principle is related to the science's tenet that each person has a primordial human right to congenial life formation. Hence, it is a violation of justice to withhold from any person the opportunity to participate in another segment of society when this change is essential for one's ongoing formation.

Violations of Formative Social Justice by Formation Segments

Formation segments of society and their members can violate justice in many ways. They are unjust when they pretend that any segment of society is in and by itself of higher human value and dignity than any other. A black formation segment, for instance, is not lower in human dignity than a white one.

Formation segments offend social justice when they try to monopolize opportunities for formation, education, power, pleasure, and possession. Such monopoly would threaten the availability of sufficient occasions to foster justice among other segments of society. It would be unjust to attempt in any way to exploit one group for the sake of another interest group. Nor can one make it inordinately difficult for people to participate in a chosen segment of society if such a move is appraised as right and just. The internal dynamism and logic of one's current formation may call for a lasting, periodic, or partial transition.

The disposition to transcend individualistic preferences in fidelity to one's deepest life call within and with a consonant formation segment of the population should be protected and fostered by social institutions. They should create, promote, and defend the facilitating conditions for such fidelity. The secret of joyous fidelity to one's life call lies not in doing what one likes but in liking what one has to do within the formation segment of the population one is called to by the mystery.

Division of Labor of Formation

The view of the science of formation pertaining to the division of labor can foster the disposition of faithfulness to one's life call. In this view, the formation of world, society, and history is based on an appropriate division of labor. The labor of formation is distributed over distinct segments of the population. These segments and their formative labors are mutually complementary. Each type of specific forming presence—characteristic of each segment—demands for its effectiveness its own style of transcendence of individualistic interests, moods, and desires. This difference in style, disposition, and tradition uniquely forms the different segments of the world population.

Those who belong to the same segment share a similar responsibility. They are called to sustain each other. They evolve an interformative style of life, constituted by specific traditions and dispositions. These include re-creative, aesthetic, and educational dispositions and facilities that enable people to maintain this style of transcendence and presence effectively.

Intersegmental Peace

Collaboration between diverse segments of the world population is another aim of the science of formation. This is the condition for a world-wide movement of justice, peace, and mercy. The emergence of a conso-nant humanity on Planet Earth depends on such collaboration. Interseg-mental peace is delayed by the obsessive preoccupation of each segment with its own gain in power and possession. This gives rise to depreciative dispositions of paranoid fear, distrust, envy, resentment, and hatred. These attitudes undermine our appreciation of the consonant facets of the lifestyles and achievements of other segments. The battle between segments may become a lethal principle of world history. The struggle among diverse dispositions and traditions could lead to a total leveling of one another in view of the weaponry now available to the human race. It could signify the end of our formation history. Peace depends on the co-operation of formation segments. They should not contest but comple-ment each other. Benediction should replace competition.

The present inspiration to interformation experienced by many people in the face of a final destruction of Planet Earth is one of the means used by the mystery of formation. This mystery is always ready to orchestrate the peaceful unfolding of humanity and history. It wisely guides the forces of formation in the macro- and microcosmic universe. Their interaction foreshadows the interformation that should harmonize the segments of this planet's population.

The movement to create a disposition of peaceful respect between seg-ments and their form traditions is tenuous and vulnerable. Its fragility should make us vigilant. We should thus avoid images, feelings, thoughts, and words that convey an underestimation of the necessity of a diversity of segments with their own distinct styles, dispositions, and traditions. Un-just, envious, resentful, or vindictive exploitation of one segment by another should be watched and opposed so that we can prevent the spiritual, eco-nomic, or physical marginalization of any consonant formation segment.

Congenial Affinity of Formation Segments

Special care should be taken not to seduce people to join, to stay with, or to minister to a segment for which they have no affinity. This caution does not deny that a number of people exhibit an ability to serve or to minister equally well to a variety of segments. Nor does affinity to any group diminish the necessity of transcendence of individualistic dispositions, moods, feelings, and aptitudes.

Affinity for social service, like congeniality, is not measured mainly by one's vital-functional aptitudes, dispositions, likes and dislikes, or by one's aspirations or inspirations that may possibly be distorted by the pride-form. It is measured mainly by the mystery calling us forth in the directive demands of our social-personal field. It is this call, first of all, that should be disclosed and wisely appraised. Then a commitment to special segments of the population may be made. Only then should one be open to more nuanced inspirations, aspirations, ambitions, pulsions, and pulsations in the light of the disclosed directives. This order should not be reversed. Individualistic ambitions, likes, and dislikes should not be mistaken for directives of the mystery. Subsequent illusions could become compulsive obsessions.

Summary Pertaining to Formation Segments

People are called to form their lives in consonance with the unique image the mystery has instilled in the secret center of their being. Opportunities for such formation should be fostered by every society. A main opportunity for this process of congenial unfolding is the development of distinct formation segments of the population. They are meant to facilitate formation as such. They advance particular form traditions, dispositions, and disciplines befitting people whose unique life-form includes similar responses to shared social situations. Such segments can only serve the mystery if they do not exploit each other. They should promote the advancement of all other consonant segments. The participants in each segment are called to sustain each other mutually. They do so by means of a distinct interformative style of life. It should be a dispositional life that offers the best possible interformative conditions for fidelity to the social call they share historically.

The various segments of a society should respect each other's differences. These are the fruit of a long sociohistorical formation. They become manifest in a distinct taste and social style of life. We should, for instance, not disparage the customs of Jewish, black, or Hispanic people. Formation segments should bring into being a harmonious yet richly varied society. Such a society would be marked by its solicitude for the congeniality of all its minorities. It would promote and defend the diverse segments in which its members are called to participate by sociohistorical destiny.

The members of all such segments should grow daily in formative justice. They should respectfully realize that the tastes, recreative needs, and dispositional lifestyle of, for example, a steelworker are different from those of an actor. The conditions that a scholar needs to make his or her best contribution to society are different from those needed by a business person or a cab driver. A poet shapes an environment distinct from that of a prize fighter. A quantum physicist or a formation scientist has to foster a mind set different from that of a theologian or philosopher. All of them need for their effective interformation compatible types of lifestyles. The greatest social injustice would be to make them feel guilty or embarrassed about the exact facilitating conditions granted to them by the formation mystery.

All segments need directors or counselors who have some affinity to their specific conditions, tastes, and dispositions. For example, not every psychologist, cleric, or counselor is ideally suited for the daily life formation of, respectively, farmers, blacks, Hispanics, emigrants, computer technicians, theologians, physicists, formation scientists, painters, actors, poets, athletes, or engineers.

The social injustice of imposing incompatible formation directors violates both the rights of the segment involved and those of the uncongenially placed director or counselor. These helping persons can be most effective only if they have a congenial affinity to those they are called to assist within the segments entrusted to their care.

A formative society fights the social injustice of marginalization of any segment of the population. A onesided attention to one or a few segments is unjust. For instance, it would be unjust for any mainline religious form tradition or church to promote favoritism, which would imply diminished attention to other segments of society, no matter how implicit and unintended this may be. This kind of attention would be a glaring example of gross injustice, both to the members of the formation segment concerned and to those who could be of assistance to them because of their own affinity and congeniality.

A prevalent pulsation in society favoring one or the other segment may be the source of much injustice. Seduced by popular pulsations, many may deny and repress the awareness of their own congeniality and affinity. They may engage in the popular service of currently favored segments of the population in spite of their personal uncongeniality. Such denial would cripple unjustly their own formation and saddle the segment concerned with counselors, directors, or clerics who can only do injustice to them by their lack of affinity.

For instance, a highly sensitive, refined, aesthetic person should not try to play the role of a miner. A classical example is that of the minister's son Vincent van Gogh, who initially played that role in the mines of Belgium in order to touch the souls of the miners. This decision resulted in serious physical and psychological illness for the oversensitive and gifted painter.

A deformative society may foster the unnatural utopia of a total leveling of all segments, their distinctive dispositions and traditions, their special contributions to history and society. Communist and fascist societies have tried such leveling, the result being that they failed to foster the open, joyous, unique life formation of people. The mystery of social formation is a mystery of unity-in-diversity. Humanity is called to be transformed in the unique image of the mystery. This image is in some way meant to shine through in every diverse formation segment.

CHAPTER 20

Practice of Social Presence

Social presence, practically speaking, reforms our inspirations, aspirations, ambitions, pulsions, and pulsations. It also affects our apparent form of life, for social concern radiates through our daily appearance in the formation field. This presence is rooted in the foundational triad of faith, hope, and consonance. The latter dispositions enable us to live in appreciative abandonment to the beneficial meaningfulness of the formation mystery. Abandonment enables us to persevere in social presence, even if it seems to be meaningless and often without visible results.

The basic orientation toward social presence is inherent in the human life-form. It is a predisposition latent in us, independent of our free choice and affirmation. Long before we make it a personal disposition, it is in us as a potential. The option for and subsequent development of this predisposition is a function of our formation freedom. As such, it is vulnerable to challenges. It can also be lost, for, like all other dispositions, it does not share in the continuity of our latent predispositions. At any moment in life, this disposition can be initiated, retracted, or reformed by our human freedom.

Were we to opt instead for the disposition of depreciative abandonment, it might seem to us as though blind forces and processes guide life and matter, history and culture, in bland indifference. Then the task of a distinctively human formation of life and society might strike us as a meaningless illusion. It would be difficult, if not impossible, to maintain a concerned presence if we believed that the process of formation was a matter of mere chance. Why then should we do anything to remedy oppression and poverty? There is thus an intimate connection between social presence and the primordial abandonment option.

The disposition to actualize our latent orientation toward such presence is a possibility for all of us. The concrete ways of incarnating this disposition vary significantly in accordance with one's preformation and predispositions, with one's social-personal formation and present formation phase, and with one's task and position in society.

The variety of dispositions and traditions of formative social presence is potentially inexhaustible. For example, movie producers, television script writers, and novelists can live and express justice, peace, and mercy in regard to their audiences and readers. They interact with them interformatively through a just, compassionate and competent use of the media. Cab drivers can interact formatively with their passengers in ways that are fair and peaceful. Their expressive dispositions of social presence are again refined, according to whether their passengers happen to be handicapped, arrogant, nervous, male, female, healthy, sick, sober, or inebriated.

Ebb and Flow of Social Presence

No matter what our concrete dispositions for this presence and its nuances are like, we may experience in ourselves and others a certain ebb and flow in the level of dedication. To disclose the sources of these shifts, we have to refer again to the connection between our decision to be present and our primordial abandonment option. Social presence leads to a confrontation with injustice. This clash can generate misgivings in regard to one's decision in favor of appreciative abandonment. It may lead to a secret crisis of faith, hope, and consonance that may erode our concern. If not resolved, this crisis could lead to total depletion. We would maintain routine dispositions of concerned behavior and expression while losing the distinctively human core of our presence. This crisis may repeat itself many times during our lives, thus accounting for the alternate fading and upsurging of wholehearted engagement.

The deepest source of this crisis is the implicit challenge we may face in regard to our primordial decision in favor of the beneficial meaningfulness of the mystery of formation. This decision is usually made in the light of our formation tradition. The deepest meaning of the crisis may remain veiled to the focal mind due to the prereflective nature of this primordial option of ours during our initial formation history. What may become more readily available to reflective focal appraisal are the occasions that evoke this crisis. Such focusing is the condition for the possibility of coping with these crises in a more reflective way.

Six Phases of the Ebb and Flow of Social Presence

The phases of the ebb and flow of presence take place within an alternating cycle of the upsurging and fading of our concern. First of all, there occurs an initial phase of exalted aspirations and ambitions. This phase is strongly influenced by the pride-form and its aggrandizing influence on our imagination. Social presence tends to be excessive and unrealistic.

The next phase is one of initial apprehension of a dissonance between two kinds of aspirations and ambitions. One consists of exalted, the other of realistic ambitions and aspirations. Such initial apprehensions of dissonance are recurrent, yet still widely spaced.

The third phase is marked by a significant increase of dissonance apprehensions. Peculiar to this phase is that we experience for the first time some noticeable erosion of our engagement as a result of these apprehensions.

The fourth phase is one of dominance of the dissonance apprehension. A dissonance crisis becomes unavoidable. It manifests itself in a temporary depletion of dedication. Meanwhile routine dispositions of conditioned behavior may be maintained.

The fifth phase is that of crisis resolution. The person is fully immersed in the crisis of presence and perhaps in a related crisis of primordial abandonment. One must move toward either a negative or a positive solution. The negative one leads to dispositions of indifference and inertia, manifesting a lasting depletion of presence, even though routine dispositions of related conditioned behavior may persist. This may be especially true of people who make their living in the helping professions, such as clergy, psychiatrists, psychologists, nurses, social workers, educators, missionaries, physicians. They may keep going through the motions of their profession, but their heart is not in it. They can be neither legally faulted nor dismissed from their positions as long as they maintain the appropriate routine dispositions and expressions.

A positive solution of this fifth phase is characterized by at least an implicit choice or reaffirmation of an appreciative, hope-filled abandonment to the mystery of formation. Exalted dispositions are gradually reformed, resulting in a more realistic, less exalted presence. A side benefit of this reformation may be that one is able in a more effective, realistic way to cope with the concrete causes that evoked the crisis in the first place.

The sixth phase in this ebb and flow of human concern is the formation of a new current form of social life, based on the reformed dispositions and their deeper rootedness in living traditions. Even if the new life-form is positive, it does not preclude challenges to this orientation in the future. Similar crises may recur many times in life. They can be evoked by any new venture, opposition, or disillusion.

Social Presence Erosion

The erosion of presence involves a progressive loss of inspiration despite the continuation of conditioned social behavior and expression. Such erosion is always related to a questioning of our primordial, appreciative abandonment in faith, hope, and consonance to the mystery of formation. Often this question is prefocal. Erosion is accompanied by the emergence or strengthening of deformative dispositions and conditions in our formation field. These challenge the meaningfulness of our concern, causing us to ask what is the use of giving so much of ourselves if the results are so little and the conditions so adverse?

The chief occasion of erosion is the experience of dissonance or disparity between the transcendent and the functional dimensions of our presence. Initially, the ambitions of the functional dimension may be forced to conform to overly exalted inspirations and aspirations. Ambitions in the functional sphere of life are embodied uncritically in the ideals of the transcendent sphere. Conversely, exalted aspirations are translated immediately into functional ambitions. What is missing is sufficient mediation by our powers of practical appraisal. We fail to take into account the information our functional and vital dimensions make available for appraisal. Such information ought to coform our final appraisal.

Our appraisal power should thus be well-informed about realistic conditions in the formation field. We have to embody our inspirations and aspirations in concrete situations. These may radically challenge our exalted ideals and remind us that we should function in life as it really is. We may become aware of the disparity between our idealistic dreams and what is feasible in everyday life. Practical appraisal of reality as resistant may discomfort us and render momentarily impotent our powers of appraisal. Disappointed by the impossibility of realizing our ideals in daily life, we may lose interest in any kind of engagement. We may refuse to reform our expectations in such a way that they are in tune with the disclosure of reality by functional appraisal. The more we experience the practical impossibility of executing our unrealistic ideals, the more our exalted inspirations and aspirations are beaten down. This loss may lead to a gradual erosion of our commitment.

The realistic conditions of our surroundings, contrasted with our exalted ideals and talents may make us feel functionally impotent in regard to the implementation of our aspirations. We may also detect a disparity between these ideals, the ambitions they inspire, and what is congenial for us in regard to our own form potencies. In this case the incompatibility of ambitions with the reality of our field of action is joined by the sense of not being congenial with who we most deeply are. Frustration then becomes doubly difficult to avoid.

A full-blown erosion may result unless we reform these exalted aspirations and ambitions. The challenge to reform social dispositions on both the transcendent and functional levels leads to a crisis of transition. We feel summoned to change our current form of presence. We must pass from one current form to another that is more congenial and compatible. Either we do so, or we may have to give up social concern entirely. Hence, we find ourselves in the midst of a transition crisis.

Unavoidability of the Crisis of Integration

We all are bound to experience dissonance between our ideals and reality. Integration of aspirations and ambitions takes time, experience, and much reality testing. This should not surprise us. The process of formation is essentially a process in time. It takes time to apprehend and appraise the uncongeniality and incompatibility of exalted ambitions and aspirations. More time is necessary to appraise and implement the right integration of these dispositions while reforming them. They have to be integrated with our core, current, and apparent forms of life. Finally, the realistic dispositions of the core, current, and apparent life forms have to be unified in our actual form of social concern. This is a big order, not to be accomplished overnight, even if it is for the most part achieved prefocally.

A crisis of integration may emerge periodically simply because our formation is ongoing. The conditions for intra-, inter-, and outer formation are always changing. Our formation field never stays the same. New aspects of preformation may be disclosed to us, thereby shedding new light on our potencies. This allows us to be more realistic in our appraisal of what is feasible for us in the field of engagement. All of these factors may initiate a crisis in regard to our current form of social concern.

Dissonance crises, therefore, seem unavoidable. We must learn to deal with them on the basis of an appreciative abandonment to the mystery. We should anticipate and welcome each crisis as an invitation to ongoing formation. Then the crisis can rekindle rather than erode our social involvement. We gain in solidity of aspiration and ambition what we lose in empty flair and excitement. Our involvement may be less conspicuous and flamboyant, more realistic and substantial, marked by quiet fidelity to the daily details of unostentatious service.

Symptoms and Deformative Consequences of Social Presence Erosion

Many physical indicators of this erosion and the crisis accompanying it can be mentioned. To name only a few: headaches, insomnia, chemical dependency, chest pains, physical exhaustion, backaches, heart and digestive disturbances, skin rashes, repeated colds, increased susceptibility to other viral infections, sexual impotence and related problems. These are joined at times by such emotional symptoms as aggravation, irritation, frustration, doubt, desperation, and revulsion.

Many other consequences of erosion could be catalogued. Just as none of us can escape the development of the social dimension of life, so we cannot escape occasional symptoms of erosion. It is part of ongoing formation. We form ourselves socially within our family, neighborhood, community, and profession. Once this presence begins to erode, the efficiency and growth of the social dimension as a whole is halted. Exalted as well as potentially realistic aspirations and ambitions are blocked by recurrent disappointments in our field of action. Besides affecting our personal growth, this erosion impedes the benefits such concern can bring to others and to the world at large. Our wholehearted participation in the process of inter and outer formation is interrupted, thus leading to deformative consequences for society and its segments.

Appealing Appearance of Exalted Social Ambitions

A special problem associated with exalted ambitions is that the resulting social concern is so appealing in appearance. It is often difficult for people to realize the exaltation behind our care. It is easier to spot exalted ambitions that are patently egocentric. Self-centered ambitions are more obviously implanted in our autarchic pride-form, whereas exalted social dispositions are more subtly related to pride. Public propriety makes it difficult for our apparent form to allow exalted, self-centered ambitions as such to shine through too blatantly. However, we can allow ourselves to manifest social ambitions more exuberantly, for they look so unselfish and generous.

Admiration or applause can reinforce our extravagant grandiosity. The seeds of erosion are contained in these false manifestations of exalted concern. We may naively believe that such ambitions will automatically be compatible with our field of formation and congenial with our life call.

Problem of Appraisal of Effectiveness of Social Presence

Another problem entails the difficulty we experience in appraising the effectiveness of our involvement. The outcome of other ambitions is easier to assess. For instance, we want to acquire the material conditions necessary for congenial intraformation, such as building or renting a house, organizing a job, furthering our career, protecting our family, providing for health care, and so on. We can appraise concretely how we are doing in the fulfillment of these ambitions because our material accomplishments in such areas are measurable and observable.

It is different in the area of social inter- and outer formation, for we cannot always see or measure the impact of our involvement on our family, community or professional environment, on our society and the world at large. Added to this low profile of visible success is the fact that social engagement is usually not highly rewarded economically. In our society economic rewards are a measure of success. But persons whose whole professional life is dedicated to social endeavors seldom enjoy the encouragement of significant economic compensation. When their exaltation wanes, they may find that economic underestimation and inequality have begun to contribute to the erosion of their dedication and to their questioning of the meaning of their service.

Concern for the inter- and outer formation of others does not take away our duty to care for our own intraformation. This implies a certain care for the material conditions that facilitate congenial unfolding. The most obvious avenue to this goal is advancement in our career. In most professions this movement upward is only possible through advancement in administrative positions, a promotion that usually removes one from direct interaction with people. This can be another occasion for questioning our aspirations and subsequently our social ambitions and anticipations.

The above problem might doubly apply to women. They may be assigned to and kept in positions of structured subservience. These assignments are often at odds with their real talents and their actual or potential contributions. Sexual discrimination may become for them an occasion to question the meaningfulness of their presence in that situation. This may lead them to a questioning of the meaningfulness of any social engagement whatsoever.

Single people, too, may have a disadvantage in this regard. A lack of respect in some circles for the calling to the single life may tempt people to abuse the generosity of single men and women in service of social causes without showing them adequate appreciation and remuneration.

A number of people try to express their social concern through large institutions, such as universities, schools, hospitals, prisons, youth camps, political parties, and charitable enterprises. They may soon find out as a fact of life that not all administrators of such institutions and organizations are moved mainly by the needs of the people they serve. Nor does an institution always live up to its stated concerns. Socially concerned people witness that their recommendations for better care are often disregarded in practice. This apprehension can again occasion an erosion of their involvement. People may feel discouraged when they realize the self-centered political or economic motivations guiding a number of administrators.

Disposition of Wise Functional Management of Social Energy

The amount and quality of formation energy available to each of us is limited in principle because we are finite. Responding to the needs of others will necessarily absorb part of that energy. This absorption should be regulated by appropriate dispositions of functional management. Otherwise we may be overwhelmed by the exigencies around us. A primary restriction of energy expenditure in this regard involves the limiting of our area of concern. What we do should be congenial with our form potencies and compatible with our field. Even within this area, we should be aware of our limits without falling into dispositions of negligence and inertia. Our concern should be focused on situations where we can be of most help without draining ourselves spiritually, emotionally, and physically. Exhaustion should be risked only temporarily in emergency situations.

We cannot relieve any and every possible need we encounter. The dream of being available to everyone is fed by the myth of overall availability, a fantasy rooted in the pride-form. Related to it is the "savior complex." Sooner or later these unrealistic tendencies will be challenged by the reality of our finitude, also in the realm of social care. Their deflation often plays a central role in the scenario of erosion of engagement.

Lack of Popular Support for Social Concern

The social dimension affects our directives, dispositions, and actions. No matter what our calling in life is, concern should be part of it. Be we millers or miners, firemen or bartenders, politicians or teachers, employers or employees, housewives or career women, we have the obligation to form ourselves in social presence.

Family members, colleagues, and friends may question our chosen realm of concern. They may disapprove of our dedication, especially if it draws us away from popular asocial directives. Society tends to be materialistic, achievement-oriented, directed by the question: What's in it for us? Hence, there is a lack of understanding of social dispositions and actions, at least in certain circles. The disapproval of others, their lack of encouragement, may erode our dedication.

Neglect of Congenial Intraformation and Its Conditions

Certain people are called to dedicate their life as a whole mainly to the relief of specific social needs, be they of an economic, aesthetic, spiritual, scientific, technical, psychological, or medical nature. They respond to the needs of one or another neglected group of the population. The danger is that specialists in such care tend to identify their entire life with their chosen realm of concern. They have no time or energy left to care for their own intraformation. Their exaltation of this social role blinds them to the necessity to replenish their inner resources. Signs of this neglect may include their failure to foster supportive friendships and other recreative resources outside their daily involvement. Sooner or later their exaltation wanes. Their presence become eroded or depleted, and, sadly for them, they have no resources to fall back upon.

In such cases, it is difficult to restore dedication. A person's physical or emotional health may suffer. Their outlook on life may become grim and onesided, determined mainly by the problems they meet daily within their small circle of specialization. Then, too, insufficient abandonment to the formation mystery at work in the history of humanity may be behind their overinvolvement.

One needs to cultivate the faith disposition that we are only meant to be engaged within the limits of our form potency, that we can let go and allow the mystery to supplement what we cannot effect by our limited powers of dedication alone. It is difficult to engage in this abandonment if we feel that the fate of the world rests on our feeble shoulders.

Subjective Formation Identification

Because we are involved simultaneously in intraformation and interformation with others, we may confuse these realms. Our needs and demands for congenial personal formation may obscure those for social care, and vice versa. We may imagine that what is congenial for us is also right for others. Our concern, while well-intentioned, may not be matched by objective knowledge, experience, and training.

For example, our formation insights may be subjectivistic, prescientific, or colored by beautiful intuitions instead of being rooted in verifiable facts. Many of our intuitions may be excellent, but we cannot be sure of them as long as they are not subjected to the objective scrutiny of critical reason in dialogue with the observations of the human and social sciences. Lacking the critical approach provided by the science of formation, many fall into the trap of subjective formation identification. In short, we identify our personal formation and its congenial demands with the formation of those for whom we care. We expect that they will react as we would. This approach leads inevitably to unrealistic anticipations, which, if not met, may lead us to experience an impasse of ineffectiveness and frustration. This gives rise in turn to erosion.

To correct this kind of identification is an arduous task. Courses in the objective approach of the science of formation, which aim to critique subjectivistic feelings and dispositions, may provide one answer. Counseling with a formation specialist trained in this science may be another means to overcome the subjectivistic bent.

Interformative Contagion

We are always in interaction with others. Whether it is horizontal with contemporaries or vertical with people in the past or the future, this interaction affects us. Briefly stated, it is contagious. This principle applies also to social commitment and its possible erosion. First, we interact with those with whom we are involved; second, with those who serve similar needs within a shared life situation; third, with other colleagues, partners, family members, and peers.

To prevent contagion from occurring, a certain emotional distance should be preserved between ourselves and those to whom we direct our care. Otherwise we may become overinvolved with them, to the point of subjectivistic identification, as described previously. This is harmful for all participants in the interformative process.

Contagion between people who share the same concern and action may be appreciative or depreciative. Appreciative contagion fosters a positive, peace-evoking, joyful atmosphere of interformation. It enhances one's readiness for appreciative presence to others. If such sharing takes place during the period of preparation for social work—for example, in a school or seminary—it will have a beneficial impact on one's presence in a future profession. The constant danger is that this appreciation may be distorted, thus giving rise to exalted aspirations and ambitions. In that event, contagious contact may kindle or enhance a similar exaltation in others.

Depreciative Contagion and Interdeformation

A worse deformation is depreciative contagion: here the atmosphere becomes negative, divisive, cynical. Soon interdeformation occurs among people who should share the same ideals. This attitude affects our relationships with one another as well as with the leaders or administrators over us. Such mutual disharmony harms the enterprises in which we are engaged.

Many factors foment this contagion. People involved in the same preparatory or actual task often live, work, and recreate together. In that case we have plenty of opportunities to rehash problems, to review disappointed expectations, to express our dissatisfactions with shared study or action. These occasions may give way to what some social scientists call "bitching sessions," which can have a devastating effect on the morale of the group, diminishing, if not destroying, the joy of commitment. Severely tested is our compassionate and merciful appraisal of each other, of the administrators over us, of the present and future patients, students, clients, and directees under us. In an atmosphere like this, it is difficult for newcomers to sustain hope and enthusiasm. Snide remarks about the uselessness of dedication may corrode any enthusiasm one brings initially to a social calling.

Administrators may lack sufficient insight and experience to identify the source of these depreciative, negative dispositions. They may not recognize in time the serious problems of pride, insecurity, immaturity, or depression dominating the life and outlook of participants in their programs of social action. Persons with these problems may become the instigators of repeated "bitching sessions." They foster negativity in subtle or open ways, often unwittingly and with the best of intentions. While these sessions may provide some relief from bottled-up negative feelings, they also tend to magnify and reinforce depreciative attitudes and appraisals.

Responsible leaders who recognize these problems may still be slow to confront them. They may fear tackling divisive, destructive participants because they are not ready to remove them from the program. In their reluctance to act, they allow this negativity to corrode the atmosphere of appreciative, confirmative coformation. They confuse tolerance of the socially disadvantaged with the kind of tolerance that is harmful within the helping group itself.

Underprivileged people may be cynical, bitter, depreciative, and conflicted. We bear with these symptoms because we know they have suffered much injustice, discrimination, and rejection. We do not blame them for their conflicts and anger. Our task is to heal these wounds, if possible. The story is much different among those who choose to become their healers. They will only be effective if they are able to grow beyond their anger, cynicism, and insecurity. Such growth is a necessary condition for the possibility of forming and maintaining the dispositions of social justice, peace, and mercy in an unjust, merciless world.

If, on the contrary, depreciating dispositions begin to prevail, the association of social healers or helpers may become a breeding ground for distrust and defeatism. Instead of growing as generous companions, graciously present to the sufferings of others, they become demanding, divisive individuals. Unwittingly, they destroy the climate of justice, peace, and mercy they intended to radiate. What should be condoned in those who seek our assistance cannot be overlooked in those who are called to create an atmosphere of peaceful understanding, compassion, and cooperation. It is the obligation of leaders and administrators of social programs of action or study to counsel destructive persons to leave the program, whenever this is necessary and possible. They should be accepted as sufferers who need help, not as actual social healers able to help others. Unless they overcome their asocial dispositions, it is better for them not to stay in this work. We should realize, of course, that these considerations should not be used by administrators to silence justified opposition against erratic behavior on their part.

Exaltation Phase

The erosion of social presence begins in the phase of exalted aspiration. Let us look at this phase in more detail. Erosion creeps up on people, so to say. It may deform their lives slowly, almost unnoticeably. Formation directors or counselors need training and experience to spot erosion in its inception. They can help counselees to deal with it creatively if they understand the phases of ebb and flow considered previously. The exaltation phase is the initial phase of this process. Here hopes run high, energy abounds, and so do unrealistic aspirations, ambitions, and anticipations.

Typical of the exaltation phase is a certain naiveté in regard to the pride-form. Exalted people may not be aware that pride is by its nature exalted and exalting. Consequently they may be ignorant of its hidden role in enthusiasm. Even if they begin to suspect it, instead of deepening their awareness, they may repudiate and ignore this danger signal.

Lack of Balance between Intraformative Factors

The phase of exaltation is marked by lack of awareness of the right balance between intraformative factors. Inspirations, aspirations, functional ambitions, situational realities, apprehension, appraisal, affirming decisions, and their related dispositions and feelings should operate in mutual consonance. Only then is consonant presence itself possible. In the exaltation phase people lack a balanced appreciation of these factors. They ignore the necessity of keeping these elements in dialogue with the demands of their engagements. Lack of insight, combined with an inclination to favor onesidedly exalted dispositions, leads to erosion.

One cannot neglect awareness of the basic relationship that governs the ebb and flow of presence, that is, the relationship between the primordial abandonment option and the presence disposition. The beginning social enthusiast may not suspect the deep impact this option has on the meaningfulness of one's engagement.

Underestimation of the Need for Other Formation Sources

Exaltation breeds unrealistic expectations. We may live in the illusion that our only need in life is the engagement for which we have opted. The exalted imagination fantasizes that social dedication will fulfill all our needs. Other sources, such as reading, meditation, recreation, exercise, friendships, and supportive relationships outside the contexts of social involvement, are ignored. Overidentification with the recipients of our care may follow. This only serves to increase our precarious isolation from formation sources outside the restricted engagement circle. In short, exalted dedication leads to excessive and inefficient use of our spiritual, functional, and vital resources and energies.

Voluntary overwork without needed rest often occurs in this phase. Repudiated or refused is the paramount question of the congeniality and compatibility of our choice of engagement. We neglect to ask: How does this type of service concretely affect me in view of my own and others' life call, prior commitments, health, talents, time limits, family, community, and so on? The moment these questions surface in focal consciousness, they may generate false guilt feelings. How dare I question the generous projects in which I am engaged? Am I not betraying a beautiful ideal by entertaining doubts, even for a moment?

Guilt feelings of this sort are bred by exalted aspirations. They share in their deceptiveness and they are as pretentious and treacherous as their source. False guilt leads to the repudiation of these basic questions, even though what hinges on them is the consonant formation of our life. Thus we should bring them to focal awareness and honestly face their directives.

Repudiation or Refusal of the Congruence of Affinity

The exalted guilt described above may pave the way for other related repudiations. Among them is our awareness of significant criteria of consonance. Formation consonance corresponds with the form dimensions of human life. Each dimension has its own type and criterion of consonance and is named accordingly. For instance, consonance is called congruence when it applies to a correspondence between functional abilities and effective acts and dispositions in regard to our formation field. A basic criterion of congruence is affinity to what we are doing. This is usually manifested in task efficiency and a certain joy in the doing.

The same criterion of affinity applies to congruent social presence. Specific engagements imply regular assignments, duties, and the tasks linked with them. If we have to spend our time and talents in these endeavors, we should have a modicum of functional affinity to them. It would be foolish not to face this question of affinity. Much depends on it, if our life formation and that of others is to remain consonant.

Take the case of a biochemist who feels inspired to spend her life in the expansion of global means of justice and mercy. She decides to devote most of her time to laboratory research, trying to develop agricultural techniques that promise better harvests to supply food for the world population. While executing this project, she experiences an habitual lack of affinity to laboratory research. She is not as effective in her research as her colleagues are. Wise appraisal of this experience may make her see that congruent affinity for continuous laboratory research is missing. Consequently her efforts are cumbersome and ineffective. She feels as if she is losing her time. The process of erosion begins, further contributing to her inefficiency. Based on the criterion of congruent consonance, she may conclude that it is advisable to incarnate her social concern in some teaching or writing task for which she feels an affinity. The same criterion can be applied to anyone in any profession—foreign missionary, social worker, nurse, public demonstrator for justice, labor organizer, peace worker, or whatever.

Like all dispositions, injustice, too, seeks articulation in a concrete formation field. Manifestations of injustice, be they economic, political, academic, material or spiritual, are secondary to the basic disposition itself. They constitute well-defined deeds of injustice with consequences that affect the related field.

Consider an expression of formation injustice in the realm of aesthetics. Parents may withhold from musically gifted children the means of the development of this disposition, even if they could easily provide them. They push the child to excel in sports and academics only. This refusal not only despoils the child's musical performance; it also contributes to an overall feeling of abandonment. Children may begin to feel deserted when they are faced with repeated acts of formation injustice. It is as if their parents have abandoned their very soul. The experience of abandonment of soul, in a self-depreciative sense, may be a response to the disposition of injustice in others, which oppresses congenial unfolding.

No matter how, when, and where this oppressive disposition vents itself in any of its nuances, it may lead to the same feeling of desertion. Later someone may try to relieve the harm done by this particular expression of injustice. Someone may give to the deprived child an opportunity for musical growth as one would give the homeless a home or the hungry food. This is a step in the direction of righting a wrong, but in and by itself it may not be sufficient to relieve the feeling of abandonment. Distrust and dejection in injured people are not that easily relieved.

Exaltation over Material Relief and Neglect of Healing Presence

In the phase of exaltation, one may rely mainly on the relief of the material effect of injustice. Yet one must go farther. Deeper wounds beg to be healed. The final results, stemming from material improvements alone, could be disappointing. Such gifts in themselves may not restore peace of soul to wounded people. Our disappointment when they do not respond in gratefulness for our material help could be another cause of the erosion of our dedication.

To be sure, our healing presence must be embodied concretely in one or more forms of economic, medical, ecological, educational, scientific, aesthetic, or spiritual care. Yet these measures can lessen abandonment of soul only if they are at the same time loving expressions of cordial presence.

Only as carriers of our care can they touch the hearts of people and resurrect in them stirrings of their own faith, hope, and consonance.

Exalted beginners may concentrate on conspicuous relief of material needs. They may even be tempted to neglect the nourishment of their own deeper presence. Yet the latter should be the source of their action, otherwise involvement becomes shallow. When the inspiration disappears, erosion of commitment may result. Therefore, movements to procure justice should be sustained by the devotion of one's heart.

Exalted aspirations and ambitions, expressed with enthusiasm, are contagious. Moved by this excitement, many want to give more and more while resourcing themselves inwardly less and less. Exaltation without deeper foundations expands until it collapses. After such dazzling beginnings, the letdown is more devastating. It may either lead to severe erosion or inspire a sober assessment of our dispositions and actions.

Inexperienced directors of formation may hesitate to question this style of excitable giving. Though caution is in order, it is hard to moderate exalted beginners. They may be lauded by fellow students and colleagues, by family members and friends. Their charming fervor may seem irresistible. Less accomplished directors may begin to identify with the idealistic dispositions of such celebrated newcomers. Understandably so, for insecure directors themselves may be in need of approval, popularity, praise, and affection from their students and directees. Unwittingly they may play a role in the scenario of exaltation and eventual erosion of social dedication.

Social and Personal Justice

We must distinguish at this point between social and personal justice. Social justice promotes the congenial unfolding of people by fostering favorable conditions in society. Personal justice deals with the congeniality rights of a specific person. These forms of justice are, of course, interwoven. They complement and facilitate each other. Social justice serves personal justice by improving the conditions of personal development. It advances the relatively unique unfolding of persons in society. Personal justice indirectly serves social justice by facilitating the congenial unfolding of the total formation of a person's life, including its social dimension. Such formation seeks to develop a presence that is compatible, compassionate, and competent. Thus one is prepared for a life of social justice in his or her own way. The experience of personal justice in one's life enables one to make specific contributions to society.

Personal justice is not immune from social deformity. For instance, a school official may grant a degree to an unqualified student because of a mistaken notion of justice and compassion. This person wants the student to feel confirmed and encouraged, to start a successful career. The official forgets that this dishonest beginning is an act of social injustice. To send an unqualified person as a trustworthy professional into society will not help future clients, students, or patients. Nor will it advance the deeper life formation of the overprotected person.

A similar case involves parents who refuse to discipline a child reasonably yet firmly. Misguided by a warped sense of personal justice and compassion, they prepare the ground for the injustice to society this child may perpetrate as a spoiled adult who is cynical or demanding. Parents may try to appease children who are not really dedicated to their chores or who are disrespectful of their teachers. To spare themselves the burden of discipline, parents may indulge a child's lack of zeal and engagement under the pretext of personal justice and compassion. By allowing children to be careless, habitually depreciative and overly critical, they impoverish in some measure the fabric of society. Their injustice toward society in these early years may saddle other families, companies, and communities later on with irresponsible parents, laborers, and professionals.

People in charge of formation should earnestly ponder the following questions: Do our well-meant acts of personal justice adversely affect social justice? Do our actions indirectly lessen the conditions of society that favor justice, peace, and mercy for all? Much societal injustice is caused by people who were unwisely appeased. By demanding, protesting, complaining, or subtly manipulating us, they obtained special treatment. They were indulged at the expense of their formation in dispositions of tolerance, humility, and self-giving service. They did not learn to substitute disciplined productivity for destructive depreciation. Nor did they establish the right balance of gracious independence and wise dependence.

Directors of formation may gain temporary peace and popularity by giving in when faced with threats of rebellion, slander, and criticism, but they betray their social responsibility. Society will have to pay the price of diminished social justice. People in charge of formation should not honor the threats that accompany unreasonable demands for acts of pseudo-justice, peace, and compassion. Appeasement only weakens the potential for social participation in the persons concerned. This potential is deepened and actualized under the guidance of wise and gentle discipline.

Persons preparing themselves for the formation of others should reflect in advance on the problems they will meet in this regard. They will have to face many immature people. Some may be clever, talented, articulate, charming, seductive. They may be members of outstanding families, of clerical establishments or religious communities, of other powerful classes of society. Such manipulative directees may be able to play on the pathologies and needs of the less gifted, anxious, and insecure students or trainees around them. Hence, they can threaten implicitly to turn an entire group in formation against their directors if they do not get their way. They may intimidate the directors by subtly indicating that they will malign their name among influential outsiders and administrators. To gain privileged treatment, they may cunningly remind them of their class, family, or community, of their relationships with powerful leaders in church or state, or of their high spiritual calling. Past success in the evasion of just demands may be one cause of their immaturity. Often they give themselves away by asking for exceptions. They simply cannot follow the rules, regulations, and demands of a program as spelled out in advance. They always want special deals.

Meeting truly just directors of formation, such types may be faced for the first time in their life with gentle yet firm representatives of equal social justice for all and its demands. They may feel driven to discredit the voice of equal justice, which threatens their requests for exceptions to the rule. Their giftedness in expression and social standing, whether it is clerical, religious, or civilian, may enable them to influence vulnerable people around them as well as to arouse persons outside the program. As a result formative directors or representatives of social justice may suffer rejection even by their peers or superiors. Yet it is better to be rejected than to betray social justice. Later in life, many of the opponents of these same just directors and masters may gain through trial and error the wisdom of heart, respect for discipline, and social responsibility they once rejected. Life may teach them the lessons of justice. Formation directors who stand firm in the midst of persecution may end up as martyrs for the cause of social justice. They are among the unsung heroes of the revolution in human rights we are witnessing.

Primary Means of Erosion Reformation

Faced with the erosion of social presence, we seek means to halt and reform this process before it leads to total depletion. One primary means of reformation is critical and creative reflection on the foundations of social presence. Do we live in personal, trusting abandonment to the beneficial meaningfulness of the mystery of formation? Is our primordial decision in favor of this abandonment strong enough to relieve our social worries? Do our faith, hope, and consonance keep this primordial decision alive despite doubts and trials? Do they sustain our trust in the formation potency given to each person? If this triad has weakened, can we rekindle its flame by dwelling in meditative presence on the mystery that evokes and nurtures it?

For the sake of congeniality, we must ask whether we still believe in our life call, and try to disclose it increasingly. Are we faithful to its message? What does it tell us about our present engagement? The same applies to compatibility. Do we appraise rightly what is compatible with our life situation and how it affects our social involvement? If we have to make some changes, have we the courage to do so? Finally, we should reflect on the right balance between congeniality and compatibility. Are we focused only on what is right for us? Do we pay sufficient attention to what is compatible with our situation? Or do we fall in the opposite extreme? Are we so eager to be compatible that we betray what we are called to be? It is essential to keep alive a creative dialogue between these two poles of social presence. Absence of a healthy tension between congeniality and compatibility will affect our involvement, its continuation or its erosion.

Secondary Means of Erosion Reformation

Critical, creative reflection on these foundations is the first means of reversing the erosion process. The secondary means for this reformation consist of needed practical interventions aimed at turning the process of erosion around.

Practical intervention can begin when we change our type of social engagement. We try to find and implement another kind of action more in tune with our congenial life direction. We become aware of the disparity between this direction, which stems from the mystery of our preformation, and our present way of social engagement. Slowly we may seek to modify our involvement, to bring it more in line with our life direction. This modification may imply a realignment of the integrative structures of our life. Our core, current, apparent, and actual forms of social presence may have to change. We need to adapt our dispositions to the concrete demands of congeniality, compatibility, and compassion. The style and measure of our social concern may have to undergo decisive alterations. A whole new current form of dedication must succeed the former one. This in turn will restyle our apparent and actual forms of presence. Such changes often result in the reversal of erosion.

Another means of reformation may involve our relationships. Within the circle of social engagement, we usually develop close connections with dependents, colleagues, superiors, and many others inside and outside this immediate ambience. Our presence is formed and reformed by this mutual interaction. The style, measure, and expression of our presence affects others as we are affected by them. Newly gained insights into the sources of erosion may imply major alterations in these relationships.

In some instances, effective renewal calls for the assistance of programs geared specifically to ongoing social formation. Participation in such programs may alleviate wholly or in part our personal predicament. Especially if these programs help us to reflect on the foundations of involvement, we may become aware of our lack of wider horizons and the need to expand our relationships outside our current engagement circle. These moves can correct and complement onesided views of life presented to us in the restricted realm of daily service. New friends, acquaintances, and interests can be sources of relaxation and recreation. They can help to restore our depleted energies and to renew our vision. They enable us to relativize what seems absolute in the areas for which we are responsible.

These, then, are a few of the practical interventions needed for the reversal of erosion. As secondary means, they are dependent on the primary means of reformation, namely, critical and creative reflection on the foundation of social presence. This alone assures the ultimate effectiveness of practical intervention. The latter should be assessed and implemented in the light of the transcendent appraisal of our presence and position. Functional appraisal follows the transcendent. It involves an assessment of the concrete conditions for care. Practical evaluation of everyday reality strikes at the heart of our exaltation. It ought to lead to new awareness. We should pay special attention as well to the wrong use of our imagination. If we use it to maintain and strengthen exaltation, it becomes the origin of unrealistic appraisals. Then fantastic transcendent appraisal replaces the realistic transcendent approach, which should guide our formation of social dispositions.

Fantastic versus Realistic Appraisal

The term *fantastic* refers to the unrealistic, fantasy-based exaltation of our appraisal of what involvement should be like. Inspirations and aspirations are blown out of proportion by exalted imagination. In the case of social visions, fantastic appraisals lead to an artificial reconstruction of our formation field that is inevitably grandiose. It is based on an exalted image of what an "idealistic" life in service of justice, peace, and mercy *should* look like. This erratic heroism may be fed by contemporary pulsations pertaining to social concern.

Realistic appraisal, by contrast, aims at what is attainable for us. It takes into account the whole situation, carefully scrutinizing the real possibilities and dispositions of the people who want to engage themselves in this or that enterprise in the light of the laws of congeniality, compatibility, compassion, and competence. It recognizes that distortions of social reality are rooted in the exalted and exalting pride-form. What is required to correct these distortions is an imaginative transcendent appraisal, informed by sound foundational appraisal.

Social formation programs should form beginners in the whole range of mutually complementary appraisal dispositions. These are linked to the dimensions of the life-form and hence are distinguished as transcendent, functional, vital, and historical appraisal dispositions. In mutual interaction they prepare future social participants to cope effectively with the crises they will have to face sooner or later.

For example, the erosion of dedication is often aggravated by a deficient appraisal of one's vital limits and capacities. This can cause premature exhaustion and weariness. Historical appraisal dispositions enable one to be cautiously and creatively critical of cultural pulsations. Are they potentially or actually onesided in their emphasis? Does this popular push contribute to one's uncongenial choice of service? Does it seduce one to develop unsuitable dispositions in regard to the type, style, measure, and expression of care in one's field of action?

Realistic preparation for engagement readies one to bestow a priceless gift on people, for it facilitates their life formation. It lays the foundations for a just, peaceful, and merciful society. It enables apprentices to be effectively present to the formation segments of society they have chosen to serve. Their sound appraisal dispositions incline them to assess realistically their basic affinity to these segments. If they find that this affinity is missing, they have the courage and wisdom to direct their care to another segment more in tune with their own preformation.

Realistic preparation also diminishes the loss in membership of socially engaged institutes, associations, or communities. It will reduce the financial costs of therapy, rehabilitation, or litigation incurred by them because of social presence erosion and depletion in their members. This fact alone makes wise formation the best long-range investment a family, association, or society can make. The responsibilities we face in the future render such formation not a luxury for a few but a survival measure for all.

Emotional Withdrawal, Transcendent Detachment, and Wise Ventilation

The erosion of social presence may manifest itself in withdrawal. Feeling disappointed, we draw back emotionally. Such evasion should not be confused with transcendent detachment. Detachment is for the sake of a deeper presence. It is a gift of enlightened tolerance. It facilitates fidelity to our concern when adverse conditions threaten our resources. Detachment keeps our engagement alive while modulating its intensity. It takes into account our limits.

The art of detachment fosters a rhythm of presence and absence. Absorption in service is prevented. We avoid the enslavement of exaltation that is liable to exhaust us prematurely. We rise above setbacks. We appreciate failing people, ourselves included, as cared for in a deeper way by the formation mystery. Detachment allows for moments of stepping back. Periods of restoration foster the continuation and quality of our care for others.

The erosion of presence is accompanied by depreciative emotions. Feelings of stress and frustration can be relieved by wise and moderate ventilation in conversation with trusted friends who have reached a sufficient level of maturity. They may share with us their own disappointments, help us regain perspective, and restore commitment. Mutual communication liberates people from the faulty feeling that they alone experience dissatisfaction. Many of them may be inclined to blame themselves for irritation, impatience, and aversion. Hearing that others suffer in the same way because of the pressures of similar situations can be a source of relief. Sharing like problems may lead participants to search together for solutions.

Depreciative emotions and appraisals can also be ventilated in ways that are deformative. Rage and indignation may be expressed destructively. As a result, depreciative appraisal intensifies, becoming a lasting disposition. This hardens and heightens the tendency to blame other people, institutions, and past formation history for the erosion of one's presence.

In this way we may induce in ourselves feelings of impotence, a slush fund of powerless rage, apathy, and despair. The outpouring of such emotional appraisals is contagious among people already touched by disappointment. As a result, adversity and failure are anxiously or cynically expected. We develop a morbid attentiveness, focusing only on those facets of the situation that confirm our depreciative expectations. We become imprisoned in a tunnel vision. Paralyzed is our sensitivity for opportunities for improvement. We are on the way from erosion to depletion of social presence.

At times some erosion seems unavoidable for all of us. We should develop dispositions to appraise and manage these crises focally and formatively. They should be turned into beneficial formation events, sources of enlightenment and disclosure. They can tell us a little more about who we basically are. They make us aware of the distortions of our calling. Penetrating our intrasphere, we may see how perhaps an inflated appreciation of social heroism is linked with the pride-form, with the demonic in our life, or with unrealistic historical pulsations. Social erosion problems can be turned into formation opportunities. They are a privileged occasion for a further unveiling of the protoform of our life.

CHAPTER 21

Key Dispositions for Effective Social Presence

W e have already referred to the global dispositions of social presence. Here we shall consider the key dispositions that articulate more concretely these general dispositions, for they help us to attain maximally effective social presence. Some of the obstacles to these dispositions will also be discussed.

Empathic Appreciation

The first concrete disposition to be mentioned is empathic appreciation. It is the ability and inclination to coexperience and wisely appraise the personal formation field of other people and the private meaning it holds for them.

Empathic Communication

Appreciation is not sufficient. It should be complemented by empathic communication. Communicating one's empathy is a great art and discipline. People open up when they feel really understood and accepted in their formation field and history. They feel relief from loneliness; they experience the security of trusted communion. Their appreciation may extend to the formation directives they perceive we represent.

Formative Social Justice

Formative justice is the disposition to apprehend, appreciate, and promote the unique form of other people's lives. It enables us to facilitate the conditions for their congenial and compatible unfolding. It includes respect for the right of others to make their own life choices in their own

322

time. Respect confirms that such options should be in tune with the consonant life directives of humanity as they come to people within their own formation tradition.

Formative also in regard to justice is the manifestation of our own disposition to be obediently congenial, to live in fidelity to the disclosures of our personal form of life. Our obedient congeniality can be an exemplary appeal to others to aspire similarly after obedient congeniality.

Formative Transcendent Joy

Another coformant of effective presence is transcendent joy. It is the fruit of our faith in the beneficence of the mystery of formation. As such it should be distinguished from the vital disposition for pleasure and the functional bent toward satisfaction. At times joy may include the latter as subordinate, if and when such inclusion is compatible. Joyousness in the face of challenges is invigorating. Its resilient quality tends to awaken or enhance in others energy, courage, and flexibility.

Joyousness may spontaneously manifest itself in our apparent life-form in various ways. These include, among others, wonder, admiration, appreciation, laughter, childlikeness, good humor, spontaneity, playfulness, pleasantness, festive celebration, graciousness, delight in the beautiful, and hope for the future (both here and in the hereafter, for those whose tradition includes faith in an afterlife).

Formative Challenge

Formative challenge is the ability and disposition to summon others gently and firmly to live in fidelity to their foundational form of life. Usually we challenge others only when they invite the gift of open communication. This may be explicit, but more commonly it is an implicit call expressed in facial or other bodily language or in veiled verbal allusion. We may question tactfully the congeniality of the life of our friends or counselees. We may respectfully comment on the deformative discrepancies we seem to apprehend in their appraisals, feelings, lifestyles, expressions, and actions.

Moderate Self-Disclosure

Helpful, too, is the disclosure of relevant incidents in one's own formation history. Certain exemplary formation events and responses in our own life may be discretely communicated. They should be selected for their aptness to benefit others in their present or anticipated formation predicament. Such disclosures should not violate the law of congeniality. For instance, they should not trespass on the privacy we experience as mandatory for our own unfolding.

Solving Compatibility Tensions

Social interformation is hindered by tensions that result from the experience of mutual incompatibility. We could call them compatibility tensions. To spot and appraise them in time, to bring them to healing and expression, may clear the air. Such real or imagined tensions mar the effectiveness, playfulness, and relaxed freedom of human exchange. Hence, it is desirable to notice and solve such tensions as soon as they emerge within freely chosen relationships. If our compatibility disposition is consonant, it takes into account the limits of our own congenial life formation.

Compassion

Compassion is another coformant of effective social presence. This disposition enables us to express genuine intentions of concern, compassion, and affection. The social disposition of compassion, if consonant, manifests in our apparent life-form nurturing attitudes without our becoming emotionally absorbed in the people for whom we truly care. Nor do we allow this disposition to interfere unwisely with the demands of congenial life formation.

Manifestation of Formation Energy

Another valuable addition to effective presence is the spontaneous manifestation of the dynamic flow of our formation energy and its invigorating power. This enhances the contagious quality of inner resilience. It radiates a spontaneous appeal that vitalizes and inspires people who seek social support and stimulation.

Manifestation of Effective Form Donation

Formative also is the revelation in our apparent form of our ability to give form to life and world concretely in effective and functionally realistic ways. This prevents our presence from deteriorating into a floating attitude divorced from everyday reality. Such an attitude would destroy the effectiveness of pure presence. It could become a power of alienation instead of liberation.

Relativity of Dispositions of Effective Social Presence

As we must realize, not all of these articulations are necessarily innate as life-form dispositions in every person who is called to be socially present. But the apparent life-form of many engaged people can be formed in some measure in the effective responses that flow spontaneously from others gifted in this way. Such apparent life formation, even if it is more willed than felt, is not necessarily deceptive or mere pretense. It is genuine to the extent that it embodies our honest will to be as formative for others as we can be within our limitations. It tends, moreover, to awaken any corresponding social ability that may be latent in our life.

Such dispositions and articulations of presence do not necessarily prevent erosion and crisis. The comforting experience of confidence that accompanies effectiveness is, however, an allied force in the effort to cope with such erosion.

Spiral of Social Exaltation

The dispositions and articulations of effective presence are easily stunted in the face of exaltation. We may ask ourselves what it is in the human life-form that gives rise to such exaltation. The answer is, of course, the pride-form of life. Pride is by its very nature exalted and exalting. It overestimates what we can do by ourselves alone. It is fascinated by isolated human projects of improvement of people and world. The blown-up fantasies of the pride-form take the place of inspiration and aspiration. They prevent a realistic appraisal of what is feasible in a concrete situation. They overstimulate our ambitions and breed an overly excitable range of social awareness and reactivity. To many these reactions may feel inspirational, but they are mainly vital.

Excessive social involvement sets into motion a spiral of exaltation. Initially it may lead to success and acknowledgment in the field of social action. Vital involvement is contagious. People on the receiving end of this action find it stimulating. Hence, do-gooders experience an expansion of vital as well as social power and effectiveness. This goads them on to more functional involvements. Ambitious overcommitment and consequent accomplishment again feed into the spiral of vital exaltation. This leads in turn to increased involvement, which winds up and up until rising anticipations crash against the ceiling of reality.

In the course of time the spiral of social exaltation will produce deformative effects. These outweigh the original benefits of the phase of unbridled enthusiasm. Overinvestment in involvement is accompanied by neglect of the intraformation of life. Our inner life deteriorates, and we are left vulnerable and defenseless when a crisis announces itself. The anticipation of accelerating change leaves us open to disappointment in the real world.

Inflation of Life Call, Savior Complex, Arrogance of Formation Ignorance

Another danger of initial success in regard to our exalted ambitions is the inflation of our life call and corresponding capacities. Grandiosity may give rise to the "social savior complex." In many cases the secret conviction that one is a charismatic savior may cover up inadequate formation knowledge. We forget easily that such knowledge should be nourished and updated continuously. The social savior may underestimate the myriad elements that enter any formation situation. Meagerness of wisdom and information is one of the sources of injustice, impatience, incompetence, and lack of compassion. Usually unintentional, this lack is simply due to the blindness caused by extravagant anticipations that unnecessarily disturb people in their surroundings.

Hence, the exaltation spiral may engender the arrogance of formation ignorance. Such arrogance gives rise to faulty appraisals and decisions. It feeds one's need to subtly pressure others to conform to one's exalted anticipations. These anticipations are subjective. For instance, they surpass the reasonable and legitimate demands any formation program should impose on those who freely commit themselves to this discipline.

Overidentification, Myth of Overall Availability, Lack of Congenial Recreation

Another effect of the spiral may be an overidentification with the people for whom we care with such exalted zeal. This may blur the boundaries between the congenial formation of our own life and the lives of those entrusted to our care. The situation thus created may in the long run become intolerable. Social do-gooders may no longer know how to extricate themselves from such suffocating relationships. Flight into the depletion of social presence may be the only solution left to them.

The spiral often gives rise to the myth of overall availability. We are duped by our own unrealistic appraisal of what the limits of sane accessibility to the socially indigent really are. This myth can deplete or diminish the richness of our intrasphere. We have no time and energy left for its restoration. It can render us vulnerable to subtle manipulation, through false feelings of social guilt, by those who take our overall availability for granted. Not only the socially indigent, but also admirers, colleagues, family, friends, students, or administrators may cleverly or unwittingly exploit our exalted aspirations and ambitions. The need to be accessible at any time to all their needs tempts us to betray our quiet fidelity to the demands of justice for ourselves and others.

Justice calls us to live in humble congeniality and compatibility with the limits of our own and others' realistic life formation. The always accessible person may neglect the demands of congeniality, wise compatibility, and compassion. In the course of time, such infidelity may cause an erosion of presence or even its depletion. This erosion is an overreaction to an exhausted existence. Our overextended life may be suddenly experienced as lost and dissonant.

One source of balanced social presence is our functional ability for sober registration of pertinent information. This disposes us to take into account what is concretely going on inside and outside our life of social engagement. The capacity to do so is overpowered by the exaltation spiral, distorted as it is by the fantasies it engenders in our imagination.

Human life has deep-seated needs for timely repose and recreation. Overengagement may blind us to what is necessary for a balanced life of formation, for relaxed effectiveness. Each of us is called to develop a refined awareness of our own congenial type, measure, and style of recreation. Only in this way can we effectively "re-create" our social presence. Overinvolvement tends to destroy this sensitivity. We may neglect recreation in misplaced zeal for our projects. We may allow ourselves to be manipulated by others into uniform types of recreation, some of which may be uncongenial to our real needs, skills, and abilities. This means that we cannot really re-create our life on basis of our own sensitivities.

The more different we are, the more we should respect our unique recreative needs. A consumer culture tends to debase people into identical recreational objects. Its atmosphere of homogenizing human recreation is socially unjust. It tends to subject people to the current recreational pulsations of the majority. Popularity and consumerism are its guidelines, not respect for the diverse recreative needs of individual persons. This mode of social injustice may invade not only the marketplace, but also clubs, communities, agencies, schools, and churches.

Universality of Social Presence Erosion

What we have discussed thus far makes it increasingly clear that social exaltation is the opposite of sober appreciation. Because of lack of reality testing, our exalted aspiration and ambitions cannot be realized in everyday life. Lack of fulfillment is their universal fate. The erosion of social presence is partly a result of this backlash of unfulfilled anticipations.

Exaltation and its erosion happen in every field of presence. We may meet its symptoms in science, art, teaching, business, publishing, medicine, spiritual animation, social work, apostolic endeavors, and administration. No formation segment of society is immune to this affliction. The spiral of exaltation and its backlash in erosion is a universal affliction.

Interformation Impotence

One painful result of the disappointment of our social ideals is the experience of a special kind of impotence. Human life is limited in its ability to form, coform, or reform people or their situations. Exaltation overlooks this limitation and makes us blandly try to reform people and places in the image of our own expectations. Sooner or later we become aware of our interformative impotence in this regard. This increasing awareness corrodes our exalted apprehension of the social dimension of the life call. It contributes to the erosion of social presence.

Administrative Opportunism and Social Presence

Erosion may be due also to the lack of administrative support we find for our social projects. Often people in charge fail to sustain, praise, reward, or kindly encourage the social presence of their scholars, authors, artists, social workers, professors, physicians, scientists, teachers, employees. As long as they function well and fulfill their duties, that is sufficient. Their social idealism may be met with condescending tolerance or benign indifference. Certain administrators may prefocally strive for power, control, and advancement, even at the price of betraying social justice. Their opportunism exceeds their wisdom, knowledge, and social concern. They are less inclined to stay in the background, humbly serving the unique unfolding of their employees in service of the common cause.

When inspired social concern is expressed, some administrators may feel threatened in their need for functional control. They may even experience the awakening of guilt feelings they have successfully refused or repudiated. Such negative characteristics may contribute to the erosion of social presence in those who work under them.

Political Power Struggle and Social Presence

A power struggle dominates the relationships of many people. The autarchic pride-form is always operative. It affects in a special way interformative situations. Such situations are not only a meeting between foundational forms of life in their nobility but also between pride-forms competing with one another for applause and control. Beneath each one's benign appearance of social presence a battle for power may lurk. This struggle is usually infra- or prefocal. The need for control and ascendancy secretly nourishes dispositions of envy, jealousy, inferiority or superiority, one-upmanship, anger, hostility, suspicion, fear, anxiety, manipulation, seduction. All of these feelings may be disguised in the apparent life-form as concern for others. For the careful observer, however, such disguised tendencies may manifest themselves as veiled infighting; charming seduction; sweet or harsh maneuvering of people and situations; gossip that demeans the expressed inspirations, aspirations, and ambitions of rivals; undercutting of reputations of people who are socially effective.

The hidden struggle for importance and control creates an undercurrent of power patterns in many institutions. In the throes of exalted presence, one may not appraise realistically the impact of these latent needs and political maneuvers. We may remain blissfully unaware that such needs are also in ourselves, that they may subtly affect our own policies. We may not sense the political patterns that already play a secret role in any formation situation, no matter how religious, humane, or idealistic it may be.

Exalted participants may discover gradually or suddenly the patterns that play such a formative role in the enterprises in which they participate. They may feel betrayed and disgusted. This discovery leads often to a crisis of social presence.

It may prove impossible to change deformative power patterns at once. In our exaltation we may overreact and strive for the abolition of political structures. A formative response, on the contrary, would be realistic acceptance of the human condition of the participants, ourselves included. Power politics are unavoidable among people. That they are easily tainted by the pride-form is unavoidable too. We can only make the best of it. On the basis of this resignation, that is, this reassignment of meaning, the effective participant tries to bring political patterns into the open, to lift them into the light of apprehension and appraisal. The purpose of appraisal is to deal with these patterns wisely, effectively, and realistically within the limits of our obedient congeniality, compatibility, compassion, and competence.

Power Politics and Social Justice in Institutions

Power politics play a special role in institutions. A great number of participants in universities, colleges, art centers, hospitals, companies, churches, or humanitarian organizations do not directly intend to diminish social presence. They may claim the opposite and genuinely intend so on the focal level. Unwittingly, however, they may be moved in their actions by such latent dispositions as these: how to look good, or at least not bad, in the eyes of administrators, colleagues, people at large, dependents, and employees; and how to be effective socially while protecting and advancing one's own position, status, income, and popularity. To the extent that such personal concerns prevail, the concern for justice and mercy may be diminished. These may become the victims of power politics.

The upsurge of power politics, as distinguished from social justice politics, is a given of the human condition and the pride-form of life. This facet of the human form can never be totally extinguished. The blindness of exaltation inclines one to deny this facet in self or others. Instead, it should be dealt with in realistic appraisal.

Pretended Affinity to Uncongenial Styles of Social Presence

The science of formation tries to trace the transcultural universal foundations of social presence. Sociohistorically, such universals will be articulated in particular styles, expressions, disciplines, or methods of presence in various form traditions. The basic aspects of such traditional styles of social presence are foundational for the articulation concerned. They are soon joined by accretions that are not fundamental for one's specific tradition but due to temporal pulsations. Popular accretions may narrow the style of social presence considerably. They may be propagated uncritically as if they were part of the fundamentals of one's form tradition.

If people have no affinity to a particular accretional approach, they cannot resonate with it deep down in the core form of their life. This alien approach—or limitation of social concern to, for instance, one formation segment—would be deformative for them. They experience inner dissonance when they succumb to popular pulsations that are at odds with the protoform of their life. An enthusiastic majority may make them feel false guilt about this inevitable experience of dissonance. The deformation is most harmful if its victims try to repudiate this experience and falsify their life by a pretense of affinity that is not truly theirs. Socially engaged persons who are the prisoners of accretional formation approaches that are uncongenial to them may experience a crisis of presence because of this lack of inner resonance.

The same deceptive identification of one type of social concern with the essence of social presence may lead to a crisis of engagement also in those who do have an affinity to this one kind of presence. They may meet a lack of spontaneous resonance in people otherwise engaged or in populations they want to imbue with their own brand of enthusiasm. Believing that such accretional approaches are fundamental for all followers of their form tradition, they are scandalized by those who cannot share their excitement. The experience of disappointment and of failure to convince others to be like they are may slowly erode their presence or breed bitterness in their hearts.

Reactions and Responses to Blocked Formation Energy

The experience of failure and disappointment in engagement tends to block the flow of our formation energy. Once this energy is dammed in or stored up by such blockage, it can be directed in deformative or formative ways.

Blockage halts the even flow of formation energy. It does not insert itself consonantly in the gentle formation of the pre-, intra-, and outer spheres of life. Instead, it becomes onesidedly mobilized around the problem at hand, in this case, how to give effective form to one's threatened ideal of social engagement; how to be effectively present in this area of formation for this specific segment of the population. The problem is compounded when we have chosen an uncongenial and incompatible field of presence. Such excessive and onesidedly mobilized energy tends to be directed deformatively into an exalted appraisal of our capacities, ideals, and duties in the situation.

Such an appraisal, strengthened by exalted memory, imagination, and anticipation, leads to exalted decisions of the will. The will, becoming willful, inclines our power of formative appraisal to keep denying vital-functional information about reality. The will compels these dimensions of the life-form to engage in a frenzy of effort aimed at forcing us, as well as other people, events, and things, into the frame of our exalted appraisals. We do not ask ourselves any longer how much we and others can vitally, functionally, and spiritually tolerate without harm or how we can function most effectively, wisely, compatibly, and compassionately in the given situation.

Exalted, frantic responses to failing presence lead to exhaustion of the formation energy abused so intensively. This hastens the emergence of a crisis that may ultimately deplete both our formation energy and our social engagement. This deformative, willful response is at the root of many precipitous departures from situations of commitment. A departure is precipitous when it happens before one is relatively certain, through sober appraisal, that one is not called to this kind of involvement with this specific segment of the population.

Mobilized formation energy in time of crisis can also be directed positively toward enlightened appraisal. It may be used to question our abandonment to the beneficial meaning of the formation mystery. After questioning this abandonment, we may use this energy to question our type, style, measure, and expression of concern, our choice of a segment of the population to serve. Is it congenial and compatible? Are failure and disappointment an invitation to a more sober and realistic adaptation of our possibly too exalted anticipations? Could they contain a disclosure that the expression of our life call should be sought elsewhere?

Mobilized formation energy can be directed, therefore, toward realistic adaptation, which would imply, among other things, the following factors:

1. assuming responsibility for a more realistic social presence in a firm and gentle way;

2. confronting courageously and wisely the objective vital and functional facts in one's social engagement and its field of action;

3. appraising objectively one's choice of population segment;

4. experimenting patiently and critically with one's style and measure of presence in order to find what seems most effective within the limits of one's capacities and engagement situation;

5. releasing in acts of tentative adaptation and in new forms of rest and recreation the emotional tension engendered by the experience of failure and disappointment;

6. scaling down exalted inspirations, aspirations, ambitions, anticipations, and actions by accommodating them to the demands of competence, effectiveness, gentleness, joyousness, congeniality, compatibility, and compassion.

CHAPTER 22

Social Presence:
Depletion, Repletion, and Restoration

S ocial presence erosion may progress to depletion. Continuous disappointment of exalted anticipations may not be worked through formatively. Finally the situation becomes intolerable. Depletion may be compounded by a deeper crisis involving our abandonment to the mystery: a hidden, more major crisis, underlying the crisis of social commitment, that was not dealt with either in time or in depth. Another cause of depletion may be a constant refusal to admit and accept the uncongeniality and incompatibility of one's style of social care.

Depletion does not necessarily manifest itself in outward withdrawal from apparent social behavior. Its primordial form is inner, not outer, withdrawal, a depletion of presence, not of action. One may rely mainly or exclusively on the manifestations of concern in one's apparent lifeform. This form, however, is no longer nourished by the core and current forms of life. The genuine will to presence is missing. As a result, corresponding feelings cannot always be activated.

Depletion affects the social functioning of our life-form. This type of functioning may go on routinely. What moves one is no longer transcendent aspirations or inspirations. Nor is one moved by the emotional modality of vital pulsions.

Depletion defeats the art and discipine of consonant formative detachment, a gentle yet firm vital-functional distancing that prevents overinvolvement and overidentification in interformative relationships. At the same time, such detachment enables us to maintain and deepen our disciplined presence and its realistic expressions.

By contrast, deformative detachment is an anxious, angry, or resentful flight from any mode or measure of presence. Engagement is experienced as a self-defeating exercise in futility. Depletion leads in this case to a shift in focus from concern for the formation needs of others to concern for one's own personal survival, appearance, popularity, monetary rewards, sanity, health, or promotion. Prefocally or focally, we may constantly appraise how we can protect and advance such personal interests by routine manifestations of apparent social concern.

Depletion implies a retreat from dedication. It is an expression of deformative detachment. This withdrawal of commitment may begin with excessive security directives, usually formed prefocally. They are meant to spare us from the pain of continual disappointment or loss of esteem for our own form potencies due to emotional and vital exhaustion.

Prevention and Correction of Social Presence Depletion

To prevent depletion we must engage in a realistic apprehension and appraisal of the social aspect of our formation field. We can never do away with all pain and suffering. Nor can we reform humanity as we would wish. Perfection is an idle dream. Nevertheless, social concern remains necessary even when our efforts fail. Without such concern hope may die in humanity. We should be a part of the chain of symbolic pointers over the millennia that keep humanity from despair by rekindling its faith in the forming mystery imaged in our concern.

One means to prevent depletion in disappointed people suffering from erosion of their engagement are sessions that serve inner repletion. Such sessions can be ineffective or effective.

Ineffective Inner Repletion Sessions

Ineffective repletion sessions offer the short-term benefits of a discharge of pent-up feelings; of relief from everyday tensions; of an artificial sense of replenishment by mutual exaltation of the "ideal" social situation; of a venting of emotional indignation about the sad state of the world and its institutions. While such venting may have some effect on these institutions, it does not prevent inner depletion; in fact, it can accelerate the process. These or like efforts may be effective in other types of sessions not oriented toward inward repletion, such as sociopolitical conventions.

Some repletion sessions lift us to a kind of "reform high." In everyday life we have to care for people who do not share the artificial elation of these meetings. One reason for the ineffectiveness of such sessions is a lack of attunement to the everyday situation. Daily life takes its course again as though nothing has happened. We have to come down from the high we shared with a select group of people. The experience of coming down may contribute to the depletion of our concern and engender false guilt feelings. Unrealistic form directives may result from such guiltiness.

Ineffective repletion sessions reinforce our depreciative appraisals. We seek relief in the mutual expression of anger, of indignant or bitter feelings about the shortcomings of administrators, colleagues, institutions, indifferent societies, and resistant students. When such expression is excessive, when it is not moderated by healing considerations, it heightens and sharpens our dispositions of depreciative appraisal of the people, events, and things that make up our daily situation. It deepens the pained and angry sensitivity that drove us to the road of depletion of social commitment in the first place.

Ineffective repletion sessions may also harm us by intensifying our exalted aspirations. The exalting pride-form deeply affects not only our personal but also our shared human life. Something like a common-pride form may be evoked in such gatherings. Shared exaltation engenders imaginary projects of elated reformation of the world. These may be expressed in loudly acclaimed speeches, slogans, position papers, and letters of indignation to various populations and authorities.

These communications may awaken outsiders to social problems, and hence they could be useful in political conventions. They are hardly helpful in inner repletion sessions for people suffering from erosion of social presence. These persons may abuse such presentations and the exciting atmosphere they evoke to fall back into the exaltation that led them into trouble in the first place. When this renewed exaltation wears off again, in spite of heightened expectations, their depreciative appraisal of the futility of their social presence may be harder than ever to overcome.

Three Types of Sessions

Sessions in service of repletion of our social presence have a character of their own. Their form is different from sessions in service of social or political changes per se. Their form differs also from awakening movements meant to evoke concern in those who are blind to the ravages of war and injustice in this world.

There are three kinds of sessions in service of repletion, and each is important. Inner life reform, world reform, and awakening sessions sustain each other but are not identical. Each implies its own distinctive purpose, scope, and means.

Awakening sessions and movements aim at the arousal of conscience in people who have little or no awareness of their responsibility for social justice in this world. World reform sessions focus primarily on particular inter- and outer conditions that foster or hinder congenial and just formation. Inner repletion sessions focus primarily on the restoration of one's personal social presence potential, which is threatened by the exaltation-erosion spiral. Inner repletion sessions aim at personal reformation of deformative patterns in our intrasphere and in the realm of social engagement.

Effective Inner Repletion Sessions

As far as possible, participants should come to repletion sessions with anticipations that are consonant with the nature and aim of these meetings. They should be clear about the basic distinction between world reform and life reform, between awakening sessions and repletion sessions. They should be willing to suspend temporarily their concerns for world reform and for the awakening of others; they should put these in parentheses, as it were. These sessions are not social-issue but social-presence oriented. Participants should wholeheartedly flow with this spirit in the hope that a replenished presence will gradually regenerate a more reasonable and dependable concern for social issues.

Repletion sessions should help participants overcome the tyranny of the obsessive idea that only the relief of certain adverse conditions in their situation will enable them to be socially present in this wounded world. Such absolutized prerequisites operate as self-fulfilling prophecies. As long as they dominate the mind and mood of the participants, repletion of social presence will remain difficult. We should rise above such debilitating "if only" conditions.

Overcoming Illusionary Responsibility

The sessions should assist us in overcoming illusions of responsibility we may nourish in ourselves. We should be liberated from the exalted notion that we can be directly responsible for all suffering and injustice done to people and reported by the media. We can only be responsible for our own congenial, compatible, and compassionate type, style, measure, expression, and implementation of social presence within this deformed world.

Nor can we be responsible for the ultimate effectiveness of our actions. This is dependent on the free form receptivity and coformative action of the people and institutions we try to assist. It also depends on the cooperation of these same people and institutions with the formation mystery at the heart of history. We should learn not to worry about ultimate effectiveness. We should live in joyous abandonment to the mystery whose advent can be neither predicted nor controlled. If we are fulfilling our responsibility of consonant concern, we can rest assured that final implementation becomes the responsibility of those who resist or receive our care. Exalted responsibility for the free decisions of others may lead to subtle social tyranny. We may experience erosion of our engagement if our coercion fails. In the end, our social presence may be depleted.

Repletion sessions should make us aware that we ourselves are responsible for our own reactions and responses, including our disappointment or resentment when our efforts prove ineffective. These sessions should be planned in such a way that participants make room in their life for relaxed reflection.

During these periods of transcendent presence to the intrasphere of our formation field, we may find relief from deformative guilt feelings that represent false accusations of our functional, pretentious ego. These may be due to pressures from the pride-form, from social pulsations that are not appraised personally, or from demonic mini-obsessions. These sessions should set us free to reappraise our mode of social presence and our choice of a segment of the population as a congenial, compatible field of social care.

We should be aided in repletion sessions to overcome our exalted fantasy. Only then may we appraise the effectiveness of social concern and action. Short-run effects can be appraised in some measure, long-run effects less so. To try to appraise our ultimate effectiveness in time and eternity is to violate the mystery of formation. When apparent failure is perceived as final failure, it is difficult, if not impossible, to maintain a hopeful presence in the midst of shattered projects.

Liberation from Alien Social Modes and Calls

Effective sessions of inner repletion should not engage in the strident propagation of popular modes of social presence. On the contrary, they should bring into the open the possible imperialistic aspects of such modes. We must be made aware that such current pulsations, while excellent for others, may be foreign to our own distinctive life direction. We must seriously ponder whether our congenial mode of presence has been unjustly absorbed by such popular modes. Our vulnerable conscience may have been skillfully manipulated into such alienation from our own congenial mode of engagement. While still faithful to our basic calling, we may have been compelled or seduced to give inordinate time, energy, and attention to uncongenial objectives of service. On the other hand, we may minister to segments of the population to which we are neither called nor qualified to serve extensively.

Effective repletion sessions should facilitate the insight that any prostitution of our own life call may aggravate the erosion we are already suffering. To admire and foster the distinctive call of others to social presence is a deed of justice; to lose oneself in a call foreign to one's makeup is a betrayal of the mystery of formation in one's own existence.

Addiction to Repletion Sessions

While inner repletion sessions are a necessity when erosion threatens our involvement in just causes, we should not become addicted to them. Our motivation for participation in such sessions should not be the sessions themselves or enjoyment of the immediate relief and elation they may engender. We should participate in them mainly to replenish our active, persistent social engagement in our daily life outside the sessions. Our prevalent purpose should not be uplifting feelings of elation but sober appreciation of personal obstacles to social presence. Otherwise repeated participation in repletion sessions may become an addiction instead of a source of reformation.

Repletion sessions should not foster the illusion that we can eliminate once and for all the threat of depletion and erosion. Instead, they should lead us to the acknowledgment that our commitment may be at stake at any time. We should learn to be gently alert for form directives that begin to erode it. We must resign ourselves (again in the sense of the reassignment of meaning) to a lifelong readiness for patient reformation of deformed directives and dispositions in the hope that we may be led by the formation mystery to a deeper, more enduring transformation.

Effective inner reformation sessions facilitate the awareness that our repletion of presence is never final. Yet at the same time such sessions should help us to make some lasting progress, first of all in the timely use of resources that enable us to replenish this presence on our own when necessary.

Repletion sessions may gain in effectiveness by implementing the general guidelines of formative direction in common, adapting them to the aim of social presence repletion as such. (These basic directives, developed both in the science of formation and in its Christian articulation, have been discussed extensively in the second part of my book *The Dynamics of Spiritual Self-Direction.*)

Primary and Secondary Reformation Acts

If we want to replenish in time our failing social concern, we should always be ready to engage in reformation. Readiness should become a lasting disposition. Our human form is vulnerable, so much so that deformative feelings, thoughts, and sensations always emerge. Therefore, the disposition for reform and replenishment implies a willingness to assume responsibility for whatever may prevent or promote the restoration of social concern.

The first reform acts we make in regard to our social engagement should be of a general nature. They help us to gain a view of the whole picture since they consist in a global apprehension and appraisal of:

1. our social situation as a whole within a formation segment of the population;

2. the congeniality of our overall mode of social presence;

3. the overall consonance of our basic strivings and affinities with the style of presence required by this situation;

4. our general effective or ineffective functioning in the situation and in regard to the segment we feel called to serve.

This first set of four initial reform acts enable us to consider critically the situation, the segment to be served, the demands made upon us and our overall response in this interacting totality. This consideration may lead to our affirmation of the situation as a point of departure for increasingly effective social engagement, or it may disclose that we have to search, if possible, for another social situation or another segment of the population to serve.

In some cases, our affirmation of a situation, segment, or demand may be based on the insight that change is impossible. We can only try to make the best of the situation. In other cases, however, we may discover that while a change in our present service situation is possible, it is also undesirable at present.

Once we have globally affirmed our situation, the formation segment we serve, and its implied demands, we have to engage in a more concrete scrutiny of what we have chosen as our field of concern. This necessity engenders a second set of concrete reform acts. These are:

1. a sober apprehension and appraisal of the concrete details of the situation, segment, and demands that become increasingly available to our understanding;

2. an affirmation of them not as an ideal but as a realistic point of departure for our social actions;

3. a critical appraisal of the exalted point of view from which we started in contrast to our concrete social reality (We may consider critically our perhaps poorly informed aspirations and ambitions.);

4. a gathering and affirmation of the resulting information as a more accurate map of our concrete point of departure: we try to apprehend, appraise, imagine, and anticipate how this detailed insight can lead to more effective social presence and action;

5. the resulting information about our point of departure should be illumined, without our distorting it, by our transcendent appraisal.

The first four of these acts may be self-evident, but what is meant by the fifth act of illumination by transcendent appraisal? This refers to appraisal that goes beyond or transcends vital-functional appraisals without repudiating them. It elevates, corrects, and complements them in the light of the formation mystery as communicated to us. Transcendent apprehensions and appraisals disclose to us the deeper meaning of the details of social situations, revealing them to us as invitations of the mystery that offer opportunities for formation. We see what changes are desirable or mandatory in the light of these disclosures.

We now come to the point of a more detailed appraisal and affirmation of our social situation, which has been illumined further by an appreciation of its deeper meanings and challenges. We have patiently affirmed the spiritually enlightened facets of our field of social care. We affirm them as the only possible point of departure for effective social engagement and action.

Once we are engaged again, we will meet with obstacles to the implementation of this affirmation of our will. Such obstacles in turn must be gently and soberly affirmed as new facets of our imperfect point of departure. They should be appraised as formation opportunities. Only after patient apprehension and appraisal of these forms of resistance can we engage in realistic attempts to reform, diminish, and remove them or to find our way gently and wisely around them. In some situations we can utilize them only as opportunities for inner growth in patience, wisdom, humility, and abandonment to the mystery.

The main obstacles, however, are not the resistances we find in the inter- and outer spheres of our formation field, no matter how serious they may be. The main obstacles are found in the intrasphere of our field of social care. They are present in our own mind and heart. They reside in exalted inner directives that interfere with the humble, realistic ones that flow from our enlightened appraisal and affirmation of our field of engagement. To reform or render impotent such exalted directives, it would be helpful to review our understanding of form directives and their dynamics in human formation.

Form Directives

To live is to receive and give form to life. To live a *human* life is to receive and give a *human* form to our existence. Unlike what happens in plants and animals, human formation does not occur by instinct, genetic inheritance, or drive alone. It has to be corrected, guided, and complemented by human form directives. Such directives can be personal, prepersonal, or impersonal. To receive and give personal human form in life is to be formed in the light of human and prehuman form directives that have been personally appraised, affirmed, and appropriated. Such directives should be in consonance with the objective ones disclosed during humanity's formation history in accordance with the cosmic, human, and transcosmic epiphanies of the mystery.

Impersonal human directives are blindly borrowed, as it were, from human persons in the past or present. The main personal and impersonal formation of human life, and implicitly of its social presence, thus finds its source in human form directives.

Impersonal Human Directives

Impersonal form directives coform our personal and social life. These are still human insofar as they have been formed by human sociohistorical pulsations and traditions, or by our personally unappraised or insufficiently appraised human inspirations, aspirations, ambitions, pulsions, and pulsations. They are impersonal insofar as they have not been subjected to our personal focal and/or prefocal apprehension and appraisal in the light of objective directives, and insofar as they have not been personally affirmed by us.

Prehuman Directives

Prehuman form directives result from certain pulsations and pulsions that by their very form cannot be subjected to any human appraisal and affirmation either by ourselves or others. For example, genetic and chemical processes in our body cells, insofar as they are still unavailable to human apprehension, appraisal, and control, illustrate this point. Yet their directives have a vital formative influence on our life. They are truly form directives, be it of a prehuman nature. In some way they affect also our social presence and its infrafocal vibrations.

Prepersonal Directives

Prepersonal form directives differ from prehuman directives in that they are in principle available to personal apprehension, appraisal, and affirmation, by ourselves or others, when historical and other conditions are favorable to their disclosure. In this regard, our personal formation history emerges in large part from the formation history of humanity. For example, at a certain moment in history neurophysiology developed biofeedback procedures. These can make certain formerly prehuman processes in our body available to our prefocal and focal apprehension. Hence, they can be indirectly subjected to personal or impersonal human directives.

Fundamental and Effectual-Qualitative Meaning of the Terms "Formation" and "Formative"

It may be helpful to clarify once again the familiar terms *formative* and *deformative*. In some sense we can say that form directives are potentially always formative; they can lead us to some form reception or donation. It does not matter whether these directives are prehuman, human, personal, prepersonal, or impersonal. They can give rise to some form.

How, then, can we make a distinction between formation and deformation? This distinction cannot apply to the fundamental meaning of formation as such. As we have seen, all formation is essentially formative regardless of its positive or negative effects. The distinction can only be made on the basis of such effects of formation, not on the basis of the intrinsic nature of formation itself.

When the qualitative effects of form directives and subsequent formation are positive, beneficial, and consonant, we call them formative in a secondary sense. This sense superimposes on the general basic meaning of formation the qualitative meaning of efficacious, wholesome formation. Such formation fosters consonant forms of life and world. However, the qualitative effects of formation can also be negative. They can give rise to dissonance in the forms of life and world. In that case we may use words like deformative and deformation. They, too, are superimposed as a secondary sense on the primal one of formation in its basic meaning.

In regard to form directives, we must thus say that they are basically always forming and formative. Yet they can be called deformative in their practical results. This is the case if they have, qualitatively speaking, dissonant effects on the formation of people or their formation field. Whether the terms formation and formative are meant in the primary or in the secondary sense, the effectual-qualitative sense can usually be inferred from the context in which they appear.

Deformative Personal Directives for Social Presence

In our discussion of the form directives that may influence our social presence in a positive or negative way, we made a distinction between prehuman and human directives. The human directives in turn were graded according to their prepersonal, impersonal, or personal form. This distinction may incline us to surmise that at least personal form directives are always formative in the effectual qualitative sense. However, this is not the case; their effects on our social presence can be deformative, too.

What is the source of the possibly deformative effects of our personal social directives? A main source would be the influence of our quasi-foundational pride-form. As we have seen, the innate pride-form is exalted and exalting. Hence, it can give rise to exalted form directives for social engagement. Initially such exalted directives may be global and general. They are a breeding ground of grandiose social ideals, schemes, and projects. Such grandiose directives engender in turn exalted subdirectives.

For example, a grandiose social-minded head of state may order professionally educated persons to be imprisoned, executed, or sent off to labor camps to foster the economic equality of all people in the country. Another example: Socially engaged people may develop as part of their grandiose project of reform of self and world the subdirective of living in such squalor that sickness overtakes the effective execution of any long-range plan for the improvement of the plight of the poor.

Reformation of Exalted Social Directives

How do we reform the exalted directives that harm our effective engagement? We made a distinction between global directives and their subdirectives. To reform these directives we have to be aware of them. Initially it may be easier to identify some of our exalted subdirectives and their adverse results. They show up more immediately than do our global directives. They effect more directly our social practice and its adverse effects on our own life and that of others. More difficult to identify are the exalted global directives that are the hidden source of such harmful subdirectives. They are often not focal in our awareness. Subdirectives are more available to focal awareness because we have to translate them directly into action. Global directives may remain pre-, infra-, and transfocal.

Such obstacles to identification are intensified by the powerful hold of the pride-form on our life. Lucid and sober appraisal is a threat to this control. It evokes anxiety. The exalted global directives, moreover, may be deeply entrenched in the infrafocal layers of the life-form. They may have their origin in primary reactions during early periods of our formation history. When we were children, our pride-form was naive, vulnerable, and uncontrollable. Our spiritual powers were not yet fully awakened.

For all of these reasons, formation direction in common or in private may be helpful for socially engaged people. Formation directors should be initiated in the art of reading subtle signs of exaltation in the expressions of their socially engaged directees. Such signs may open for the directors avenues along which they can trace exalted subdirectives from which such symptoms may arise. In the end these signs may lead them to the exalted global directives that are the ultimate source of such subdirectives and their diversified expressions.

Like all global form directives, the exalted social ones are not necessarily or clearly expressed in inner or outer language. They may be totally or partially preverbal. We may approach their meaning by translating them in linguistic expressions that somehow approximate the intraspheric talk that people engage in prefocally. Exalted social directives can be positive, negative, or conditional. Hence, we will give examples of possible verbal translations of each of these categories of social exaltation.

Exalted Positive Social Form Directives

We call exalted social form directives positive when they result in exalted positive anticipations. They are based on idealizations of what our own social presence and the responses of others could and should be like. These idealizations dispose us to apprehensions and appraisals that are excessively optimistic, if not utopian. They give rise to unrealistic decisions and actions. These are bound to meet with failure and disappointment. They dispose us for a crisis of social commitment that may lead to depletion if it is not solved in time.

Examples of such exalted positive directives are the following: "I should be loved, appreciated, or at least respected by all people to whom I try to be socially present." "If I am socially engaged and give myself wholeheartedly to my job, I should always enjoy the understanding, cooperation, and encouragement of every superior, employer, administrator, chairperson, or colleague." "If I truly try to live a graced life of asceticism, prayer, and presence to God, I do not have anything else to learn to be socially present in a formatively effective way in any situation." "If I am an ordained minister or know theology and philosophy, I do not have to know anything else to deal wisely with social problems." "If I simply follow popular pulsations of social concern I will be socially relevant in any situation."

Exalted Negative Social Form Directives

We call exalted social form directives negative when they breed negative anticipations. They are caused by a depreciation of what our own social presence and the response of others to it may be like. They dispose us to exaggerate the limits of our own or of others' social potential and effectiveness. They make us overrate the power of people, institutions, and events to paralyze our own social presence, action, and effectiveness. Such negative anticipations give rise to pessimistic apprehensions and appraisals. These influence negatively our decisions and actions. Disposing us to self-doubt, discouragement, and disappointment, they hasten the moment of social depletion.

Examples of such exalted negative directives are the following: "My social engagement cannot be worthwhile or useful when I am not fully competent in the social work I am doing." "People who do not share my kind of social interest are selfish and out of touch with the times. They should be looked down upon and dismissed as irrelevant, especially when my kind of social involvement happens to be 'in' with some contemporary pulsation in church or society." "People who do not do something for the segment of the population I am involved in are prejudiced, socially blind, and behind the times. They are to be despised and ridiculed, especially when the segment to which I feel an affinity happens to be the object of popular concern in church or society." "I have the right to be aggravated with the problems and failings of people for whom I do so much." "People or institutions do not deserve my attention and effort when they do not behave as my involvement in their cause gives me the right to expect." "The ineffectiveness and disappointment that I experience in my engagement is always due to others and to social institutions." "I have little or no power to control my negative reactions and responses to failure and disappointment." "People and institutions should manifest some improvement in response to my concern; if not, there is no excuse for their failure and, therefore, I am no longer bound to continue my efforts on their behalf.''

Exalted Conditional Social Form Directives

Exalted conditional social form directives foster the anticipation that we cannot be effective in our commitment if certain exalted conditions are not fulfilled. They are "if only" conditions. Our subsequent unrealistic apprehensions, appraisals, decisions, and actions tend to paralyze effective presence. When the exalted conditions are not met, we feel justified in allowing our commitment to be eroded and depleted.

The following are some examples of exalted conditional directives: "If only my family were more cooperative or if my education were more extensive, I could be effective in my concern." "If only they gave me a better position, my commitment would be easy, spontaneous, and yield ample results." "If only administrators, superiors, and supervisors did not interfere with my job, I would be really successful in my enterprise." "If only the people under my care were more receptive and appreciative, I could commit myself to enduring concern for their needs." "If only the institution I have to work with settled its political or doctrinal disputes, it would be possible for me to spend time and energy in social presence and action."

Disclosure and Reformation of Exalted Social Form Directives

We discussed the danger of unrealistic directives for the effectiveness of social presence and action. By means of examples, we illustrated such exalted ideals in a general way. It is important to disclose similar compulsions in our own life. They compel us to make the wrong moves. Only when we know them can we reform them. Only when we reform them can our engagement become more beneficial.

One road to disclosure is reflection on our interformation with those to whom we are present. Our life does not form itself in isolation. Its unfolding is modulated by the formation of others. Conversely, our own formation affects theirs. This general law of interformation applies also to our interaction with those for whom we socially care. It, too, is marked by formative mutuality. We influence each other for better or worse. Therefore, candid consideration of what goes on in this process offers us an opportunity to find out how tenuous our directives are.

When we look more closely at this interaction, we see that our position as caretakers is different from that of the recipients of our concern. We are more active, they more passive; we act as the givers, they as the recipients. This does not mean that they are not active at all. They give something to us in this relationship. To benefit from their gift, we should not isolate their role and ours from the mystery of formation. Isolation makes us arrogant, secretly filled with self-importance, unduly pleased with our own generosity. We should see ourselves as agents of the mystery. The recipients of our care should not be seen merely as the beneficiaries of our own generosity. They should be revered as the recipients of the flow of the formation mystery itself. We are unworthy instruments inspired and used by this loving, beneficial presence in the universe. The more we look at it this way, the more we realize that the same loving mystery uses these beneficiaries also as channels of our own formation.

The mystery forms us through the recipients of our care in many ways. For example, their response to our concern may facilitate our own process of becoming focally aware of the directives in the situation that call for social justice, peace, and mercy and that move us to engagement. The reactions of people can inform us that we affect them in the wrong way. Asking ourselves why this is so, we may become aware that we are driven by exaltation. This germinal awareness can be repudiated or refused. It can also be appreciated and affirmed as the blessed beginning of reformation. The seed can only blossom if we grow in humble wisdom, enabling us to flow gently with this interformative gift of the mystery.

Stages of Gently Nursing the Seed of Interformative Disclosure

To appreciate and affirm the gift of seminal insight is not sufficient. This seed should be nursed effectively. Nursing is a work of patience. It demands the art of waiting for just-noticeable signs of improvement. It is not an all-or-nothing affair. Nursing is a gradual process marked by many successive stages. Fidelity to unfolding insight depends on gentle willingness and humble readiness on our part.

We should be ready to apprehend and appraise interformative events as possible opportunities for disclosure. We must foster awareness of emergent exaltation. We should soberly appraise its effects. Then we must be willing to dive deeper. We have to examine directives that may be the hidden source of our exalted apprehension and appraisal of social possibilities. Once we have disclosed such deeper motivations we should question why and how they give rise to a proliferation of ineffective subdirectives and corresponding actions. Finally, on the basis of gained insights, we can begin to develop directives of dedication that are more realistic. This stage of actual reformation demands circumspection and patient testing. We must consider circumspectly the potential effects of our new directives. We should cautiously test them out and be ready to modulate them in consonance with the responses of reality.

Formative Effects of Utilizing Interformative Disclosure Opportunities

The road to reformation of directives is arduous. We should consider its ultimate purpose: the illumination of our life and its service. This will help us to muster the courage to persevere on the path of purification.

Purification enables us to illumine the presuppositions that interfere with the effectiveness of our presence. It facilitates the continuation of our commitment in the midst of adversity. The enlightenment that follows purification will shed light on our call to responsibility. We become able to develop responsibly directives that are congenial, just, and compassionate. We take responsibility also for their effects. We become less inclined to blame our negative responses on people, events, and institutions that do not meet our exalted anticipations.

Another fruit of such illumination is liberation from the tyranny of an exalted conscience. We are no longer enslaved to the false demands and anticipations that it generates. We can let go of our frantic attempts to control the situation in which we are called to flow gently with the modest possibilities that the mystery allows to emerge.

Another benefit of this illumination is a freeing from manipulation by the recipients of our care. Such control is usually prefocal; hence, it is more insidious. We invite manipulation by our false feelings of social guilt. An exalted conscience lays excessive demands on self and others. These are accompanied by an irrational sense of guilt when our projects fail. The recipients of our concern spot our vulnerability. They are tempted to play on these feelings. They sense how they can arouse potential or actual pressures of imagined guiltiness within us. Our lack of gentle realism seduces them to try to manipulate our generosity toward them in ways that are in the long run harmful to them and to ourselves. Before we realize it, our oversensitive conscience imprisons us in a web of subtle manipulations by social care recipients, administrators, colleagues, students, or family members.

Social Formation Conscience and Social Presence Repletion

The foregoing considerations raise the question of our conscience in relation to social formation. To understand what our conscience should be in regard to the social form of our life, we should first reflect on conscience insofar as it directs our formation in general. We could call this our "formation conscience."

Simply defined, formation conscience encompasses all the directives that guide our formation. It translates such directives in demands and prohibitions that enable us to appraise our acts and dispositions. It makes us aware of our responsibilities. It tells us how to respond to various formation events. Indeed this conscience is the matrix of formation responsibility. Our formation conscience should be consonant, which implies that it should be obedient, congenial, compatible, compassionate, and firm.

Formation conscience is obedient insofar as it is in tune with universal, objective form directives. Objectivity cannot be attained by exclusive attention to each formation directive in isolation. A certain objective hierarchy should be maintained among directives. According to this hierarchy, certain directives are objectively higher than others. For example, we should form our conscience first of all in obedience to pneumatic and transcendent directives. Should this lead to a conflict between them and certain functional-vital directives, objectivity demands that the transcendent prevail. The consonance of obedience assures the universal, objective quality of our responsibility.

Our formation conscience should also take into account the unique way in which each of us is called to give form to life and world. We can call this the congeniality of conscience. It gives our formation responsibility its quality of relative uniqueness. This congeniality, however, should be subordinated to our obedience to universal, objective directives and their hierarchy. For example, it may be our unique call to give form to life and world by means of writing in a style that is lucid yet original. Still our publications must obey universal, objective directives of consonant life and world formation. For instance, no matter how we personally feel, it would be objectively against a well-formed conscience to write an immoral book that did grave injustice to people of other religions by misrepresenting or ridiculing their intentions or practices.

Our formation conscience is compatible insofar as it takes into account the reasonable demands of people we meet in shared situations. Compatibility grants our responsibility its communal quality. Take a situation in which the common good demands that we delay the congenial fulfillment of our aspirations: our wife and children may be in need of the necessities of life and they can only obtain them when we take a job less in keeping with what we really can do best.

Compatibility should be complemented by compassion. Compassion makes our conscience aware of our own and others' limitations, fallibility, and vulnerability. Formation directives should be tempered, made gentle and flexible in their execution by this awareness. Compassion moderates responsibility and makes it gentle. It rescues responsibility from willfulness, stubbornness, harshness, and fanaticism. It enables a person, for instance, to bear gently with the slow recuperation from alcoholism within programs designed for this purpose.

Finally, we must aim at a formation conscience that is firm. One of the main means toward this disposition is to raise our directives to the level of focused consciousness. This will enable us to appraise, ratify, reject, or modify our directives in relative freedom. After such appraisal, affirmation, and focal appropriation through exercise, they may sink back again in our prefocal consciousness. We presuppose, of course, that they have obtained sufficient firmness to be maintained prefocally in our everyday formation. They are firm insofar as their execution is not thwarted by timidity, fastidiousness, or fear of opposition and misunderstanding.

Firmness grants responsibility its endurance, its sober steadfastness. For example, the demands to be imposed on students in service of the population they have to serve later in life cannot be diminished simply because the student in question is ordained to the clergy or is a member of a religious community or an important family, or because the student threatens to complain to an administrator. Giving in would be a betrayal of formation conscience under its aspect of firmness.

Alienated Formation Conscience

To understand our conscience in relation to social formation, we ought to consider the general problem of alienation of conscience. We have seen that the formation of a consonant conscience is facilitated by raising its directives to the level of focal appraisal. The omission of such appraisal carries the danger of forming life and world in the light of a conscience that is in some measure alienated. In this context *alienated* means that we have not personally appropriated and ratified the conscience that gives form to our acts and dispositions. It is still alien to what we are personally called to be. While our unappraised directives may be consonant, probably some of them are dissonant because they are disobedient, uncongenial, incompatible, without compassion, or lacking in firmness.

The same can happen, of course, to appraised directives. We may have misappraised them. In that case, they contribute to the alienation of our conscience from what it uniquely should be. The difference is that appraised directives are, at least in principle, more open to focused conscious reformation or purification and subsequent illumination.

We may ask ourselves from whence we gathered such alien directives of formation? They were probably borrowed, usually prefocally, from various sources. We may have been fascinated by formation models to such a degree that they were no longer prototypes for us to be creatively and selectively appraised but became models to be blindly imitated. We may have absorbed thoughtlessly subjectivistic codes of form directives or sociohistorical pulsations that are at odds with objective universal directives or are uncongenial with our life call. Formative literature, the media, formative propaganda, and pressure groups in community and society may have had a similar alienating impact on our conscience.

Some of these blindly borrowed directives may prove to be consonant and congenial. They deserve our personal ratification with or without correction. Others may be congenial to people we rightly admire. Admiration evokes imitation. Yet on closer inspection these life directives may prove to be alien to both our own preformation and to our unfolding call and situation.

Social Formation Conscience

Our considerations of conscience have readied us for further reflection on social conscience, a dimension of the conscience that guides all of our formation. This dimension forms and maintains social directives, which are the guiding light of our presence and action. This conscience develops in us a sense of personal responsibility in the social sphere, which should share in the consonance of obedience, congeniality, compatibility, compassion, and firmness that are the necessary qualities of our formation conscience as a whole. We should appraise soberly whether our social responsibility is in tune with these qualities. Such appraisal will be helpful for the rescue or replenishment of an engagement that has lost its inspiration.

Disobedient Social Conscience

We may be tempted to betray or pretend to betray the universal, objective hierarchy of directives in which we believe. This betrayal may be caused by a mood to please or accommodate others. We may be the victims of an excessive need to gain their trust, affection, approval, applause, or collaboration. Betrayal of directives will resonate inwardly in a conflict of refused conscience that can drain our inner peace and energy. In subtle ways it mars our social relationships. In the end it may erode and deplete our social presence itself.

We can reverse this process of deterioration by facing our infidelity to the universal hierarchy of basic directives. We should not underestimate the impact of our infidelity on others. We may tempt them by word or example to share our betrayal. This would be an act of injustice against their right of consonant formation in the light of foundational directives.

Uncongenial Social Conscience

There are three main ways of uncongeniality that can deform our social conscience. First, we may naively or willfully assume responsibility for social problems or for particular formation segments of the population that we are not personally called to serve. We may also not be called to serve them in a more or less exclusive, permanent, or preferential fashion. Second, we may be tempted to take full responsibility for the actions of other people and institutions for which we feel personally responsible. Third, we may accumulate so much responsibility for the formation of others that we have no time and energy left to take care of the necessary conditions for our own congenial formation. As a result, we begin to neglect timely attendance to our own spiritual, intellectual, emotional, aesthetic, vital, and recreative needs.

Our development of uncongenial responsibility may adversely affect our relationships with the social institutions with which we labor. The institution that employs us may serve the relief of spiritual, academic, aesthetic, educational, physical, or economic needs of a population. A deceptive sense of social guiltiness may pervade our lives and make us feel responsible for anything that goes wrong in the institution. Normally we should feel responsible only for our own social presence and for what we can reasonably improve in the institution. We cannot be responsible for all possible actions of the institution itself and of each of its members.

Such an irrational identification with any institution, such as a charitable organization, university, school, or labor movement, leads sooner or later to a curious reversal. We begin gradually to believe that the institution in turn is totally responsible for our own effectiveness in relation to the institution and others. Hence, when it does not respond to our own efforts by immediate manifest improvement, we may feel betrayed in our trust. Erosion and depletion of our presence may set in as a result of this disappointment.

Uncongenial responsibility also affects adversely our relationships with others. We cannot be ultimately responsible for their final decisions. It is foolish to appraise their formation as if it were the formation of our own life. We cannot be responsible for all possible effects of our social engagement on people. Their reactions to our efforts are not within our control. Parents may feel guilty for the mistakes of their children and their families; spiritual directors in private or in common direction may berate themselves for the loss of vocations among their directees; teachers may feel they have failed because of the failure of students to apply themselves; doctors and nurses may be plagued by irrational guilt about the deterioration of patients who do not follow their instructions.

Briefly, when the anticipated beneficial effects of our commitment are not apparent in others' lives, we may feel personally responsible, guilty, disappointed, and upset. Their responses begin to control our own feelings of guilt, shame, embarrassment, and failure. We lose inner freedom and relaxed effectiveness. Our life is weighed down by an alien responsibility for the free formation decisions of others.

Reformation Response to Loss of Formation Freedom through Uncongenial Social Conscience

We should try patiently to regain our freedom and congenial responsibility once it becomes clear that they are lost or diminished. Our style of anticipation needs to be restructured. We must learn to expect soberly that our social presence can *only potentially* affect the consonant life formation of others. Realistic anticipation makes us ready to maintain our dedication within the limits of our congeniality, regardless of its *actual* effect on others or on the way in which they ultimately respond. The firmness of steady dedication greatly depends on the art and discipline of detachment from the observed or imagined reactions and responses of others.

We must cultivate the conviction that the *actual* life formation or reformation of others is *their* final responsibility, that we can only be facilitating agents of *possible* changes of mind and heart. Social presence is the genuine, effective, inspired, and well-informed will to assist others in *their* free self-formation and its facilitating conditions. We can only assist them within the limits of our preformed and unfolding congeniality. Social dedication can never mean that we surrender the emotional modality of our life to overdependent or excessively independent people for their manipulation. Such surrender would spell deformation for both agents and recipients in interformative relationships.

Lack of congeniality may lead to loss of social justice. We tempt the recipients of our care to trespass increasingly not only on our own congeniality rights but also on those of others. It becomes their lasting deformative disposition. This contributes to the spread of the evil and the ailment of social injustice in society. Social injustice leads indirectly to an erosion and depletion of social presence in many people.

Balance between Congeniality Protection and Tolerance of Manipulation

While we should never foster manipulation, we cannot totally avoid its presence in our relationships. The temptation to manipulate is one of the consequences of the fallen human condition. We have to tolerate it within limits. The inclination to manipulate should never be accepted as ideal. We should apprehend and appraise it as a realistic point of departure. We have to take it into account as a possible obstruction of the consonant interformative flow of our relationships.

In other words, we have to find a fine balance between the protection of our congeniality and the tolerance of manipulation. If we tried to eliminate or prevent all temptations to manipulation, we might paralyze any emergent relationships. What should be aimed at gently is the development of an interformative balance. Helpful is the awareness that we, too, as social agents, are inclined to manipulation. The purpose of this balance is to keep the manipulation within the limits of tolerance while acknowledging its presence. Social interaction may only gradually attain sufficient depth and trust to enable it to purify itself from prefocal manipulation strivings in the parties involved.

We are now able to give a descriptive definition of congenial, interformative balance. It could be described as our gentle but firm maintenance of a congenial yet tolerant type, measure, style, and expression of social presence, mainly to a formation segment of the population to which we have some affinity by grace and nature.

Such balance tolerates attempts to manipulate our dedication as long as these do not significantly erode our capacity for social presence and its necessary conditions. The concrete measure of our congenial interformation varies periodically. The bearable balance between protection of congeniality and threats of manipulation depends on many changing conditions. What changes periodically is the state of our own pre-, intra-, inter-, and outer formation and that of the recipients of our care. This change in turn affects our sensitivity to false social guilt feelings. What makes us vulnerable are significant changes in our formation field, such as the loss of a family member or an intimate friend; harassment by envy and jealousy; lack of encouragement by administrators; the emergence of a strong personal attraction to a care recipient; an inspiration by the formation mystery to seek periods of stillness in our life. Such events cannot help but influence the delicate balance between fidelity to what we are called to be in such situations and the seductive manipulation to be something else.

Incompatible Social Conscience

Social conscience is uncongenial when it directs us in ways that are not in tune with our call by the formation mystery as it speaks silently in our intrasphere. Social conscience is incompatible when it guides us in a fashion that is out of tune with the formation mystery as it announces itself in our inter- and outer spheres. The compatible aspect of social conscience and its congenial aspect modulate each other. In mutual consonance they complement and balance each other.

Each life situation in which we are involved has its own inherent demands and limits, whether they arise from our family, community, profession, or other social institutions. We must make a distinction between foundational demands and limits and those that are peripheral. A job has certain basic demands that we cannot neglect without being unfaithful to our obligations; other aspects, such as the amount and kind of socializing with colleagues, are not as basic. Compatible social conscience is primarily concerned with the foundational demands. It maintains a greater latitude in regard to its peripheral aspects.

In respect to the basics of our job or family life, we may have to sacrifice things that are more congenial to us while in peripheral aspects congeniality may prevail. For example, a university professor who is a gifted thinker and writer must organize life in a fashion that is compatible with availability to students as a well-prepared lecturer and academic adviser. In regard to socializing with administrators, colleagues, or students, the formation mystery may ask the professor to sacrifice whatever does not serve the congenial unfolding of the talents for thinking and writing.

We may only gradually apprehend, appraise, and affirm what is basically compatible with the essence of our life situation. These situations may be overlaid with peripheral accretions that are popularly misapprehended as basic demands. The popular apprehension, appraisal, and affirmation of the "natural" demands of any situation is coformed by historical institutions or communities. Many demands are not basic at all but simply accidental accretions. Many people may abide by such specific accretions as though they were foundational. This should not be decisive for the final appraisal by our conscience of what is foundationally compatible with our social presence and action.

Our social conscience becomes incompatible if it makes us maintain social responsibilities that conflict with the essential responsibilities inherent in our basic life situation. Such dissonance breeds conflicts in our intrasphere. These conflicts eat away at our social presence potential. They will continue to deplete this potential and its spontaneous animation unless the conflict is faced and solved in wise appraisal.

Social concern implies the promotion of peace not only among nations but also among people and their situations and companions. The diminishment of compatibility of our own social conscience diminishes our capacity to promote peace among those who follow our word and example. We may neglect to promote in our counselees or directees sensitivity for compatibility with the basic demands of their own life situation. This may prolong or deepen unnecessary conflicts with their families or other surroundings.

Conformity or Nonconformity to Peripheral Accretions

As noted earlier, peripheral accretions do not necessarily fall under the compatibility demand of conscience. Nonetheless, many people conditioned by historical pulsations perceive such accidentals as essentials. When we bypass them lightly, it may seem to them that we forsake the principle of basic compatibility. They may be shocked, saddened, angered, or scandalized by our deviation from familiar details. We should not forget that such circumstantial accretions may be the result of well-intentioned pressures or superstitions of past or present majorities in the country, community, or institution concerned. They may be due to past and present, strong, popular pulsations in church and society.

At times it may be wise and charitable to keep peace by conforming at least publicly, to peripheral accretions. This is especially the case when such accretions are meaningful and worthwhile for many. At other times it may be necessary in service of congeniality with the call of the mystery not to conform. Some participants in our life situation may respond negatively to our lack of peripheral conformity. A conformity conflict between them and us may be unavoidable.

One question to ask ourselves is whether we are able to handle this conflict without too much detriment to our intrasphere. Are we able to bear with rejection in such a way that it does not make us bitter or constantly distressed both inwardly and physically? Such tension can contribute indirectly to the erosion and depletion of our presence.

We have thus to appraise whether we are really ready for the rejection that may follow our refusal to conform to certain peripheral accretions. This appraisal should be directed by a growing insight into our life call as disclosed thus far. It should also be illumined by an insight in our present ability to cope with eventual disapproval and rejection by critical majorities or minorities deeply attached to such accretions. Our appraisal, if possible, should be enlightened by the counsel of mature friends who know us, our situation, and the reactions of the people involved. Well-prepared, experienced formation counselors and directors can also be of assistance.

It may become evident in such appraisal and consultation that the demands and the gifts of grace and nature clearly dispose us to be less dependent on accretions. Even then we should not display our independence unnecessarily. The needless pain of scandal and irritation among people dependent on accretions should be avoided. We should realize that for them such dependence may be necessary. Subtle tact and charity should lighten our way in the delicate art of bypassing accretions revered by others. Usually we should exercise moderation in the manifestation of independence from accretions.

Compassionate Social Conscience

A social conscience that is compassionate takes into account the fallibility and vulnerability of people. We may only gradually apprehend what compassion and mercy demand of us in this regard. Subsequent appraisal will structure our social conscience in its compassionate dimension. It takes experience and wisdom to distinguish clearly between two kinds of compassion: foundational, or primary, and secondary compassion.

Primary compassion directs itself to the deepest poverty of self and others. The most profound indigence is the abandonment of soul or of our unique foundational life form. The first volume of this series, chapter 15, entitled "Abandonment to the Formation Mystery," discussed our factual or experienced abandonment of soul. When we abandon this core of selfhood, our soul itself is abandoned; it loses living contact with its center.

Such abandonment of soul is abetted by the erosion of the pneumatic, transcendent, functional, vital, or sociohistorical conditions that sustain our own or others' congenial and compatible life formation. There exists a hierarchy between these five formation dimensions. The word hierarchy means that each dimension on this ascending or descending scale has its own superordinate or subordinate rank. To each dimension corresponds the appropriate negative abandonment condition.

For example, abandonment of infants in the vital-functional dimension may predispose them to the experience of total abandonment of soul. In later formation years, withholding of transcendent formation is an injustice that may lead to an experience of inner emptiness, a lack of what is distinctively human. Such abandonment, too, can predispose people to the experience of abandonment of soul. Oppression or impoverishment in the sociohistorical dimension may lead to a resentment, despair, and rage that prepare for the experience of abandonment of soul.

Secondary modes of compassion are directed to such adverse conditions of any of the five formation dimensions. A compassionate conscience is in principle concerned not only with the foundational abandonment of soul but with the conditions in these dimensions that may dispose people for this abandonment. Compassionate social conscience directs us to use consonant means that may replenish the conditions for people's congenial and compatible formation. These restored conditions may strengthen one or more of the five formation dimensions. Their effective functioning will diminish the danger of a continued abandonment of soul. We ourselves, or the recipients of our social care, will be less tempted to betray our foundational life-form as it authentically emerges from its mysterious center.

Primacy of the Foundational Mode of Compassion

From all of this it may be clear that the foundational mode of compassion comes first. In principle, secondary modes of compassionate conscience can never replace or substitute for the primary mode of compassion in regard to the abandoned foundational life-form itself. For example, we cannot take care of food and housing for poor people and forget about the abandonment of soul they may experience. Rather, we should pay attention to both aspects of their abandonment.

All authentic secondary modes of compassion and mercy receive their meaning and strength from their rootedness in the primary mode of compassion. The secondary modes of compassion and mercy cannot *in principle* reverse the fivefold hierarchy of formation dimensions and their conditions. For instance, we can never declare that political freedom is in principle more important than spiritual freedom. We should strive for both. If political freedom can only be attained by sacrificing transcendent beliefs and convictions, we must opt for the transcendent dimension of our life, no matter the consequences.

In practice, however, the hierarchy of facilitating conditions for reprieve from abandonment of soul may be temporarily reversed. We could call this a strategic, passing revision, as in the case of periodic emergencies. For example, the need for political freedom, vital health, or functional sustenance in dire poverty may be so overwhelming and pressing that our compassionate concern for them may temporarily seem to engage our energies more than the transcendent needs of the same population. Moreover, some social agents seem uniquely called by grace and nature to specialize in the relief of one or more of these lower needs. To keep their compassionate conscience balanced, they should not isolate their concerns from the higher needs of the recipients of their care. Their marvelous work is preparatory to the resolution of transcendent and pneumatic needs by themselves or others. Reprieve of the primary abandonment of soul should remain the ultimate, if implicit, aim of the compassionate conscience.

Awareness of this primary responsibility—a responsibility in principle— does not imply that we should not concentrate on the acts of mercy to which we may be uniquely called. It demands chiefly that we subordinate them in our heart and conscience, at least implicitly, to the aims to which they are subordinated by the very nature of the fundamental indigence of fallen humanity. The danger exists that secondary acts and strategies of compassion and mercy may block our awareness, even on a prefocal level, that they should be rooted in foundational compassion and mercy. If that happens, these secondary modes may become increasingly isolated from transcendent and pneumatic sources of meaning. Our compassionate conscience then becomes distorted. As a result our acts of compassion tend to become exclusively functional in execution and exclusively vital in emotional motivation. This will make our social presence onesidedly dependent on functional effectiveness and vital moods. When these are low, the loss of transcendent and pneumatic rootedness begins to announce itself painfully. It gives rise to conflict in our intrasphere. One pole of the conflict represents the refused or forgotten transcendent directives of compassion. The other pole is formed by the vital-functional directives of compassion that actually and exclusively guide our social actions. Such conflict contributes to the erosion and depletion of our social presence. Unless this conflict is solved, our social conscience is not a safe light by which to travel.

CHAPTER 23

Formation Counseling and Social Presence

Formation counseling is a particular form of social presence. It awakens and sustains in counselees the art and discipline of formative apprehension and appraisal. This type of appraisal relates directly to their actual life formation. People who come to counselors with the normal problems of consonant form reception and donation in our culture do not necessarily have to be referred to intensive psychotherapeutic treatment. They may be helped by formation counseling, which draws upon the insights and findings of the science of formation and its theory of social presence. This does not mean that certain principles of formation counseling could not be relevant to or for psychotherapy. Appropriately, this final chapter, on formation counseling, offers us the opportunity to review and summarize some of the main concepts covered so far.

Formative Apprehension and Appraisal

One of the problems of counselees in our culture is that they are accustomed mainly to informative thinking. They have lost or have never acquired the art of formative apprehension and appraisal that is fostered in the great formation traditions of humanity.

Counselees have to realize that they are always receiving or giving form in their lives, albeit usually in a prefocal or unfocused fashion. In counseling sessions they learn to focus on this process in a way that is primarily formative instead of informative. They become aware that many experiences manifest and foster this formation process, but that people are inclined to deny these experiences, to bypass them as insignificant, or to use them merely as neutral matter for informative thinking.

Formation counseling assists them in the disclosure of the unique meaning of their experiences for their formation. It enables them to gain insight into the structures, dimensions, conditions, and dynamics of their formation process, its consonant and dissonant directions. This type of counseling creates space for an enlightened dwelling on their experiences in order to appraise them as helpful or harmful for consonant human unfolding. Gradually counselees come to see that their excessive dependence on informative-functional thought is not sufficient for the full flowering of their life. This thought should be balanced by formative reflection as the gentle master of human existence.

Until now, formative thinking has been represented for the most part by spiritual masters in the East and West. The science of formation integrates their insights with the relevant contributions of the arts and sciences that emerged more recently in history. The science itself and the formation counseling sessions it fosters, either in common or in private, highlight humanity's primary tendency to give and receive form in life and world in relative freedom together with others. These sessions bring into the open the obstacles and facilitating conditions that the counselees meet on this journey, the ever present threat of deformation, and the ability to cope with it effectively.

Emergence of the Need for Formation Counseling

At certain times in our life, a congenial and compatible form of existence seems to emerge almost effortlessly. Formative inspirations, aspirations, ambitions, pulsions, and pulsations arise spontaneously in natural consonance with one another. We sense that we are growing wisely and graciously. We feel in harmony with the world. Life flows easily. Formation is not problematic.

At other moments, however, we may feel compelled to think about what happens to us in our formation. Often we are brought to reflection by some crisis that interrupts the spontaneous flow of life, or by a conflict that disrupts our daily routine. These problems may continue because we do not know how to solve the tension between the spontaneous formation of our life and the formative reflection that should guide it at moments of decisive redirection. We may have lost contact with the great formation traditions of humanity that could awaken this formative wisdom. Nor is this wisdom made available to us in a living way by theological propositions or psychological theories, if these are not illumined by the age-old treasure of human formation experience. Hence, we may have to turn to formation counseling to receive the light needed for the solution of normal problems of growth in contemporary humanity.

Counseling sessions help us to question the sense of the situations we are facing. What do these formation events really mean for us? We begin to ask ourselves how we may foster consonant formation. Can we do something about it by means of meditative reflection or recourse to formation wisdom and tradition; to formative reading; to the exercise of formative apprehension, appraisal, affirmation, and other means of disclosing consonant form directives? Counselees begin to feel increasingly the need to appraise who they are and where they are going. The moment they begin to reflect on their formation experience, they initiate the possibility of critically appraising their life direction.

Formation Field

The human life-form, as we know, is always involved in a field of formation. This field is the totality of all the factors that have a formative impact on a person's inner and outer life. The life of our counselees is interwoven with this field. They live in it as an oyster in its shell, a fish in its pond, a fetus in the womb. The human form of life is always in ongoing formation, but only in and through its formation field. Each human life-form, and each community of human forms, develops its own field through unique dialogue.

For example, the field in which our American counselees give form to their life differs from that of the Indians, Bantus, or Eskimos. Things have a different formative meaning for them. Even if the information about these things is the same, their *formative meaning*, the real difference they make in one's spiritual, functional, vital, and sociohistorical life, may be quite different. The fact that people everywhere are increasingly participating in the same information about things makes us too ready to assume that this information has the same formative impact on all people. This is not necessarily the case. For instance, African converts to Islam or Christianity may be informed about the tenets of their new religion. Yet its formative impact will be modulated, subtly and usually prefocally, by the interiorized formative meanings of their tribal traditional formation field. Briefly, formation fields are not the same for people of different cultures and historical periods.

The animal form of life, on the other hand, seems to maintain basically the same type of formation field. Hence, we do not see much change in patterns of building shelter, mating, or rearing young. However, humans are changing all the time the ways in which we receive and give form in our field. We dress in new fashions, cultivate the earth with new machines, differentiate our sciences into ever more refined ones, create new forms of aesthetic expression, soar off into space. The human life-form does not seem as bound to a naturally inherited formation field as that of animals. In some way we keep giving form to our own field. We cannot realize our own form potencies without giving form to the very potencies of the field in which we live. In short, we form ourselves by forming our field. We are people in constant reformation.

For example, we formed ourselves as city dwellers by building cities, as industrialists by developing mills and plants. We became readers by printing books; travelers by giving form to trains, cars, and planes; astronauts by producing spacecrafts and satellites. Our formation field is the domain of our form potencies. They are ours in and through this field. Without our formation field, we would be nothing potentially. We experiment with our formation field in innumerable ways because this is our only road to ongoing formation. Each time we are formatively in touch with our formation field in a new manner, we receive or give form to a new mode of our humanity. When we probe our field, we actualize our form potency for empirical investigation; when we care for people, we grow in love; when we admire the beauty of nature, our aesthetic sense is formed in depth. When we dig a hole, chop down a tree, fly a kite, or cook a new dish, we are formed in practical insight, aptitude, and agility. In short, we are formed humanly by our manifold formative engagement in our fields of action and contemplation.

Form Potencies

A human form potency is thus a dynamic tendency to give or receive form. Definite form potencies permeate the life-form of our counselees; their apprehensions, appraisals, and affirmations of their formation field; their actions and apparent behavior. Counselees may be oblivious to the pressure of denied potencies. Such awareness is due to repudiation or refusal of the call inherent in their form potencies. This lack of awareness leads inevitably to disturbance. The relief of such disturbance presupposes that one face the denied potency and its urgent call. It does not necessarily mean that a person will realize this invitation. A free and insightful decision to forego a certain formation possibility in favor of another can be healthy and invigorating, provided this option ties in with an overall consonant project of life that makes sense to a person here and now at this juncture of his or her formation history.

Our counselees cannot find consonance of life so long as they repudiate or refuse to face their emergent form potencies. They must come to terms with them realistically in accordance with their formation field as apprehended and appraised in the light of their freely chosen formation traditions.

Power of Emergent Formation Potencies

The emergence of a form potency implies a powerful motive to give or receive form accordingly. For example, at a certain age children experience a challenge to give new form to their movements in the playpen. Their formation field becomes structured momentarily around this awakening of their form potency. Their field becomes different in the light of this potency that presses for a new modulation of their bodily form. In their field the open arms of inviting and encouraging parents appear as a harbor to which they can safely travel; chairs become instruments to lean on in their first awkward attempts at new form donation; safety belts with which they may be bound are resented as obstacles to formation.

Later on in life, we may apprehend and appraise similar reformations of our field when challenged by other emergent potencies. Consider the field of the adolescent who experiences the first stirrings of love; of executives who sense that they could reach the top; of scholars or artists who feel they may achieve something great in their field. At such moments other form potencies seem to recede toward the background, at least temporarily. The human form involved in such an emergent tendency is mainly aware of what may lead to the desired form of life and achievement.

Ultimately, it is our transcendent personal choice that should freely decide what kinds of form donation and reception should receive priority. We should not allow ourselves to be overcome by the pressure of emergent form potencies. Prefocally, mutually incompatible kinds of potencies may dominate our actions. We become confused and erratic, irrational and tense. Our formation journey is no longer smooth and even. A great deal of formation counseling is taken up with making these prefocal pressures of emergent form potencies focal and in assisting the counselees to decide on their priorities in the light of the secular or religious formation traditions to which they have freely committed themselves. Such commitment implies necessarily that counselees become aware of what these implicit secular or religious traditions mean for them, formatively speaking.

We conclude that a human form potency is a focal or prefocal (in some instances, an infra- or transfocal) dynamic tendency toward a specific form reception or donation in one's formation field. As a motivating force, it colors one's apprehension, appreciation, and affirmation. Which particular form potencies gain priority in our life depends to a large extent on our prefocal hierarchy of form potencies. This hierarchy is formed under the influence of one's formation history, formation phase, innate affinities, form traditions, and personal affirmations. Many if not all of these forming influences may enter into the dialogue of formation counseling.

Formation Counseling as Such

Formation counseling is essentially a process of helping people become free for their[1] own formation. They come to us because, under the usual pressures of deformative accretions and pulsations of some of their form traditions, they have lost their formation freedom in certain sectors of life. They can no longer transcend the formative directives imposed by socio-historical pulsations in their formation field. They have repudiated or refused to allow emergent form potencies to come into awareness. This repudiation is embodied in dissonant reactions and responses. These may be extinguished gradually after insight into their inhibitory power is gained during the counseling sessions. Dissonant reactions and responses may be replaced through the conditioning of other responses generated by new consonant form directives. The latter should correspond to a new and freer apprehension, appraisal, and affirmation of their formation field.

Counselees can be known from their unique field of formation, not from an isolated and interior intrasphere. Therefore, from the very beginning, the formation counselor orients the attention of the counselees toward themselves as receiving and giving form in their unique field of self, people, events, and things in the light of the formation mystery. They are encouraged not to escape their ongoing formation by a flight into the past, where there are no decisions to make and where there is no necessity to reform freely the present field of form reception and donation, where one's life-form seems explained and justified by inescapable determinants. Instead of forcing counselees to revise the fixed form history of their past, they are invited to face their formation field today, not to excuse themselves but to realistically confront their actual field of life in a new mode of presence and to accept its challenges. Past formation history will only be referred to in service of a clarification of the challenges of the present.

The aim of formation counseling is to make the counselees feel at home in their real field by reforming their unrealistic apprehensions, appraisals, affirmations, aspirations, ambitions, pulsions, and pulsations. Transcending the barriers to free formation, they learn how to move with a new freedom and consonance in daily life. Only people who can call their real field their dwelling place can cope with formation anxiety. They accept and affirm their whole field, not only its bright side but its dark side as well.

Formative Dispositions and Expressions

Formation counselors translate these objectives into appropriate dispositions that are in turn embodied in speech, posture, facial expression, and bodily movement. Such dispositions and expressions are formed in the light of the purpose of formation counseling as well as of the formation field of the counselees. *Their* modes of forming apprehension, appraisal, and affirmation must be clarified. *Their* personal field of presence has to be explored and expressed by means of the counseling relationship. To sense which dispositions and expressions of ours may give effective form to our directives for specific counselees, we should gradually gain an appreciation of their field of formation. Subsequently, we will grow during the sessions into the right appraisal of the kinds of relationships that may induce our counselees to explore and express their field and their formation projects in the light of the form traditions to which they have implicitly or explicitly committed themselves. Such crucial commitment itself will often be the focus of shared exploration.

Formation Project

As mentioned earlier, the main characteristic of the human form of life is its ongoing formation by means of a succession of current formation projects. These are tentative answers to its unfolding formation field. The feelings, desires, hopes, ideas, imaginations, memories, and anticipations of counselees are embedded in such projects, usually prefocally. They form together a system of formation directives. Every directive that becomes the focus of our shared exploration has a place somewhere in this system. It sheds light on all other directives.

The structure of a formation project as a differentiated whole explains partly the formative power and orientation of every single directive that participates in it. Each directive in turn colors all directives that make up the current formation project of the counselee. Counselees are gradually able to apprehend and express the main lines of their current formation project. As formation anxiety diminishes, they may finally see and appraise the deformative impact of dissonant directives within this system. On the basis of this appraisal, they may be ready to develop a new current formation project more congenial with who they are as a unique constellation of form potencies and more compatible with their actual formation field here and now, including the traditions to which they are committed.

Interformative Relationship

The interformative relationship between counselor and counselee is the principal means for bringing to expression the current formation project of the counselee. The quality of the interformative relationship influences the degree to which one's project of formation as well as one's personal field will find adequate expression. The counselor establishes a relationship that leads to diminishment of formation anxiety and to optimal communication.

In order to protect themselves from being misunderstood, humiliated, ridiculed, condemned, or abused, people learn to use security directives to hide their personal formation projects. To disclose their personal project is in a sense to surrender their life-form, to expose their sensitivity, and to unveil their vulnerability when certain directives that they cherish are at odds with the form directives appreciated by their environment. Fear of disapproval and depreciation limits the free admission not only of base inclinations but also of sublime aspirations. It is difficult for many to verbalize their finer sentiments. They fear that the communication of refined feelings would sound ridiculous in the field of onesided functionalistic appreciation shared with their contemporaries.

This refusal of higher aspirations under the pressure of a shared functionalistic field of action may be terribly effective. Counselees themselves may not be aware of the deepest personal aspirations at the root of their preformed life that cry out for expression in their empirical life-form. Counselors may mistakenly make themselves the allies of this sociohistorical, functionalistic field. They may joke lightly about "noble sentiments" in order to reassure *apparently* functionalistic counselees that they are "regular fellows" like the rest of the population. As a result, the hidden aspirations of their counselees may remain a closed book. Some counselors may cherish the illusion that such "open-mindedness" breaks down barriers. They forget that an exclusive openness to the contemporary scene may mean closure to the denied personal aspirations of the counselee.

Imposition of One's Own Form of Life

Every one of us has his or her own current project of formation. This implies, among other things, the formation traditions in accordance with which we embody our strivings in everyday formative efforts. Such form traditions have been absorbed through the dispositions and expressions of the culture in which we are inserted by our birth and initial formation. Our form traditions permeate our interformative relationships with others. This connection is particularly pervasive in the encounter between us as counselors and the counselees who come to us for the facilitation of their formation journey. The subtle influence of our own form traditions could be confusing. Our personal embodiment of life formation is not the only possible or desirable one for others. The identification of our own formation project as "the" project for all may limit our relevance to that segment of the population which is spontaneously in touch with our own traditions and our personal version of them. At the same time, we risk repelling others who are not similarly disposed.

Therefore, counselors should grow increasingly in the appraisal of their own dispositions. Of course, they cannot do away with a personal form of life. They must embody their presence in some apparent expression that is of necessity limited in time and space and, therefore, necessarily onesided. But they can increasingly free themselves from the identification of consonant human formation as such with their own formation project. This inner freedom will enable them to sense the unique form potencies, form directives, and formation field of those who differ from them.

Formation counselors should be aware of the impact of their own traditions, their cultural and subcultural stereotypes, their antipathies and sympathies, their affinities. Emotional blocks will become manifest to them in this maturity. They may disclose, for instance, that they feel uneasy with people who have aesthetic inclinations because the folks at home confused artistry with frivolity. Such confusion may be traced to an historical overreactive rejection of all art and beauty due to the danger of an idolizing of secular aestheticism during a certain cultural period. This threat may have generated a deformative accretion of their formation tradition. Such dissonant accretions, if not worked through, render counselors less effective and unnecessarily inhibitive in their formative presence.

Some counselors may realize that they onesidedly prefer "regular guys" because as high-school or college students they disliked some companions who were delighted more by books than by baseballs. Others, on the contrary, may find that they are enamored of scholarly types because they are fed up with more pragmatic colleagues who make fun of them. Still others may discover during the process of ongoing formation that they lean toward compulsiveness because they have identified the compulsive form of life with sound discipline and firmness. Hence, they distrust spontaneity in themselves and their counselees.

Formation Counselor and Formation Traditions

Formation happens from infancy on. It may start in the fetal stage of life. It is influenced by our interformative interaction with our parents or guardians. They communicate to us in words, gestures, and actions what people in their secular and/or religious traditions appraise as advantageous in the formation of acts and dispositions. Our initial life orientation is not fashioned in isolation but in dialogue with the lifestyle of representatives of one or more form traditions.

Thus it is not true that children develop their formation project with a wary eye on their real form potencies. Children are not faced with the ideal directives of formation as such, but with their parents' appraisal of desirable life formation. The parents' appraisal is coformed in turn by the view of formation that prevails in their traditions. No human life-form is an island in the great sea of formation. Directives are deeply interwoven with the interests of humanity and of each human community in their formation history.

We ought to assimilate the directives of form traditions in a unique and congenial way. They should become truly our own in the course of our formation history. The basic directives of the great classical traditions are not ordinarily contrary to the givenness of the human form in its fundamental dimensions and articulations. These directives are the fruit of revered wisdom, revelation, and the experiences of generations. The sober core of such age-old wisdom is usually consonant with at least the main foundations of human life. This wisdom, however, is incorporated in directives, dispositions, and customs that change with historical situations. Its adaptive embodiment in concrete styles of life may be at odds with what we foundationally are called to be by the formation mystery. These concrete expressions of form traditions are dictated not only by the foundations of the vision of generations. They are influenced also by the temporal or regional demands of the changing situations in which this vision has to be realized.

Our counselees often confuse the core of the accumulated wisdom of their form traditions with its historical accretions, some of which may be dissonant and deformative. These accretions may represent safeguards or secondary security directives. Our counselees may have made them ends in themselves. Safeguards have perhaps taken the place of the directives they were designed to protect. They take on a life of their own. Their growth is no longer rooted in the fundamental directives of their traditions; rather, they loom as isolated powers. Thus the myriad safeguards developed over the centuries may have become for some counselees a stern police force hemming in their distinctively human formation. Safety directives may have become excessive in extent and intensity. They may even contradict the very directives they were meant to protect.

Formation counselors should carefully watch their own prefocal dispositions. They should not depreciate the consonant foundations of the tradition to which their counselees have committed themselves in their style of formation. They should help people clarify the formation potential of the tradition they have chosen and encourage the unique way in which persons try to implement such foundations.

Formation counselors ought to distinguish in their appraisal between the truly fundamental and the merely personal. They may discover that certain people live the directives of their tradition in an unwholesome, over-anxious fashion that elicits dissonant dispositions and actions. Inexperienced or uninformed counselors may identify this unhealthy expression with the directives themselves. They may be appalled by the deforming consequences. Implicitly or explicitly, counselors may then communicate to the counselee their lack of appreciation for the fundamental directives of the tradition of the counselee. By doing so they may drain away the motivating and integrating power of the traditional infrastructure of a person's life. However, it is in the light of this traditional introjected structure that counselees may eventually be able to integrate their life formation more wholesomely with the entire formation field. Outside their form tradition they may lose their possibility for consonant integration. It may be replaced by the opposite of integration, by a syncretism that is intrinsically dissonant and deformative.

Syncretism in formation is the attempt to force selected life directives from intrinsically different form traditions into an artificial unity that in fact is nothing more than an arbitrary collection of incompatible elements. Syncretic formation is usually prefocal. It is a source of dissonance in many people who live in a pluralistic society.

Form Traditions of the Formation Counselor
Formation counselors are rooted in subcultures of their own and are influenced implicitly by one or various traditions. These subcultures and their underlying traditions may differ from those of their counselees.

They may implicitly impose on their counselees their own subcultural view of formation. An unguarded reaction, a certain look, a smile, a slight impatience or surprise may communicate more than words what they really feel. They may unwittingly suggest that their counselees should develop their formation project on the basis of the subcultural structure that nourishes the counselor's own directives and dispositions. If counselees attempt to follow this suggestion, they may fail because the counselor's directives of formation may flow from form traditions that the counselees do not share.

The formation project that the counselor personally cultivates will be for such counselees an abstract ideal, not enfleshed in their own formation history. Such an imposition of alien form directives may result in a new dissonance between the counselees' formative dispositions. Their own formation project may flow from their own tradition as embodied in their culture or subculture, but they may try to develop an alien project of formation suggested to them by a tactless counselor. Their formation project will then be directed from two conflicting centers: the directives of their own subculturally embodied traditions and those of their counselor's subculture. (We presuppose, of course, that the counselees have not freely decided to change to another subculture, formation segment, or tradition.)

Formation counselors can prevent such dissonance if they remain aware of the implicit impact of their personal directives on their communications. Simultaneously they should try to apprehend and appraise the background of the counselee's life formation. This appraisal should be guided by the distinction made between the infrastructure of the tradition of their counselees, its current cultural embodiment, and the personally consonant or dissonant manner in which counselees try to implement this structure.

Structure of the Interformative Relationship

The interformative relationship of counseling differs in structure from other interformative relationships. First, it is different because of its objectives (as discussed earlier); second, it is different because of the dispositions the counselor brings to the relationship.

Counseling sessions are meant to facilitate the expression and appraisal of the formation field of the counselee. The basic disposition is one of genuine acceptance of counselees, regardless of what features of their field they may disclose to us. Any sign of depreciation awakens formation anxiety. However, focal apprehension and appraisal of one's full field of formation can also be impeded by overly emphatic involvement of the counselor in one or another sphere of this field. Such emotional focusing on one facet may impede the communication of other facets that may be of equal or greater significance for full apprehension and appraisal. The counselor prompts counselees by this accepting disposition to lift into the light of shared focal attention vague and confused apprehensions, appraisals, affirmations, memories, imaginations, anticipations, and accompanying feelings, all of which play a role in their current project of formation.

The formation counselor should be affectively present to the extent necessary to keep the counselees motivated in the exploration of their field and project. Yet his affective presence should be modulated by the necessary strategic distance. Distance in the midst of affective presence makes the interformative relationship of counseling different from other affective relationships interformative in their own fashion. Strategic distance facilitates the relaxed acceptance of all facets of the field and project of the counselees without the counselor reacting to them emotionally in a favorable or unfavorable fashion. Either reaction may evoke an appreciative or depreciative fixation on some particular facet of field or project at the expense of the disclosure of other significant aspects. The counselor must be simultaneously an interformative participant in the field and project of the counselee and a respectful appraiser.

The description of the ideal relationship elicits the question of dispositions that may facilitate this kind of encounter between counselor and counselee. Hence, it may be helpful to end this chapter with a consideration of two main dispositions a formation counselor should develop in service of this relationship: the formative disposition and the interformative disposition.

Formative Disposition

The center of our presence is not our own form of life or our own formation. It is the emergent life-form of our counselee—its congenial, compatible, and compassionate unfolding within its own formation field.

Counseling becomes formative when we refuse to consider our counselees as mere compilations of symptoms, problems, diagnostic indicators, constellations of personality theories, or exponents of philosophical or theological propositions. This kind of information should remain available in the background of our competent attention. It should not dominate our relationship exclusively.

We must continually transcend such functional evaluations, no matter how significant they are in their own right. We should be disposed to hear primarily the distinctively human appeal of counselees, to be wholly with and for them as struggling forms of life called forth uniquely by a transcendent mystery. The care of formation counseling may be summarized by saying that its motivation is the consonant self-formation of the counselees in the free core of their life formation by our participation in that core.

It would be impossible to appraise fully a unique formation story by means of the methods of the exact sciences alone. Such approaches accept as significant only what is reducible to measurement. The unique formation call of a person cannot be disclosed in this way. Only a loving respectful presence to each life-form in its gifted uniqueness can disclose this call insofar as it is knowable at this moment.

Every meaningful description presupposes our loving apprehension, appreciation, and confirmation of the present limited disclosure of the counselee's calling. The disposition of loving respect fosters our shared reflection on this disclosure and on the inner and outer obstacles to and facilitating conditions for fidelity to this inner light.

A positivistic approach reduces ongoing life formation to a summary of functional and vital qualities, to a list of symptoms, to an inventory of significant incidents, to a static profile of character, temperament, or personality type. It may freeze an unfolding human form in a filled-out questionnaire, test, protocol, or case history.

The life-form as mystery and call is beyond categorization. Yet formation counseling should take into account the information provided by these positive approaches. In their light, counselors realize the background and the environmental conditions of their counselees, the inner and outer scenery of their struggle, so to speak. They become aware of their symptoms and problematic self-expressions. However, they do not merely identify such conditions and symptoms. They reach out to their deepest roots in the preformative and intraformative regions of the life-form of their counselees.

The formation approach enables them to apprehend holistically both the symptoms of deformation and the repudiated or refused facets of the life call of the counselees as disclosed at this moment of their formation history. They interrelate this disclosure of the call and the symptoms of dissonance as mutually illuminating aspects of the same formation story. The counselee is not reduced to a series of functional categories or test scores. Formative concern keeps the counselor present to something more than symptoms, personality profiles, and problems of adjustment without denying the relative significance of such facets. No diagnostic category by itself alone can do justice to the emergent disclosure of the unique call of a human life-form in its personal formation field.

Interformative Disposition

Formative counseling can give new form to the life of the counselee. To understand what this means in the context of the science of formation, we must realize that counseling is not only interformative but that every human meeting shares in some way in that quality. The manner in which we give form to the life of others is influenced first of all by the kind of meeting in which we engage. Take, for example, the simple situation of two men meeting each other in a bar. The first phase of this meeting may be one of casual informality. One man makes a pleasant remark to the other; the other responds in kind. Further talk ensues, and for each expression of interest and companionship, there is evoked a counterexpression of interest in the other. As a result of these increasingly pleasant exchanges, the two feel at ease with each other. Then, one man says something about a current political controversy that has lots of people stirred up. He says it in a way that leaves no doubt about which side he is on. The other holds the opposite opinion. He feels threatened, offended, hurt. He answers this challenge hotly with an equally forceful argument of his own. His voice is a shade louder than that of his challenger. The other responds in kind. Before either of them realizes it, the friendly meeting has become a heated debate. Soon it turns into a shouting match.

Let us look more closely at the interformative development of this encounter. Notice how the disposition and expression of each person gave form at every moment to the disposition and expression of the other. The two started out as superficial acquaintances. This mode of peripheral interformation was succeeded by one of companionship between mutually interested people. They interformed one another in this mode of presence by friendly dispositions and expressions. Then they switched to giving form mutually to an encounter of heated discussants. Finally, they interformed each other as boisterous fighters.

The point is that they interformed their mutual presence *through* or *by* each other. They really formed each other, first as casual acquaintances, then as sympathetic friends, next as irate debaters, and finally as shouting opponents.

We are so used to modulating the form of one another's lives that we are rarely focally aware that one can give form to another's life and its manifestations in a specific fashion and that the other gives form to our life similarly. We cannot think realistically about our life assuming a form on the basis of our own form donation alone. We can apprehend ourselves only as born from others; as nourished and formed by others; as speaking the language others formed before us; as wearing clothes designed and produced by others; and as cultivating dispositions generated and unfolded by many others preceding us in the history of human formation.

Take, for example, infants born black. They do not assume inwardly the form of an unjustly treated minority until they are treated differently from children who are not black. This treatment forms their life in a different way. It makes them feel, think, and act in a different fashion. It changes their life-form. Note well that it was the interformative encounter which effected this change.

Principle of Interformation Applied to Counseling

We can apply this principle of the science of formation to the counseling situation. The interformative disposition we bring to counseling forms the counselees and ourselves in a way no other encounter (except the love encounter) can give form to our lives.

Interforming encounters that are not encounters of love or of respectful counseling imply prefocal classifications. These unspoken categories subtly influence the way in which we give form to others and in which others receive the form we impose upon them.

Say we take a test such as IQ or a profile of aptitudes test. When testers communicate to us the results of the test, they give form to us in a certain mode, namely as persons who from now on are more conscious of the limitations of their "intelligence" or of a range of "skills." Similar communications by medical doctors, teachers, and moralists do indeed indicate a certain number of valid facts about our life. They certainly make us aware of these realities. Doing so, they modulate somewhat the form of our life and of our self-appraisal in relation to concrete data we cannot deny or ignore. For example, our life-form has been significantly modulated when we leave the office of the physician who tells us that we have cancer, high blood pressure, diabetes, or an ulcer. We are certainly different than we were before we learned about these physical facts. Our response to this communication in some way affected interformatively our physician too, if we had a real encounter. The doctor may feel compassion and concern, and may experience anew the effect of being medically competent.

In formation counseling, the interformative relationship gains a far deeper dimension. This disposition as cultivated by counselors makes them rise above mere facts. They apprehend the counselees primarily as called to relatively free life formation, as people endowed with hidden form potencies and a unique life call. This endowment challenges them to give form to their life in a way not determined exclusively by deformative symptoms, problems, and deficits. Formation counseling interforms the counselees in this relative freedom of formation. It makes them appraise their factual determinants no longer as mere hindrances to human growth. They begin to appreciate them as opportunities for formation of their life in some admittedly limited yet meaningful direction. This creation of new meaning allows them to use limiting formation events inventively to create new modulations of their existence in consonance with the present disclosure of their life call. They become increasingly able to turn obstacles into opportunities. Briefly, when formation counseling is effective, the counselees become ready to affirm themselves as sources of initiative in the midst of seemingly invincible determinants and failures.

Interformation as Participation in the Core Form

Interformation means that we participate in the core form of the life of our counselees. By our cordial presence, we foster the free unfolding of this core, which is hampered by irrational inhibitions, fears, stereotypes, compulsions, vital pulsions, and popular pulsations. Thanks to interformation, counselees no longer feel like lonely, threatened individuals overwhelmed by the responsibility to devise their formation projects in isolation. Because we are wholeheartedly with them, they dare to open up to their form potencies. We present them, as it were, to themselves. We enable their own fundamental life-form to emerge, to take hold of their potencies and limitations. Anxiety-evoking events lose their aura of insurmountability. Our counselees begin to emerge as the flexible masters of their field of form reception and donation.

The interformative disposition of the counselor, if shared by the counselee, generates a "we" experience, a companionship which is different from that of daily situations. This interformative "we" marks the art and discipline of formation counseling. Before this healing encounter, our counselees may have experienced their field of formation as frightening or desolate. They may have felt choked and oppressed, smothered by formation anxiety.

In interformation we become a new appearance in the field of the counselee. Our sustaining presence is a source of inner freedom. They will be touched sooner or later by the absence of any forcing, imposing, or overpowering on our part. In us their now expanded field of formation shows to them a confirming face. Finally, they may begin to believe in the possibility that not all people, events, and things are as untrustworthy as they tend to anticipate. Our interformative disposition helps to make their field become a home for them.

Before our confirmation of their uniqueness, they may have succumbed to an anxious conformity to the wishes of others. The compulsion to be indiscriminate people pleasers made them lose the relative freedom needed for distinctively human formation. They may have become parrots of popular pulsations, inviting control and enslavement by their surroundings. The repudiation or refusal of their fundamental life-form may have generated an impotent rage against real or imagined oppressors. Their flow of formation energy may have been halted or fixated.

In interformation we restore and foster respectfully this oppressed life-form of the person. We try to break the vicious circle of deformative self-apprehension, appraisal, and affirmation, to release their encapsulated energy into a free formation flow.

Interformation makes us vulnerable. We are exposed by our generosity. Initially, it may lead to the eruption of stored-up resentment, hostility, and aggression in our counselees. These emotions are directed toward us, their formation counselors, as the only persons in their present formation field against whom they can dare to live out these angry feelings. The interformative mode of presence implies that we maintain our manifestation of loving respect for the unique formation call others are as human persons, even though this call may first reveal itself in a negative fashion.

Free Participation of the Counselee in Interformation

Interformation in counseling can be effective only when counselees accept freely their counselors' loving concern and gradually come to share in it by focusing with them on their problems. Otherwise it would not really be interformation. The "yes" of the counselees must ratify the concern of the counselor to make true interformation possible. Formation counselors desire the freedom and transcendence of their counselees. Hence, they can only hope that counselees will enter into interformation by freely collaborating with the loving care extended to them.

Formation counseling amounts to wanting, above all, this formation freedom of the counselees. When the counselees do simply what they are told because of the fact that to them the counselor is an expert or "sees through them" or is "such a nice fellow," the subtle process of growth to freedom is stillborn.

Interformation is fertile only when the person who has to grow chooses to grow. Interformation in depth is an interchange between two human forms of life in which both are actively involved in form reception and donation. Without this free participation by the counselees, interformative counseling cannot occur. This "yes" of the counselees to a freely interforming relationship is their gift to the counselor.

Afterword

This volume on the formation of the human heart ends our considerations of the dispositions of the heart. This seems an appropriate
juncture to bring into view once more the project of this series as a whole
on formation science and its articulation in the Christian formation tradition.

Such a recapitulation can start out from different perspectives. The
one chosen here is an examination of five fundamental problems that
religious and secular formation traditions are faced with today. A brief
consideration of each of them may highlight the whole of this undertaking
and its urgency in the contemporary situation.

The fundamental issues confronting these traditions are the following:
1. the nonfocal and focal pluralistic formation of their adherents;
2. the relevance for their adherents of certain proximate pluralistic form
   directives;
3. the emergent necessity of not stimulating indirectly war and social
   injustice;
4. the emergent necessity of interformative missionary dialogue;
5. formative implications of the theologies of scientifically articulated
   traditions.

Nonfocal and Focal Pluralistic Formation of Adherents of Traditions

Formation traditions are concerned with the distinctively human or
spiritual, proximate, and immediate formation of their adherents. This
formation is increasingly modulated by the formative implications of
philosophies, of arts and sciences, and of contemporary pulsations, all of
which permeate our pluralistic societies through education, the media,
and numerous interformative contacts. Most adherents of most traditions
are formed to some extent by such pluralistic directives before being

sufficiently formed by the tradition of their own religion or ideology. They may be formed this way focally or nonfocally. This nonfocal antecedent formation may be infra-, trans-, or prefocal.

This pluralistic formation is not in every facet compatible with the religious or secular form tradition of such adherents. Even when compatible, it needs to be complemented by and integrated in one's own form tradition. Such articulation should be in consonance with the formative implications of its doctrine, theology, or philosophy.

Pluralistic form directives modulate the proximate and immediate formation of the adherents of any tradition. Such modulations cannot be reduced to the fallout of only one or another formation source in our pluralistic societies. They cannot be fully accounted for by the formative implications of only one or a few form traditions, such as Buddhism, Hinduism, Sufism, humanism, Marxism, or scientism. Nor can they be reduced to the forming influence of only one or another philosophy, art, or science, such as contemporary theater, television plays, existentialism, dialectical materialism, linguistic analysis, phenomenology, Freudianism, Jungianism, Rogerianism, psychology, psychiatry, anthropology, medicine, or modern physics. Hence, form traditions should engage in a responsible, critical dialogue with all modulating pluralistic form directives that affect their adherents. They can do so only through an integrative critical science of formation. Among other things, this science appraises systematically all such form directives. One of its central questions is: In what way do such form directives modulate the distinctively human or spiritual formation of various populations?

In principle, no formation tradition can articulate, correct, complement, and integrate in a systematic fashion pluralistic form directives if their students have no way of knowing systematically and critically what these directives are and what their experiential impact is on their adherents.

Relevance of Certain Proximate Pluralistic Form Directives

Certain proximate, pluralistic form directives, modulating experientially the lives of adherents of various form traditions may be truly relevant for their overall proximate and immediate life formation. Their form tradition may not be able to deduce such practical form directives directly from its own doctrine and its theological or philosophical propositions. However, once such directives become known as formatively consonant they should be articulated, elevated, complemented, and, if necessary, corrected in the light of one's religious or secular form tradition. In such an articulation the formative implications, potential or actual, of the theology or philosophy of one's tradition should be taken into account.

Emergent Necessity of Stimulating Indirectly War and Social Injustice

The nuclear threat has raised the consciousness of humanity regarding the necessity of peace on our pluralistic planet. We witness also an increasing hunger for social justice in a diversified world in spite of, or perhaps because of, its division in a variety of distinct formation segments of the population. Contemporary awareness makes it mandatory for all religious and secular form traditions to initiate attempts to establish a common minimum base of distinctively human formation. Ideally, it should become a base that a significant majority can accept without betraying their own traditions.

All traditions are challenged today to reverse their incidental roles as sources of aggressive division, war, and social injustice by religious or secular discrimination. This sharing of a minimum of distinctively human directives will counteract the implicit, unintended formation of prefocal dispositions of mutual alienation between diverse religious or secular formation segments, of disrespect for each other, of distrust and hostility. Such deformation often makes religious and secular form traditions major sources of war, social injustice, discrimination, and persecution.

Fortunately, centuries of accumulation of insights and findings regarding distinctively human formation by various traditions, philosophies, arts, sciences and formative practices offer at our crucial moment in history the possibility of an integrative science of proximate, distinctively human formation. This science may eventually present an acceptable minimum of humane form directives for congenial, compatible, and compassionate living together on this planet. A majority of form traditions may agree upon them to secure a climate of peace and respectful cooperation. This may prevent the wars fomented or motivationally intensified by religious and secular form traditions up to this moment in the formation history of the human race. The threat of our final extinction may be diminished significantly by such a basic formation consensus.

An articulation and enrichment of this minimum in terms of each tradition may motivate adherents not only to live in fidelity to this shared minimum but to transcend and deepen this commitment in the light of their own cherished directives.

Of course, we are aware that significant groups of contemporary Christians are already transcending the minimum demand of not stimulating indirectly war and social injustice. They are actively engaged in the concrete formation of a just, peaceful, and compassionate world. Yet not all Christians, all religions, or all secular ideologies have reached that stage. Realistically, we may hope that at least a first stage of nonstimulation of war and injustice may eventually be adopted by a majority of traditions and incorporated in their formation traditions and projects. The next positive steps may then follow naturally.

Emergent Necessity of Interformative Missionary Dialogue

Many traditions imply a mission to witness for their faith and form directives. Such missionary witnessing does not exclude openness to other consonant, distinctively human directives wherever they are found. Witnessing is not imposition by force of arms, display of cultural superiority, economic handouts, free education for the indigent in underdeveloped countries, care of the sick, sociopolitical manipulation, court decisions, legal punishment, or inquisition.

Formation traditions today are faced with the challenge to halt such secondary missionary methods insofar as they are exclusively directed at conversion. At the same time they should enhance their disinterested care for the sick, the poor, and the uneducated, no matter their segmental convictions.

The modern missionary mentality starts out from where people really are in regard to the distinctively human formation of their life. If their witness does not move people to join their tradition, they respectfully foster in them fidelity to the spiritual formation wisdom attained by humanity today and known to the missionary by the diligent study of formation science.

Over and above the missionaries' promotion of this foundational human spirituality and their witnessing for their own convictions, they engage in interformative missionary dialogue. This dialogue implies first of all that we take the dialogical partners seriously, manifesting this in our respectful listening, thoughtful response, and studious reflection on their spiritual form directives and their sources. Dialogue implies the presence of reverence for the actual or potential goodwill of the partners, in the conviction that people may be subjectively consonant while objectively dissonant. True interformative dialogue is characterized by relaxed openness to any proximate, consonant directives our partners in dialogue may be able to offer us as an enrichment of our own formation traditions. We accommodate compatibly and compassionately the forms of thought, imagination, language, and symbols congenial to our dialogical partners. We search together for a common ground in the distinctively human experience of our formation journey. This search can be facilitated by the science of formation.

Interformative dialogue implies that any adherent of a formation tradition who functions as missionary should avoid false irenicism. People can only learn from each other or be freely converted to a faith and form tradition when they communicate naturally about where they agree and where they honestly and respectfully disagree. This applies not only to intellectual propositions: far more significant is the spontaneous disclosure of the convictions of the heart. Hence, true missionary dialogue implies the living witness of how one really feels about one's form tradition. In Christian thinking such witnessing may be used by grace to appeal to the grace of Christ at work in the dialogical partners. If this does not amount to a calling to a conversion to membership in public Christianity, this grace may deepen the fundamental distinctively human form directives to which the dialogue partners already adhere.

Formative Implications of the Theologies of Scientifically Articulated Traditions

Theology is the science of the ultimate truth as revealed in the religion concerned. As a science of ultimate revealed truth, theology contains ultimate formation directives. These have practical implications for the proximate and immediate spiritual formation of the adherents of a particular faith and form tradition. Hence, the study of theology *in its formative implications* must permeate through and through the articulation research, teaching, and applications of formation science in regard to a specific religious formation tradition. For example, the Institute of Formative Spirituality teaches, in all its courses of Christian articulation, theology in its *proximate-formative implications*.

Theology can be approached from many perspectives. The particular perspective (*objectum formale quo*) through which articulation researchers, students, practitioners, and writers approach theology is their concern for its proximate implications, actual or potential. Potential formative implications of theology may be disclosed in the light of the insights and findings of formation science. In that event, formation science becomes auxiliary to theology. Conversely, theology becomes auxiliary to the articulation of formation science when its already pronounced, actual ultimate form directives and their formative implications are studied in articulation research.

To be sure, professional systematic theology in turn may approach spiritual formation and the findings of formation science from the perspective of systematic theology much as it may approach any art or science. It seems unnecessary to say that these arts and sciences do not thereby become mere subdivisions of theology. Nor does formation science.

The strong, all-pervading theological orientation of a formation institute or department—or any other science department insofar as it engages in articulation research—does not make it a theology department. One could compare this with a department of religious education: its students approach theology from the perspective of the transmission of the truth content of the faith tradition in a way that is educational. They study theology, but not exactly as a professional theologian studies theology. They are professional religious educators not professional theologians. The same applies to formation scientists who engage in complementary articulation research. They study theology from the perspective of distinctively human or spiritual formation. This does not make them professional theologians. Their specialized interest as articulation students is not in the ultimate truth of theology as ultimate but in the formative implications of such ultimate truth for the proximate and immediate formation of human life as concretely lived in its everyday formation field and as illumined by formation science.

These reflections on science and theology lead us into the theme of the next volume in this series, which will deal with the science of formation *as science*. The rationale for this emergent science will be discussed and its position within the constellation of human sciences will be delineated. The volume will also describe finely developed methods of research and the constitution of an appropriate metalanguage, both meeting the theoretical standards demanded of a legitimate human science.

In the final chapters of the next volume, the demands of valid articulation research in regard to specific form traditions will be considered at length. Those considerations will bring us back to the theme of the relation between the theological sciences and formation science, their essential difference and autonomy, and their mutually auxiliary possibilities.

Bibliography

Books

Adler, A. *The Individual Psychology of Alfred Adler*. New York: Harper Torch-books, 1964.

Aelred of Rievaulx. *Spiritual Friendship*. Kalamazoo, Mich.: Cistercian Publications, 1977.

Allport, G. *Personality and Social Encounter*. Boston: Beacon Press, 1960.

Anderson, R. *On Being Human: Essays in Theological Anthropology*. Grand Rapids, Mich.: William B. Eerdmans, 1982.

Andrews, E. D. *The Gift to Be Simple*. New York: Dover Publications, 1967.

Arendt, H. *The Human Condition*. Chicago: University of Chicago Press, 1958.

Argyris, C. *Personality and Organization: The Conflict between System and Individual*. New York: Harper Torchbooks, 1970.

Axline, V. *Dibs: In Search of Self*. New York: Ballantine Books, 1964.

Ayer, A *The Concept of a Person and Other Essays*. London: Macmillan, 1963.

Barron, F. *Creative Person and Creative Process*. New York: Holt, Rinehart & Winston, 1969.

Baum, G. *Religion and Alienation: A Theological Reading of Sociology*. New York: Paulist Press, 1975.

Bellah, R. N. *Beyond Belief: Essays on Religion in a Post-Traditional World*. New York: Harper and Row, 1970.

Bennis, W. G., and others, eds. *Interpersonal Dynamics*. Homewood, Ill.: The Dorsey Press, 1968.

Benson, A. C. *The Silent Isle*. New York: G. P. Putnam's Sons, 1910.

Berdiaev, N. *Solitude and Society*. London: The Centenary Press, 1938.

Berger, P. *The Social Construction of Reality*. Garden City, N.Y.: Doubleday, 1967.

Barron, F. *Creativity and Personal Freedom*. Princeton, N.J.: Van Nostrand, 1968.

_____ . *Creativity and Psychological Health: Origins of Personal Vitality and Creative Freedom*. Princeton, N.J.: Van Nostrand, 1963.

Beha, M. *The Dynamics of Community*. New York: Corpus Books, 1970.

Bergson, H. *The Two Sources of Morality and Religion*. Translated by R. Audra, C. Brereton, and the assistance of W. Carter. New York: Henry Holt, 1935.

Bidney, D. *Theoretical Anthropology*. New York: Columbia University Press, 1953.

Bonhoeffer, D. *Life Together*. London: SCM Press, 1949.

Bugental, J. *The Search for Authenticity*. New York: Holt, Rinehart & Winston, 1965.

Chermayeff, S., and C. Alexander. *Community and Privacy*. Garden City, N.Y.: Doubleday, 1965.

Cole, P. *The Problematic Self in Kierkegaard and Freud*. New Haven and London: Yale University Press, 1971.

Crom, S. *On Being Real: A Quest for Personal and Religious Wholeness*. Wallingford, Pa.: Pendle Hill Publications, 1967.

Crowne, D., and D. Marlowe. *The Approval Motive: Studies in Evaluative Dependence*. New York and London: John Wiley, 1964.

Cuzzort, R. *Humanity and Modern Sociological Thought*. New York: Holt, Rinehart & Winston, 1969.

Dabrowski, K. *Personality Shaping Through Positive Disintegration*. London: J. and A. Churchill, 1967.

_____ . *Positive Disintegration*. London: J. and A. Churchill, 1967.

Dalton, R. H. *Personality and Social Interaction*. Boston: D. C. Heath, 1961.

Dessauer, P. *Natural Meditation*. Translated by J. H. Smith. New York: J. P. Kennedy, 1965.

Downie, R. S., and E. Telfer. *Respect for Persons*. London: George Allen & Unwin, 1969.

Drucher, P. *The Age of Discontinuity: Guidelines to Our Changing Society*. London: Heinemann, 1969.

DuQuoc, C., and C. Geffre., eds. *Dimensions of Spirituality*. New York: Herder and Herder, 1970.

Edelwich, J., and A. Brodsky. *Burn-Out: Stages of Disillusionment in the Helping Professions*. New York: Human Sciences Press, 1980.

Eisley, L. *The Unexpected Universe*. New York: Harcourt, Brace, Jovanovich, 1969.

Eliade, M. *The Sacred and the Profane*. New York: Harper and Row, 1961.

_____ . *Shamanism*. Princeton, N.J.: Princeton University Press, 1972.

Ellis, A., and R. A. Harper. *A New Guide to Rational Living*. N. Hollywood, Calif.: Wilshire, 1975.

Eller, V. *The Simple Life*. Grand Rapids, Mich.: William B. Eerdmans, 1973.

Ellul, J. *Prayer and Modern Man*. Translated by C. E. Hopkins. New York: Seabury Press, 1970.

Erikson, Erik. *Identity, Youth and Crisis*. New York: W. W. Norton, 1963.

Fernandez, R., ed. *Social Psychology Through Literature*. New York: John Wiley, 1972.

Franck, F. *Pilgrimage to Now/Here*. Maryknoll, N.Y.: Orbis Books, 1974.

French, R. M., trans. *The Way of a Pilgrim and the Pilgrim Continues His Way*. New York: The Seabury Press, 1968.

Freud, S. *The Ego and the Id*. New York: W. W. Norton, 1962.

Freudenberger, H. J. *Burn-Out*. New York: Bantam Books, 1980.

Fromm, E. *Creativity and Its Cultivation*. Edited by H. H. Anderson. New York: Harper and Row, 1959.

_____ . *The Art of Loving*. New York: Harper and Row, 1956.

_____ . *The Revolution of Hope: Toward a Humanized Technology*. New York: Harper and Row, 1968.

Gardner, J. W. *Self-Renewal: The Individual and the Innovative Society*. New York: Harper and Row, 1963.

_____ . *Reality Therapy*. New York: Harper Colophon Books, 1975.

Goffman, E. *Behavior in Public Place*. London: Free Press of Glencoe, 1963.

_____ . *The Presentation of Self in Everyday Life*. New York: Anchor Books/Doubleday, 1959.

Goode, W. J. *The Family*. Englewood Cliffs, N. J.: Prentice-Hall, 1964.

Gordon, M. *Final Payments*. New York: Ballantine Books, 1980.

Gratton, C. *Trusting: Theory and Practice*. New York: Crossroad, 1982.

Greenleaf, R. K. *Servant Leadership*. New York: Paulist Press, 1977.

Greeley, A. M. *The Friendship Game*. Garden City, N.Y.: Doubleday, 1970.

Guardini, R. *The World and the Person*. Chicago: Regnery, 1965.

Guntrip, H. *Personality Structures and Human Interaction*. New York: International Universities Press, 1961.

_____ . *Schizoid Phenomena, Object Relations and Self*. New York: International Universities Press, 1969.

Jourard, S. *Disclosing Man to Himself*. Princeton, N.J.: Van Nostrand, 1968.

Jung, C. *The Undiscovered Self*. Translated by R. F. C. Hull. Boston: Little, Brown, 1958.

Hall, C. S., and G. Lindzey, eds. *Theories of Personality*. New York: John Wiley, 1978.

Halmos, P. *Solitude and Privacy: A Study of Social Isolation, Its Causes and Therapy*. London: Routledge and Paul, 1952.

Harper, R. *The Seventh Solitude*. Baltimore: Johns Hopkins Press, 1965.

Harrison, A. F., and R. M. Bramson. *Styles of Thinking*. New York: Anchor Books/Doubleday, 1982.

Haughton, R. *The Passionate God*. London: Darton, Longman & Todd, 1981.

Heidegger, M. *Discourse on Thinking*. New York: Harper and Row, 1966.

Henson, R. D., ed. *Landmarks of Law*. Boston: Beacon Press, 1960.

Horney, K. *Neurosis and Human Growth*. New York: W. W. Norton, 1970.

_____ . *Our Inner Conflicts*. New York: W. W. Norton, 1945.

Huxley, A. *The Doors of Perception*. New York: Harper and Row, 1970.

Hyers, C. *Zen and the Comic Spirit*. Philadelphia: Westminster Press, 1973.

Jourard, S. *The Transparent Self*. Princeton, N.J.: Van Nostrand, 1964.

Kahler, E. *The Tower and the Abyss: An Inquiry into the Transformation of the Individual*. New York: Braziller, 1957.

Kaltenmark, M. *Lao Tsu and Taoism*. Stanford, Calif.: Stanford University Press, 1969.

Kaplan, A., ed. *Individuality and the New Society*. Seattle and London: University of Washington Press, 1970.

Katz, R. L. *Empathy, Its Nature and Uses*. New York: Free Press of Glencoe, 1963.

Keniston, K. *The Uncommitted: Alienated Youth in American Society*. New York: Brace and World, 1965.

Kierkegaard, S. *Purity of Heart Is to Will One Thing: Spiritual Preparation for the Office of Confession*. Translated by D. Steere. New York: Harper Torchbooks, 1956.

Kitaro, N. *Fundamental Problems of Philosophy*. Translated by D. A. Dilworth. Tokyo: Monumenta Nipponica, Sophia University, 1970.

Klubertanz, G. P. *The Philosophy of Human Nature*. New York: Appleton-Century-Crofts, 1953.

Krech, D., R. S. Crutchfield, and E. L. Ballachey. *Individual in Society: A Textbook of Social Psychology*. New York: McGraw-Hill, 1962.

Kubie, L. S. *Neurotic Distortion of the Creative Process*. New York: The Noonday Press, 1961.

Kwant, R. *Encounter*. Pittsburgh, Pa.: Duquesne University Press, 1960.

_____ . *Phenomenology of Social Existence*. Translated by H. J. Koren. Pittsburgh, Pa.: Duquesne University Press, 1965.

Laing, R. D. *The Divided Self*. Baltimore: Penguin Books, 1965.

Lao Tzu. *The Simple Way of Lao Tzu*. Fintry, England: Shrine of Wisdom, 1951.

Lazarus, A. *In the Mind's Eye: The Power of Imagery for Personal Enrichment*. New York: Rawson Associates Publisher, 1977.

Leech, K. *Soul Friend*. London: Sheldon Press, 1977.

Lepp, I. *A Christian Philosophy of Existence*. Dublin: Gill and Son, 1965.

_____ . *The Ways of Friendship*. Translated by B. Burchland. Toronto: Macmillan, 1969.

Levinas, E. *Totality and Infinity*. Pittsburgh, Pa.: Duquesne University Press, 1969.

Levinson, D. J. *The Seasons of a Man's Life*. New York: Ballantine Books, 1978.

Levi-Strauss, C. *The Savage Mind*. Translated by G. Weidenfeld and L. Nicholson. Chicago: University of Chicago Press, 1966.

Lewin, K. *Resolving Social Conflicts*. New York: Harper and Row, 1948.

Lindbergh, A. M. *Gift From the Sea*. New York: Random House, 1955.

_____ . *War Within and Without*. New York: Harcourt, Brace, Jovanovich, 1980.

Lowen, A. *The Betrayal of the Body*. New York: Macmillan, 1967.

Macquarrie, J. *Paths to Spirituality*. London: SCM Press, 1972.

MacMurray, J. *Persons in Relation*. London: Faber and Faber, 1961.

Mannheim, K. *Diagnosis of Our Time*. New York: Oxford University Press, 1944.

Marcel, G. *Being and Having: An Existential Diary*. New York: Harper and Row, 1965.

_____ . *Homo Viator*. New York: Harper and Row, 1968.

_____ . *The Mystery of Being*. Vol. 1, *Reflection and Mystery*. Chicago: Henry Regnery, 1960.

Maslow, A. *Toward a Psychology of Being*. New York: Van Nostrand, 1968.

May, R. *Love and Will*. New York: W. W. Norton, 1969.

Mayeroff, M. *On Caring*. New York: Harper and Row, 1971.

McConnell, T. A. *The Shattered Self: The Psychological and Religious Search for Selfhood*. Philadelphia: Pilgrim, 1971.

McCurdy, H. G. *The Personal World*. New York: Harcourt, Brace and World, 1961.

McGinley, P. *Province of the Heart*. New York: Viking Press, 1957.

Mead, G. H. *Mind, Self and Society: From the Standpoint of a Social Behaviorist*. Chicago: University of Chicago Press, 1938.

Metz, J. B. *Poverty of Spirit*. Translated by J. Drury. New York: Newman Press, 1968.

Miller, D. L. *Individualism: Personal Achievement and the Open Society*. Austin and London: University of Texas Press, 1967.

Moustakas, C. E. *Creativity and Conformity*. Princeton, N. J.: Van Nostrand, 1967.

_____ . *Individuality and Encounter*. Cambridge, Mass.: Howard A. Doyle, 1968.

_____ . *Loneliness*. Englewood Cliffs, N.J.: Prentice-Hall, 1961.

Mullahy, P., ed. *A Study of Interpersonal Relations: New Contributions to Psychiatry*. New York: Science House, 1967.

Mumford, L. *The Culture of Cities*. New York: Harcourt Brace, 1966.
————. *The Transformation of Man*. New York: Collier Books, 1962.
Munz, P. *Relationship and Solitude*. Middletown, Conn.: Wesleyan University Press, 1965.
Muto, S. A. *Celebrating the Single Life*. New York: Crossroad, 1982.
Nouwen, H. J. M. *Reaching Out*. Garden City, N.Y.: Doubleday, 1975.
O'Neill, D. *What Do You Say to a Child When You Meet a Flower?* St. Meinrad, Ind.: Abbey Press, 1972.
Ortega y Gasset, J. *On Love*. New York: World Publishing Company, 1957.
Packard, V. *The Naked Society*. New York: D. Mckay, 1964.
Pfuetze, P. *The Social Self*. New York: Bookman Associates, 1954.
Pieper, J. *About Love*. Chicago: Franciscan Herald Press, 1971.
Polanyi, M. *Personal Knowledge*. Chicago: The University of Chicago Press, 1958.
Powell, J. *A Reason to Live! A Reason to Die*. Chicago: Argus Communications, 1972.
————. *Why Am I Afraid to Tell You Who I Am?* Chicago: Argus Communications, 1969.
Rabin, A. I. *Growing up in the Kibbutz*. New York: Springer Publishing Company, 1965.
Reich, C. A. *The Greening of America*. New York: Random House, 1970.
Richards, M. C. *Centering in Pottery, Poetry and the Person*. Middletown, Conn.: Wesleyan University Press, 1962.
Ricoeur, P. *Freedom and Nature: The Voluntary and the Involuntary*. Evanston, Ill.: Northwestern University Press, 1966.
————. *The Symbolism of Evil*. New York: Harper and Row, 1967.
Riesman, D. *The Lonely Crowd*. New Haven, Conn.: Yale University Press, 1961.
Rubin, T. *The Angry Book*. New York: Collier Books, 1969.
Ruesch, J. *Disturbed Communication*. New York: W. W. Norton, 1957.
Ruitenbeek, H. M. *The Individual and the Crowd*. New York: Mentor Books, 1965.
Sadler, W. A. *Existence and Love*. New York: Charles Scribner's Sons, 1969.
Schachtel, E. *Metamorphosis in the Development of Affect, Perception, Attention and Memory*. New York: Basic Books, 1959.
Scheler, M. *Ressentiment*. New York: The Free Press, 1961.
Schnapper, E. B. *The Inward Odyssey: The Concept of the Way in the Great Religions of the World*. London: George Allen & Unwin, 1965.
Schoeck, H. *Envy: A Theory of Social Behavior*. Translated by M. Glenny and B. Ross. London: Secker and Warburg, 1969.
Schutz, A. *Collected Papers, I*. The Hague: Nijhoff, 1967.
————. *On Phenomenology and Social Relations*. Chicago: University of Chicago Press, 1970.
Schwartz, A. U., and M. L. Ernst. *Privacy: The Right to Be Let Alone*. New York: Macmillan, 1962.
Simon, S. B., L. Howe, and H. Kirschenbaum. *Values Clarification*. New York: Hart, 1972.
Silverstein, L. M. *Consider the Alternative*. Minneapolis, Minn.: CompCare Publications, 1977.
Slater, R. L. *World Religions and World Community*. New York: Columbia University Press, 1963.
Smith, H. *Realism in Renewal*. Ill.: Divine Word Publications, 1969.

Sommer, R. *Personal Space*. Englewood Cliffs, N.J.: Prentice-Hall, 1969.

Steiner, G. *Language and Silence: Essays*. New York: Atheneum, 1967.

Strasser, S. *Phenomenology of Feeling: An Essay on the Phenomena of the Heart*. Pittsburgh, Pa.: Duquesne University Press, 1977.

Streng, F. J., ed. *Understanding Religious Man*. Belmont, Calif.: Dickenson Publishing, 1969.

Strunk, O. *Privacy: Experience, Understanding, Expression*. Lanham, Md.: University Press of America, 1982.

Tillich, P. *A History of Christian Thought: From Its Judaic and Hellenistic Origins to Existentialism*. Edited by C. E. Braaten. New York: Simon & Schuster, 1972.

—————— . *Dynamics of Faith*. New York: Harper Torchbooks, 1957.

—————— . *The Courage to Be*. New Haven: Conn. Yale University Press, 1963.

—————— . *Systematic Theology*. Chicago: The University of Chicago Press, 1951.

Toffler, A. *Future Shock*. New York: Random House, 1970.

Troeltsch, E. *The Absoluteness of Christianity and the History of Religions*. Translated by D. Reid. Richmond, Va.: John Knox Press, 1971.

Underhill, E. *Practical Mysticism*. New York: Dutton, 1943.

van Croonenburg, B. J. *Don't Be Discouraged*. Denville, N.J.: Dimension Books, 1972.

Van der Post, L. *The Lost World of the Kalahari*. Middlesex, England: Penguin Books, 1962.

van Leeuwen, A. T. *Christianity in World History: The Meeting of the Faiths of East and West*. Translated by H. H. Hoskins. New York: Charles Scribner's Sons, 1964.

von Hildebrand, D. *Transformation in Christ: On the Christian Attitude of Mind*. New York: Longmans, Green and Company, 1948.

Von Durckheim, K. *Daily Life as Spiritual Exercise*. New York: Harper and Row, 1972.

—————— . *Hara, The Vital Centre of Man*. London: George Allen & Unwin, 1962.

Wagner, C. *The Simple Life*. Translated by M. L. Hendee. New York: McClure, Phillips and Company, 1901.

Watts, A. W. *The Book: On the Taboo Against Knowing Who You Are*. New York: Collier Books, 1967.

Weil, S. *The Need for Roots*. Boston: Beacon Press, 1955.

Westcott, M. R. *Toward a Contemporary Psychology of Intuition*. New York: Holt, Rinehart and Winston, 1958.

White, W. *Beyond Conformity*. New York: The Free Press of Glencoe, 1961.

Wienpahl, P. *Zen Diary*. New York: Harper & Row, 1970.

Wild, R. W. *Intuition*. London: Cambridge University Press, 1938.

Williams, R. J. *Biochemical Individuality*. New York: John Wiley and Sons, 1956.

—————— . *You Are Extraordinary*. New York: Random House, 1967.

Wolff, K. H., ed. and trans. *The Sociology of George Simmel*. Glencoe, Ill.: Free Press, 1950.

Wood, M. M. *Paths of Loneliness: The Individual Isolated in Modern Society*. New York: Columbia University Press, 1953.

Ziegler, E. K. *Simple Living*. Elgan, Ill.: Brethren Press, 1974.

Zimmerman, J. G. *On Solitude*. Baltimore: George McDowell and Son, 1832.

Articles

Arndt, H. W. "The Cult of Privacy." *Australian Quarterly* 21 (September 1949): 69–71.

Bennet, C. C. "What Price Privacy?" *American Psychologist* 22 (May 1967): 371–76.

Calhoun, J. B. "A Behavioral Sink." In *Roots of Behavior*, edited by E. L. Bliss. New York: Harper and Brothers, 1962.

Ching, J. "Chu Hsi's Theory of Human Nature." *Humanitas* 15 (February 1979): 77–100.

Conrad, H. S. "Clearance of Questionnaires with Respect to 'Invasion of Privacy,' Public Sensitivities, Ethical Standards, etc." *American Psychologist* 22 (May 1967): 356–59.

Dibzhansky, T. "The Pattern of Human Evolution." In *The Uniqueness of Man*, edited by J. Rolansky. Amsterdam: North-Holland Publishing Company, 1960.

Dubos, R. "Biological Determinants of Individuality." In *Individuality and the New Society*, edited by A. Kaplan. Seattle and London: University of Washington Press, 1970.

Ellison, K. W., and J. L. Genz "The Police Officer as Burned-Out Samaritan." *FBI Law Enforcement Bulletin* (March 1978): 1–7.

Farrell, E. J. "The Journal: A Way into Prayer." *Review for Religious* 30 (September 1971): 751–56.

Felipe, N. J., and R. Sommet "Invasions of Personal Space." *Social Problems* 14 (Fall 1966): 206–14.

Fischer, W. "The Problem of Unconscious Motivation." In *Duquesne Studies in Phenomenological Psychology*, edited by Giorgi, and others. Pittsburgh, Pa.: Duquesne University Press, 1967.

Freudenberger, H. J. "Staff Burn-Out." *Journal of Social Issues* 30 (1974): 159–65.

_____. "The Staff Burn-Out Syndrome in Alternative Institutions." *Psychotherapy: Theory, Research and Practice* 12 (Spring 1975): 73–82.

Gotesky, J. "Aloneness, Loneliness, Isolation, Solitude." In *An Invitation to Phenomenology*, edited by J. Edie. Chicago: Quadrangle Books, 1965.

Green, A. "The Middle-Class Male Child and Neurosis." *American Sociological Review* 2 (February 1946): 34–41.

Gregor, T. A. "Exposure and Seclusion: A Study of Institutionalized Isolation Among the Mehinacu Indians of Brazil." *Ethnology* 9 (July 1970): 234–50.

Goffman, E. "On Face-Work: An Analysis of Ritual Elements in Social Interaction." *Psychiatry* 18 (August 1955): 213–31.

Gross, H. "The Concept of Privacy." *New York University Law Review.* 42 (March 1967): 35–36.

Harvey, A. "The Pious Ones." *National Geographic* 148 (August 1975): 276–98.

Jager, B. "Horizontality and Verticality." In *Duquesne Studies in Phenomenological Psychology*, edited by Giorgi, and others. Pittsburgh, Pa.: Duquesne University Press, 1967.

Jolivet, R. "Neighbor: Communication to Communion." *Philosophy Today* 2 (Summer 1958): 113–18.

Kahn, R. "Job Burnout: Prevention and Remedies." *Public Welfare* 36 (Spring 1978): 61–63.

Kalven, H., Jr. "The Problem of Privacy in the Year 2000." *Daedalus* 96 (Summer 1967): 876–82.

Kirkendall, L. A., and P. B. Anderson "Authentic Selfhood Basis of Tomorrow's Sexual Morality." *Pastoral Psychology* 21 (November 1970): 9–32.

Koch, S. "The Image of Man in Encounter Groups." *American Scholar* 23 (Autumn 1983): 636–52.

LeClerq, J. "Prayer and Speed-Spirituality for the Man of Today." In *Prayer*, edited by C. Mooney. New York: Paulist Press, 1969.

LeKachman, R. "Vance Packard, Defender of Privacy." *Christianity and Crisis* 24 (May 1964): 102–104.

Masao, A. "Non-Being and Mu: The Metaphysical Nature of Negativity in the East and in the West." *Religious Studies* 11 (June 1975): 181–92.

Maslach, C., and A. Pines "The Burn-Out Syndrome in the Day Care Setting." *Child Care Quarterly* 6 (1977): 100–13.

_____ . "The Client Role in Staff Burn-Out." *Journal of Social Issues* 34 (Fall 1978): 111–24.

_____ . "Job Burnout: How People Cope." *Public Welfare* 36 (Spring 1978): 56–58.

Maslow, A. "The Need to Know and the Fear of Knowing." *Journal of General Psychology* 68 (1963): 111–25.

Mead, M. "Margaret Mead Re-examines Our Rights to Privacy." *Redbook* 124 (April 1965): 15–16.

Misner, P. "Two Ecumenisms of Friedrich Heiler." *Andover Newton Quarterly* 15 (March 1975): 238–49.

O'Shea, K. "Enigma and Tenderness." *Spiritual Life* 21 (Spring 1975): 8–21.

Pilpel, H. "The Challenge of Privacy." In *The Price of Liberty*, edited by A. Reitman. New York: W. W. Norton, 1968.

Pines, A., and C. Maslach. "Characteristics of Staff Burnout in Mental Health Settings." *Hospital and Community Psychiatry* 29 (1978): 233–37.

Rapaport, A. "The Search for Simplicity." *Main Currents in Modern Thought* 28 (January-February 1972): 79–84.

Ruitenbeek, H. "Mechanization Versus Spontaneity: Which Will Survive?" *Humanitas* 2 (Winter 1967): 261–69.

Schwartz, B. "The Social Psychology of Privacy." *American Journal of Sociology* 73 (May 1968): 741–52.

Shaw, F. J. "Laughter: Paradigm of Growth." *Journal of Individual Psychology* 16 (November 1960): 151–57.

_____ . "The Problem of Acting and the Problem of Becoming." *Journal of Humanistic Psychology* 1 (January 1961): 64–69.

Shil, E. "Social Inquiry and the Autonomy of the Individual." In *The Human Meaning of the Social Sciences*, edited by D. Lerner. New York: Meridian Books, 1959.

Shine, D. J. "The Analogy of Individuality and 'Togetherness'." *The Thomist* 33 (July 1969): 497–518.

Shubin, S. "Burnout: The Professional Hazard You Face in Nursing." *Nursing* 78 (July 1978): 22–27.

Simmel, G. "The Sociology of Secrecy and of Secret Societies." *American Journal of Sociology* 2 (January 1906): 462–98.

Van den Berg, J. H. "What Is Psychotherapy?" *Humanitas* 7 (Winter 1971): 321–70.

Weinstein, M. "The Uses of Privacy in the Good Life." In *Privacy* edited by J. R. Pennock and J. W. Chapman. New York: Atherton Press, 1971.

Westin, A. F. "Science, Privacy and Freedom: Issues and Proposals for the 1970's." *Columbia Law Review* 66 (June 1966): 1003-50.

Unpublished Theses

Byrne, R., OCSO. "Christian Formation Tradition: Its Selective, Critical and Creative Utilization in Service of a Christian Articulation of the Science of Foundational Human Formation." Doctoral dissertation, Institute of Formative Spirituality, Duquesne University, Pittsburgh, Pa., 1982.

Foley, P. "Remember Who You Most Deeply Are: The Role of Memory in the Unfolding of Foundational Identity and Commitment." Doctoral dissertation, Institute of Formative Spirituality, Duquesne University, Pittsburgh, Pa., 1981.

Leavy, M., OSB. "Reforming Dispositions: A Formative Approach to Habit Change." Doctoral dissertation, Institute of Formative Spirituality, Duquesne University, Pittsburgh, Pa., 1981.

Lewis, L., MM. "The Formative Experience of Waiting: Moving from Living in Illusion to Living with Reality." Doctoral dissertation, Institute of Formative Spirituality, Duquesne University, Pittsburgh, Pa., 1983.

Lockwood, T., CFC. "The Formative Experience of Taking Responsibility for an Unfamiliar Task." Doctoral dissertation, Institute of Formative Spirituality, Duquesne University, Pittsburgh, Pa., 1981.

Muto, S. A. "The Symbolism of Evil: A Hermeneutic Approach to Milton's Paradise Lost." Doctoral dissertation, University of Pittsburgh, Pa., 1970.

Reuter, M., OSB. "Transformation through Our Encounters of Ordinary Life." Doctoral dissertation, Institute of Formative Spirituality, Duquesne University, Pittsburgh, Pa., 1982.

Agnew, U., SSL. "Originality and Spirituality: The Art of Discovering and Becoming Oneself." Master's thesis, Institute of Formative Spirituality, Duquesne University, Pittsburgh, Pa., 1974.

Aliquo, M. R., RSM. "Coming to a Readiness to Respond to New Situations." Master's thesis, Institute of Formative Spirituality, Duquesne University, Pittsburgh, Pa.,1978.

Bellport, M. F., OCD. "Asceticism and Esthetics Conjoined Toward Wholeness of Person." Master's thesis, Institute of Formative Spirituality, Duquesne University, Pittsburgh, Pa., 1981.

Bellerose, Y., SSA. "A Gracious Presence in Daily Living: Preparing the Way for Human and Spiritual Growth." Master's thesis, Institute of Formative Spirituality, Duquesne University, Pittsburgh, Pa., 1978.

Bindewald, A., O. Carm. "Spirituality in a Technical Environment." Master's thesis, Institute of Formative Spirituality, Duquesne University, Pittsburgh, Pa., 1977.

Biscotti, M., OCD. "Creative Response to Limitedness: The Movement from Anger to Compassion." Master's thesis, Institute of Formative Spirituality, Duquesne University, Pittsburgh, Pa., 1980.

Blank, G., SDR. "On the Relationship of Embodiment to Spiritual Unfolding." Master's thesis, Institute of Formative Spirituality, Duquesne University, Pittsburgh, Pa., 1976.

Bomberger, R. P., SSJ. "Tradition: A Way to Creative Original Living." Master's thesis, Institute of Formative Spirituality, Duquesne University, Pittsburgh, Pa., 1981.

Breaud, B., OC. "The Experience of Guilt: Implications for Religious Life." Master's thesis, Institute of Formative Spirituality, Duquesne University, Pittsburgh, Pa., 1972.

Carfagna, R., OSU. "Empathy and Personal Responsiveness: The Way of Spirit-Enlightened Relatedness." Master's thesis, Institute of Formative Spirituality, Duquesne University, Pittsburgh, Pa., 1976.

Casey, B., RSM. "Obedience and the Autonomy of the Religious Sister." Master's thesis, Institute of Formative Spirituality, Duquesne University, Pittsburgh, Pa., 1970.

Chin, M., RSM. "Lived Privacy: An Avenue to True Encounter." Master's thesis, Institute of Formative Spirituality, Duquesne University, Pittsburgh, Pa., 1974.

Dirkx, B., SSM. "Compulsive Living: Challenged and Effected by Spirituality." Master's thesis, Institute of Formative Spirituality, Duquesne University, Pittsburgh, Pa., 1976.

Dube, E., SASV. "Spirituality and Being Courageous." Master's thesis, Institute of Formative Spirituality, Duquesne University, Pittsburgh, Pa., 1980.

Earner, M. A., SDR. "Life as Communication: Saying, Silence and the Spiritual Life." Master's thesis, Institute of Formative Spirituality, Duquesne University, Pittsburgh, Pa., 1972.

Fernandes, M., OP. "Spirituality and Humor: Accepting and Living the Limitation of Everyday Life." Master's thesis, Institute of Formative Spirituality, Duquesne University, Pittsburgh, Pa., 1975.

Finn, M., HVM. "Religious Autonomy and the Spirituality of the Novitiate." Master's thesis, Institute of Formative Spirituality, Duquesne University, Pittsburgh, Pa., 1969.

Guerin, E., RSM. "Spirituality and Fatigue." Master's thesis, Institute of Formative Spirituality, Duquesne University, Pittsburgh, Pa., 1977.

Gunelson, M. C., CPPS. "Interpersonal Reconciliation: Moving Toward Right Relations Through Spiritual Living." Master's thesis, Institute of Formative Spirituality, Duquesne University, Pittsburgh, Pa., 1974.

Hageman, L., OP. "Suffering and Its Significance for Personal and Spiritual Life." Master's thesis, Institute of Formative Spirituality, Duquesne University, Pittsburgh, Pa., 1972.

Hamilton, J., CFX. "Stepping Aside: Formative Self-presence." Master's thesis, Institute of Formative Spirituality, Duquesne University, Pittsburgh, Pa., 1980.

Hanlon, M. C., SC. "Custom: A Way of Life—Creative Renewal of Religious Living." Master's thesis, Institute of Formative Spirituality, Duquesne University, Pittsburgh, Pa., 1970.

Helak, A., CSSF. "Spirituality and Becoming Patient with Oneself." Master's thesis, Institute of Formative Spirituality, Duquesne University, Pittsburgh, Pa., 1979.

Helldorfer, M. C., FSC. "The Participative Religious as Worker." Master's thesis, Institute of Formative Spirituality, Duquesne University, Pittsburgh, Pa., 1970.

Hever, D., FMS. "Self-Acceptance: Basis for Authentic Response to Life." Master's thesis, Institute of Formative Spirituality, Duquesne University, Pittsburgh, Pa., 1976.

Iacobucci, S., CSSF. "Man's Search for Security: Implications for Religious Living." Master's thesis, Institute of Formative Spirituality, Duquesne University, Pittsburgh, Pa., 1974.

Jezik, J., OSF. "Spirituality and the Experience of Failure." Master's thesis, Institute of Formative Spirituality, Duquesne University, Pittsburgh, Pa., 1979.

Jokerst, C. A., CCVI. "On the Way Toward a Trusting Response: Implications for Spiritual Living." Master's thesis, Institute of Formative Spirituality, Duquesne University, Pittsburgh, Pa., 1974.

Jordan, G., SSL. "Spirituality and Lived Time." Master's thesis, Institute of Formative Spirituality, Duquesne University, Pittsburgh, Pa., 1976.

Kelly, M., SSL. "Spirituality and Human Spatial Surroundings." Master's thesis, Institute of Formative Spirituality, Duquesne University, Pittsburgh, Pa., 1973.

Kuzmickus, M., SSC. "Authentic Detachment in Religious Living." Master's thesis, Institute of Formative Spirituality, Duquesne University, Pittsburgh, Pa., 1971.

Lyons, K., CSJ. "Moving from Envious Comparisons Towards Respectful Community Living." Master's thesis, Institute of Formative Spirituality, Duquesne University, Pittsburgh, Pa.,1977.

McKay, M., CSJ. "Spiritual Life and the Call to Leadership." Master's thesis, Institute of Formative Spirituality, Duquesne University, Pittsburgh, Pa., 1977.

McKeever, C., SSL. "Functionality and the Spirituality of the Religious Sister." Master's thesis, Institute of Formative Spirituality, Duquesne University, Pittsburgh, Pa., 1970.

Mester, M., RSM. "Spiritual Awakening and a Sense of Wonder." Master's thesis, Institute of Formative Spirituality, Duquesne University, Pittsburgh, Pa., 1975.

Miceli, P. E. "The Formative Experience of Detachment: The Threshold of Transcendent Living." Master's thesis, Institute of Formative Spirituality, Duquesne University, Pittsburgh, Pa., 1980.

Mulholland, G., SCIC. "Spirituality and Living with Loneliness." Master's thesis, Institute of Formative Spirituality, Duquesne University, Pittsburgh, Pa., 1976.

Newport, M. C., OLM. "The Journey to Freedom Through Affirmation: A Formative Experience." Master's thesis, Institute of Formative Spirituality, Duquesne University, Pittsburgh, Pa., 1980.

O'Reardon, M., OSF. "Living in the Spirit of Justice." Master's thesis, Institute of Formative Spirituality, Duquesne University, Pittsburgh, Pa., 1977.

Parsons, M. A., CSC. "Consideration of Autonomy Within the Formal Organizational Structures of Religious Communities of American Women." Master's thesis, Institute of Formative Spirituality, Duquesne University, Pittsburgh, Pa., 1969.

Pepera, G., CSFN. "Spirituality and Homecoming: On the Way Toward Being at Home Where One Is." Master's thesis, Institute of Formative Spirituality, Duquesne University, Pittsburgh, Pa., 1978.

Peters, R., CFC. "Breaking Away: A Formative Movement From Embeddedness Towards Transcendence." Master's thesis, Institute of Formative Spirituality, Duquesne University, Pittsburgh, Pa., 1981.

Rake, J.M., CDP "Friendship in Religious Life." Master's thesis, Institute of Formative Spirituality, Duquesne University, Pittsburgh, Pa., 1969.

Richardt, S., DC. "Towards an Understanding of Human Receptivity: Implications for Religious Formation." Master's thesis, Institute of Formative Spirituality, Duquesne University, Pittsburgh, Pa., 1972.

Satala, M., D.C. "Compassionate Living." Master's thesis, Institute of Formative Spirituality, Duquesne University, Pittsburgh, Pa., 1972.

Schaut, M. R., OSB. "Spirituality and the Role of the Family." Master's thesis, Institute of Formative Spirituality, Duquesne University, Pittsburgh, Pa., 1973.

Semple, B., SJSM. "The Experience of Solitude: Implications for Spirituality." Master's thesis, Institute of Formative Spirituality, Duquesne University, Pittsburgh, Pa., 1976.

Sharpe, M. J., RSM. "Life Form and Its Transforming Influence Upon the Person." Master's thesis, Institute of Formative Spirituality, Duquesne University, Pittsburgh, Pa., 1971.

Sheehan, W., OMI. "The Ongoing Movement of Integration and the Spiritual Life." Master's thesis, Institute of Formative Spirituality, Duquesne University, Pittsburgh, Pa., 1973.

Sherman, S. M., RSM. "The Lived Experience of Personal Conflict: Implications for Spirituality." Master's thesis, Institute of Formative Spirituality, Duquesne University, Pittsburgh, Pa., 1973.

Sinnott, M., MMM. "The Emotional Response to Separation From Loved Persons." Master's thesis, Institute of Formative Spirituality, Duquesne University, Pittsburgh, Pa., 1978.

Springer, M., SSJ. "Moving from Constancy to Fidelity in Everyday Life." Master's thesis, Institute of Formative Spirituality, Duquesne University, Pittsburgh, Pa., 1977.

Steadman, J. M., CSC. "Spirituality and Responding to the Gift of Vulnerable Creaturehood: A Dimension of the Cross in Daily Life." Master's thesis, Institute of Formative Spirituality, Duquesne University, Pittsburgh, Pa., 1979.

Storms, K., SSND. "Simplicity of Life as Lived Everyday." Master's thesis, Institute of Formative Spirituality, Duquesne University, Pittsburgh, Pa., 1976.

Thames, M. C., FMI. "Interpersonal Listening: Implications for Community Living." Master's thesis, Institute of Formative Spirituality, Duquesne University, Pittsburgh, Pa., 1974.

Tracy, M. F., CDP. "Man Responding to Changes: Implications for Spirituality." Master's thesis, Institute of Formative Spirituality, Duquesne University, Pittsburgh, Pa., 1973.

Ulica, J., OSF. "The Dynamics of Hoping: A Fundamental Attitude of Spirituality." Master's thesis, Institute of Formative Spirituality, Duquesne University, Pittsburgh, Pa., 1978.

Viens, A., SSCH. "Lived Inner Silence: An Attitude of Expectancy." Master's thesis, Institute of Formative Spirituality, Duquesne University, Pittsburgh, Pa., 1976.

Wangler, B., OSB. "Spirituality and Self Concept." Master's thesis, Institute of Formative Spirituality, Duquesne University, Pittsburgh, Pa., 1978.

Zeleznik, C., OSB. "Be Who You Are: Self Acceptance and the Life of the Spirit." Master's thesis, Institute of Formative Spirituality, Duquesne University, Pittsburgh, Pa., 1975.

Index